Also by Charles P. Curtis

THE OPPENHEIMER CASE

The Trial of a Security System, by

CHARLES P. CURTIS

SIMON AND SCHUSTER · NEW YORK

1955

FIRST PRINTING
LIBRARY OF CONGRESS CATALOG CARD NUMBER: 55-8808
DEWEY DECIMAL CLASSIFICATION NUMBER: 973.92
MANUFACTURED IN THE UNITED STATES OF AMERICA
PRINTED BY MURRAY PRINTING COMPANY, WAKEFIELD, MASS.
BOUND BY AMERICAN BOOK-STRATFORD PRESS, INC., NEW YORK, N. Y.

For Frances

Contents

Foreword

THE *Oppenheimer case is the first opportunity we have had to understand how our security system works, and this book is an attempt to seize it.*

It is too easy to condemn our security system simply on the basis of the bare results in a number of cases, even important cases, where the results have been stupid, mischievous and unjust. To be sure, things are known by their fruits, but knowledge is not enough. We've got to understand how the present security system works before we can make it better. We can't junk it.

It is equally easy, and just as useless, to sit back and fold our hands around our confidence, or our complacence in the integrity and wisdom of those who are working with our security system. Even a good workman may do shoddy work with bad tools.

I am not talking about Congressional investigating committees. We know very well what has been the matter with them. The publicity in which they flourished soon showed us what the trouble was, and now we are curing their distemper. What I am talking about is the Loyalty-Security Program we set up in 1947, eight years ago, and which in 1953 we expanded into the present Federal Employees Security Program.

We can't hope to understand what's the matter with this program unless we are told more about it. Unlike Congressional committees, it has been growing in the darkness of secrecy, in the cellar of public opinion. Secrecy, indeed, seems to be part of the system.

A foreign-service officer of twenty-odd years' standing, John Paton Davies, is dismissed. The security board which gave him a hearing tells us only that "the continued employment of Mr. Davies is not clearly consistent with the interests of national security." The Secretary of State refuses to make public the transcript of the hearings because "at the present time he believed it would not be desirable from the point of view of national interest to make the full record public, and at the same time it would be unfair to Mr. Davies if only a partial record were disclosed." (The New York Times, November 10, 1954.) All that the Secretary will tell us is that the reason for Davies' dismissal was not disloyalty. This may be some comfort to Davies, but is less than reassuring to us.

In 1948 the Director of our National Bureau of Standards, Dr. Edward Condon, was charged with being "one of the weakest links in our atomic security." The Atomic Energy Commission promptly investigated and promptly cleared him. So did the Department of Defense. Later, in 1951, he left the government service and was engaged by the Corning Glass Works. In July 1954 he was again cleared, under the new program, by a security board. Three months later the Secretary of the Navy announced that "there was sufficient evidence to warrant my requesting a complete reconsideration of this action." The Secretary refused to indicate what this evidence was. (The New York Times, October 22, 1954.)

Dr. Condon lost patience and withdrew his application for clearance. He moved to Berkeley to engage in a long-range program of research into the structure and properties of glass for the Corning Glass Works. At the annual meeting of the American Association for the Advancement of Science, in Berkeley in December 1954, Condon was given a long ovation.

When Wolf Ladejinsky, who had been praised by General MacArthur for his work on land reform in Japan and who had been cleared by the State Department, was denied clearance by the Department of Agriculture, the Secretary of Agriculture defended the decision of his security officer in a written summary of the case, which he brought to the President to meet the protests of the State Department. But all the President told us at his next press conference about this summary was that it would "scare him." (The New York Times, January 13, 1955.) Then Harold Stassen, the Foreign Operations Administrator, cleared Ladejinsky to do the same thing in Vietnam that he had done for MacArthur in Japan, and Stassen gave the press a statement of his reasons for clearing him, which are entirely convincing. (The New York Times, January 19, 1955.) Something went obviously and appallingly wrong in the handling of this case. Our trouble is, we don't know yet what it was.

In only one case, that of J. Robert Oppenheimer, have we been vouchsafed a transcript of the proceedings before a security board. Something less than the complete transcript, to be sure, for every now and then we find a row of stars in the transcript, indicating the omission of classified material. Nor have we any of the F.B.I. reports. But here in the Oppenheimer case we have a good deal to go on—enough, I think, to give us a pretty clear understanding of how our security system works. For we have also the opinions of the security board and the opinions of the Atomic Energy Commissioners stating the reasons, particular and specific, why Oppenheimer was denied security clearance.

This case is our first opportunity to give our security system a fair trial, and this book is an attempt to seize it.

CHARLES P. CURTIS

Stonington, Connecticut
May 1955

"There is more than Dr. Oppenheimer on trial in this room. . . . The Government of the United States is here on trial also. Our whole security process is on trial here. . . ."
—LLOYD K. GARRISON to the Security Board

"We are acutely aware that in a very real sense this case puts the security system of the United States on trial, both as to procedures and as to substance."
—The Security Board to the Atomic Energy Commission

1. ABOUT THIS BOOK

IT IS NOW a year and more since June 29, 1954, when the Atomic Energy Commission announced that "concern for the defense and security of the United States" required it to deny Professor J. Robert Oppenheimer further access to restricted data, and so bring his service to his government to an end. The next day, June 30, Oppenheimer's contract as adviser and consultant to the A.E.C. was to terminate unless it was renewed, and with its termination would have ended any access to the restricted data which the Commission was taking away from him.

It was then about eleven years since, in the spring of 1943, a like concern for the defense and security of the United States required Oppenheimer's appointment as the director of the atomic laboratory at Los Alamos, the most secret, and the most successful, of our efforts to defend and secure ourselves against totalitarian aggression. For there, under his direction, the first atomic bomb was devised.

Why did the A.E.C. refuse to clear Oppenheimer? On what grounds and for what good reasons? We do not yet seem to understand, even now after the transcript of the proceedings and the opinions have been before us for all these months. This book is an attempt to understand.

To begin with, you should know what this book is based on—in other words, what lies behind it. What usually lies behind a book is mainly the opinions, the prejudices and the experiences of the author. I am not going to keep either my opinions or my prejudices out of this book. I don't want to. I couldn't anyhow. I know Oppenheimer. I don't know him well. I have met him half a dozen times. But I know him well enough to start with an opinion—or, if you prefer, a prejudice—in his favor. And the transcript of the proceedings and the decisions have confirmed my opinion and my prejudice.

I will try to indicate my presence behind this book, wherever it is not obvious, by speaking in the first person. Elsewhere, when I write in the third person, what lies behind the book is the transcript of the proceedings, all of its 992 closely printed pages, the majority and minority opinions of the Personnel Security Board, the briefs of Oppenheimer's counsel—the rules did not permit counsel for the A.E.C. to file a brief—the five opinions of the Atomic Energy Commissioners, who split four to one over the final decision, and what I have read in the papers, in a number of current periodicals and in some few books. I will indicate, wherever I can remember, what else I have read in order to write this book.

This, then, is an account of the trial of J. Robert Oppenheimer on charges of being a security risk.

I know that our security regulations prefer not to call such proceedings a "trial" but rather an "inquiry." Yet Roger Robb, who was counsel for the A.E.C., although Chairman Gordon Gray referred to him as counsel for the Security Board at the outset of the hearings, behaved as if he were a prosecuting attorney trying a case. Though the Board kept protesting that it was conducting an inquiry—and I am sure they thought they were—the proceedings, as the Board allowed them to progress, were not simply and properly inquisitorial. At best, they were neither wholly an inquiry nor wholly a trial. The Board permitted them to fall into a muddled middle course, which was not satisfactory. I don't believe a combination of the inquisitorial process with the adversary process of a trial can ever be satisfactory. A hearing ought to be one or the other.

You will understand that I am not speaking disrespectfully of the process of inquiry. *Inquisitorial* is the technical and appropriate adjective. Please don't take the word *inquisitorial* in any invidious or derogatory sense.

I know, too, that our security regulations prefer to call the charges on which an alleged security risk is tried "a statement of substantial derogatory information."

Is this simply semantics? Yes. But see where the words lead us. We say "derogatory information" when we are talking about "charges." We call the proceedings an "inquiry" and we allow them to become a "trial." We say that the issue is whether or not Oppenheimer's access to restricted data is to be reinstated. We are diverted from the obvious fact that the issue really is whether or not Oppenheimer is fit to serve the country. The question you and I are going to discuss is whether Oppenheimer was to be convicted or acquitted on this issue. You and I don't need to be prim about it.

I propose first to tell you whom we are talking about—that is, try to make Oppenheimer something more than a name. Then I want to explain what we are talking about—that is, what a security risk is. This will lead me into the law, but after you've read a couple of pages you will find that I have skipped the rest of it until later, which, being a lawyer, I cannot help telling you. I ask you not to think the less of it. What there is of it is gravely important.

I will then ask you to read the charges against Oppenheimer. I will ask you to read them in full, together with Oppenheimer's reply. Read them as practical men of affairs who are called on to make sound decisions, common-sense judgments, in your own lives. This is what you would do anyway, but it is also, as you will see, the sum and substance of the applicable law.

Then there is the evidence and the testimony before the Personnel Security Board to which Oppenheimer's case was referred by the Atomic Energy Commission. He was employed by the Commission as a consultant, and this was the regular and prescribed procedure. Luckily an indulgent providence brought about the publication of the transcript of the testimony, all of it that was not classified by the security officers; and it has been said that they might well have classified more.

The Commission had promised not to publish it, not even the charges, and the Board had announced at the opening of the hearings that the proceedings and the stenographic record were to be strictly confidential. The chairman repeated this to each witness, and expressed the hope that they would take the same view. He said, "The Atomic Energy Commission will not take the initiative in public release of any information relating to the proceedings before this board."

But the story had already become known. The suspension of Oppenheimer's clearance had been cabled and broadcast to submarine commanders and to Army posts over the world. Senator McCarthy knew about it. Plainly the charges would be published after his fashion. So, shortly after the hearings opened, Lloyd K. Garrison, Oppenheimer's counsel, decided he had to give a copy of the charges and a copy of Oppenheimer's reply to James Reston of the New York *Times*. There they were printed in full, on April 13, 1954.

This was as proper as it was inevitable, and yet the Board expressed "very deep concern." The chairman questioned Oppenheimer and his counsel closely about how it had happened and why they had done it, and said he thought it "very prejudicial to the spirit of inquiry that I tried to establish as an atmosphere for this hearing as we started yesterday." I shall have much to say about this spirit of inquiry later.

The Commission issued a short statement to the press later the same day. It was Dr. Oppenheimer's privilege, the Commission said, to make public an account of the matter; and it went on to give an account of the inception of the proceedings under the Executive Order of April 27, 1953. The Commission pointed out that the President had been consulted and that he had "directed that pending a security review of the material in the file, a blank wall be placed between Dr. Oppenheimer and any secret data and that, without prejudging the outcome, established procedures should be followed." It was a good statement, and the Commission was well advised to make it. This remark about the President can be regarded as in the nature of a retort courteous to the publication by Oppenheimer's counsel of the charges against Oppenheimer and of his reply.

The transcript of the testimony, which ran to over 3,000 typed pages—nearly a thousand printed pages—remained secret for more than a month after the hearings closed on May 6. The Board had made its recommendations, and the General Manager had filed his report with the Commission, when a curious thing happened. On June 15 the Commission, on its own initiative and in spite of the promise which the Chairman of the Board had made on the Commission's behalf, with only a few hours' notice to Oppenheimer and his counsel, gave the full transcript to the press for release at noon the next day, June 16. Garrison and John W. Davis, who had joined him as counsel for Oppenheimer, were still preparing their brief for the Commission, and they hurriedly made it public too, in time to have much of it published in the New York *Times* for June 16, when the transcript was released.

The Commission announced that the release of the transcript was being made "in advance of the time—later this month—when the Commission will reach its decision." The Commission said, "The wide national interest and concern in the matter make inevitable and desirable close public examination of the final determination." Yes, but why before, instead of with, the Commission's decision? The *Times* reported that the Commission had done this by a vote of four to one, Smyth dissenting.

The Commission continued:

A.E.C. security clearance proceedings are conducted in privacy. The Commission's personnel security regulations provide for closed hearings. The Commission protects the privacy of the individuals concerned in such proceedings if they so desire. In this instance, Dr. Oppenheimer's attorneys, as was their privilege, have issued texts of some documents. In the present circumstances, release of the transcript, within the limits of security, will in the opinion of the Commission best serve the public interest.

It is true, as we have seen, that Oppenheimer's attorneys had published the charges and Oppenheimer's reply. As the Commission had recognized, both here and in its statement of April 13, this was his privilege. Certainly the exercise of Oppenheimer's privilege was no good reason why the Commission should break its word, which the Board had given to each witness. I understand that the Commission talked with them and got their assent on the telephone. What it said and what they said I do not, of course, know. Nor how reluctantly, or happily, they gave their assent.

The Commission must have had some urgent reason for acting so abruptly. It will not do to say merely that "the wide national interest and concern in the matter make inevitable and desirable close public examination of the final determination." Nor is what C. A. Rolander, Jr., said later—reported in the *U.S. News and World Report* for December 24, 1954—any better. Rolander, who assisted Robb in the hearings and who was the A.E.C.'s Deputy Director of Security, said that the transcript was released "so that A.E.C. personnel and the public could review the facts of the case." For this is just what the witnesses were assured would not be done. However, you and I now have the transcript, and I, for one, am loath to look a gift horse in the mouth.

There was a story in the newspapers about one of the commissioners leaving part of the transcript on a train. No security bones were broken, for it turned up again safe and sound in Lost and Found. What, if anything, this had to do with the release of the whole transcript by the Commission I do not know. Even if what was lost had not been found, a careless disclosure of one witness' testimony, given in the assurance that it would be confidential, does not justify the publication of the others' or of all. The Commission surely had a better reason than this, some particular reason that the public interest would be best served by the Commission doing what it had undertaken not to do, some reason which overrode its assurance to each witness, not to speak of Oppenheimer and his counsel, that it would not take the initiative in public release of any information relating to the proceedings. What it was I do not know. It has never been announced. Another, and it seems to me a graver, question is whether the public interest is best served by the Commission's giving assurances to the witnesses which it could not be sure of keeping.

Whatever doubts you and I may have about the propriety of the Commission's publication of the transcript, let us be grateful to the Commission that we have it. It is good reading. It is the most interesting transcript of a trial I have read since the transcript of the proceedings in the trial of Joan of Arc. The transcript of her trial, I believe, was not published for four hundred years. The trial took place in 1431, and Guicherat's edition of the proceedings was published in 1841. You and I got the Oppenheimer transcript in little more than four weeks.

I am going to give long passages verbatim, a great part of Oppenheimer's testimony and much from the testimony of many of the other witnesses. Where I have abridged, I have done so sparingly and dutifully. You will listen to such people as Vannevar Bush, James B. Conant, Gordon Dean, Lee A. DuBridge, Enrico Fermi, George F. Kennan, David E. Lilienthal, John J. McCloy, I. I. Rabi, Edward Teller. There were forty witnesses. They talked through most of the nearly 1,000 pages, and what they said was more than ordinarily interesting, partly, I must surmise, because they were told that it was not going to be published. It's not often that we get such testimony. It is like listening to a brilliant as well as serious after-dinner conversation. We ought to be as grateful to the Commission for making its promise as we are for its breaking it.

We will discuss the considerations which led a majority of the Board, two of its three members, to the conclusion that the reinstatement of Oppenheimer's clearance would not be clearly consistent with the security interests of the United States. After that you can read Dr. Ward V. Evans' short dissent without need of interruption.

It was the recommendation of the Board, two against one, to the General Manager of the Atomic Energy Commission that Oppenheimer's clearance should not be reinstated. He in turn made his recommendation to the Commission. I will discuss his memorandum, which came to the same conclusion for different reasons, along with the opinion of the majority of the Commission. Their opinion ran along much the same lines as the General Manager's. This will call for a reconsideration of the significance of some of the evidence. For they take quite a different view of the significance of many of the facts than the Board had taken. They lay stress on things in which the Board saw nothing significant or derogatory; and on the other hand, the Commission took no interest in things which had given the Board great concern. One important charge, Oppenheimer's opposition to the development of an H-bomb in 1949, which the Board found disturbing, the Commission totally rejected. We shall pass close enough to this wrangle to see why the Commission kept out of it. I will tell you about it.

After the opinion of the majority of the Commission, which the chairman, Lewis L. Strauss, wrote, we shall look at the separate opinions of each of the other four commissioners. Eugene M. Zuckert and Joseph Campbell joined in Strauss's opinion, but each had something to add. Thomas E. Murray agreed that clearance should be denied, but only for his own particular reasons, which seem to me of the highest importance. Dr. Henry D. Smyth dissented.

You will then have before you as fair an account of the trial as I can give you and as complete an account as I can get within the covers of a book.

2. WHO IS OPPENHEIMER?

I DON'T KNOW whether I may take it for granted that you know who Oppenheimer is and what he has done. You are going to make his acquaintance as soon as you read his own reply to the charges which the A.E.C. made against him, and some of his testimony. I hope you will read his letter of reply as a whole, and I hope you will read it as if you were listening to it, as you would to the man speaking, and then try to get a picture of the man, the whole individual. I will now simply introduce him.

If you were asked to meet Oppenheimer, you might very well want to look him up in Who's Who. You'd find that at the time of his trial he was just fifty, that he'd had an enviable education—Harvard, Cambridge and Göttingen—that he had at the same time taught at the California Institute of Technology and at the University of California and had become a full professor at thirty-two. Fourteen years of teaching. Then came the race against the Nazis for an atomic bomb. Vannevar Bush, James B. Conant and General Leslie R. Groves chose Oppenheimer to lead and direct our laboratory at Los Alamos. He was not the father and mother of the A-bomb, but I think we may say that he was its midwife and its wet nurse. In his own way, he seems to have the same obstetrical virtues that Socrates had; or, as a scientist might put it, he is a catalyst. Better, a demiurge.

After the war was over, Oppenheimer became the Chairman of the General Advisory Committee to the Atomic Energy Commission. This was in 1947. That fall he was made, and he now is, Director of the Institute for Advanced Study in Princeton. This is not Princeton University. The Institute is a wholly separate and independent affair in the town of Princeton, New Jersey. Einstein was there, and also John von Neumann and George F. Kennan, both of whom we are going to hear testify. The Institute is governed by a board of trustees, and Lewis Strauss is its president. He was an Atomic Energy Commissioner in 1947, when Oppenheimer was appointed Director of the Institute and Chairman of the Commission's General Advisory Committee. He wrote the opinion in this case for the majority of the A.E.C. Another of the trustees is Lloyd K. Garrison, Oppenheimer's counsel in these proceedings.

This is only an introduction. You will judge for yourself what sort of man Oppenheimer is when you get to know him, and how important his services and his influence are to us. As to his influence, which is a difficult thing to judge, he is intelligent enough, candid enough and objective enough to make his own judgment its best measure. When Roger Robb, the attorney for the A.E.C., pressed him to admit that he was the "most experienced, most powerful, and most effective member" of the opposition to the development of the hydrogen bomb in 1949, Oppenheimer said this: "Well, I would say that I was not the most powerful, I was not the most experienced, and I was not the most influential. But, if you take all three factors together, perhaps I combined a little more experience, a little more power, and a little more of influence than anyone else." Robb had asked him the same question, in broader terms, before, and Oppenheimer had answered, "With some people I was very influential. With others not at all. I was an influential physicist and put it anywhere you want."

3. WHAT IS A
SECURITY RISK?

WE MUST KNOW what we are talking about as well as who it is we are talking about. What is a security risk? Whose security are we concerned with? Is it ours, our country's security? Or is it the security of our secrets?

In this case, we are going to be concerned with the hard core of it, the security of our secrets. For plainly the way Oppenheimer could have endangered our security was either by revealing our secrets or by allowing them to escape him. Who else had so many of our most precious secrets in his possession? There was no question of sabotage or subversion—unless you want to see something like one or the other, as some did in the way he criticized our official military strategy.

But the meaning of security cannot be bounded in a nutshell, for some of us are having bad dreams. The Atomic Energy Act speaks largely of "the common defense and security." So the derogatory information which the Board was asked to consider and on which the Commission had to pass was dispersed over an equally wide field.

We must keep a watchful eye on this large and expansive meaning of security. As we shall see, fear as well as actual danger has a way of making our common security all but synonymous with our general welfare. Then the question of whether a man is a security risk blows up into the question of whether we want to employ him instead of somebody else.

This confronts us with the law. The basic law is Section Ten of the Atomic Energy Act of 1946. It says that a person shall not have access to restricted data until the F.B.I. "shall have made an investigation and report to the Commission on the character, associations and loyalty of such individual and the Commission shall have determined that permitting such person to have access to restricted data will not endanger the common defense or security."

The A.E.C. went into particulars in what it called "A.E.C. Personnel Security Clearance Criteria for Determining Eligibility." These have not been revised since September 1950. (*Federal Register*, September 19, 1950.) The Commission saw no need of revising or changing them even after President Eisenhower made his Executive Order 10450 on April 27, 1953, although it revoked and superseded President Truman's Order 9835 of March 21, 1947, under which the criteria had first been drafted.

If you are not a lawyer, I think you will get an adequate and living understanding of the A.E.C.'s criteria, so far as they are immediately applicable to this case, from two colloquies between the Chairman of the Board and Garrison, counsel for Oppenheimer.

One came toward the close of the testimony of Dr. Harry A. Winne, a witness for Oppenheimer. Dr. Winne had been until 1953 vice-president in charge of engineering of the General Electric Company, in charge of General Electric's part in Oak Ridge and its operation of Hanford Works. At the conclusion of Dr. Winne's cross-examination the chairman, Gordon Gray, had the following to say:

Mr. GRAY. Mr. Winne, your convictions are pretty deep about this matter. That is apparent.

The WITNESS. Yes.

Mr. GRAY. I know you are here to be helpful to this board in the discharge of a really very difficult task. There has been some discussion about the Nichols letter and Dr. Oppenheimer's reply which quite apart from the record of this proceeding establish certain facts. There are certain things reported and adverted to in General Nichols' letter and which are said to be true in Dr. Oppenheimer's reply.

Mr. Winne, against the background of the exchange of letters, I would like to read you certain pertinent excerpts from the personnel security clearance criteria for determining eligibility which was issued by the Commission and which we are required, as I understand it, to consider in the course of these deliberations.

I would be glad if counsel for Dr. Oppenheimer would watch me closely in this because I don't want to leave out anything that might be pertinent and therefore mislead Mr. Winne.

This is a very serious question I am addressing to you. This document establishes the fact, or rather, recites the fact that the Commission in September 1950, issued its procedure for administrative review—that is the reason for which we are convened—and points out also that this procedure places considerable responsibility on the managers of operations, and it is to provide uniform standards for their use that the Commission has adopted the criteria described herein.

I might interrupt to say that I am sure it is true that managers of operations here would be in this case the General Manager of the Commission, General Nichols.

Mr. ROBB. That is correct.

Mr. GRAY. Then reading from the document:

"Under the Atomic Energy Act of 1946, it is the responsibility of the Atomic Energy Commission to determine whether the common defense or security will be endangered by granting security clearance to individuals either employed by the Commission or permitted access to restricted data."

Then omitting some language: "Cases must be carefully weighed in the light of all the information and a determination must be reached which gives due recognition to the favorable as well as to the unfavorable information concerning the individual and which balances the cost of the program of not having his services against any possible risks involved."

I believe you, in your testimony, put some emphasis on the point of great services and values that Dr. Oppenheimer has been to the program.

The WITNESS. Yes.

Mr. GRAY. Then it says, "To assist in making these determinations on the basis of all the information in a particular case, there are set forth below a number of specific types of derogatory information. The list is not exhaustive, but it contains the principal types of derogatory information which indicate a security risk." Then it says that they are divided into two categories.

Category (A) includes certain things. I am going to read paragraph No. 1 and parts of paragraph No. 3.

"Category (A) includes those cases in which there are grounds sufficient to establish a reasonable belief that the individual or his spouse has:

"1. Committed or attempted to commit, or aided or abetted another who committed or attempted to commit, any act of sabotage, espionage, treason, or sedition.

*   *   *   *   *   *   *

"3. Held membership in or joined any organization which has been declared by the Attorney General to be totalitarian, Fascist, Communist, subversive * * * or, prior to the declaration by the Attorney General, participated in the activities of such an organization in a capacity where he should reasonably have had knowledge as to the subversive aims or purposes of the organization;".

*   *   *   *   *   *   *

"6. Violated or disregarded security regulations to a degree which would endanger the common defense or security;".

There are a lot of other types of derogatory information which I am not reading. I hope it does not distort it to take those out of context. Then I would go to the last two or three paragraphs of this document:

"The categories outlined hereinabove contain the criteria which will be applied in determining whether information disclosed in investigation reports shall be regarded as substantially derogatory. Determination that there is such information in the case of an individual establishes doubt as to his eligibility for security clearance.

"The criteria outlined hereinabove are intended to serve as aids to the Manager of Operations in discharging his responsibility in the determination of an individual's eligibility for security clearance. While there must necessarily be an adherence to such criteria, the Manager of Operations is not limited thereto, nor precluded in exercising his judgment that information or facts in a case under his cognizance are derogatory although at variance with, or outside the scope of the stated categories. The Manager of Operations upon whom the responsibility rests for the granting of security clearance, and for recommendation in cases referred to the Director of Security, should bear in mind at all times, that his action must be consistent with the common defense or security."

I suppose it is true that the Executive order of the President, which I think has somewhat more restrictive criteria, must also be taken into account in these proceedings. I will not take the time now to take you through all of those.

I have indicated this is a serious inquiry and I am asking for your help to this board.

The WITNESS. Yes.

Mr. GRAY. It seems to me pretty clear that some of these criteria have been met, if you will, by the exchange of letters that I read. Would you agree with that?

The WITNESS. It seems to me that the exchange of letters indicates that in the earlier years under consideration—I think it is 1942 and earlier—that Dr. Oppenheimer—I forget the exact wording there—did support to some extent some of the organizations which have since been declared subversive or perhaps were at that time. I do not know.

Mr. GRAY. This is quite a serious question. One of our difficulties is that it does not say "is a member."

The WITNESS. I recognize that.

Mr. GRAY. It says "The individual or his spouse," and then "done these things."

The WITNESS. Of course, Dr. Oppenheimer does admit that his wife had been a member of the Communist Party.

Mr. MARKS. That is correct.

The WITNESS. That is in the letter. So taking the strictly legal interpretation perhaps you have no alternative there.

Then Garrison had this to say:

Mr. Chairman, just a word about these criteria which I am so glad that you raised. It has been on my own mind to say something about it, but I didn't want to interrupt the flow of the testimony.

I would like to read into the record and just for a moment bring to the attention of the board rather forcibly the two paragraphs that follow the rescription of the general nature of the Atomic Energy Act. These are taken from the Atomic Energy Commission criteria for determining eligibility from which the chairman read particular excerpts from category (A).

"Under the act, the Federal Bureau of Investigation has the responsibility for making an investigation and report to the Commission on the character, associations, and loyalty of individuals who are to be permitted to have access to restricted data. In determining any individual's eligibility for security clearance other information available to the Commission should also be considered, such as whether the individual will have direct access to restricted data or work in proximity to exclusion areas, his past association with the atomic energy program, and the nature of the job he is expected to perform (certainly something we have here before us). The facts of each case must be carefully weighed and determination made in the light of all the information presented whether favorable or unfavorable. The judgment of responsible persons as to the integrity of the individuals should be considered. The decision as to security clearance is an overall, commonsense judgment, made after consideration of all the relevant information as to whether or not there is risk that the granting of security clearance would endanger the common defense or security. If it is determined that the common defense or security will not be endangered, security clearance will be granted; otherwise, security clearance will be denied.

"Cases must be carefully weighed in the light of all the information, and a determination must be reached which gives due recognition to the favorable as well as unfavorable information concerning the individual and which balances the cost to the program of not having his services against any possible risks involved. In making such practical determination, the mature viewpoint and responsible judgment of Commission staff members, and of the contractor concerned are available for consideration by the general manager."

I think that last sentence, of course, is particularly pertinent to the general manager's consideration, but I am sure that this board is expected to provide the general manager with all of this kind of information that is here set forth. This would include, for example, responsible judgment of a man like Dr. Bradbury who is a Commission staff member.

I would like to stress in summary that it seems to me that quite pertinent to this proceeding is Dr. Oppenheimer's past association with the atomic energy program, the nature of his job as a consultant, the judgment of responsible persons who have appeared here and will appear here as to his integrity and the responsible mature viewpoint and responsible judgment of Commission staff members who have testified—only one of them actually—and that the case must be carefully weighed in the light of all of the information.

There is one other thing I would like to point out. That is, if category (A) is considered, as, of course, it must be, it is said to include those classes of derogatory information which establish a presumption of security risk.

I take it that it is quite clear from this that if the board should find a derogatory item which it felt had been established under category (A), which I hope the board will not and believe it should not on the evidence—but if it should— that would establish a presumption which, I take it under this overall judgment that is referred to here, would be rebuttable by other evidence such as what Dr. Oppenheimer has actually done for his country and the opinion of responsible people who know him and the like. In other words, it is not a final and conclusive matter but a rebuttable presumption.

Mr. GRAY. I assume, Mr. Garrison, that at the conclusion of the testimony you possibly may wish to address yourself to some of these matters. I would not at this time respond to any request for an interpretation of the criteria either in this document or in the President's order.

I frankly have received this statement of yours at this time in the record because I initiated all this by bringing it up with Mr. Winne. I think I would like to say why I did that.

I believe it is true and I say this now not in the presence of any witness that we have had some witnesses who have come before the board and in effect have said, "I know this man to be loyal; clear him." That is the sum of some of the testimony we have had.

There has been an inclination to be impatient with procedures and regulations and things of that sort. I just wanted to make clear that everybody understands that the board must take into account all rules, regulations, and procedures in the course of its proceedings and I would not wish you to draw any conclusion now from anything I might have said in talking to Mr. Winne.

Mr. GARRISON. Mr. Chairman, speaking for Dr. Oppenheimer, we agree that any light waving aside of what are serious matters or what may be requirements of the regulations we are not in sympathy with. We take this just as seriously as does the board. That goes for all of us.

I think apart from that, the mere testimony from a witness that having known Dr. Oppenheimer closely for many years he has a conviction about his loyalty, I would say that in itself is pertinent.

Mr. GRAY. I quite agree it is pertinent. Speaking at least for one member of the board, these deep convictions held by responsible people are important in these deliberations. They are important to me and I am sure to the other members of the board.

The other colloquy came at the end of McCloy's testimony. John J. McCloy was then the chairman of the board of the Chase National Bank. Throughout the war he had been Assistant Secretary of War under Henry L. Stimson and Stimson's right-hand man. He had later been our High Commissioner in Germany. McCloy had this to say:

There is another aspect to this question of security, if I may just go on, that troubles me and I have been thinking about it a good bit since I have read the charges and the reply of Dr. Oppenheimer, and have talked to a number of people who are somewhat familiar with this whole subject. It seems to me that there are two security aspects. One is the negative aspect. How do you gage an individual in terms of his likelihood of being careless with respect to the use of documents or expressions, if he is not animated by something more sinister? There is also for want of a better expression the positive security. I remember very vividly the early days when the warnings that Neils Bohr—I was not in Washington when Neils Bohr first came over, but I saw him from time to time after that—when he announced to us and to the President that the uranium atom had been split, and we might look forward with some concern to the possibility that the Germans would have an atomic weapon, and our eagerness at that time to take on, practically speaking, anyone who had this quality of mind that could reach in back of and beyond, from the layman's point of view, at least, and deal with this concept and reduce it to reality.

As I try to look back to that period, I think we would have taken pretty much anybody who had certainly the combination of those qualities, the theoretical ability, plus the practical sense, to advance our defense position in that field. In those days we were on guard against the Nazis and the Germans. I think we would have grabbed one of them if we thought he had that quality, and surrounded him with as much security precautions as we could. Indeed, I think we would have probably taken a convicted murderer if he had that capacity. There again is this question of the relative character of security. It depends somewhat on the day and age that you are in.

I want to emphasize particularly this affirmative side of it. The names we bandied about at that time included a number of refugees and a number of people that came from Europe. I have the impression—I may be wrong about it—but I have the impression that a very large element of this theoretical thinking did emanate from the minds of those who immigrated from this country, and had not been generated here as far as it had been in Europe. There were names like Fermi and Wigner and Teller, Rabi, another queer name, Szilard, or something like that—but I have the impression they came over here, and probably embued with a certain anti-Nazi fervor which tended to stimulate thinking, and it is that type of mind that we certainly needed then.

We could find, so to speak, practical atomic physicists, and today there are great quantities of them being trained, and whether we are getting this finely balanced imagination which can stretch beyond the practicalities of this thing is to my mind the important aspect of this problem. The art is still in its infancy and we still are in need of great imagination in this field.

In a very real sense, therefore, I think there is a security risk in reverse. If anything is done which would in any way repress or dampen that fervor, that verve, that enthusiasm, or the feeling generally that the place where you can get the greatest opportunity for the expansion of your mind and your experiments in this field is the United States, to that extent the security of the United States is impaired.

In other words, you can't be too conventional about it or you run into a security problem the other way. We are only secure if we have the best brains and the best reach of mind in this field. If the impression is prevalent that scientists as a whole have to work under such great restrictions and perhaps great suspicion, in the United States, we may lose the next step in this field, which I think would be very dangerous for us.

From my own experience in Germany, although they were very backward in this field, and in that respect there is a very interesting instance which I have seen referred to in print——

Mr. Gray. Mr. McCloy, may I interrupt you for a minute? As a lawyer, you must observe we allow very considerable latitude in these hearings, and we have tried in no way to circumscribe anything that any witness wishes to say, and in fact, almost anything the lawyers wanted to say has gone into the record. You were asked a question, I believe, by Mr. Garrison, about Dr. Oppenheimer's— it has been a long time and I have forgotten.

Mr. Garrison. Loyalty, and him as a security risk.

Mr. Gray. Yes. Whereas I think your views are entitled to great weight on these matters generally, I would respectfully and in the most friendly spirit, suggest that we not wander too far afield from this question.

The Witness. I didn't mean to wander too far.

Mr. Gray. Yes, sir.

The Witness. I did want to make one point. I have been asked this recently in New York frequently: Do you think that Dr. Oppenheimer is a security risk, and how would I answer that. This is long before I had any idea I was going to be called here. What do you mean by security, positive, negative, there is a security risk both ways in this thing. It is the affirmative security that I believe we must protect here. I would say that even if Dr. Oppenheimer had some connections that were somewhat suspicious or make one fairly uneasy, you have to balance his affirmative aspect against that, before you can finally conclude in your own mind that he is a reasonable security risk, because there is a balance of interest there; that he not only is himself, but that he represents in terms of scientific inquiry—I am very sorry if I rambled on about that and I didn't mean to.

Mr. Gray. I don't want to cut you off at all, but you were getting back about something of the Nazis during the war.

The Witness. Yes. Let me tell you why I did that, if I may.

Mr. Robb. Mr. Chairman, may I interpose one thought. I think the rules do provide that no witness will be allowed to argue from the witness stand. I think the witness should bear that in mind, if I might suggest it.

The Witness. Yes. I don't mean to argue. I am trying honestly to answer the question whether this man is a security risk in my judgment from what I know of him.

Mr. Robb. I understand.

The Witness. One of my tasks in Germany was to pick up Nazi scientists and send them over to the United States. These Nazi scientists a few years before were doing their utmost to overthrow the United States Government by violence. They had a very suspicious background. They are being used now, I assume—whether they are still, I don't know, because I am not in contact with it—on very sensitive projects in spite of their background. The Defense

Department has been certainly to some extent dependent upon German scientists in connection with guided missiles. I suppose other things being equal, you would like to have a perfectly pure, uncontaminated chap, with no background, to deal with these things, but it is not possible in this world. I think you do have to take risks in regard to the security of the country. As I said at the beginning, even if they put you—I won't be personal about it—but let us say put Mr. Stimson or anybody in charge of the innermost secrets of our defense system, there is a risk there. You can't avoid the necessity of balancing to some degree.

So I reemphasize from looking at it, I would think I would come to the conclusion if I were Secretary of War, let us balance all the considerations here and take the calculated risk. It is too bad you have to calculate sometimes. But in the last analysis, you have to calculate what is best for the United States, because there is no Maginot Line in terms—it is just as weak as the Maginot Line in terms of security.

Mr. GRAY. Do you understand that it is beyond the duty of this board to make the ultimate decision as to who shall be employed by the Government on the basis of his indispensability or otherwise?

The WITNESS. Surely.

Mr. GRAY. We are more narrowly concerned with the field of security as we understand the term.

The WITNESS. I understand that.

Mr. GRAY. I think I have no more questions. Dr. Evans.

Dr. EVANS. Mr. McCloy, you say you talked to Bohr?

The WITNESS. Yes; Neils Bohr.

Dr. EVANS. Where did you talk to Neils?

The WITNESS. I talked to him abroad and here. He visited Washington, you know.

Dr. EVANS. I know. Did he tell you who split the uranium atom over there?

The WITNESS. Wasn't it Hahn and Straussman?

Dr. EVANS. Yes. I am just giving you a little quiz to find out how much you associated.

The WITNESS. You terrify me.

Dr. EVANS. Did you read Smyth's book?

The WITNESS. Yes; I did. I·was also tutored by Rabi; I may say that when Dr. Oppenheimer gave me up as a poor prospect.

Dr. EVANS. And you think we should take some chances for fear we might disqualify someone who might do us a lot of good?

The WITNESS. Yes; I do.

Dr. EVANS. You do?

The WITNESS. Yes.

4. THE CHARGES

THESE PROCEEDINGS against Oppenheimer began to emerge and take shape in the spring of 1953. In June 1953, shortly before Gordon Dean retired as chairman of the A.E.C., the Commission had renewed Oppenheimer's contract as consultant for another year. On July 7, 1953, within a week after Strauss succeeded Dean as chairman, at Strauss's request the Commission "initiated steps to organize the removal of classified documents" from Oppenheimer's custody at Princeton. (The A.E.C.'s statement on April 13, 1954.) This was the first open step toward these proceedings.

I don't know just what was done, but the Commission was in no great hurry to remove the classified documents from Oppenheimer's custody. Rolander, in a memorandum to the General Manager dated October 25, 1954, which was published in the *U.S. News and World Report* of December 24, 1954, says that it was not till December 24, 1953, the day after Oppenheimer's clearance was suspended, the day before Christmas, that two security officers delivered a letter to him directing all his A.E.C. classified documents be returned. This was done beginning the next Monday and completed before the new year. Oppenheimer told one of the security men that "what he had at first feared would be an unpleasant duty had turned out to be somewhat of a pleasure." This is Rolander's account. I wonder whether it was not Oppenheimer who made the proceedings "somewhat of a pleasure."

There is sometimes, and there was here, an irony in the passage and carriage of things. Oppenheimer was also a consultant to the Department of Defense, and that same June the question of his reappointment came up there too. The security officers brought this to the attention of Dr. Walter G. Whitman, the chairman of the

Research and Development Board in the Pentagon. He told them that he would personally review the whole case and leave his recommendation for his successor under the recent reorganization of the department. He chose a quiet Saturday and went through the file himself. It was the first Saturday of the same July 1953, three days before Strauss took this first step toward the removal of Oppenheimer's classified papers from his custody. Whitman made his recommendation on July 10, three days later. One hand did not know what the other hand was doing. Dr. Whitman's recommendation was ". . . I am convinced that he can be of great service as a consultant to the research and developmental work of the Department of Defense. I unqualifiedly recommend his reappointment as a consultant."

In November 1953 William L. Borden, who up to a short time before had been secretary of the Joint Committee of Congress on Atomic Energy, wrote a letter to the F.B.I. I think you will want to read it.

"DEAR MR. HOOVER: This letter concerns J. Robert Oppenheimer.

"As you know, he has for some years enjoyed access to various critical activities of the National Security Council, the Department of State, the Department of Defense, the Army, Navy, and Air Force, the Research and Development Board, the Atomic Energy Commission, the Central Intelligence Agency, the National Security Resources Board, and the National Science Foundation. His access covers most new weapons being developed by the Armed Forces, war plans at least in comprehensive outline, complete details as to atomic and hydrogen weapons and stockpile data, the evidence on which some of the principal CIA intelligence estimates is based, United States participation in the United Nations and NATO and many other areas of high security sensitivity.

"Because the scope of his access may well be unique, because he has had custody of an immense collection of classified papers covering military, intelligence, and diplomatic as well as atomic-energy matters, and because he also possesses a scientific background enabling him to grasp the significance of classified data of a technical nature, it seems reasonable to estimate that he is and for some years has been in a position to compromise more vital and detailed information affecting the national defense and security than any other individual in the United States.

"While J. Robert Oppenheimer has not made major contributions to the advancement of science, he holds a respected professional standing among the second rank of American physicists. In terms of his mastery of Government affairs, his close liaison with ranking officials, and his ability to influence high-level thinking, he surely stands in the first rank, not merely among scientists but among all those who have shaped postwar decisions in the military, atomic energy, intelligence, and diplomatic fields. As chairman or as an official or unofficial member of more than 35 important Government committees, panels, study groups, and projects, he has oriented or dominated key policies involving every principal United States security department and agency except the FBI.

"The purpose of this letter is to state my own exhaustively considered opinion, based upon years of study, of the available classified evidence, that more probably than not J. Robert Oppenheimer is an agent of the Soviet Union.

"This opinion considers the following factors, among others:

"(a) He was contributing substantial monthly sums to the Communist Party;

"(b) His ties with communism had survived the Nazi-Soviet Pact and the Soviet attack upon Finland;

"(c) His wife and younger brother were Communists;

"(d) He had no close friends except Communists;

"(e) He had at least one Communist mistress;

"(*f*) He belonged only to Communist organizations, apart from professional affiliations;

"(*g*) The people whom he recruited into the early wartime Berkeley atomic project were exclusively Communists;

"(*h*) He had been instrumental in securing recruits for the Communist Party; and

"(*i*) He was in frequent contact with Soviet espionage agents.

"2. The evidence indicating that—

"(*a*) In May 1942, he either stopped contributing funds to the Communist Party or else made his contributions through a new channel not yet discovered;

"(*b*) In April 1942 his name was formally submitted for security clearance;

"(*c*) He himself was aware at the time that his name had been so submitted; and

"(*d*) He thereafter repeatedly gave false information to General Groves, the Manhattan District, and the FBI concerning the 1939–April 1942 period.

"3. The evidence indicating that—

"(*a*) He was responsible for employing a number of Communists, some of them nontechnical, at wartime Los Alamos;

"(*b*) He selected one such individual to write the official Los Alamos history;

"(*c*) He was a vigorous supporter of the H-bomb program until August 6, 1945 (Hiroshima), on which day he personally urged each senior individual working in this field to desist; and

"(*d*) He was an enthusiastic sponsor of the A-bomb program until the war ended, when he immediately and outspokenly advocated that the Los Alamos Laboratory be disbanded.

"4. The evidence indicating that:

"(*a*) He was remarkably instrumental in influencing the military authorities and the Atomic Energy Commission essentially to suspend H-bomb development from mid-1946 through January 31, 1950.

"(*b*) He has worked tirelessly, from January 31, 1950, onward, to retard the United States H-bomb program;

"(*c*) He has used his potent influence against every postwar effort to expand capacity for producing A-bomb material;

"(*d*) He has used his potent influence against every postwar effort directed at obtaining larger supplies of uranium raw material; and

"(*e*) He has used his potent influence against every major postwar effort toward atomic power development, including the nuclear-powered submarine and aircraft programs as well as industrial power projects."

From such evidence, considered in detail, the following conclusions are justified:

"1. Between 1929 and mid-1942, more probably than not, J. Robert Oppenheimer was a sufficiently hardened Communist that he either volunteered espionage information to the Soviets or complied with a request for such information. (This includes the possibility that when he singled out the weapons aspect of atomic development as his personal specialty, he was acting under Soviet instructions.)

"2. More probably than not, he has since been functioning as an espionage agent; and

"3. More probably than not, he has since acted under a Soviet directive in influencing United States military, atomic energy, intelligence, and diplomatic policy.

"It is to be noted that these conclusions correlate with information furnished by Klaus Fuchs, indicating that the Soviets had acquired an agent in Berkeley who informed them about electromagnetic separation research during 1942 or earlier.

"Needless to say, I appreciate the probabilities identifiable from existing evidence might, with review of future acquired evidence, be reduced to possibilities; or they might also be increased to certainties. The central problem is not whether J. Robert Oppenheimer was ever a Communist; for the existing evidence makes abundantly clear that he was. Even an Atomic Energy Commission analysis prepared in early 1947 reflects this conclusion, although some of the most significant derogatory data had yet to become available. The central problem is assessing the degree of likelihood that he in fact did what a Communist in his circumstances, at Berkeley, would logically have done during the crucial 1939–42 period—that is, whether he became an actual espionage and policy instrument of the Soviets. Thus, as to this central problem, my opinion is that, more probably than not, the worst is in fact the truth.

"I am profoundly aware of the grave nature of these comments. The matter is detestable to me. Having lived with the Oppenheimer case for years, having studied and restudied all data concerning him that your agency made available to the Atomic Energy Commission through May 1953, having endeavored to factor in a mass of additional data assembled from numerous other sources, and looking back upon the case from a perspective in private life, I feel a duty simply to state to the responsible head of the security agency most concerned the conclusions which I have painfully crystalized and which I believe any fairminded man thoroughly familiar with the evidence must also be driven to accept.

"The writing of this letter, to me a solemn step, is exclusively on my own personal initiative and responsibility.

"Very truly yours,

"(Signed)   William L. Borden,
"(Typed)   WILLIAM L. BORDEN."

On receipt of Borden's letter, the F.B.I. prepared a summary report on Oppenheimer and on November 30, 1953, distributed it, with copies of Borden's letter, to the interested agencies of the Government, including the Office of the President. You have read the letter. We have not, of course, got the summary, nor Hoover's covering letter. On December 3, 1953, Strauss, the chairman of the A.E.C., Charles E. Wilson, the Secretary of Defense, and Arthur S. Flemming, the Director of Defense Mobilization, conferred with the President; and then, as the A.E.C. announced later, the President directed that "a blank wall be placed between Dr. Oppenheimer and any secret data" and that the established procedures be followed (April 13, 1954).

Later, the day after the Commission's decision, on June 30, 1954, the President was asked about this meeting at his news conference:

MR. RESTON—Mr. President, could I ask you just one more question about Oppenheimer in order to keep the record straight? You said the case was the responsibility of the Atomic Energy Commission.

As I understand it, the Atomic Energy Commission never discussed the case until it received a letter from you on the 3d of December ordering the investigation.

Could you tell us about that December 3 meeting, what the background of that was?

A.—Well, he didn't recall any meeting. He recalled that he had received a report that was very disturbing to him, and he had forwarded it to the Atomic Energy Commission with the certainty in his own mind that it would be thoroughly investigated.

Now, exactly what they had said at that time, Mr. Reston, he hadn't the slightest idea. It was—he took the action that seemed almost compulsory under the circumstances.

I don't at all like to think that such a letter as Borden's could make such action compulsory on the President. I wish we knew what Strauss, Wilson and Flemming advised.

On December 10, 1953, the A.E.C. voted unanimously to institute the regular procedure of the Commission "to determine the veracity or falsity of the charges." I take it these are Borden's charges. Oppenheimer was abroad. He had gone to England to deliver the Reith Lectures. On December 17, Oxford gave him an honorary degree. He and his wife spent a few days in Paris, and they had supper with their old friend Haakon Chevalier, of whom we shall hear more.

On December 21, 1953, soon after the Oppenheimers got home, Strauss called Oppenheimer in and told him that his clearance by the A.E.C. was "about to be suspended." Strauss gave him one day to consider and decide what he wanted to do about it. Oppenheimer replied the next day. Here is his letter:

"DEAR LEWIS: Yesterday, when you asked to see me, you told me for the first time that my clearance by the Atomic Energy Commission was about to be suspended. You put to me as a possibly desirable alternative that I request termination of my contract as a consultant to the Commission, and thereby avoid an explicit consideration of the charges on which the Commission's action would otherwise be based. I was told that if I did not do this within a day, I would receive a letter notifying me of the suspension of my clearance and of the charges against me, and I was shown a draft of that letter.

"I have thought most earnestly of the alternative suggested. Under the circumstances this course of action would mean that I accept and concur in the view that I am not fit to serve this Government, that I have now served for some 12 years. This I cannot do. If I were thus unworthy I could hardly have served our country as I have tried, or been the Director of our Institute in Princeton, or have spoken, as on more than one occasion I have found myself speaking, in the name of our science and our country.

"Since our meeting yesterday, you and General Nichols told me that the charges in the letter were familiar charges, and since the time was short, I paged through the letter quite briefly. I shall now read it in detail and make appropriate response.

"Faithfully yours,

ROBERT OPPENHEIMER."

The day after that, December 23, Oppenheimer's clearance was suspended and formal charges were made against him in a letter to him from General Nichols, the General Manager of the A.E.C. This letter you must read now and in full. You will note, if you have read Borden's letter, that, for all you can see, Nichols paid no more attention to it than the Board did. And yet I suppose Borden can claim to be the can of kerosene that started the conflagration. The "derogatory information" in the General Manager's letter is the kindling.

"DEAR DR. OPPENHEIMER: Section 10 of the Atomic Energy Act of 1946 places upon the Atomic Energy Commission the responsibility for assuring that individuals are employed by the Commission only when such employment will not endanger the common defense and security. In addition, Executive Order 10450 of April 27, 1953, requires the suspension of employment of any individual where there exists information indicating that his employment may not be clearly consistent with the interests of the national security.

"As a result of additional investigation as to your character, associations, and loyalty, and review of your personnel security file in the light of the requirements of the Atomic Energy Act and the requirements of Executive Order 10450, there has developed considerable question whether your continued employment on Atomic Energy Commission work will endanger the common defense and security and whether such continued employment is clearly consistent with the interests of the national security. This letter is to advise you of the steps which you may take to assist in the resolution of this question.

"The substance of the information which raises the question concerning your eligibility for employment on Atomic Energy Commission work is as follows:"

Let the record show at this point that Mr. Garrison asked to be excused for a few minutes.

"It was reported that in 1940 you were listed as a sponsor of the Friends of the Chinese People, an organization which was characterized in 1944 by the House Committee on Un-American Activities as a Communist-front organization. It was further reported that in 1940 your name was included on a letterhead of the American Committee for Democratic and Intellectual Freedom as a member of its national executive committee. The American Committee for Democracy and Intellectual Freedom was characterized in 1942 by the House Committee on Un-American Activities as a Communist front which defended Communist teachers, and in 1943 it was characterized as subversive and un-American by a special subcommittee of the House Committee on Appropriations. It was further reported that in 1938 you were a member of the Western Council of the Consumers Union. The Consumers Union was cited in 1944 by the House Committee on Un-American Activities as a Communist-front headed by the Communist Arthur Kallet. It was further reported that you stated in 1943 that you were not a Communist, but had probably belonged to every Communist front organization on the west coast and had signed many petitions in which Communists were interested.

"It was reported that in 1943 and previously you were intimately associated with Dr. Jean Tatlock, a member of the Communist Party in San Francisco, and that Dr. Tatlock was partially responsible for your association with Communist-front groups.

"It was reported that your wife, Katherine Puening Oppenheimer, was formerly the wife of Joseph Dallet, a member of the Communist Party, who was killed in Spain in 1937 fighting for the Spanish Republican Army. It was further reported that during the period of her association with Joseph Dallet, your wife became a member of the Communist Party. The Communist Party has been designated by the Attorney General as a subversive organization which seeks to alter the form of Government of the United States by unconstitutional means, within the purview of Executive Order 9835 and Executive Order 10450.

"It was reported that your brother, Frank Friedman Oppenheimer, became a member of the Communist Party in 1936 and has served as a party organizer and as educational director of the professional section of the Communist Party in Los Angeles County. It was further reported that your brother's wife, Jackie Oppenheimer, was a member of the Communist Party in 1938; and that in August 1944, Jackie Oppenheimer assisted in the organization of the East Bay branch of the California Labor School. It was further reported that in 1945 Frank and Jackie Oppenheimer were invited to an informal reception at the Russian consulate, that this invitation was extended by the American-Russian Institute of San Francisco and was for the purpose of introducing famous American scientists to Russian scientists who were delegates to the United Nations Conference on International Organization being held at San Francisco at that time, and that Frank Oppenheimer accepted this invitation. It was further reported that Frank Oppenheimer agreed to give a 6 weeks course on The Social Implications of Modern Scientific Development at the California Labor School, beginning May 9, 1946. The American-Russian Institute of San Francisco and the California Labor School have been cited by the Attorney General as Communist organizations within the purview of Executive Order 9835 and Executive Order 10450.

"It was reported that you have associated with members and officials of the

Communist Party including Isaac Folkoff, Steve Nelson, Rudy Lambert, Kenneth May, Jack Manley, and Thomas Addis.

"It was reported that you were a subscriber to the Daily People's World, a west coast Communist newspaper, in 1941 and 1942.

"It was reported in 1950 that you stated to an agent of the Federal Bureau of Investigation that you had in the past made contributions to Communist-front organizations, although at the time you did not know of Communist Party control or extent of infiltration of these groups. You further stated to an agent of the Federal Bureau of Investigation that some of these contributions were made through Isaac Folkoff, whom you knew to be a leading Communist Party functionary, because you had been told that this was the most effective and direct way of helping these groups.

"It was reported that you attended a housewarming party at the home of Kenneth and Ruth May on September 20, 1941, for which there was an admission charge for the benefit of The People's World, and that at this party you were in the company of Joseph W. Weinberg and Clarence Hiskey, who were alleged to be members of the Communist Party and to have engaged in espionage on behalf of the Soviet Union. It was further reported that you informed officials of the United States Department of Justice in 1952 that you had no recollection that you had attended such a party, but that since it would have been in character for you to have attended such a party, you would not deny that you were there.

"It was reported that you attended a closed meeting of the professional section of the Communist Party of Alameda County, Calif., which was held in the latter part of July or early August 1941, at your residence, 10 Kenilworth Court, Berkeley, Calif., for the purpose of hearing an explanation of a change in Communist Party policy. It was reported that you denied that you attended such a meeting and that such a meeting was held in your home.

"It was reported that you stated to an agent of the Federal Bureau of Investigation in 1950, that you attended a meeting in 1940 or 1941, which may have taken place at the home of Haakon Chevalier, which was addressed by William Schneiderman, whom you knew to be a leading functionary of the Communist Party. In testimony in 1950 before the California State Senate Committee on Un-American Activities, Haakon Chevalier was identified as a member of the Communist Party in the San Francisco area in the early 1940's."

Let the record show that Mr. Garrison has returned to the hearing room.

"It was reported that you have consistently denied that you have ever been a member of the Communist Party. It was further reported that you stated to a representative of the Federal Bureau of Investigation in 1946 that you had a change of mind regarding the policies and politics of the Soviet Union about the time of the signing of the Soviet-German Pact in 1939. It was further reported that during 1950 you stated to a representative of the Federal Bureau of Investigation that you had never attended a closed meeting of the Communist Party; and that at the time of the Russo-Finnish War and the subsequent break between Germany and Russia in 1941, you realized the Communist Party infiltration tactics into the alleged anti-Fascist groups and became fed up with the whole thing and lost what little interest you had. It was further reported, however, that:

"(*a*) Prior to April 1942, you had contributed $150 per month to the Communist Party in the San Francisco area, and that the last such payment was apparently made in April 1942, immediately before your entry into the atomic-bomb project.

"(*b*) During the period 1942–45 various officials of the Communist Party, including Dr. Hannah Peters, organizer of the professional section of the Communist Party, Alameda County, Calif., Bernadette Doyle, secretary of the Alameda County Communist Party Steve Nelson, David Adelson, Paul Pinsky, Jack Manley, and Katrina Sandov, are reported to have made statements indicating that you were then a member of the Communist Party; that you could not be active in the party at that time; that your name should be removed from the party mailing list and not mentioned in any way; that you had talked the atomic-bomb question over with party members during this period; and that several years prior to 1945 you had told Steve Nelson that the Army was working on an atomic bomb.

"(*c*) You stated in August of 1943 that you did not want anybody working for you on the project who was a member of the Communist Party, since 'one always had a question of divided loyalty" and the discipline of the Communist Party was very severe and not compatible with complete loyalty to the project.

You further stated at that time that you were referring only to present membership in the Communist Party and not to people who had been members of the party. You stated further that you knew several individuals then at Los Alamos who had been members of the Communist Party. You did not, however, identify such former members of the Communist Party to the appropriate authorities. It was also reported that during the period 1942–45 you were responsible for the employment on the atom-bomb project of individuals who were members of the Communist Party or closely associated with activities of the Communist Party, including Giovanni Rossi Lomanitz, Joseph W. Weinberg, David Bohm, Max Bernard Friedman, and David Hawkins. In the case of Giovanni Rossi Lomanitz, you urged him to work on the project, although you stated that you knew he had been very much of a Red when he first came to the University of California and that you emphasized to him that he must forego all political activity if he came to the project. In August 1943, you protested against the termination of his deferment and requested that he be returned to the project after his entry into the military service.

"It was reported that you stated to representatives of the Federal Bureau of Investigation on September 5, 1946, that you had attended a meeting in the East Bay and a meeting in San Francisco at which there were present persons definitely identified with the Communist Party. When asked the purpose of the East Bay meeting and the identity of those in attendance, you declined to answer on the ground that this had no bearing on the matter of interest being discussed.

"It was reported that you attended a meeting at the home of Frank Oppenheimer on January 1, 1946, with David Adelson and Paul Pinsky, both of whom were members of the Communist Party. It was further reported that you analyzed some material which Pinsky hoped to take up with the legislative convention in Sacramento, Calif.

"It was reported in 1946 that you were listed as vice chairman on the letterhead of the Independent Citizens Committee of the Arts, Sciences, and Professions, Inc., which has been cited as a Communist front by the House Committee on Un-American Activities.

"It was reported that prior to March 1, 1943, possibly 3 months prior, Peter Ivanov, secretary of the Soviet consulate, San Francisco, approached George Charles Eltenton for the purpose of obtaining information regarding work being done at the Radiation Laboratory for the use of Soviet scientists; that George Charles Eltenton subsequently requested Haakon Chevalier to approach you concerning this matter; that Haakon Chevalier thereupon approached you, either directly or through your brother, Frank Friedman Oppenheimer, in connection with this matter; and that Haakon Chevalier finally advised George Charles Eltenton that there was no chance whatsoever of obtaining the information. It was further reported that you did not report this episode to the appropriate authorities until several months after its occurrence; that when you initially discussed this matter with the appropriate authorities on August 26, 1943, you did not identify yourself as the person who had been approached, and you refused to identify Haakon Chevalier as the individual who made the approach on behalf of George Charles Eltenton; and that it was not until several months later, when you were ordered by a superior to do so, that you so identified Haakon Chevalier. It was further reported that upon your return to Berkeley following your separation from the Los Alamos project, you were visited by the Chevaliers on several occasions; and that your wife was in contact with Haakon and Barbara Chevalier in 1946 and 1947.

"It was reported that in 1945 you expressed the view that 'there is a reasonable possibility that it (the hydrogen bomb) can be made,' but that the feasibility of the hydrogen bomb did not appear, on theoretical grounds, as certain as the fission bomb appeared certain, on theoretical grounds, when the Los Alamos Laboratory was started; and that in the autumn of 1949 the General Advisory Committee expressed the view that 'an imaginative and concerted attack on the problem has a better than even chance of producing the weapon within 5 years.' It was further reported that in the autumn of 1949, and subsequently, you strongly opposed the development of the hydrogen bomb; (1) on moral grounds, (2) by claiming that it was not feasible, (3) by claiming that there were insufficient facilities and scientific personnel to carry on the development, and (4) that it was not politically desirable. It was further reported that even after it was determined, as a matter of national policy, to proceed with development of a hydrogen bomb, you continued to oppose the project and declined to cooperate fully in the project. It was further reported that you departed from your proper role as an adviser to the Commission by causing the distribution separately and in private, to top personnel at Los Alamos of the majority and minority reports of the General Advisory Committee on development of the hydrogen bomb for the purpose of trying to turn such top personnel against the development of the hydrogen bomb. It was further reported that you were instrumental in persuading other outstanding scientists not to work on the hydrogen-bomb project, and that the opposition to the hydrogen bomb, of which you are the most experienced, most powerful, and most effective member, has definitely slowed down its development.

"In view of your access to highly sensitive classified information, and in view of these allegations which, until disproved, raise questions as to your veracity, conduct and even your loyalty, the Commission has no other recourse, in discharge of its obligations to protect the common defense and security, but to suspend your clearance until the matter has been resolved. Accordingly, your employment on Atomic Energy Energy Commission work and your eligibility for access to restricted data are hereby suspended, effective immediately, pending final determination of this matter.

"To assist in the resolution of this matter, you have the privilege of appearing before an Atomic Energy Commission personnel security board. To avail yourself of the privileges afforded you under the Atomic Energy Commission hearing procedures, you must, within 30 days following receipt of this letter, submit to me, in writing, your reply to the information outlined above and request the opportunity of appearing before the personnel security board. Should you signify your desire to appear before the board, you will be notified of the composition of the board and may challenge any member of it for cause. Such challenge should be submitted within 72 hours of the receipt of notice of composition of the board.

"If no challenge is raised as to the members of the board, you will be notified of the date and place of hearing at least 48 hours in advance of the date set for hearing. You may be present for the duration of the hearing, may be represented by counsel of your own choosing, and present evidence in your own behalf through witnesses, or by documents, or by both.

"Should you elect to have a hearing of your case by the personnel security board, the findings of the board, together with its recommendations regarding your eligibility for employment on Atomic Energy Commission work, in the light of Criteria for Determining Eligibility for Atomic Energy Commission Security Clearance and the requirements of Executive Order 10450, will be submitted to me.

"In the event of an adverse decision in your case by the personnel security board, you will have an opportunity to review the record made during your appearance before the board and to request a review of your case by the Commission's personnel security review board.

"If a written response is not received from you within 30 days it will be assumed that you do not wish to submit any explanation for further consideration. In that event, or should you not advise me in writing of your desire to appear before the personnel security board, a determination in your case will be made by me on the basis of the existing record.

"I am enclosing herewith, for your information and guidance, copies of the Criteria and Procedures for Determining Eligibility for Atomic Energy Commission Security Clearance and Executive Order 10450.

"This letter has been marked 'Confidential' to maintain the privacy of this matter between you and the Atomic Energy Commission. You are not precluded from making use of this letter as you may consider appropriate.

"I have instructed Mr. William Mitchell, whose address is 1901 Constitution Avenue NW., Washington, D. C., and whose telephone number is Sterling 3–8000, Extension 277, to give you whatever further detailed information you may desire with respect to the procedures to be followed in this matter.

"Very truly yours,

"K. D. NICHOLS, *General Manager.*

"2 Enclosures. 1. Criteria and Procedures. 2. Executive Order 10450."

You must now read Oppenheimer's reply, again exactly as it was read during the hearings.

"DEAR GENERAL NICHOLS: This is in answer to your letter of December 23, 1953, in which the question is raised whether my continued employment as a consultant on Atomic Energy Commission work 'will endanger the common defense and security and whether such continued employment is clearly consistent with the interests of the national security.'

"Though of course I would have no desire to retain an advisory position if my advice were not needed. I cannot ignore the question you have raised, nor accept the suggestion that I am unfit for public service.

"The items of so-called derogatory information set forth in your letter cannot be fairly understood except in the context of my life and my work. This answer is in the form of a summary account of relevant aspects of my life in more or less chronological order, in the course of which I shall comment on the specific items in your letter. Through this answer, and through the hearings before the personnel security board, which I hereby request, I hope to provide a fair basis upon which the questions posed by your letter may be resolved.

"THE PREWAR PERIOD

"I was born in New York in 1904. My father had come to this country at the age of 17 from Germany. He was a successful businessman and quite active in community affairs. My mother was born in Baltimore and before her marriage was an artist and teacher of art. I attended Ethical Culture School and Harvard College, which I entered in 1922. I completed the work for my degree in the spring of 1925. I then left Harvard to study at Cambridge University and in Goettingen, where in the spring of 1927 I took my doctor's degree. The following year I was national research fellow at Harvard and at the California Institute of Technology. In the following year I was fellow of the international education board at the University of Leiden and at the Technical High School in Zurich.

"In the spring of 1929, I returned to the United States. I was homesick for this country, and in fact I did not leave it again for 19 years. I had learned a great deal in my student days about the new physics; I wanted to pursue this myself, to explain it and to foster its cultivation. I had had many invitations to university positions, 1 or 2 in Europe, and perhaps 10 in the United States. I accepted concurrent appointments as assistant professor at the California Institute of Technology in Pasadena and at the University of California in Berkeley. For the coming 12 years, I was to devote my time to these 2 faculties.

"Starting with a single graduate student in my first year in Berkely, we gradually began to build up what was to become the largest school in the country of graduate and postdoctoral study in theoretical physics, so that as time went on, we came to have between a dozen and 20 people learning and adding to quantum theory, nuclear physics, relativity and other modern physics. As the number of students increased, so in general did their quality; the men who worked with me during those years hold chairs in many of the great centers of physics in this country; they have made important contributions to science, and in many cases to the atomic-energy project. Many of my students would accompany me to Pasadena in the spring after the Berkeley term was over, so that we might continue to work together.

"My friends, both in Pasadena and in Berkeley, were mostly faculty people, scientists, classicists, and artists. I studied and read Sanskrit with Arthur Rider. I read very widely, must mostly classics, novels, plays, and poetry; and I read something of other parts of science. I was not interested in and did not read about economics or politics. I was almost wholly divorced from the contemporary scene in this country. I never read a newspaper or a current magazine like Time or Harper's; I had no radio, no telephone; I learned of the stock-market crack in the fall of 1929 only long after the event; the first time I ever voted was in the presidential election of 1936. To many of my friends, my indifference to contemporary affairs seemed bizarre, and they often chided me with being too much of a highbrow. I was interested in man and his experience; I was deeply interested in my science; but I had no understanding of the relations of man to his society.

"I spent some weeks each summer with my brother Frank at our ranch in New Mexico. There was a strong bond of affection between us. After my mother's death, my father came often, mostly in Berkeley, to visit me; and we had an intimate and close association until his death.

"Beginning in late 1936, my interests began to change. These changes did not alter my earlier friendships, my relations to my students, or my devotion to physics; but they added something new. I can discern in retrospect more than one reason for these changes. I had had a continuing, smoldering fury about the treatment of Jews in Germany. I had relatives there, and was later to help in extricating them and bringing them to this country. I saw what the depression was doing to my students. Often they could get no jobs, or jobs which were wholly inadequate. And through them, I began to understand how deeply political and economic events could affect men's lives. I began to feel the need to participate more fully in the life of the community. But I had no framework of political conviction or experience to give me perspective in these matters.

"In the spring of 1936, I had been introduced by friends to Jean Tatlock, the daughter of a noted professor of English at the university; and in the autumn, I began to court her, and we grew close to each other. We were at least twice close enough to marriage to think of ourselves as engaged. Between 1939 and her death in 1944 I saw her very rarely. She told me about her Communist Party memberships; they were on again, off again affairs, and never seemed to provide for her what she was seeking. I do not believe that her interests were really political. She loved this country and its people and its life. She was, as it turned out, a friend of many fellow travelers and Communists, with a number of whom I was later to become acquainted.

"I should not give the impression that it was wholly because of Jean Tatlock that I made leftwing friends, or felt sympathy for causes which hitherto would have seemed so remote from me, like the Loyalist cause in Spain, and the organization of migratory workers. I have mentioned some of the other contributing causes. I liked the new sense of companionship, and at the time felt that I was coming to be part of the life of my time and country.

"In 1937, my father died; a little later, when I came into an inheritance, I made a will leaving this to the University of California for fellowships to graduate students.

"This was the era of what the Communists then called the United Front, in which they joined with many non-Communist groups in support of humanitarian objectives. Many of these objectives engaged my interest. I contributed to the strike fund of one of the major strikes of Bridges' union; I subscribed to the People's World; I contributed to the various committees and organizations which were intended to help the Spanish Loyalist cause. I was invited to help establish the teacher's union, which included faculty and teaching assistants at the university, and school teachers of the East Bay. I was elected recording secretary. My connection with the teacher's union continued until some time in 1941, when we disbanded our chapter.

"During these same years, I also began to take part in the management of the physics department, the selection of courses, and the awarding of fellowships, and in the general affairs of the graduate school of the university, mostly through the graduate council, of which I was a member for some years.

"I also became involved in other organizations. For perhaps a year, I was a member of the western council of the Consumer's Union which was concerned with evaluating information on products of interest on the west coast. I do not recall Arthur Kallet, the national head of the Consumer's Union; at most I could have met him if he made a visit to the west coast. I joined the American Committee for Democracy and Intellectual Freedom. I think it then stood as a protest against what had happened to intellectuals and professionals in Germany. I listed, in the personal security questionnaire that I filled out in 1942 for employment with the Manhattan District, the very few political organizations of which I had ever been a member. I say on that questionnaire that I did not include sponsorships. I have no recollection of the Friends of the Chinese People, or of what, if any, my connection with this organization was.

"The statement is attributed to me that, while I was not a Communist, I 'had probably belonged to every Communist-front organization on the west coast and had signed many petitions in which Communists were interested.' I do not recall this statement, nor to whom I might have made it, nor the circumstances. The quotation is not true. It seems clear to me that if I said anything along the lines quoted, it was a half-jocular overstatement.

"The matter which most engaged my sympathies and interests was the war in Spain. This was not a matter of understanding and informed convictions. I had never been to Spain; I knew a little of its literature; I knew nothing of its history or politics or contemporary problems. But like a great many other

Americans I was emotionally committed to the Loyalist cause. I contributed to various organizations for Spanish relief. I went to, and helped with, many parties, bazaars, and the like. Even when the war in Spain was manifestly lost, these activities continued. The end of the war and the defeat of the Loyalists caused me great sorrow.

"It was probably through Spanish relief efforts that I met Dr. Thomas Addis, and Rudy Lambert. As to the latter, our association never became close. As to the former, he was a distinguished medical scientist who became a friend. Addis asked me, perhaps in the winter of 1937–38, to contribute through him to the Spanish cause. He made it clear that this money, unlike that which went to the relief organizations, would go straight to the fighting effort, and that it would go through Communist channels. I did so contribute; usually when he communicated with me, explaining the nature of the need, I gave him sums in cash, probably never much less than a hundred dollars, and occasionally perhaps somewhat more than that, several times during the winter. I made no such contributions during the spring terms when I was in Pasadena or during the summers in New Mexico. Later—but I do not remember the date—Addis introduced me to Isaac Folkoff, who was, as Addis indicated, in some way connected with the Communist Party, and told me that Folkoff would from then on get in touch with me when there was need for money. This he did, in much the same way that Addis had done before. As before, these contributions were for specific purposes, principally the Spanish War and Spanish relief. Sometimes I was asked for money for other purposes, the organization of migratory labor in the California valleys, for instance. I doubt that it occurred to me that the contributions might be directed to other purposes than those I had intended, or that such other purposes might be evil. I did not then regard Communists as dangerous; and some of their declared objectives seemed to me desirable.

"In time these contributions came to an end. I went to a big Spanish relief party the night before Pearl Harbor; and the next day, as we heard the news of the outbreak of war, I decided that I had had about enough of the Spanish cause, and that there were other and more pressing crises in the world. My contributions would not have continued much longer.

"My brother Frank married in 1936. Our relations thereafter were inevitably less intimate than before. He told me at the time—probably in 1937—that he and his wife Jackie had joined the Communist Party. Over the years we saw one another as occasions arose. We still spent summer holidays together. In 1939 or 1940 Frank and Jackie moved to Stanford; in the autumn of 1941 they came to Berkeley, and Frank worked for the Radiation Laboratory. At that time he made it clear to me that he was no longer a member of the Communist Party.

"As to the alleged activities of Jackie and Frank in 1944, 1945, and 1946: I was not in Berkeley in 1944 and 1945; I was away most of the first half of 1946; I do not know whether these activities occurred or not. and if I had any knowledge of them at the time it would have been very sketchy. After Christmas of 1945 my family and I visited my brother's family for a few days during the holidays, and I remember that we were there New Year's Eve and New Year's Day in 1946. On New Year's Day people were constantly dropping in. Pinsky and Adelson, who were at most casual acquaintances of mine, may have been among them, but I cannot remember their being there, nor indeed do I remember any of the others who dropped in that day or what was discussed.

"It was in the summer of 1939 in Pasadena that I first met my wife. She was married to Dr. Harrison, who was a friend and associate of the Tolmans, Lauritsens, and others of the California Institute of Technology faculty. I learned of her earlier marriage to Joe Dallet, and of his death fighting in Spain. He had been a Communist Party official, and for a year or two during their brief marriage my wife was a Communist Party member. When I met her I found in her a deep loyalty to her former husband, a complete disengagement from any political activity, and a certain disappointment and contempt that the Communist Party was not in fact what she had once thought it was.

"My own views were also evolving. Although Sidney and Beatrice Webb's book on Russia, which I had read in 1936, and the talk that I heard at that time had predisposed me to make much of the economic progress and general level of welfare in Russia, and little of its political tyranny, my views on this were to change. I read about the purge trials, though not in full detail, and could never find a view of them which was not damning to the Soviet system. In 1938 I met three physicists who had actually lived in Russia in the thirties. All were eminent scientists, Placzek, Weisskopf, and Schein; and the first two have become close friends. What they reported seemed to me so solid, so unfanatical, so true, that it made a great impression; and it presented Russia, even when seen from their limited experience, as a land of purge and terror, of ludicrously bad management and of a long-suffering people. I need to make clear that this changing opinion of Russia, which was to be reinforced by the Nazi-Soviet Pact, and the behavior of the Soviet Union in Poland and in Finland, did not mean a sharp break for me with those who held to different views. At that time I did not fully understand—as in time I came to understand—how completely the Communist Party in this country was under the control of Russia. During and after the battle of France, however, and during the battle of England the next autumn, I found myself increasingly out of sympathy with the policy of disengagement and neutrality that the Communist press advocated.

"After our marriage in 1940, my wife and I for about 2 years had much the same circle of friends as I had had before—mostly physicists and university people. Among them the Chevaliers, in particular, showed us many acts of kindness. We were occasionally invited to more or less obviously leftwing affairs, Spanish relief parties that still continued; and on two occasions, once in San Francisco and once in Berkeley, we attended social gatherings of apparently well to do people, at which Schneiderman, an official of the Communist Party in California, attempted, not with success as far as we were concerned, to explain what the Communist line was all about. I was asked about the Berkeley meeting in an interview in 1946 with agents of the FBI. I did not then recall this meeting, and in particular did not in any way connect it with Chevalier, about whom the agents were questioning me; hence it seemed wholly irrelevant to the matter under discussion. Later my wife reminded me that the Berkeley meeting had occurred at the house of the Chevaliers; and when I was asked about it by the FBI in 1950, I told them so.

"We saw a little of Kenneth May; we both liked him. It would have been not unnatural for us to go to a housewarming for May and his wife; neither my wife nor I remember such a party. Weinberg was known to me as a graduate student; Hiskey I did not know. Steve Nelson came a few times with his family to visit; he had befriended my wife in Paris, at the time of her husband's death in Spain in 1937. Neither of us has seen him since 1941 or 1942.

"Because of these associations that I have described, and the contributions mentioned earlier, I might well have appeared at the time as quite close to the Communist Party—perhaps even to some people as belonging to it. As I have said, some of its declared objectives seemed to me desirable. But I never was a member of the Communist Party. I never accepted Communist dogma or theory; in fact, it never made sense to me. I had no clearly formulated political views. I hated tyranny and repression and every form of dictatorial control of thought. In most cases I did not in those days know who was and who was not a member of the Communist Party. No one ever asked me to join the Communist Party.

"Your letters sets forth statements made in 1942–45 by persons said to be Communist Party officials to the effect that I was a concealed member of the Communist Party. I have no knowledge as to what these people might have said. What I do know is that I was never a member of the party, concealed or open. Even the names of some of the people mentioned are strange to me, such as Jack Manley and Katrina Sandow. I doubt that I met Bernadette Doyle, although I recognize her name. Pinsky and Adelson I met at most casually, as previously mentioned.

"By the time that we moved to Los Alamos in early 1943, both as a result of my changed views and of the great pressure of war work, my participation in leftwing organizations and my associations with leftwing circles had ceased and were never to be reestablished.

"In August 1941, I bought Eagle Hill at Berkeley for my wife, which was the first home we had of our own. We settled down to live in it with our new baby. We had a good many friends, but little leisure. My wife was working in biology at the university. Many of the men I had known went off to work on radar and other aspects of military research. I was not without envy of them; but it was not until my first connection with the rudimentary atomic-energy enterprise that I began to see any way in which I could be of direct use."

Let the record show that Mr. Oppenheimer has asked to be excused briefly.

"Ever since the discovery of nuclear fission, the possibility of powerful explosives based on it had been very much in my mind, as it had in that of many other physicists. We had some understanding of what this might do for us in the war, and how much it might change the course of history. In the autumn of 1941, a special committee was set up by the National Academy of Sciences under the chairmanship of Arthur Compton to review the prospects and feasibility of the different uses of atomic energy for military purposes. I attended a meeting of this committee; this was my first official connection with the atomic-energy program.

"After the academy meeting, I spent some time in preliminary calculations about the construction and performance of atomic bombs, and became increasingly excited at the prospects. At the same time I still had a quite heavy burden of academic work with courses and graduate students. I also began to consult, more or less regularly, with the staff of the Radiation Laboratory in Berkeley on their program for the electromagnetic separation of uranium isotopes. I was never a member or employee of the laboratory; but I attended many of its staff and policy meetings. With the help of two of my graduate students, I developed an invention which was embodied in the production plants at Oak Ridge. I attended the conference in Chicago at which the Metallurgical Laboratory (to produce plutonium) was established and its initial program projected.

"In the spring of 1942, Compton called me to Chicago to discuss the state of work on the bomb itself. During this meeting Compton asked me to take the responsibility for this work, which at that time consisted of numerous scattered experimental projects. Although I had no administrative experience and was not an experimental physicist, I felt sufficiently informed and challenged by the problem to be glad to accept. At this time I became an employee of the Metallurgical Laboratory.

"After this conference I called together a theoretical study group in Berkeley, in which Bethe, Konopinski, Serber, Teller, Van Fleck, and I participated. We had an adventurous time. We spent much of the summer of 1942 in Berkeley in a joint study that for the first time really came to grips with the physical problems of atomic bombs, atomic explosions, and the possibility of using fission explosions to initiate thermonuclear reactions. I called this possibility to the attention of Dr. Bush during the late summer; the technical views on this subject were to develop and change from them until the present day.

"After these studies there was little doubt that a potentially world-shattering undertaking lay ahead. We began to see the great explosion at Alamogordo and the greater explosions at Eniwetok with a surer foreknowledge. We also began to see how rough, difficult, challenging, and unpredictable this job might turn out to be.

"When I entered the employ of the Metallurgical Laboratory I filled out my first personnel security questionnaire."

Let the record show that Dr. Oppenheimer has returned to the hearing room.

"Later in the summer, I had word from Compton that there was a question of my clearance on the ground that I had belonged to leftwing groups; but it was indicated that this would not prove a bar to my further work on the program.

"In later summer, after a review of the experimental work, I became convinced, as did others, that a major change was called for in the work on the bomb itself. We needed a central laboratory devoted wholly to this purpose, where people could talk freely with each other, where theoretical ideas and experimental findings could affect each other, where the waste and frustration and error of the many compartmentalized experimental studies could be eliminated, where we could begin to come to grips with chemical, metallurgical, engineering, and ordnance problems that had so far received no consideration. We therefore sought to establish this laboratory for a direct attack on all the problems inherent in the most rapid possible development and production of atomic bombs.

"In the autumn of 1942 General Groves assumed charge of the Manhattan Engineer District. I discussed with him the need for an atomic-bomb laboratory. There had been some thought of making this laboratory a part of Oak Ridge. For a time there was support for making it a Military Establishment in which key personnel would be commissioned as officers; and in preparation for this course I once went to the Presidio to take the initial steps toward obtaining a commission. After a good deal of discussion with the personnel who would be needed at Los Alamos and with General Groves and his advisers, it was decided that the laboratory should, at least initially, be a civilian establishment in a military post. While this consideration was going on, I had showed General Groves Los Alamos; and he almost immediately took steps to acquire the site.

"In early 1943, I received a letter signed by General Groves and Dr. Conant, appointing me director of the laboratory, and outlining their conception of how it was to be organized and administered. The necessary construction and assembling of the needed facilities were begun. All of us worked in close colloboration with the engineers of the Manhattan District.

"The site of Los Alamos was selected, in part at least, because it enabled those responsible to balance the obvious need for security with the equally important need of free communication among those engaged in the work. Security, it was hoped, would be achieved by removing the laboratory to a remote area, fenced and patrolled, where communication with the outside was extremely limited. Telephone calls were monitored, mail was censored, and personnel who left the area—something permitted only for the clearest of causes—knew that their movements might be under surveillance. On the other hand, for those within the community, fullest exposition and discussion among those competent to use the information was encouraged.

"The last months of 1942 and early 1943 had hardly hours enough to get Los Alamos established. The real problem had to do with getting to Los Alamos the men who would make a success of the undertaking. For this we needed to understand as clearly as we then could what our technical program would be, what men we would need, what facilities, what organization, what plan.

"The program of recruitment was massive. Even though we then underestimated the ultimate size of the laboratory, which was to have almost 4,000 members by the spring of 1945, and even though we did not at that time see clearly some of the difficulties which were to bedevil and threaten the enterprise, we knew that it was a big, complex and diverse job. Even the initial plan of the laboratory called for a start with more than 100 highly qualified and trained scientists, to say nothing of the technicians, staff, and mechanics who would be required for their support, and of the equipment that we would have to beg and borrow since there would be no time to build it from scratch. We had to recruit at a time when the country was fully engaged in war and almost every competent scientist was already involved in the military effort.

"The primary burden of this fell on me. To recruit staff I traveled all over the country talking with people who had been working on one or another aspect of the atomic-energy enterprise, and people in radar work, for example, and underwater sound, telling them about the job, the place that we were going to, and enlisting their enthusiasm.

"In order to bring responsible scientists to Los Alamos, I had to rely on their sense of the interest, urgency, and feasibility of the Los Alamos mission. I had to tell them enough of what the job was, and give strong enough assurance that it might be successfully accomplished in time to affect the outcome of the war, to make it clear that they were justified in their leaving other work to come to this job.

"The prospect of coming to Los Alamos aroused great misgivings. It was to be a military post; men were asked to sign up more or less for the duration; restrictions on travel and on the freedom of families to move about to be severe; and no one could be sure of the extent to which the necessary technical freedom of action could actually be maintained by the laboratory. The notion of disappearing into the New Mexico desert for an indeterminate period and under quasi military auspices disturbed a good many scientists, and the families of many more. But there was another side to it. Almost everyone realized that this was a great undertaking. Almost everyone knew that if it were completed successfully and rapidly enough, it might determine the outcome of the war. Almost everyone knew that it was an unparalleled opportunity to bring to bear the basic knowledge and art of science for the benefit of his country. Almost everyone knew that this job, if it were achieved, would be a part of history. This sense of excitement, of devotion and of patriotism in the end prevailed. Most of those with whom I talked came to Los Alamos. Once they came, confidence in the enterprise grew as men learned more of the technical status of the work; and though the laboratory was to double and redouble its size many times before the end, once it had started it was on the road to success.

"We had information in those days of German activity in the field of nuclear fission. We were aware of what it might mean if they beat us to the draw in the development of atomic bombs. The consensus of all our opinions, and every directive that I had, stressed the extreme urgency of our work, as well as the need for guarding all knowledge of it from our enemies. Past Communist connections or sympathies did not necessarily disqualify a man from employment, if we had confidence in his integrity and dependability as a man.

"There are two items of derogatory information on which I need to comment at this point. The first is that it was reported that I had talked the atomic-bomb question over with Communist Party members during this period (1942–45). The second is that I was responsible for the employment of the atomic-bomb project of individuals who were members of the Communist Party or closely associated with activities of the Communist Party.

"As to the first, my only discussions of matters connected with the atomic bomb were for official work or for recruiting the staff of the enterprise. So far as I knew none of these discussions were with Communist Party members. I never discussed anything of my secret work or anything about the atomic bomb with Steve Nelson.

"As to the statement that I secured the employment of doubtful persons on the project: Of those mentioned, Lomanitz, Friedman, and Weinberg were never employed at Los Alamos. I believe that I had nothing to do with the employment of Friedman and Weinberg by the Radiation Laboratory; I had no responsibility for the hiring of anyone there. During the time that I continued to serve as a consultant with the Radiation Laboratory and to advise and direct the work of some of the graduate students, I assigned David Bohm and Chaim Richman to a problem of basic science which might prove useful in analyzing experiments in connection with fast neutrons. That work has long been published. Another graduate student was Rossi Lomanitz. I remember vaguely a conversation with him in which he expressed reluctance to take part in defense research, and I encouraged him to do what other scientists were doing for their country. Thereafter he did work at the Radiation Laboratory. I remember no details of our talk. If I asked him to work on the project, I would have assumed that he would be checked by the security officers as a matter of course. Later, in 1943, when Lomanitz was inducted into the Army, he wrote me asking me to help his return to the project. I forwarded a copy of this letter to the Manhattan District security officers, and let the matter rest there. Still latter, at Lomanitz' request, I wrote to his commanding officer that he was qualified for advanced technical work in the Army.

"I asked for the transfer of David Bohm to Los Alamos; but this request, like all others, was subject to the assumption that the usual security requirements would apply; and when I was told that there was objection on security grounds to this transfer, I was much surprised, but of course agreed. David Hawkins was known to the personnel director at the laboratory, and I had met and liked him and found him intelligent; I supported the suggestion of the personnel director that he come to Los Alamos. I understand that he had had leftwing associations; but it was not until in March of 1951, at the time of his testimony, that I knew about his membership in the Communist Party.

"In 1943 when I was alleged to have stated that 'I knew several individuals then at Los Alamos who had been members of the Communist Party,' I knew of only one; she was my wife, of whose disassociation from the party, and of whose integrity and loyalty to the United States I had no question. Later, in 1944 or 1945, my brother Frank, who had been cleared for work in Berkeley and at Oak Ridge, came to Los Alamos from Oak Ridge with official approval.

"I knew of no attempt to obtain secret information at Los Alamos. Prior to my going there my friend Haakon Chevalier with his wife visited us on Eagle Hill, probably in early 1943. During the visit, he came into the kitchen and told me that George Eltenton had spoken to him of the possibility of transmitting technical information to Soviet scientists. I made some strong remark to the effect that this sounded terribly wrong to me. The discussion ended there. Nothing in our long standing friendship would have led me to believe that Chevalier was actually seeking information; and I was certain that he had no idea of the work on which I was engaged.

"It has long been clear to me that I should have reported the incident at once. The events that led me to report it— which I doubt ever would have become known without my report—were unconnected with it. During the summer of 1943, Colonel Lansdale, the intelligence officer of the Manhattan District, came to Los Alamos and told me that he was worried about the security situation in Berkeley because of the activities of the Federation of Architects, Engineers,

Chemists, and Technicians. This recalled to my mind that Eltenton was a member and probably a promoter of the FAECT. Shortly thereafter, I was in Berkeley and I told the security officer that Eltenton would bear watching. When asked why, I said that Eltenton had attempted, through intermediaries, to approach people on the project, though I mentioned neither myself nor Chevalier. Later, when General Groves urged me to give the details, I told him of my conversation with Chevalier. I still think of Chevalier as a friend.

"The story of Los Alamos is long and complex. Part of it is public history. For me it was a time so filled with work, with the need for decision and action and consultation, that there was room for little else. I lived with my family in the community which was Los Alamos. It was a remarkable community, inspired by a high sense of mission, of duty and of destiny, coherent, dedicated, and remarkably selfless. There was plenty in the life of Los Alamos to cause irritation; the security restrictions, many of my own devising, the inadequacies and inevitable fumblings of a military post unlike any that had ever existed before, shortages, inequities, and in the laboratory itself the shifting emphasis on different aspects of the technical work as the program moved forward; but I have never known a group more understanding and more devoted to a common purpose, more willing to lay aside personal convenience and prestige, more understanding of the role that they were playing in their country's history. Time and again we had in the technical work almost paralyzing crises. Time and again the laboratory drew itself together and faced the new problems and got on with the work. We worked by night and by day; and in the end the many jobs were done.

"These years of hard and loyal work of the scientists culminated in the test on July 16, 1945. It was a success. I believe that in the eyes of the War Department, and other knowledgeable people, it was as early a success as they had thought possible, given all the circumstances, and rather a greater one. There were many indications from the Secretary of War and General Groves, and many others, that official opinion was one of satisfaction with what had been accomplished. At the tme, it was hard for us in Los Alamos not to share that satisfaction, and hard for me not to accept the conclusion that I had managed the enterprise well and played a key part in its success. But it needs to be stated that many others contributed the decisive ideas and carried out the work which led to this success and that my role was that of understanding, encouraging, suggesting and deciding. It was the very opposite of a one-man show.

"Even before the July 16 test and the use of the bombs in Japan, the members of the laboratory began to have a new sense of the possible import of what was going on. In the early days, when success was less certain and timing unsure, and the war with Germany and Japan in a desperate phase, it was enough for us to think that we had a job to do. Now, with Germany defeated, the war in the Pacific approaching a crisis, and the success of our undertaking almost assured, there was a sense both of hope and of anxiety as to what this spectacular development might portend for the future. This came to us a little earlier than to the public generally because we saw the technical development at close range and in secret; but its quality was very much the same as the public response after Hiroshima and Nagasaki.

"Thus it was natural that in the spring of 1945 I welcomed the opportunity when I was asked by Secretary Stimson to serve, along with Compton, Lawrence, and Fermi, on an advisory panel to his Interim Committee on Atomic Energy. We met with that committee on the 1st of June 1945; and even during the week when Hiroshima and Nagasaki were being bombed, we met at Los Alamos to sketch out a prospectus of what the technical future in atomic energy might look like: atomic war heads for guided missiles, improvements in bomb designs, the thermonuclear program, power, propulsion, and the new tools available from atomic technology for research in science, medicine, and technology. This work absorbed much of my time, during September and October; and in connection with it I was asked to consult with the War and State Departments on atomic-energy legislation, and in a preliminary way on the international control of atomic energy.

"I resigned as directór of Los Alamos on October 16, 1945, after having secured the consent of Commander Bradbury and General Groves that Bradbury should act as my successor.

"There were then on the books at the laboratory, embodied in memoranda and reports and summarized by me in letters to General Groves, developments in atomic weapons, which could well have occupied years for their fulfillment, and which have in fact provided some, though by no means all, of the themes for Los Alamos work since that time. It was not entirely clear whether the future of atomic weapons work in this country should be continued at or confined to Los Alamos or started elsewhere at a more accessible and more practical site, or indeed what effect international agreements might have on the program. But in the meantime Los Alamos had to be kept going until there was created an authority competent to decide the question of its future. This was to take almost a year.

"THE POST WAR PERIOD

"In November 1945, I resumed my teaching at the California Institute of Technology, with an intention and hope, never realized, that this should be a full-time undertaking. The consultation about postwar matter which had already begun continued, and I was asked over and over both by the Executive and the Congress for advice on atomic energy. I had a feeling of deep responsibility, interest, and concern for many of the problems with which the development of atomic energy confronted our country.

"This development was to be a major factor in the history of the evolving and mounting conflict between the free world and the Soviet Union. When I and other scientists were called on for advice, our principal duty was to make our technical experience and judgment available. We were called to do this in a context and against a background of the official views of the Government on the military and political situation of our country. Immediately after the war, I was deeply involved in the effort to devise effective means for the international control of atomic weapons, means which might, in the words of those days, tend toward the elimination of war itself. As the prospects of success receded, and as evidence of Soviet hostility and growing military power accumulated, we had more and more to devote ourselves to finding ways of adapting our atomic potential to offset the Soviet threat. In the period marked by the first Soviet atomic explosion, the war in Korea and the Chinese Communist intervention there, we were principally preoccupied, though we never forgot long-term problems, with immediate measures which could rapidly build up the strength of the United States under the threat of an imminent general war. As our own atomic potential increased and developed, we were aware of the dangers inherent in comparable developments by the enemy; and preventive and defensive measures were very much on our minds. Throughout this time the role of atomic weapons was to be central.

"From the close of the war, when I returned to the west coast until finally in the spring of 1947 when I went to Princeton as the director of the Institute for Advanced Study, I was able to spend very little time at home and in teaching in California. In October 1945, at the request of Secretary of War Patterson, I had testified before the House Committee on Military Affairs in support of the May-Johnson bill, which I endorsed as an interim means of bringing about without delay the much needed transition from the wartime administration of the Manhattan District to postwar management of the atomic-energy enterprise. In December 1945, and later, I appeared at Senator McMahon's request in sessions of his Special Committee on Atomic Energy, which was considering legislation on the same subject. Under the chairmanship of Dr. Richard Tolman, I served on a committee set up by General Groves to consider classification policy on matters of atomic energy. For 2 months, early in 1946, I worked steadily as a member of a panel, the Board of Consultants to the Secretary of State's Committee on Atomic Energy, which, with the Secretary of State's Committee, prepared the so-called Acheson-Lilienthal report. After the publication of this report, I spoke publicly in support of it. A little later, when Mr. Baruch was appointed to represent the United States in the United Nations Atomic Energy Committee, I became one of the scientific consultants to Mr. Baruch, and his staff in preparation for and in the conduct of our efforts to gain support for the United States' plan. I continued as consultant to General Osborn when he took over the effort.

"At the end of 1946 I was appointed by the President as a member of the General Advisory Committee to the Atomic Energy Commission. At its first meeting I was elected Chairman, and was reelected until the expiration of my term in 1952. This was my principal assignment during these years as far as the atomic-energy program was concerned, and my principal preoccupation apart from academic work.

"A little later I was appointed to the Committee on Atomic Energy of the Research and Development Board, which was to advise the Military Establishment about the technical aspects of the atomic-energy program; I served on it for 7 years; and twice was designated Chairman of special panels set up by the Committee.

"Meanwhile I had become widely regarded as a principal author or inventor of the atomic bomb, more widely, I well knew, than the facts warranted. In a modest way I had become a kind of public personage. I was deluged as I have been ever since with requests to lecture, and to take part in numerous scientific activities and public affairs. Most of these I did not accept. Some, important for the promotion of science or learning or of public policies that corresponded to my convictions, I did accept: the Council of the National Academy of · Sciences, the Committee on the Present Danger; the board of overseers of Harvard College, and a good number of others.

"A quite different and I believe unique occurrence is cited as an item of derogatory information—that in 1946 I was 'listed as vice chairman on the letterhead of the Independent Citizens Committee of the Arts, Sciences, and Professions, Inc. * * * cited as a Communist front by the House Committee on Un-American Activities.' The fact is that in 1946, when I was at work on the international control of atomic energy, I was notified that I had been nominated and then elected as vice chairman of this organization. When I began to see that its literature included slogans such as 'Withdraw United States troops from China' and that it was endorsing the criticism enunciated by the then Secretary Wallace of the United States policy on atomic energy, I advised the organization in a letter of October 11, 1946, that I was not in accord with its policy, that I regarded the recommendations of Mr. Wallace as not likely to advance the cause of finding a satisfactory solution for the control of atomic energy, and that I wished to resign. When an effort was made to dissuade me from this course I again wrote on December 2, 1946, insisting upon resignation.

"Later in the postwar period an incident occurred which seems to be the basis of one of the items of derogatory information. In May 1950, Paul Crouch, a former Communist official, and Mrs. Crouch, testified before the California State Committee on Un-American Activities that in July 1941 they had attended a Communist Party meeting at a house in Berkeley, of which I was then the tenant. On the basis of pictures and movies of me which they saw some 8 years later, they said they recognized me as having been present. When the FBI first talked to me about this alleged incident, I was quite certain that no such meeting as Crouch described had occurred. So was my wife, when I discussed it with her. Later, when I saw the testimony, I became even more certain. Crouch had described the gathering as a closed meeting of the Communist Party. I was never a member of the party. Crouch said that no introductions had been made. I could not recall ever having had a group of people at my home that had not been introduced. In May of 1952, I again discussed this alleged meeting with the United States attorney in the Weinberg case (an indictment against Joseph Weinberg for perjury for having among other things denied membership in the Communist Party). I again said that I could not have been present at a closed meeting of the Communist Party because I was not a member of the party: that I had searched my memory and that the only thing that conceivably could be relevant was the vaguest impressions that someone on the campus might at some time have asked permission to use our home for a gathering of young people; that, however, I could recall no such gathering, nor any meeting even remotely resembling the one described by Crouch; that I thought it probable that at the time of the meeting, which by then had been fixed by Crouch as approximately July 23, my wife and I were away from Berkeley. Shortly thereafter, with the aid of counsel, we were able to establish that my wife and I left Berkeley within a few days after July 4, 1941, and did not return until toward the end of the first week in August.

"I need to turn now to an account of some of the measures which, as Chairman of the General Advisory Committee, and in other capacities, I advocated in the years since the war to increase the power of the United States and its allies to resist and defeat aggression.

"The initial members of the General Advisory Committee were Conant, then president of Harvard, DuBridge, president of the California Institute of Technology, Fermi of the University of Chicago, Rabi of Columbia University, Rowe, vice president of the United Fruit Co., Seaborg of the University of California, Cyril Smith of the University of Chicago, and Worthington of the duPont Co. In 1948 Buckley, president of the Bell Telephone Laboratories, replaced Worthington; in the summer of 1950, Fermi, Rowe, and Seaborg were replaced by Libby of the University of Chicago, Murphree, president of Standard Oil Development Co., and Whitman of the Massachusetts Institute of Technology. Later Smith resigned and was succeeded by von Neumann of the Institute for Advanced Study.

"In these years from early 1947 to mid-1952 the Committee met some 30 times and transmitted perhaps as many reports to the Commission. Formulation of policy and the management of the vast atomic-energy enterprises were responsibilities vested in the Commission itself. The General Advisory Committee had the role, which was fixed for it by statute, to advise the Commission. In that capacity we gave the Commission our views on questions which the Commission put before us, brought to the Commission's attention on our initiative technical matters of importance, and encouraged and supported the work of the several major installations of the Commission.

"At one of our first meetings in 1947 we settled down to the job of forming our own views of the priorities. And while we agreed that the development of atomic power and the support and maintenance of a strong basic scientific activity in the fields relevant to it were important, we assigned top priority to the problem of atomic weapons. At that time we advised the Commission that one of its first jobs would be to convert Los Alamos into an active center for the development and improvement of atomic weapons. In 1945–46 during the period immediately following the war, the purposes of Los Alamos were multiple. It was the only laboratory in the United States that worked on atomic weapons. Los Alamos also had wide interests in scientific matters only indirectly related to the weapons program. We suggested that the Commission recognize as the laboratory's central and primary program the improvement and diversification of atomic weapons, and that this undertaking have a priority second to none. We suggested further that the Commission adopt administrative measures to make work at Los Alamos attractive, to assist the laboratory in recruiting, to help build up a strong theoretical division for guidance in atomic-weapons design, and to take advantage of the availability of the talented and brilliant consultants who had been members of the laboratory during the war. In close consultation with the director of the Los Alamos Laboratory, we encouraged and supported courses of development which would markedly increase the value of our stockpile in terms of the destructive power of our weapons, which would make the best use of existing stockpiles and those anticipated, which would provide weapons suitable for modern combat conditions and for varied forms of delivery and which in their cumulative effect would provide us with the great arsenal we now have.

"We encouraged and supported the building up of the laboratory at Sandia whose principal purpose is the integration of the atomic warhead with the weapons system in which it is to be used. In agreement with the Los Alamos staff we took from the very first the view that no radical improvement in weapons development would be feasible without a program of weapons testing. We strongly supported such a program, helped Los Alamos to obtain authorization for conducting the tests it wished, and encouraged the establishment of a permanent weapons testing station and the adoption of a continental test station to facilitate this work. As time went on and the development of atomic weapons progressed, we stressed the importance of integrating out atomic warheads and the development of the carriers, aircraft, missiles, etc., which could make them of maximum effectiveness.

"We observed that there were opportunities which needed to be explored for significantly increasing our arsenal of weapons both in numbers and in capabilities by means of production plant expansion and by ambitious programs to enlarge the sources of raw materials. It was not our function to formulate military requirements. We did regard it as our function to indicate that neither the magnitude of existing plant nor the mode of operation of existing plant which the Commission inherited, nor the limitation of raw materials to relatively well known and high-grade sources of ore, need limit the atomic-weapons program

"The four major expansion programs which were authorized during the 6 years 1946 to 1952 reflect the decision of the Commission, the Military Establishment, the Joint Congressional Committee and other agencies of the Government to go far beyond the production program that was inherited in 1946. And the powerful arsenal of atomic weapons and the variety of their forms adaptable to a diversity of military uses which is today a major source of our military strength in turn reflect the results of these decisions. The record of minutes, reports and other activities of the General Advisory Committee will show that that body within the limits of its role as an advisory group played a significant, consistent, and unanimous part in encouraging and supporting and sometimes initiating the measures which are responsible for these results.

"As a committee and individually, our advice was sought on other matters as well. As early as October 1945 I had testified before a Senate committee on the Kilgore-Magnuson bill—the initial measure for a National Science Foundation; like most scientists I was concerned that steps be taken for recreating in the United States a healthy scientific community after the disruption of the war years. In the General Advisory Committee we encouraged the Commission to do everything that it properly could to support atomic science, both in its own laboratories and in the university centers to which we felt we must look for the training of scientists for advances of a basic character. Throughout the postwar period my colleagues and I stressed the importance of continuing support and promotion of basic science so that there might be a healthy balance between the effort invested in military research and applied science, and that invested in pure scientific training and research which is indispensable to all else. We supported the Commission's decision to make available for distribution in appropriate form and with appropriate safeguards the tracer materials, isotopes, and radioactive substances which have played so constructive a part in medicine, in biological research, in technology, in pure science, and in agriculture.

"We took an affirmative view on the development of reactors for submarines and naval propulsion not only for their direct military value but also because this seemed a favorable and forward-looking step in the important program of reactor development. We were, for the most part, skeptical about the initially very ambitious plans for the propulsion of aircraft. though we advocated the studies which in time brought this program to a more feasible course. We frequently pointed out to the Commission the technical benefits which would accrue to the United States by closer collaboration with the atomic energy enterprise in Canada and the United Kingdom.

"During all the years that I served on the General Advisory Committee, however, its major preoccupation was with the production and perfection of atomic weapons. On the various recommendations which I have described, there were never, so far as I can remember, any significant divergences of opinion among the members of the committee. These recommendations, of course, constitute a very small sample of the committee's work, but a typical one.

"In view of the controversies that have developed I have left the subject of the super and thermonuclear weapons for separate discussion—although our committee regarded this as a phase of the entire problem of weapons.

"The super itself had a long history of consideration, beginning, as I have said, with our initial studies in 1942 before Los Alamos was established. It continued to be the subject of study and research at Los Alamos throughout the war. After the war, Los Alamos itself was inevitably handicapped pending the enactment of necessary legislation for the atomic energy enterprise. With the McMahon Act, the appointment of the Atomic Energy Commission and the General Advisory Committee, we in the committee had occasion at our early meetings in 1947 as well as in 1948 to discuss the subject. In that period the General Advisory Committee pointed out the still extremely unclear status of the problem from the technical standpoint, and urged encouragement of Los Alamos' efforts which were then directed toward modest exploration of the super and of thermonuclear systems. No serious controversy arose about the super until the Soviet explosion of an atomic bomb in the autumn of 1949.

"Shortly after that event, in October 1949, the Atomic Energy Commission called a special session of the General Advisory Committee and asked us to consider and advise on two related questions: First, whether in view of the Soviet success the Commission's program was adequate, and if not, in what way it should be altered or increased; second, whether a crash program for the development of the super should be a part of any new program. The committee considered both questions, consulting various officials from the civil and military branches of the executive departments who would have been concerned, and reached conclusions which were communicated in a report to the Atomic Energy Commission in October 1949.

"This report, in response to the first question that had been put to us, recommended a great number of measures that the Commission should take the increase in many ways our overall potential in weapons.

"As to the super itself, the General Advisory Committee stated its unanimous opposition to the initiation by the United States of a crash program of the kind we had been asked to advise on. The report of that meeting, and the Secretary's notes, reflect the reasons which moved us to this conclusion. The annexes, in particular, which dealt more with political and policy considerations—the report proper was essentially technical in character—indicated differences in the views of members of the committee. There were two annexes, one signed by Rabi and Fermi, the other by Conant, DuBridge, Smith, Rowe, Buckley and myself. (The ninth member of the committee, Seaborg, was abroad at the time.)

"It would have been surprising if eight men considering a problem of extreme difficulty had each had precisely the same reasons for the conclusion in which we joined. But I think I am correct in asserting that the unanimous opposition we expressed to the crash program was based on the conviction, to which technical considerations as well as others contributed, that because of our overall situation at that time such a program might weaken rather than strengthen the position of the United States.

"After the report was submitted to the Commission, it fell to me as chairman of the committee to explain our position on several occasions, once at a meeting of the Joint Congressional Committee on Atomic Energy. All this, however, took place prior to the decision by the President to proceed with the thermonuclear program.

"This is the full story of my 'opposition to the hydrogen bomb.' It can be read in the records of the general transcript of my testimony before the joint congressional committee. It is a story which ended once and for all when in January 1950 the President announced his decision to proceed with the program. I never urged anyone not to work on the hydrogen bomb project. I never made or caused any distribution of the GAC reports except to the Commission itself. As always, it was the Commission's responsibility to determine further distribution.

"In summary, in October 1949, I and the other members of the General Advisory Committee were asked questions by the Commission to which we had a duty to respond, and to which we did respond with our best judgment in the light of evidence then available to us.

"When the President's decision was announced in January 1950, our committee was again in session and we immediately turned to the technical problems facing the Commission in carrying out the President's directive. We sought to give our advice then and in ensuing meetings as to the most promising means of solving these problems. We never again raised the question of the wisdom of the policy which had now been settled, but concerned ourselves rather with trying to implement it. During this period our recommendations for increasing production facilities included one for a dual-purpose plant which could be adapted to make materials either for fission bombs or materials useful in a thermonuclear program. In its performance characteristics, the Savannah River project, subsequently adopted by the Commission, was foreshadowed by this recommendation.

"While the history of the GAC opposition to a crash program for the super ended with the announcement of the President's decision, the need for evaluation and advice continued. There were immense technical complications both before and after the President's decision. It was of course a primary duty of the committee, as well as other review committees on which I served, to report new developments which we judged promising, and to report when a given weapon or family of weapons appeared impractical, unfeasible or impossible. It would have been my duty so to report had I been alone in my views. As a matter of fact, our views on such matters were almost always unanimous. It was furthermore a proper function for me to speak my best judgment in discussion with those responsibly engaged in the undertaking.

"Throughout the whole development of thermonuclear weapons, many occasions occurred where it was necessary for us to form and to express judgments of feasibility. This was true before the President's decision, and it was true after the President's decision. In our report of October 1949, we expressed the view, as your letter states, that 'an imaginative and concerted attack on the problem has a better than even chance of producing the weapon within 5 years.' Later calculations and measurements made at Los Alamos led us to a far more pessimistic view. Still later brilliant inventions led to the possibility of lines of development of very great promise. At each stage the General Advisory Committee, and I as its Chairman and as a member of other bodies, reported as faithfully as we could our evaluation of what was likely to fail and what was likely to work.

"In the spring of 1951 work had reached a stage at which far-reaching decisions were called for with regard to the Commission's whole thermonuclear program. In consultation with the Commission, I called a meeting in Princeton in the late spring of that year, which was attended by all members of the Commission and several members of its staff, by members of the General Advisory Committee, by Dr. Bradbury and staff of the Los Alamos Laboratory, by Bethe, Teller, Bacher, Fermi, von Neumann, Wheeler, and others responsibly connected with the program. The outcome of the meeting, which lasted for 2 or 3 days, was an agreed program and a fixing of priorities and effort both for Los Alamos and for other aspects of the Commission's work. This program has been an outstanding success.

"In addition to my continuing work on the General Advisory Committee there were other assignments that I was asked to undertake. Late in 1950 or early in 1951 the President appointed me to the Science Advisory Committee to advise the Office of Defense Mobilization and the President in 1952 the Secretary of State appointed me to a panel to advise on armaments and their regulation; and I served as consultant on continental defense, civil defense, and the use of atomic weapons in support of ground combat. Many of these duties led to reports in the drafting of which I participated, or for which I took responsibility. These supplement the record of the General Advisory Committee as an account of the counsel that I have given our government during the last eight years.

"In this letter, I have written only of those limited parts of my history which appear relevant to the issue now before the Atomic Energy Commission. In order to preserve as much as possible the perspective of the story, I have dealt very briefly with many matters. I have had to deal briefly or not at all with instances in which my actions or views were adverse to Soviet or Communist interest, and of actions that testify to my devotion to freedom, or that have contributed to the vitality, influence and power of the United States.

"In preparing this letter, I have reviewed two decades of my life. I have recalled instances where I acted unwisely. What I have hoped was, not that I could wholly avoid error, but that I might learn from it. What I have learned has, I think, made me more fit to serve my country.

"Very truly yours,

J. ROBERT OPPENHEIMER.

PRINCETON, N. J., MARCH 4, 1954."

Do you get the impression I do—that although this letter is addressed to Nichols, according to the established procedures, Oppenheimer is speaking to you and me? The letter has nothing of a press release about it. Possibly this was a mistake. Another man might have taken the occasion as an opportunity to turn his defense against these charges into a cause. It seems plain to me that Oppenheimer was speaking quietly, candidly and as persuasively as he knew how, to those he believed would understand him. This is why I asked you to read it now.

5. THE HEARINGS

THE BOARD opened its proceedings early in April by spending a week with Robb over the F.B.I. and other secret files. It was an inquiry, not a trial, but it seems to me that the Board blundered when it refused Garrison's request to meet the Board informally to discuss the procedure and to add what he could to the picture of the case which Oppenheimer had drawn in his reply to Nichols' letter. They could not, of course, let Garrison see any of these classified files, which Robb was able to share with them. But here they were, exposing themselves to derogatory information. They would have been prudent to inoculate their minds with Garrison's answers to their queries and with his explanations of their unavoidable suspicions and surmises. It might, moreover, have shortened the hearings, as courts have found that pre-trial conferences shorten trials. I have said, and we shall see, that Robb was going to treat this inquiry as if it were a trial.

The hearings—that is, the taking of testimony—were held in Room 2022 in Building T-3 of the Atomic Energy Commission in Washington. The Board sat almost day to day from the middle of April to the end of May. It sat, as lawyers would say, in chambers, avoiding publicity so far as it could. The witnesses came and went, one by one. The Board had no power of subpoena, and they came voluntarily at the request of counsel or, in the case of those from the Air Force, under oral orders. As each one appeared, the chairman asked him whether he preferred to be sworn or not. They all did. Then the chairman admonished each one that the proceedings were to be regarded as confidential.

Except for each witness, and the occasional presence of a classification officer to cover classified papers or to warn or advise a witness, there were only a handful in the room: the three members of the Board; two attorneys for the Commission; three or four attorneys for Oppenheimer; a reporter at a stenotype; William Mitchell, the general counsel of the A.E.C., sitting silently in a corner; and

Oppenheimer. The Board allowed Mrs. Oppenheimer to be present on the first day and on the day she testified. A small and an exceedingly distinguished group in a small and rather drab setting.

Gordon Gray, the chairman, is a Baltimorean, forty-five years old, a graduate of the University of North Carolina and of the Yale Law School. He practiced law for two years in New York and for two more in North Carolina. Then he was elected to the state senate, published two newspapers and ran a radio station. In the war he rose from private to captain of infantry. In 1947 President Truman appointed him Assistant Secretary of the Army, in 1949 Secretary, and in 1950 a special assistant to the President. Then Gray was elected president of the University of North Carolina, which he was when he was appointed to the Board.

The other two members of the Board were older men, and neither had Gray's experience in public life. Thomas A. Morgan is a North Carolinian. When he left high school he enlisted in the Navy, and after one enlistment he went to the Sperry Gyroscope Company as sales manager. He rose to be general manager and then president, and from 1932 to 1947 he was chairman of the board of directors. When the Sperry Corporation was formed in 1933 Morgan became its president and later chairman of its board. The Sperry Corporation is one of the best-known producers of high-precision specialized equipment for the armed services and the Atomic Energy Commission. It operates a guided missile plant for the Navy in Tennessee. Morgan retired in 1952 and since then has been director of a number of corporations, among them the Bankers Trust Company, the Lehmann Corporation, Bulova Watch Company; Pressed Steel Car, Western Union, and Shell Oil.

The third member was Ward V. Evans. Born and reared in Rawlinsville, Pennsylvania, Evans was educated at Franklin and Marshall College, graduating in 1907. In 1916 he was given his Ph.D. in chemistry by Columbia, and he served in the Army in the First World War. After that he resumed his teaching career at Northwestern University, and he retired as head of its Department of Chemistry in 1945. Since then he has been a professor at Loyola University in Chicago.

It would be hard to find a better board, even for a less thankless task. Here were three men from three different careers who had each reached its respective top. Gray stood high in public service, as a newspaper publisher, as Secretary of the Army, as a college president. Morgan had risen to the top of a great business, which, appropriately, was engaged in our national defense. Evans had mounted as high on the ladder of an academic career as one could climb, and he was still teaching. Their willingness to serve on this Board was vivid evidence of the truth of the ancient observation that the best public service springs from a reluctant devotion to duty. Certainly our security system had never had a better-manned security board.

A word on the attorneys: Roger Robb, the attorney for the Atomic Energy Commission, was born in Vermont, went to Yale, where he was graduated in 1928, and then to the Yale Law School. He began his law practice as Assistant United States Attorney in the District of Columbia, and after seven years of that he served for a time, in 1934–1940, as associate counsel for a Congressional committee investigating the National Labor Relations Board. Then he joined the firm of Bingham, Collins, Porter, and Kistler in Washington. He was assisted by C. A. Rolander, Jr., Deputy Director of the A.E.C. Division of Security.

As I have said, Gray was uncertain at first whether Robb was counsel for the Commission or for the Board, and finally decided he was the attorney for the Commission. Whichever he was, his duties were defined by the A.E.C. Rules:

Where the nature of the case is complicated or the Board desires assistance in conducting the hearing, the Manager should designate such person or persons to aid the Board as may be necessary, the person then named shall not be a member of the Board, shall not participate in the deliberations of the Board, shall express no opinion to the Board concerning the merits of the case, but shall assist the Board in such manner as to bring out a full and complete disclosure of all facts having any bearing upon the issues before the Board.

Lloyd K. Garrison was Oppenheimer's attorney. Later, before the Commission, John W. Davis joined him on the brief. Garrison was in the midst of a career as varied as it was distinguished. Born in New York, he went to Harvard, was graduated in 1919, and then to the Harvard Law School. He started practice in New York with Root, Clark, Buchner, and Howland. In 1932 he became Dean of the Wisconsin Law School. From 1942 he was on leave with the National War Labor Board, as general counsel, public member, and finally as its chairman. In 1946 he resumed general practice of law in New York as partner in the firm of Paul, Weiss, Rifkind, Wharton, and Garrison. He was treasurer of the National Urban League

from 1926 to 1932, and its president from 1947 to 1952. He served
in the Navy in the First World War. A trustee of Howard University, of Sarah Lawrence College, and an overseer of Harvard University, and since 1953 a trustee of the Institute for Advanced
Study, of which Oppenheimer is the director and of which Strauss,
the chairman of the A.E.C., is the president.

Garrison's partner, Samuel J. Silverman, and his associate, Allan
B. Ecker, assisted him in the trial.

With Garrison, an associate counsel, was Herbert S. Marks. Marks
had been general counsel for the A.E.C. in 1947, and before that
Assistant General Counsel to the War Production Board, from 1941
to 1945, and then Special Assistant to Dean G. Acheson when he
was Under Secretary of State in 1945. For years he had been
Oppenheimer's lawyer.

I will give you the whole of the opinion of the Board—that is, the
majority opinion of Gray and Morgan—and later Evans' dissent,
but I am going to rearrange the sections and some of the paragraphs of the majority opinion to suit myself, in order to put them
in the appropriate places in the course of my text. This seems an
appropriate place for the Introduction. Their opinion took the form
of a letter to Nichols, the General Manager:

UNITED STATES ATOMIC ENERGY COMMISSION,
Washington, D. C., May 27, 1954.

Subject: Findings and recommendation of the Personnel Security Board in the
case of Dr. J. Robert Oppenheimer.

Mr. K. D. NICHOLS,
    General Manager, U. S. Atomic Energy Commission,
        1901 Constitution Avenue NW., Washington 25, D. C.

DEAR MR. NICHOLS: On December 23, 1953, Dr. J. Robert Oppenheimer was
notified by letter that his security clearance had been suspended. He was furnished a list of items of derogatory information and was advised of his rights
to a hearing under AEC procedures. On March 4, 1954, Dr. Oppenheimer requested that he be afforded a hearing. A hearing has been conducted by the
Board appointed by you for this purpose, and we submit our findings and
recommendation.

Dr. Ward V. Evans dissents from the recommendation of the majority of the
Board, and his minority report is attached. He specifically subscribes to the
"Findings" of the majority of the Board, and to a portion of the material entitled
"Significance of the Findings."

INTRODUCTION

It must be understood that in our world in which the survival of free institutions and of individual rights is at stake, every person must in his own way
be a guardian of the national security. It also must be clear that, in the exercise

of this stewardship, individuals and institutions must protect, preserve, and defend those human values for which we exist as a nation, as a government, and as a way of life.

The hard requirements of security, and the assertion of freedoms, together thrust upon us a dilemma, not easily resolved. In the present international situation, our security measures exist, in the ultimate analysis, to protect our free institutions and traditions against repressive totalitarianism and its inevitable denial of human values. Thoughtful Americans find themselves uneasy, however, about those policies which must be adopted and those actions which must be taken in the interests of national security, and which at the same time pose a threat to our ideals. This Board has been conscious of these conflicts, presenting as they do some of the grave problems of our times, and has sought to consider them in an atmosphere of decency and safety.

We share the hope that some day we may return to happier times when our free institutions are not threatened and a peaceful and just world order is not such a compelling principal preoccupation. Then security will cease to be a central issue; man's conduct as a citizen will be measured only in the terms of the requirements of our national society; there will be no undue restraints upon freedom of mind and action; and loyalty and security as concepts will cease to have restrictive implications.

This state of affairs seems not to be a matter of early hope. As we meet the present peril, and seek to overcome it, we must realize that at no time can the interests of the protection of all our people be less than paramount to all other considerations. Indeed, action which in some cases may seem to be a denial of the freedoms which our security barriers are erected to protect, may rather be a fulfillment of these freedoms. For, if in our zeal to protect our institutions against our measures to secure them, we lay them open to destruction, we will have lost them all, and will have gained only the empty satisfaction of a meaningless exercise.

We are acutely aware that in a very real sense this case puts the security system of the United States on trial, both as to procedures and as to substance. This notion has been strongly urged upon us by those who recommended clearance for Dr. J. Robert Oppenheimer, and no doubt a similar view is taken by those who feel he should not be cleared.

If we understand the two points of view, they may be stated as follows: There are those who apprehend that our program for security at this point in history consists of an uneasy mixture of fear, prejudice, and arbitrary judgments. They feel that reason and fairness and justice have abdicated and their places have been taken by hysteria and repression. They, thus, believe that security procedures are necessarily without probity and that national sanity and balance can be served only by a finding in favor of the individual concerned. On the other hand, there is a strong belief that in recent times our government has been less than unyielding toward the problem of communism, and that loose and pliable attitudes regarding loyalty and security have prevailed to the danger of our society and its institutions. Thus, they feel that this proceeding presents the unrelinquishable opportunity for a demonstration against communism, almost regardless of the facts developed about the conduct and sympathies of Dr. Oppenheimer.

We find ourselves in agreement with much that underlies both points of view. We believe that the people of our country can be reassured by this proceeding that it is possible to conduct an investigation in calmness, in fairness, in disregard of public clamor and private pressures, and with dignity. We believe that it has been demonstrated that the Government can search its own soul and the soul of an individual whose relationship to his Government is in question with full protection of the rights and interests of both. We believe that loyalty and security can be examined within the frameworks of the traditional and inviolable principles of American justice.

The Board approached its task in the spirit of inquiry, not that of a trial. The Board worked long and arduously. It has heard 40 witnesses including Dr. J. Robert Oppenheimer and compiled over 3,000 pages of testimony in addition to having read the same amount of file material.

Dr. Oppenheimer has been represented by counsel, usually four in number, at all times in the course of the proceedings. He has confronted every witness appearing before the Board, with the privilege of cross-examination. He is familiar with the contents of every relevant document, which was made available to the Board, except those which under governmental necessity cannot be disclosed, such as reports of the Federal Bureau of Investigation. He has, in his own words, received patient and courteous consideration at the hands of the Board. The Board has, in the words of his chief counsel, displayed fairness in the conduct of the hearings. And, finally, perhaps it should be said that the investigation has been conducted under the auspices of the responsible agency which has the obligation of decision.

As it considered substance, the Board has allowed sympathetic consideration for the individual to go hand in hand with an understanding of the necessities for a clear, realistic, and rugged attitude toward subversion, possible subversion, or indeed broader implications of security.

It was with all these considerations in mind that we approached our task.

PROCEDURES GOVERNING THE HEARINGS

This proceeding is based upon the Atomic Energy Act of 1946; upon the Atomic Energy Commission's published Security Clearance Procedures, dated September 12, 1950; and Personnel Security Clearance Criteria for Determining Eligibility, dated November 17, 1950; and upon Executive Order No. 10450, dated April 27, 1953.

Subparagraphs (ii) and (iv) of section 10 (b) (5) (B) of the Atomic Energy Act provide that, except as authorized by the Commission in case of emergency, no individual shall be employed by the Commission until the Civil Service Commission or (in certain instances) the Federal Bureau of Investigation shall have made an investigation and report to the Commission on the "character, associations, and loyalty" of such individual.

The AEC published Procedures provide, among other things, for written notice to the individual (1) listing the items of derogatory information and (2) explaining his rights (*a*) to reply in writing to the information set forth in the Commission's letter, (*b*) to request a hearing before a personnel security board, (*c*) to challenge the appointment of the members of the Board for cause, (*d*) to be present for the duration of the hearing, (*e*) to be represented by counsel of his own choosing, and (*f*) to present evidence in his own behalf through witnesses, or by documents, or by both. The Commission's Procedures further provide that in the event of a recommendation for a denial of security clearance, the individual shall be immediately notified of that fact and of his right to request a review of his case by the AEC Personnel Security Review Board, with the right to submit a brief to that Board before the case goes to the general manager for final determination.

The AEC published Criteria establish the uniform standards to be applied in determining eligibility for clearance. These Criteria, which, of course, are binding on this Board, provide that it is the responsibility of the Atomic Energy Commission to determine whether the common defense or security will be endangered by granting security clearance.

The Executive order requires the head of each department and agency of the Government to establish and maintain within his department or agency an effective program to insure that "the employment and retention in employment of any civilian officer or employee within the department or agency is clearly consistent with the interests of the national security." The Executive order further provides that information on this issue shall relate, but shall not be limited, to certain categories of information set forth in the order.

6. EARLY DEROGATORY ASSOCIATIONS

YOU HAVE READ the charges in Nichols' letter and Oppenheimer's reply. The Board numbered them, one through twenty-four, and followed each with a specific finding. I am going to ask you now to read the first twenty-two in conjunction with the Board's findings, and then in the next chapter the twenty-third, which the Board treated at some length. The twenty-fourth and last charge concerned Oppenheimer's attitude toward the development of the H-bomb up to the spring of 1951. It was a new charge. You may have heard it for the first time when you read Borden's letter. If you are a reader of *Fortune*, you may have read something about it in the issue of May 1953. Now it was making its first official appearance. We will come to it later.

In compliance with section 4.16 (c) of the Commission's Security Clearance Procedures, the Board makes the following specific findings as to the allegations contained in Mr. K. D. Nichols' letter of December 23, 1953 to Dr. J. Robert Oppenheimer:

1. It was reported that in 1940 you were listed as a sponsor of the Friends of the Chinese People, an organization which was characterized in 1944 by the House Committee on Un-American Activities as a Communist-front organization.

The Board concludes that this allegation is true.

Dr. Oppenheimer in his answer replied that he had no recollection of the Friends of the Chinese People, or of what, if any, his connection with this organization was.

The Board had before it a four page pamphlet (undated) entitled, "American Friends of the Chinese People." The fourth page contains a list of sponsors which includes "Prof. J. R. Oppenheimer."

2. It was further reported that in 1940 your name was included on a letter-head of the American Committee for Democracy and Intellectual Freedom as a member of its National Executive Committee. The American Committee for Democracy and Intellectual Freedom was characterized in 1942 by the House Committee on Un-American Activities as a Communist-front which defended Communist teachers, and in 1943 it was characterized as subversive and Un-American by a Special Subcommittee of the House Committee on Appropriations.

The Board concludes that this allegation is true.

Dr. Oppenheimer testified before the Board to having joined the American Committee for Democracy and Intellectual Freedom in 1937. He said that it

then stood as a protest against what had happened to intellectuals and professionals in Germany. The Board had before it a letterhead of the "American
Committee for Democracy and Intellectual Freedom." The letterhead contains
a printed list of the National Executive Committee, which includes "Prof. J. R.
Oppenheimer." Dr. Oppenheimer testified that he supposed he accepted membership on this Executive Committee although he did not meet with it.

Dr. Oppenheimer stated in his personnel security questionnaire, which he
executed on April 28, 1942, for the purpose of obtaining a clearance for work
on the atomic program, that he had joined the "American Committee for Democratic Intellectual Freedom" in 1937 and was still a member on the date the
PSQ was executed. He testified that he did not know how long after that
he continued to be a member; that, in any event, he was not active thereafter.

3. It was further reported that in 1938 you were a member of the Western
Council of the Consumers Union. The Consumers Union was cited in 1944
by the House Committee on Un-American Activities as a Communist-front
headed by the Communist Arthur Kallet.

The Board concludes that this allegation is true.

Dr. Oppenheimer in his answer stated that for perhaps a year he had been
a member of the Western Council of the Consumers Union. In his personnel
security questionnaire, which he executed on April 28, 1942, Dr. Oppenheimer
stated that he had been a member of the Consumers Union (Western) in
1938–39.

The Board had before it a photostat of a four-page pamphlet (undated)
entitled, "Western Consumers Union," containing a list of Western sponsors,
which included the name "Dr. Robert J. Oppenheimer—Internationally-known
Physicist at the University of California."

4. It was further reported that you stated in 1943 that you were not
a Communist, but had probably belonged to every Communist-front organization on the west coast and had signed many petitions in which Communists
were interested.

The Board concludes that this statement was made by Dr. Oppenheimer, and
the Board had before it considerable evidence indicating Dr. Oppenheimer's
membership in, and association with, Communist-front organizations and activities on the west coast. However, Dr. Oppenheimer, in his answer, claimed that
the quotation was not true and that if he had said anything along the lines
quoted, it was a half-jocular overstatement.

The Board had before it a memorandum, dated September 14, 1943, prepared
by Lt. Col. John Lansdale, Jr., who was then head of Security and Intelligence
for the Manhattan District, which reported "Oppenheimer categorically stated
(to General Groves) that he himself was not a Communist and never had been,
but stated that he had probably belonged to every Communist-front organization on the west coast and signed many petitions concerning matters in which
Communists were interested.

The Board also had before it a transcript of an interview between Colonel
Lansdale and Dr. Oppenheimer on September 12, 1943, which reflected that
Colonel Lansdale had asked Dr. Oppenheimer, "You've probably belonged to
every front organization on the coast," to which Dr. Oppenheimer replied,
"Just about." The transcript further records that Dr. Oppenheimer also stated
that he thought we would have been considered at one time a fellow-traveler
and that "my association with these things was very brief and very intense."

Dr. Oppenheimer in his testimony defined "fellow-traveler" as "someone who
accepted part of the public program of the Communist Party, who was willing
to work with and associate with Communists, but who was not a member of the
party." He testified to having been a fellow-traveler from late 1936 or early
1937, with his interest beginning to taper off after 1939, and with very little
interest after 1942. He further stated that within the framework of his definition of a fellow-traveler, he would not have considered himself as such after
1942.

He further stated that with respect to things that the Communists were
doing, in which he still had an interest, it was not until 1946 that it was clear
to him that he would not collaborate with Communists no matter how much
he sympathized with what they pretended to represent.

5. It was reported that in 1943 and previously you were intimately asso-

ciated with Dr. Jean Tatlock, a member of the Communist Party in San Francisco, and that Dr. Tatlock was partially responsible for your association with Communist-front groups.

The Board concludes that this allegation is true.

Dr. Oppenheimer in his testimony before this Board admitted having associated with Jean Tatlock from 1936 until 1943. He stated that he saw her only rarely between 1939 and 1943, but admitted that the association was intimate. He admitted having seen Jean Tatlock under most intimate circumstances in June or July of 1943, during the time when he was Director of the Los Alamos Laboratory, and admitted that he knew she had been a Communist and that there was not any reason for him to believe that she was not at that time still a Communist. He named several Communists, Communist functionaries or Communist sympathizers whom he had met through Jean Tatlock, or as a result of his association with her.

6. It was reported that your wife, Katherine Puening Oppenheimer, was formerly the wife of Joseph Dallet, a member of the Communist Party, who was killed in Spain in 1937 fighting for the Spanish Republican Army.

The Board concludes that this allegation is true.

Mrs. Oppenheimer testified that she was married to Joseph Dallet from 1934 until he was killed in Spain, fighting for the Spanish Republican Army in 1937.

Mrs. Oppenheimer admitted knowing that Dallet was a member of the Communist Party and was actively engaging in Communist Party activities.

7. It was further reported that during the period of her association with Joseph Dallet, your wife became a member of the Communist Party. The Communist Party has been designated by the Attorney General as a subversive organization which seeks to alter the form of government of the United States by unconstitutional means, within the purview of Executive Order 9835 and Executive Order 10450.

The Board concludes that this allegation is true.

Mrs. Oppenheimer testified to having been a member of the Communist Party from about 1934 to June 1936 and having engaged in Communist Party activities in the Youngstown, Ohio, area.

8. It was reported that your brother Frank Friedman Oppenheimer became a member of the Communist Party in 1936 and has served as a party organizer and as educational director of the professional section of the Communist Party in Los Angeles County.

The Board concludes that this allegation is true.

Dr. Frank Friedman Oppenheimer admitted in testimony before the Committee on Un-American Activities of the House of Representatives, on June 14, 1949, that he had been a member of the Communist Party from about 1937 until the early spring of 1941. He testified that he joined under the name of "Frank Folsom."

From information before it, the Board concludes that Dr. Frank Oppenheimer had served as a party organizer and as educational director of the professional section of the Communist Party in Los Angeles County.

9. It was further reported that your brother's wife, Jackie Oppenheimer, was a member of the Communist Party in 1938.

The Board concludes that this allegation is true.

Mrs. Jacquenette Oppenheimer in testimony before the Committee on Un-American Activities, House of Representatives, on June 14, 1949, admitted having been a member of the Communist Party from 1937 until the spring of 1941.

10. and that in August, 1944, Jackie Oppenheimer assisted in the organization of the East Bay branch of the California Labor School.

On the basis of information before it, the Board concludes that this allegation is true.

11. It was further reported that in 1945 Frank and Jackie Oppenheimer were invited to an informal reception at the Russian Consulate, that this invitation was extended by the American-Russian Institute of San Francisco and was for the purpose of introducing famous American scientists to Russian scientists who were delegates to the United Nations Conference on

International Organization being held at San Francisco at that time, and that Frank Oppenheimer accepted this invitation.

On the basis of information before it, the Board concludes that this allegation is true.

12. It was further reported that Frank Oppenheimer agreed to give a 6-week course on The Social Implications of Modern Scientific Development at the California Labor School, beginning May 9, 1946, The American-Russian Institute of San Francisco and the California Labor School have been cited by the Attorney General as Communist organizations within the purview of Executive Order 9835 and Executive Order 10450.

On the basis of information before it, the Board concludes that this allegation is true.

13. It was reported that you have associated with members and officials of the Communist Party, including Isaac Folkoff, Steve Nelson, Rudy Lambert, Kenneth May, Jack Manley, and Thomas Addis.

The Board concludes that this allegation is substantially true.

Dr. Oppenheimer in his answer and in his testimony admitted having associated with Isaac Folkoff, Steve Nelson, Rudy Lambert, Kenneth May, and Thomas Addis. He testified that he knew at the time of his association with them that Folkoff, Nelson, Lambert, and May were Communist Party functionaries, and that Addis was either a Communist or close to one. He admitted that his associations with these persons continued until 1942. There was no evidence before the Board with respect to an association with Jack Manley.

Dr. Oppenheimer testified that he made contributions to the Spanish War and Spanish Relief through Isaac Folkoff and Thomas Addis. He testified that he had seen Lambert on half a dozen occasions, and that he discussed such contributions once or twice at luncheon with Lambert and Folkoff.

Dr. Oppenheimer testified that Steve Nelson and his family visited his home on several occasions, the last being probably in 1942; that such visits lasted "a few hours;" that he had met Steve Nelson through his (Oppenheimer's) wife since Nelson had befriended her in Paris at the time of Dallet's death; that he had nothing in common with Nelson "except an affection for my wife."

14. It was reported that you were a subscriber to the Daily People's World, a west coast Communist newspaper, in 1941 and 1942.

The Board concludes that this allegation is true.

Dr. Oppenheimer testified that he had subscribed to the People's World "for several years." He could not recall when the subscription expired and stated that he did not believe he had canceled the subscription. He testified that he knew the Daily People's World was the west coast Communist newspaper.

15. It was reported in 1950 that you stated to an agent of the Federal Bureau of Investigation that you had in the past made contributions to Communist-front organizations, although at the time you did not know° of Communist Party control or extent of infiltration of these groups. You further stated to an agent of the Federal Bureau of Investigation that some of these contributions were made through Isaac Folkoff, whom you knew to be a leading Communist Party functionary, because you had been told that this was the most effective and direct way of helping these groups.

The Board finds that Dr. Oppenheimer made the statements attributed to him by the Federal Bureau of Investigation.

The Board concludes that Dr. Oppenheimer in the past made contributions to Communist-front organizations and that some of these contributions were made through Isaac Folkoff, a leading Communist Party functionary.

Dr. Oppenheimer testified that he contributed to Spanish causes through Communist Party channels from the winter of 1937–38 until early in 1942. He said that he had contributed more than $500 and less than $1,000 each year during this period. He testified that he had made the contributions in cash and, in explaining how these contributions came to an end, he said (in referring to Pearl Harbor) that he "didn't like to continue a clandestine operation of any kind at a time when I saw myself with the possibility or prospect of getting more deeply involved in the war."

Dr. Oppenheimer in his answer admitted making the contributions through

Thomas Addis and Isaac Folkoff. He testified that he knew Addis was a Communist or very close to a Communist. He knew that Folkoff was connected with the Communist Party. In addition, Dr. Oppenheimer admitted having contributed about $100 in cash to the Strike fund of one of the major strikes of "Bridges' Union" about 1937 or 1938.

16. It was reported that you attended a house-warming party at the home of Kenneth and Ruth May on September 20, 1941, for which there was an admission charge for the benefit of The Peoples World, and that at this party you were in the company of Joseph W. Weinberg and Clarence Hiskey, who were alleged to be members of the Communist Party and to have engaged in espionage on behalf of the Soviet Union. It was further reported that you informed officials of the United States Department of Justice in 1942 that you had no recollection that you had attended such a party, but that since it would have been in character for you to have attended such a party, you would not deny that you were there.

The Board concludes on the basis of information before it, that it was probable that Dr. Oppenheimer attended "the house-warming party" at the home of Kenneth and Ruth May. The Board concludes that Dr. Oppenheimer made the statements to the United States Department of Justice officials attributed to him.

Dr. Oppenheimer did not deny having attended such a party and testified that he knew Kenneth May. He denied knowing Hiskey but testified that he, Oppenheimer, was at parties at which Weinberg was present.

17. It was reported that you attended a closed meeting of the professional section of the Communist Party of Alameda County, Calif., which was held in the latter part of July or early August 1941, at your residence, 19 Kenilworth Court, Berkeley, Calif., for the purpose of hearing an explanation of a change in Communist Party policy. It was further reported that you denied that you attended such a meeting and that such a meeting was held in your home.

The Board is of the opinion that the evidence with respect to this meeting is inconclusive. The Board finds that Dr. Oppenheimer did deny that he attended such a meeting and that such a meeting was held in his home.

18. It was reported that you stated to an agent of the Federal Bureau of Investigation in 1950 that you attended a meeting in 1940 or 1941, which may have taken place at the home of Haakon Chevalier, which was addressed by William Schneiderman, whom you knew to be a leading functionary of the Communist Party. In testimony in 1950 before the California State Senate Committee on Un-American Activities, Haakon Chevalier was identified as a member of the Communist Party in the San Francisco area in the early 1940's.

The Board finds that Dr. Oppenheimer made the statements attributed to him by the Federal Bureau of Investigation.

Dr. Oppenheimer testified that on December 1, 1940, he attended an evening meeting at the home of Haakon Chevalier at which perhaps 20 people were present and at which William Schneiderman, secretary of the Communist Party in California, gave a talk about the Communist Party line. He testified that he thought that possibly Isaac Folkoff, Dr. Addis, and Rudy Lambert were there.

He also testified that "after the end of 1940" he attended a similar meeting at the home of Louise Bransten, "a Communist sympathizer," at which some of the same people were present and at which Schneiderman also spoke and expounded the Communist Party line.

Dr. Oppenheimer testified that sometime between 1937 and 1939 as a guest he attended a Communist Party meeting at the home of his brother, Frank.

19. It was reported that you have consistently denied that you have ever been a member of the Communist Party. It was further reported that you stated to a representative of the Federal Bureau of Investigation in 1946 that you had a change of mind regarding the policies and politics of the Soviet Union about the time of the signing of the Soviet-German Pact in 1939. It was further reported that during 1950 you stated to a representative of the Federal Bureau of Investigation that you had never attended a closed meeting of the Communist Party; and that at the time of the Russo-

Finnish War and the subsequent break between Germany and Russia in 1941, you realized the Communist Party infiltration tactics into the alleged anti-Fascist groups and became fed up with the whole thing and lost what little interest you had.

Dr. Oppenheimer testified that he had never been a member of the Communist Party. The Board finds that Dr. Oppenheimer made the statements attributed to him by the Federal Bureau of Investigation.

It was further reported, however, that:

19. (a) Prior to April 1942 you had contributed $150 per month to the Communist Party in the San Francisco area, and that the last such payment was apparently made in April 1942 immediately before your entry into the atomic bomb project.

The Board concludes on the basis of testimony and other information before it that Dr. Oppenheimer made periodic contributions through Communist Party functionaries to the Communist Party in the San Francisco area in amounts aggregating not less than $500 nor more than $1,000 a year during a period of approximately 4 years ending in April 1942. As of April 1942, Dr. Oppenheimer had been for several months participating in Government atomic energy research activities. He executed a questionnaire for Government clearance on April 28, 1942, and subsequently assumed full-time duties with the atomic energy project.

19. (b) During the period 1942–45 various officials of the Communist Party, including Dr. Hannah Peters, organizer of the Professional Section of the Communist Party, Alameda County, Calif., Bernadette Doyle, secretary of the Alameda County Communist Party, Steve Nelson, David Adelson, Paul Pinsky, Jack Manley, and Katrina Sandow, are reported to have made statements indicating that you were then a member of the Communist Party; that you could not be active in the party at that time; that your name should be removed from the Party mailing list and not mentioned in any way; that you had talked the atomic bomb question over with Party members during this period; and that several years prior to 1945 you had told Steve Nelson that the Army was working on an atomic bomb.

The Board finds that during the period 1942–45, Dr. Hannah Peters, Bernadette Doyle, Steve Nelson, Jack Manley, and Katrina Sandow made statements indicating that Dr. Oppenheimer was then a member of the Communist Party; and that the other statements attributed to officials of the Communist Party in this allegation were made by one or more of them. The Board does not find on the basis of information available to it that such statements were made by David Adelson and Paul Pinsky.

19. (c) You stated in August of 1943 that you did not want anybody working for you on the project who was a member of the Communist Party, since "one always had a question of divided loyalty" and the discipline of the Communist Party was very severe and not compatible with complete loyalty to the project. You further stated at that time that you were referring only to present membership in the Communist Party and not to people who had been members of the party. You stated further that you knew several individuals then at Los Alamos who had been members of the Communist Party. You did not, however, identify such former members of the Communist Party to the appropriate authorities. It was also reported that during the period 1942–45 you were responsible for the employment on the atomic bomb project of individuals who were members of the Communist Party or closely associated with activities of the Communist Party, including Giovanni Rossi Lomanitz, Joseph W. Weinberg, David Bohm, Max Bernard Friedman, and David Hawkins. In the case of Giovanni Rossi Lomanitz, you urged him to work on the project, although you stated that you knew he had been very much of a "Red" when he first came to the University of California and that you emphasized to him that he must forego all political activity if he came on to the project. In August 1943 you protested against the termination of his deferment and requested that he be returned to the project after his entry into the military service.

The Board concludes that Dr. Oppenheimer did state in 1943 that he did not want anybody working for him on the project who was a member of the Communist Party, since "one always had a question of divided loyalty" and the discipline of the Communist Party was very severe and not compatible with complete loyalty to the project. He further stated at that time he was referring only to present membership in the Communist Party and not to people who had been members of the party. He stated further that he knew several individuals then at Los Alamos who had been members of the Communist Party. He did not, however, identify such former members of the Communist Party to the appropriate authorities.

The Board concludes that Dr. Oppenheimer was responsible for the employment on the atom bomb project of Giovanni Rossi Lomanitz at Berkeley and David Hawkins at Los Alamos.

The Board concludes that Dr. Oppenheimer asked for the transfer of David Bohm to Los Alamos, although Bohm was closely associated with the Communist Party. In his answer, Dr. Oppenheimer admitted that while at Berkeley he had assigned David Bohm to a problem of basic science having a bearing on atomic research.

Dr. Oppenheimer testified that he understood that Hawkins had left-wing associations; and that Hawkins "talked about philosophy in a way that indicated an interest and understanding and limited approval anyway of Engels."

The Board does not conclude that Dr. Oppenheimer was responsible for the employment of Friedmann or Weinberg on the atomic energy program.

Dr. Oppenheimer testified that Joseph W. Weinberg was a graduate student of his; that he had heard that Weinberg had been a member of the Young Communist League before coming to Berkeley and the Board had before it a transcript of a conversation with Dr. Oppenheimer indicating that at least by August 1943, he knew Weinberg to be a member of the Communist Party and that he "suspected that before but was not sure." Weinberg gave Oppenheimer as a reference at the time he (Weinberg) obtained employment at the Radiation Laboratory on April 22, 1943.

Dr. Oppenheimer testified that he asked General Groves for the transfer of David Bohm to Los Alamos in 1943, but was told by General Groves that he could not be transferred since he had relatives in Nazi Germany. In March 1944 after a conversation with Bohm at Berkeley (a surveillance report indicated that the talk took place at a sidewalk meeting), he checked with the security officer at Los Alamos to see whether the objections to Bohm still obtained.

Dr. Oppenheimer testified that he thought that in 1946 or 1947 he helped Bohm get a job as Assistant Professor of Physics at Princeton. He testified that he happened to meet Bohm and Lomanitz on the street in Princeton in 1949 just prior to their testifying before the House Committee on Un-American Activities; that he said that "they should tell the truth"; that he later saw Bohm at Princeton and attended a farewell party for him in Princeton; that he would, if asked, have written a letter of recommendation for Bohm as a competent physicist in connection with a job in Brazil, although he knew and was worried about Bohm having pleaded the Fifth Amendment when he testified.

The Board finds that Dr. Oppenheimer did urge Lomanitz to work on the project although he knew he had been very much a "Red" when he first came to the University of California and, in fact, during his attendance at the University, and that Dr. Oppenheimer later stated to a Manhattan District official that he had warned Lomanitz that he must forego all political activity if he came to the project. The Board finds further that in August 1943, Dr. Oppenheimer protested against the termination of Lomanitz' deferment and urgently requested that he be returned to the project after his entry into the military service. It appears from the testimony that Dr. Oppenheimer first learned of the impending induction of Lomanitz in a letter from Dr. E. U. Condon who wrote to him "About it in a great sense of outrage."

20. It was reported that you stated to representatives of the Federal Bureau of Investigation on September 5, 1946, that you had attended a meeting in the East Bay and a meeting in San Francisco at which there were present persons definitely identified with the Communist Party. When asked the purpose of the East Bay meeting and the identity of those in attendance, you declined to answer on the ground that this had no bearing on the matter of interest being discussed.

The Board concludes that this allegation is true. The Board finds that Dr. Oppenheimer did attend a meeting in the East Bay and a meeting in San Francisco (see item 18 above) at which there were present persons definitely identified with the Communist Party and that when he was asked about this meeting by representatives of the Federal Bureau of Investigation on September 5, 1946, he declined to answer on the ground that this had no bearing on the matter of interest being discussed.

The Board finds that Dr. Oppenheimer advised representatives of the FBI of this meeting in a subsequent interview in 1950.

21. It was reported that you attended a meeting at the home of Frank Oppenheimer on January 1, 1946, with David Adelson and Paul Pinsky, both of whom were members of the Communist Party. It was further reported that you analyzed some material which Pinsky hoped to take up with the Legislative Convention in Sacramento, Calif.

The Board concludes that this allegation is true.

22. It was reported in 1946 that you were listed as vice chairman on the letterhead of the Independent Citizens Committee of the Arts, Sciences, and Professions, Inc., which has been cited as a Communist-front by the House Committee on Un-American Activities.

The Board concludes that this allegation is true, although the Board finds that Dr. Oppenheimer advised the organization in a letter on October 11, 1946, that he was not in accord with its policy and wished to resign. He wrote again on December 2, 1946, insisting upon resignation. The resignation was accepted on December 10, 1946.

These charges were far from new. They were old. They were stale. They were historical. They belonged to Oppenheimer's past and to our past—the era of the 1930s and early 1940s, pre-Pearl Harbor days and pre-Stalingrad. Who was then so anti-Communist as we all are now? Only the very astute, or the bitterly prejudiced, or xenophobes who, like General Groves, had much the same attitude toward England as they had toward Russia. In the fine phrase of the editor of *Nature*, in its issue of September 25, 1954, these charges were "revived now from the irrelevance to which a brilliant record of national service had relegated them."

Oppenheimer too had changed. He was then as callow and naïve as he was idealistic. He was now mature and still idealistic. May it not be a sign of true maturity that you do not so much change as develop, leaving behind you only your immaturity? The man had better not be too different from the youth. He had better not shift his base. He had better secure it and build on it. When we grow up it had better be up than sideways.

Oppenheimer told Robb in the course of his cross-examination:

Q. Doctor, I notice in your answer on page 5 you use the expression "fellow travelers." What is your definition of a fellow traveler, sir?

A. It is a repugnant word which I used about myself once in an interview with the FBI. I understood it to mean someone who accepted part of the public program of the Communist Party, who was willing to work with and associate with Communists, but who was not a member of the party.

Q. Do you think though a fellow traveler should be employed on a secret war project?

A. Today?

Q. Yes, sir.

A. No.

Q. Did you feel that way in 1942 and 1943?

A. My feeling then and my feeling about most of these things is that the judgment is an integral judgment of what kind of a man you are dealing with. Today I think association with the Communist Party or fellow traveling with the Communist Party manifestly means sympathy for the enemy. In the period of the war, I would have thought that it was a question of what the man was like, what he would and wouldn't do. Certainly fellow traveling and party membership raised a question and a serious question.

Q. Were you ever a fellow traveler?

A. I was a fellow traveler.

Q. When?

A. From late 1936 or early 1937, and then it tapered off, and I would say I traveled much less fellow after 1939 and very much less after 1942.

Q. How long after 1942 did you continue as a fellow traveler?

A. After 1942 I would say not at all.

Q. But you did continue as a fellow traveler until 1942?

A. Well, now, let us be careful.

Q. I want you to be, Doctor.

A. I had no sympathy with the Communist line about the war between the spring of 1940 and when they changed. I did not admire the fashion of their change.

Q. Did you cease to be a fellow traveler at the time of the Nazi-Russian Pact in 1939?

A. I think I did, yes.

Q. Now, are you changing ——

A. Though there were some things that the Communists were doing which I still had an interest in.

Q. Are you now amending your previous answer that you were more or less a fellow traveler until 1942?

A. Yes, I think I am.

Mr. GARRISON. Mr. Chairman, I think he testified that he tapered off; did he not?

Mr. ROBB. I said more or less a fellow traveler. I was trying to paraphrase.

By Mr. ROBB:

Q. Do you want to say something more, Doctor?

A. Yes.

Q. Doctor, I don't intend to cut you off at any time. If I ask a question and if you have not completed your answer, I wish you would stop me and finish your answer.

A. Let me give you a couple of examples.

Q. Yes, sir.

A. The Communists took an interest in organizing the valley workers. I think this was long after the Nazi-Soviet Pact. That seemed fine to me at the time. They took an interest in extricating and replanting the refugee loyalists fighters from Spain. That seemed fine to me at the time. I am not defending the wisdom of these views. I think they were idiotic. In this sense I approved of some Communist objectives. Beating the drums about keeping out of war, especially after the battle of France, did not seem fine to me.

Q. You continued your contributions to Communist causes through Communist channels until approximately 1942?

A. I don't remember the date. I have no reason to challenge the date in the Commission's letter.

Q. When did you fill out and file your first personnel security questionnaire?

A. It was in June or July, I guess, of 1942.

Q. Was that about the time when you ceased to be a fellow traveler?

A. No.

Q. How much before that?

A. I have tried to tell you that this was a gradual and not a sharp affair. Any attempt by me to make it sharp would be wrong. I tried in my answer to spell out some of the steps in my understanding, first, of what it was like in Russia. Second, the apparent pliability of American Communist positions to Russian interests, and my final boredom with the thing. It was not something that I can put a date on. I did not write a letter to the papers.

Q. Is it possible, Doctor, for you to set a date when you were sure you were no longer fellow traveling?

A. In that I had no sympathy for any cause the Communists promoted?

Q. Yes, sir.

A. I think I can put it this way. After the war and about the time of this letter——

Q. Which letter?

A. My letter to the Independent Citizens Committee, I was clear that I would not collaborate with Communists no matter how much I sympathized with what they pretended to be after. This was absolute. I believe I have not done so since.

Q. So that would be the Ultima Thule of your fellow traveling, that date?

A. Yes, but I think to call me a fellow traveler in 1944 or 1946 would be to distort the meaning of the word as I explained it.

The fact is, Oppenheimer is the better and the sounder now for his early immaturity. "For God's sake," Robert Louis Stevenson said in his *Virginibus Puerisque*, "give me the young man who has brains enough to make a fool of himself!" Were there stains on the linen of Oppenheimer's character, he has long since washed them out. But were they stains? Unless young men can see visions, old men can only dream dreams.

If these charges have any rational bearing now on Oppenhiemer's fitness to serve his country, how is it that they did not prevent him from serving his country in 1943 as director of Los Alamos and again in 1947 as chairman of the G.A.C.? They were fresher then and the more relevant, and Oppenheimer himself was less mature.

General Groves knew pretty much all there was to know about Oppenheimer in 1943 and cleared him to be director of Los Alamos. "I think I was thoroughly familiar with everything that was reported about Dr. Oppenheimer," he said; and later, in 1950, after General Groves had retired and gone to Remington Rand, he wrote Oppenheimer this letter:

"Dr. J. ROBERT OPPENHEIMER,
  "*The Institute for Advanced Study, Princeton, N. J.*

"DEAR Dr. OPPENHEIMER: If at any time you should feel that it were wise, I would be pleased to have you make a statement of the general tenor of that which follows:

" 'General Groves has informed me that shortly after he took over the responsibility for the development of the atomic bomb, he reviewed personally the entire file and all known information concerning me and immediately ordered that I be cleared for all atomic information in order that I might participate in the development of the atomic bomb. General Groves has also informed me that he personally went over all information concerning me which came to light during the course of operations of the atomic project and that at no time did he regret his decision.'

"I don't believe that you will find any need to make use of any such statement, but you might. You might wish to show it to some individual for his use in handling unpleasant situations, if any arise.

"I have been very much pleased with the comments that have been made by various persons in whose judgment I have more than average faith, such as the reported statement of Representative Nixon that he had 'complete confidence in Dr. Oppenheimer's loyalty.' This was made in a speech at Oakdale, Calif.

"I am sure of one thing, and that is, that this type of attack, while it is unpleasant, does not in the end do real damage to one's reputation.

"I wonder if you saw the editorial in the Washington Post to the effect that the way to cripple the United States atomic energy program would be to single out a few of the foremost nuclear physicists and dispose of them by character assassination. When I remember how the Post has written about me, it makes me wonder just who wrote this particular editorial.

"I do hope that you are finding life enjoyable and not too hectic and that I will have the pleasure of seeing you again before too long.

"My very best to Mrs. Oppenheimer.

"Sincerely yours" signed "L. R. Groves, Lt. General U. S. Army (Retired)."

General Groves did not mean that he would clear Oppenheimer now or at any time after the Atomic Energy Act of 1946. The general said, "I don't care how important the man is, if there is any possibility other than a tortured one that his associations or his loyalty or his character might endanger the [common defense or security]. In this case I refer particularly to associations and not to the associations as they exist today but the past record of the associations. I would not clear Dr. Oppenheimer today if I were a member of the Commission on the basis of this interpretation. If the interpretation is different, then I would have to stand on my interpretation of it." The general is an honest man and a good general.

The whole A.E.C. knew all about Oppenheimer's past when it cleared him for the General Advisory Committee in 1947. I will go into this in detail in a moment.

In 1950 Gordon Dean, when he became chairman of the A.E.C., went through Oppenheimer's personnel file. He testified:

Q. Did you go through Dr. Oppenheimer's personnel file?
A. I did. This is the first occasion I ever had to look at Dr. Oppenheimer's personnel file. Ordinarily Commissioners don't go through the files of people unless there is some real reason. Here, however, was a person who was chairman of the committee; he had been cleared in 1947 by the Commission, and I for the first time picked it up and went through it personally myself.
I then asked Dr. Oppenheimer if he could come in and see me about this, and I personally asked him about the Crouch incident. He said substantially what I have said he said in reply to Mr. Volpe, and I believed him.
Q. Did you continue to read matters that went into his personnel file after this?
A. I told the security officer, I believe, or perhaps my secretary, that anything coming from the FBI concerning Dr. Oppenheimer I wanted to see, and file in my own mind at least.
Two or three did come in. Because here was a file with a lot of early association evidence, I thought he was too important a man for me to overlook him, and it was my responsibility as Chairman, also. So I did see, I am sure, every memorandum from the FBI. But there were only 2 or 3, and there was nothing particularly new in them, as I recall, from that point on.
Q. What was your belief as to Dr. Oppenheimer's loyalty after you had been through the file and had talked with him?
A. There was no question in my mind—I must say when I first looked at the file, I had doubts, largely growing out of these early associations—but there was never any doubt in my mind after I examined the file and based partly on my knowledge of Dr. Oppenheimer, which was very close, there was never

any doubt as to his loyalty in my opinion. None. That decision had to be made one way or the other. It could not be half way. There were some very unpleasant early associations when you look at them in retrospect, but as far as his loyalty I was convinced of it, not that the file convinced me so much, but the fact that here was a man, one of the few men who can demonstrate his loyalty to his country by his performance. Most people illustrate their loyalty in negative terms. They did not see somebody. Here is a man who had an unusual record of performance. It is much broader than I have indicated so far.

Q. Would you state to the board your general impression of his character as well as his loyalty, his integrity and sense of discretion? How would you rate those qualities?

A. I would say that he is a very human man, a sensitive man, a very well educated man, a man of complete integrity in my association with him. And a very devoted man to his country, and certainly to the Commission. No question of these things in my mind.

And then, as we know, Dr. Walter G. Whitman, the head of the Chemical Engineering Department of M.I.T., as Chairman of the Research and Development Board of the Department of Defense, himself reviewed Oppenheimer's record that Saturday in July 1953.

But the Board was quite right to take these early and callow associations and interests seriously, as we have heard the chairman tell Dr. Winne. They could not properly be shrugged off. The security rules and regulations were not the same. For one thing, they now put the burden on Oppenheimer of proving he was not a security risk. It was up to him. Shift the burden of proof and you shift the responsibility. Lawyers, who are used to an adversary process of justice, take the come and go of the burden of proof lightly. Between adversaries the burden, one way or the other, simply makes it easier or harder to win the case. The presumption of innocence makes it harder to convict. A presumption of guilt simply makes it easier. But in an inquiry, when you shift the burden of proof you change the whole nature of the proceeding. The tribunal is no longer asked to seek the truth. It is told to stop as soon as it reaches a doubt. This is what it has been told to look for, all it is expected to find. With the burden of proof, the burden of the inquiry itself has been laid on the defendant. For the only way to allay or dissipate a doubt is to demonstrate the truth. The roles are, in effect, reversed. The seeker after the truth becomes a man who has to be shown. It is then up to the truth to come to him. For he has been told not to pursue her.

7. THE CHEVALIER
AFFAIR

THE LAST of these twenty-three items of derogatory information was far and away the most derogatory. This was the Chevalier affair. If Oppenheimer had not himself complicated it, there would have been little to it. But he did, and most effectually, for his friends as well as for his enemies. Here are Nichols' allegations, followed by the Board's findings:

> 23. It was reported that prior to March 1, 1943, possibly 3 months prior, Peter Ivanov, secretary at the Soviet Consulate, San Francisco, approached George Charles Eltenton for the purpose of obtaining information regarding work being done at the Radiation Laboratory for the use of Soviet scientists; that George Charles Eltenton subsequently requested Haakon Chevalier to approach you concerning this matter; that Haakon Chevalier thereupon approached you, either directly or through your brother, Frank Friedman Oppenheimer, in connection with this matter; and that Haakon Chevalier finally advised George Charles Eltenton that there was no chance whatsoever of obtaining the information. It was further reported that you did not report this episode to the appropriate authorities until several months after its occurrence; that when you initially discussed this matter with the appropriate authorities on August 26, 1943, you did not identify yourself as the person who had been approached, and you refused to identify Haakon Chevalier as the individual who had made the approach on behalf of George Charles Eltenton; and that it was not until several months later, when you were ordered by a superior to do so, that you so identified Haakon Chevalier. It was further reported that upon your return to Berkeley following your separation from the Los Alamos project, you were visited by the Chevaliers on several occasions; and that your wife was in contact with Haakon and Barbara Chevalier in 1946 and 1947.

The Board concludes that this allegation is substantially true.

The Board had before it a recording of a conversation between Dr. Oppenheimer and Lt. Col. Boris T. Pash, War Department intelligence officer, who had the responsibility for investigating subversive activities at the Radiation Laboratory, University of California at Berkeley. This conversation took place on August 26, 1943, at the Radiation Laboratory.

It was on this occasion that Dr. Oppenheimer reported the incident to Government authorities. He named Eltenton but refused to identify Chevalier. He also stated that the unnamed contact (Chevalier) had approached three persons on the atomic project and in the course of the interview mentioned other factors, such as the use of microfilm or other means and the involvement of the Russian Consulate.

The Board also had before it a transcript of a conversation between Dr. Oppenheimer and Lieutenant Colonel Lansdale which records that on September 12, 1943, Dr. Oppenheimer again refused to name Chevalier but reported the involvement of three others.

It was not until December 1943, that Dr. Oppenheimer, after being told by General Groves that he would be ordered to divulge the identity of the contact, reported the name of Chevalier. However, the record shows that having been told of the identity of Chevalier by Dr. Oppenheimer, the Manhattan District officials were still of the opinion that Chevalier had contacted three employees on the atomic project.

Dr. Oppenheimer, in his answer, stated that his friend, Haakon Chevalier, with his wife, visited him at his home on Eagle Hill probably in early 1943. He stated further that during the visit Chevalier came into the kitchen and told him that George Eltenton had spoken to him of the possibility of transmitting technical information to Soviet scientists. Dr. Oppenheimer said that he made some strong remark to the effect that this sounded terribly wrong to him, and the discussion ended there.

Dr. Oppenheimer's answer further states that nothing in his long-standing friendship would have led him to believe that Chevalier was actually seeking information, and he was certain that Chevalier had no idea of the work on which Dr. Oppenheimer was engaged.

Dr. Oppenheimer testified that the detailed story of the Chevalier incident which he told to Colonel Pash on August 26, 1943, and affirmed to Colonel Lansdale on September 12, 1943, was false in certain material respects. Dr. Oppenheimer testified that this story was "a cock-and-bull story"; that "the whole thing was a pure fabrication except for the one name, Eltenton." He said that his only explanation for lying was that he "was an idiot" and he "was reluctant to mention Chevalier" and "no doubt somewhat reluctant to mention myself." He admitted on cross examination, however, that if the story he told Colonel Pash had been true, it would have shown that Chevalier "was deeply involved"; that it was not just a casual conversation; that Chevalier was not an innocent contact, and that it was a criminal conspiracy.

Dr. Oppenheimer admitted that if this story to Colonel Pash had been true, it made things look very bad for both Chevalier and himself. He acknowledged that he thought the request for information by Eltenton was "treasonable." He admitted that he knew when he talked to Colonel Pash that his falsification impeded Colonel Pash's investigation.

Dr. Oppenheimer testified that in June or July of 1946 shortly after Chevalier was interviewed by the FBI about the Eltenton-Chevalier Incident, Chevalier came to Oppenheimer's home in Berkeley and told Oppenheimer about the interview; that Chevalier said the FBI had pressed him about whether he talked to anyone besides Oppenheimer; that quite awhile later Dr. Oppenheimer was interviewed by the FBI about the same matter, and at this time he knew from Chevalier substantially what Chevalier had said to the FBI about the incident.

Dr. Oppenheimer testified that he recalled getting a letter from Chevalier in 1950 asking him about Dr. Oppenheimer's testimony before the House Un-American Activities Committee concerning the Chevalier-Eltenton incident. He responded, giving Chevalier a summary of what he, Dr. Oppenheimer, had testified. This letter was later used by Chevalier in support of his application for a passport. Dr. Oppenheimer further testified that at about that time, Chevalier came to Princeton and spent 2 days with Dr. Oppenheimer, discussing Chevalier's personal affairs and that he also then mentioned the matter of his passport. Dr. Oppenheimer said that on this occasion he recommended to Chevalier a lawyer named Joseph Fanelli, who, cross examination disclosed, was the attorney who represented Joseph Weinberg at his trial for perjury. Dr. Oppenheimer testified that he did not know Mr. Fanelli at this time but he had represented Frank Oppenheimer at his appearance before the House Committee on Un-American Activities.

Dr. Oppenheimer testified further that in December of 1953, when he and Mrs. Oppenheimer were in Paris, they had dinner with Dr. and Mrs. Chevalier and, on the following day, went with the Chevaliers to visit a Dr. Malraux. According to Dr. Oppenheimer, Dr. Malraux had given a speech at a "Spanish Relief" meeting in California at which Chevalier presided in about 1938. Dr. Oppenheimer said that since that time, Malraux had undergone "rather major political changes"; that "Malraux became a violent supporter of DeGaulle and his great brainman and deserted politics and went into purely philosophic and literary work." It appears also that subsequent to his meeting with Dr. Oppenheimer in Paris in December 1953, Chevalier wrote a letter to an official of the United States Embassy in Paris, reading as follows:

"My friend—and yours—Robert Oppenheimer, gave me your name when he was up for dinner here in our apartment early last December, and urged me to get in touch with you if a personal problem of mine which I discussed with him became pressing. He gave me to understand that I could speak to you with the same frankness and fullness as I have with him, and he with me, during the 15 years of our friendship.

"I should not have presumed to follow up such a suggestion if it had come from anyone else. But, as you know, Opje never tosses off such a suggestion lightly.

"If you are in Paris, or will be in the near future, I should, then, like to see you informally and discuss the problem.

"On rereading what I have written, I have a feeling that I have made the thing sound more formidable than it really is. It's just a decision that I have to make, which is fairly important to me, and which Opje in his grandfatherly way suggested that I shouldn't make before consulting you.

"Very sincerely,

"HAAKON CHEVALIER."

Dr. Oppenheimer testified that the problem which was bothering Chevalier and his wife was that Chevalier was employed as a translator for UNESCO, and he understood that if he continued this work as an American citizen, he would have to be cleared after investigation, and he was doubtful as to whether he would be cleared. He did not wish to renounce his American citizenship but did wish to keep his job, and he was in a conflict about it. Dr. Oppenheimer in his testimony denied going to the American Embassy to assist Dr. Chevalier in getting a passport to return to the United States although he admitted having had lunch with the official in question.

Dr. Oppenheimer also denied discussing with the official in question or anyone else the matter of Chevalier's passport.

Dr. Oppenheimer in his testimony has stated that his association with Chevalier has continued and that he still considers him to be his friend.

Early in 1943, a month or more before Oppenheimer went to Los Alamos and while the Oppenheimers were still living in Eagle Hill in Berkeley, the Haakon Chevaliers came for a visit. Chevalier was a colleague of Oppenheimer's at the University of California, a professor of French, and he and his wife had been quite close friends of the Oppenheimers for five or six years. Oppenheimer first met him when Chevalier presided at a meeting for Spanish relief at which the French writer André Malraux was the speaker. While they were there—but Oppenheimer can tell just what happened better than I can. Robb cross-examined him on the passage in his reply.

Q. Yes, sir. Doctor, on page 22 of your letter of March 4, 1954, you speak of what for convenience I will call the Eltenton-Chevalier incident.
A. That is right.
Q. You describe the occasion when Chevalier spoke to you about this matter. Would you please, sir, tell the board as accurately as you can and in as much detail as you can exactly what Chevalier said to you, and you said to Chevalier, on the occasion that you mention on page 22 of your answer?
A. This is one of those things that I had so many occasions to think about that I am not going to remember the actual words. I am going to remember the nature of the conversation.
Q. Where possible I wish you would give us the actual words.
A. I am not going to give them to you.
Q. Very well.
A. Chevalier said he had seen George Eltenton recently.
Mr. GRAY. May I interrupt just a moment? I believe it would be useful for Dr. Oppenheimer to describe the circumstances which led to the conversation, whether he called you or whether this was a casual meeting.

Mr. ROBB. Yes, sir.

The WITNESS. He and his wife——

By Mr. ROBB:

Q. May I interpose, Doctor? Would you begin at the beginning and tell us exactly what happened?

A. Yes. One day, and I believe you have the time fixed better than I do in the winter of 1942–43, Haakon Chevalier came to our home. It was, I believe, for dinner, but possibly for a drink. When I went out into the pantry, Chevalier followed me or came with me to help me. He said, "I saw George Eltenton recently." Maybe he asked me if I remembered him. That Eltenton had told him that he had a method, he had means of getting technical information to Soviet scientists. He didn't describe the means. I thought I said "But that is treason," but I am not sure. I said anyway something, "This is a terrible thing to do." Chevalier said or expressed complete agreement. That was the end of it. It was a very brief conversation.

Q. That is all that was said?

A. Maybe we talked about the drinks or something like that.

Q. I mean about this matter, Doctor, had Chevalier telephoned you or communicated with you prior to that occasion to ask if he might see you?

A. I don't think so. I don't remember. We saw each other from time to time. If we were having dinner together it would not have gone just this way. Maybe he called up and said he would like to come.

Q. It could have been that he called you and you said come over for dinner; is that correct?

A. Any of these things could have been.

Q. You said in the beginning of your recital of this matter that you have described that occasion on many, many occasions; is that right?

A. Yes.

Q. Am I to conclude from that that it has become pretty well fixed in your mind?

A. I am afraid so.

Q. Yes, sir. It is a twice told tale for you.

A. It certainly is.

Q. It is not something that happened and you forget it and then thought about it next, 10 years later, is that correct?

A. That is right.

Q. Did Chevalier in that conversation say anything to you about the use of microfilm as a means of transmitting this information?

A. No.

Q. You are sure of that?

A. Sure.

Q. Did he say anything about the possibility that the information would be transmitted through a man at the Soviet consulate?

A. No; he did not.

Q. You are sure about that?

A. I am sure about that.

Q. Did he tell you or indicate to you in any way that he had talked to anyone but you about this matter?

A. No.

Q. You are sure about that?

A. Yes.

Q. Did you learn from anybody else or hear that Chevalier had approached anybody but you about this matter?

A. No.

Q. You are sure about that?

A. That is right.

Q. You had no indication or no information suggesting to you that Chevalier had made any other approach than the one to you?

A. No.

Q. You state in your description of this incident in your answer that you made some strong remarks to Chevalier. Was that your remark, that this is treasonous?

A. It was a remark that either said—this is a path that has been walked over too often, and I don't remember what terms I said this is terrible.

Q. Didn't you use the word "treason"?

A. I can tell you the story of the word "treason."
Q. Would you answer that and then explain?
A. I don't know.
Q. You don't know now?
A. No, I don't know.
Q. Did you think it was treasonous?
A. I though it was terrible.
Q. Did you think it was treasonous?
A. To take information from the United States and ship it abroad illicitly, sure.
Q. In other words, you though that the course of action suggested to Eltenton was treasonous.
A. Yes.
Q. Since Eltenton was not a citizen, if it was not treasonous, it was criminal; is that correct?
A. Of course.
Q. In other words, you thought that the course of conduct suggested to Eltenton was an attempt at espionage; didn't you?
A. Sure.

There the matter lay for some time. Oppenheimer did nothing, reported nothing. Chevalier was Oppenheimer's friend. Oppenheimer trusted him. Finally, but not until some months later, Oppenheimer told the authorities. In August 1943 he went to a security officer and tried to get it off his conscience; and he did it in the worst possible way.

In August there was an investigation of some suspicious activities of a group in the Radiation Laboratory at Berkeley. One of them was a man named Rossi Lomanitz, who was a member of a leftish union there and who, the security officers believed, was also a member of the Communist party. Oppenheimer's relations with Lomanitz—and how Oppenheimer and Dr. Ernest Lawrence tried to get Lomanitz' induction into the Army deferred and keep him working in the laboratory at Berkeley—is another story, to which we shall come.

Anyhow, in August 1943 Oppenheimer came back from Los Alamos to the Radiation Laboratory in Berkeley on some errand or other. He went to the intelligence officer there, a Lieutenant Lyall Johnson, and told him about a possible espionage effort in connection with the laboratory. Lieutenant Johnson at once reported this to his superior, a Lieutenant Colonel Boris T. Pash, who was in charge of the investigation, and Pash came to Berkeley. Johnson and Pash interviewed Oppenheimer on August 26, 1943.

Pash arranged to have the interview recorded. I am going to ask you to read the transcript of the recording. It is far from being as clear and as accurate a representation of what was said as we wish it were. Counsel did their best to make it as nearly correct as possible, but they had to put asterisks to indicate where the recording was unintelligible. Then I will give you Robb's cross-examination.

Here, as nearly as Robb and Garrison could understand the recording, is a transcription of Oppenheimer's interview with Pash. I warn you, it is harder reading than it would have been listening.

"UNCLASSIFIED, 4/19/54 CAR,
"*San Francisco, Calif., August 27, 1943.*

"MEMORANDUM FOR THE OFFICER IN CHARGE

"Subject: D. S. M. Project.
"Re: Transcript of Conversation between Dr. J. R. Oppenheimer, Lt. Col. Boris T. Pash, and Lt. Lyall Johnson.

"Transmitted herewith is the transcript of conversation between Dr. J. R. Oppenheimer, Lt. Colo. Boris T. Pash, and Lt. Lyall Johnson, held in Lt. Johnson's office in the New Class Room Building, University of California, Berkeley, Calif., on August 26, 1943. It is to be noted that in some places the conversation was very indistinct and that the running commentary may be indecisive in these places, but the substance of the material discussed is herewith presented:

"P. This is a pleasure, because I am interested to a certain extent in activities and I feel I have a certain responsibility in a child which I don't know anything about. General Groves has, more or less, I feel, placed a certain responsibility in me and it's like having a child, that you can't see, by remote control. I don't mean to take much of your time——

"O. That's perfectly all right. Whatever time you choose.

"P. Mr. Johnson told me about the little incident, or conversation, taking place yesterday in which I am very much interested and it had me worried all day yesterday since he called me.

"O. I was rather uncertain as to whether I should or should not talk to him [Rossi] when I was here. I was unwilling to do it without authorization. What I wanted to tell this fellow was that he had been indiscreet. I know that that's right that he had revealed information. I know that saying that much might in some cases embarrass him. It doesn't seem to have been capable of embarrassing him—to put it bluntly.

"P. Well, that is not the particular interest I have. It is something a little more, in my opinion, more serious. Mr. Johnson said there was a possibility that there may be some other groups interested.

"O. I think that is true, but I have no first-hand knowledge that would be, for that reason, useful, but I think it is true that a man, whose name I never heard, who was attached to the Soviet consul, has indicated indirectly through intermediary people concerned in this project that he was in a position to transmit, without any danger of a leak, or scandal, or anything of that kind, information, which they might supply. I would take it that it is to be assumed that a man attached to the Soviet consulate might be doing it but since I know it to be a fact, I have been particularly concerned about any indiscretions which took place in circles close enough to be in contact with it. To put it quite frankly—I would feel friendly to the idea of the Commander in Chief informing the Russians that we were working on this problem. At least, I can see that there might be some arguments for doing that, but I do not feel friendly to the idea of having it moved out the back door. I think that it might not hurt to be on the lookout for it.

"P. Could you give me a little more specific information as to exactly what information you have? You can readily realize that phase would be, to me, as interesting, pretty near, as the whole project is to you.

"O. Well, I might say that the approaches were always to other people, who were troubled by them, and sometimes came and discussed them with me; and that the approaches were always quite indirect so I feel that to give more, perhaps, than one name, would be to implicate people whose attitude was one of bewilderment rather than one of cooperation. I know of no case, and I am fairly sure that in all cases where I have heard of these contacts, would not have yielded a single thing. That's as far as I can go on that. Now there is a man, whose name was mentioned to me a couple of times—I don't know of my own knowledge that he was involved as an intermediary. It seems, however, not impossible and if you wanted to watch him it might be the appropriate thing to do. He spent quite a number of years in the Soviet Union. He's an English * * * I think he's a chemical engineer. He was—he may not be here now—at the time I was with him here, employed by the Shell development. His name is Eltenton. I would think that there was a small chance—well, let me put it this way: He has probably been asked to do what he can to provide information. Whether he is successful or not, I do not know, but he talked to a friend of his who is also an acquaintance of one of the men on the project, and that was one of the channels by which this thing went. Now I think that to go beyond that would be to put a lot of names down, of people who are not only innocent but whose attitude was 100-percent cooperative.

"P. Now here's a point. You can readily realize that if we get information like that we have to work in an absolutely discreet manner. In other words we can't afford to even indicate——

"O. That you are concerned.

"P. That we are concerned or through whom we get information. However anything that we may get which would eliminate a lot of research work on our part would necessarily bring to a closer conclusion anything that we are doing.

"O. Well, I'm giving you the one name that I think is, or isn't—I mean I don't know the name of the man attached to the consulate—I think I may have been told or I may not have been told and I have, at least not purposely, but actually forgotten. He is—and he may not be here now. These incidents occurred of the order of about 5, 6, 7, months ago.

"J. I was wondering, Dr. Oppenheimer, if there was a particular person—maybe a person on the project that they were trying to pump information from—that if we knew who those were, would at least know where to look for a leak, not from the standpoint of * * *, but looking at a certain picture

"P. Here's the point that I would feel.

"O. I would feel that the people that they tried to get information from were more or less an accident [interpolation] and I believe I would be making some harm by saying that——

"P. Yes. Here's the thing—we, of course, assume that the people who bring this information to you are 100 percent with you, and therefore, there is no question about their intentions. However, if——

"O. Well, I'll tell you one thing—I have known of 2 or 3 cases, and I think two of the men were with me at Los Alamos—they are men who are very closely associated with me.

"P. Have they told you that either they thought they were contacted for that purpose or they were actually contacted for that purpose?

"O. They told me they were contacted for that purpose.

"P. For that purpose.

"O. That is, let me give you the background. The background was—well, you know how difficult it is with the relations between these two allies, and there are a lot of people who don't feel very friendly to Russia, so that the information—a lot of our secret information, our radar and so on, doesn't get to them, and they are battling for their lives and they would like to have an idea of what is going on and this is just to make up, in other words, for the defects of our official communication. That is the form in which it was presented.

"P. Oh, I see.

"O. Of course, the actual fact is that since it is not a communication which ought to be taking place, it is treasonable. But it wasn't presented in that method. [Garble.] It is a method carrying out a policy which was more or less a policy of the Government and the form in which it came was that an interview be arranged with this man Eltenton who had very good contacts with a man from the embassy attached to the consulate who was a very reliable guy (that's his story) and who had a lot of experience in microfilm work, or whatever the hell.

"P. Well, now. I may be getting back to a little systematic picture. * * * These people whom you mentioned, who (two?) are down with you now * * * were they contacted by Eltenton direct?

"O. No.

"P. Through another party?

"O. Yes.

"P. Well, now, could we know through whom that contact was made?

"O. I think it would be a mistake, that is, I think I have told you where the initiative came from and that the other things were almost purely accident and that it would involve people who ought not to be involved in this.

"P. This will not involve the people but it would indicate to us Eltenton's channel. We would have to, now that this is definite on Eltenton. We, of course——

"O. It is not definite in the sense that I have seen him do the thing. He may have been misquoted. I don't believe so. Now Eltenton is a member of the FAECT or not?

"P. That's the union.

"O. That's the CIO union. He's a man whose sympathies are certainly very far "left," whatever his affiliations, or he may or may not have regular contacts with a political group.

"P. Well, here's how I feel——

"O. I doubt it. In any case, it is a safe thing to say that the channels that would be followed in this case are those involving people who have been generally sympathetic to the Soviet and somehow connected peripherally with the Communist movements in this country. That's obvious. I don't need to tell you that.

"P. Well, yes, the fact is, this second contact—the contact that Eltonton had to make with these other people—is that person also a member of the project?

"O. No.

"P. That also is an outsider?

"O. It's a member of the faculty, but not on the project.

"P. A member of the faculty here? Eltenton made it through a member of the faculty to the project.

"O. As far as I know—these approaches were—there may have been more than one person involved. I don't know.

"P. Here's how I feel about this leftist inclination. I think that whether a man has "left" or "right" inclinations, if his character which is back of it—if he's willing to do this, it doesn't make any difference what his inclinations are. It's based on his character primarily and not——

"O. A thing like this going on, let us say, with the Nazis would have a somewhat different color. I don't mean to say that it would be any more deserving of attention, or any more dangerous. but it would involve rather different motives.

"P. Oh, yes, sure.

"O. I'm pretty sure that none of the guys here, with the possible exception of the Russian, who is doing probably his duty by his country—but the other guys really were just feeling they didn't do anything but they were considering the step, which they would have regarded as thoroughly in 'line with the policy of this Government, just making up for the fact that there were a couple of guys in the State Department who might block such communications. You may or may not know that in many projects we share information with the British and some we do not, and there is a great deal of feeling about that, and I don't think that the issues involved here seem to the people very different, except that of course, the people on the project realize the importance and that this is a little bigger and the whole procedure gets away. [Garble.]

"P. Now. Do you feel that would affect—and there could be continued attempts now to establish this type of contract?

"O. I haven't any idea.

"P. You haven't any idea?

"O. As I say, if the guy that was here may by now be in some other town and all that I would have in mind is this—I understood that this man to whom I feel a sense of responsibility, Lomanitz, and I feel it for two reasons. One, he is doing work which he started and which he ought to continue, and, second, since I more or less made a stir about it when the question of his induction came up, that this man may have been indiscreet in circles which would lead to trouble. That is the only thing that I have to say. Because I don't have any doubt that people often approach him, with whom he has contact, I mean whom he sees, might feel it their duty if they got word of something, to let it go further and that is the reason I feel quite strongly that association with the Communist movement is not compatible with the job on a secret war project, it is just that the two loyalties cannot go.

"P. Yes—well——

"O. That is an expression of political opinion, I think that a lot of very brilliant and thoughtful people have seen something in the Communist movement, and that they maybe belong there, maybe it is a good thing for the country. I hope it doesn't belong on the war project——

"P. I get your point. I don't want to seem to you insistent. I want to again sort of explore the possibility of getting the name of the person of the faculty—

I'll tell you for what reason. Not for the purpose of taking him to task in any way whether its nonofficially, officially, or openly or not but to try to see Eltenton's method of approach. You may not agree with me, but I can assure you that that is one of the most important steps.

"O. I understand that, but I have to take the following points of view: I think in mentioning Eltenton's name I essentially said about the man that I think that he may be acting in a way which is dangerous to this country, and which should be watched. I'm not going to mention the name of anyone in the same breath, even if you that you will make a distinction. I just can't do that, because in the other cases, I am convinced from the way in which they handled the thing that they themselves thought it was a bad business.

"P. These other people, yes; I realize—but if—here is the point—if that man is trying to make other contacts for Eltenton, it would take us some time to try to——

"O. My honest opinion is that he probably isn't—that he ran into him at a party and they saw each other or something and Eltenton said, "Do you suppose you could help me? This a very serious thing because we know that important work is going on here, and we think this ought to be made available to our allies, and would you see if any of those guys are willing to help us with it—and then it wouldn't have to be much." You see, that is the kind of thing. [Remaining statement unintelligible.]

"P. Were these two people you mentioned—were they contacted at the same time?

"O. They were contacted within a week of each other.

"P. They were contacted at two different times?

"O. Yes; but not in each other's presence.

"P. That's right. And then from what you first heard, there is someone else who probably still remains here who was contacted as well?

"O. I think that is true.

"P. What I am driving at is that means that there was a plan, at least for some length of time, to make these contacts—and we may not have known all the contacts.

"O. That is certainly true. That is why I mentioned it. If I knew all about it, then I would say forget it. I thought it would be appropriate to call to your attention the fact that these channels at one time existed.

"P. Yes.

"O. I really think that I am drawing [garbled].

"P. You see, you understand that I am sort of—you picture me as a bloodhound on the trail, and that I am trying to get out of you everything I possibly can.

"O. That's your duty to a certain extent.

"P. You see what I mean.

"O. It is also my duty not to implicate these people, who are acquaintances, or colleagues and so on of whose position I am absolutely certain—myself and my duty is to protect them.

"P. Oh, yes.

"O. If I thought that—I won't say it—it might be slightly off.

"P. Well, then here's another point, Doctor, if we find that in making these various contacts, that we get some information which would lead us to believe that certain of these men may have either considered it or are still considering it (mind you I do not even know these men, so it can't be personal)——

"O. Well, none of them that I had anything to do with considered it. They were just upset about it. * * * [Garbled.] They have a feeling toward this country and have signed the Espionage Act; they feel this way about it for I think that the intermediary between Eltenton and the project, thought it was the wrong idea, but said that this was the situation. I don' think he supported it. In fact I know it.

"P. He made about at least three contacts that we knew of.

"O. Well, I think that's right, yes.

"P. And two of these contacts are down there. That means we can assume at least there is one of these men contacted still on the project here.

"O. Yes, I believe that this man has gone, or is scheduled to go to Site X.

"P. This third man?

"O. I think so.

"P. Well that is, as I say, if I can't get across that line, I even certainly appreciate this much, because it——

"O. I think it's a thing you ought to know.

"P. Oh, no doubt.

"O. I think it's probably one of those sporadic things and I do not think—I have no way of thinking it was systematic but I got from the way in which it was handled, which was rather loosely, and frankly if I were an agent I would not put much confidence in people who are loose-mouthed or casual. I would not think that this was a very highly organized or very well put-together plan but I don't know and I was very much afraid when I heard of Lomanitz' indiscretion that it might very well be serious. I hope that isn't the case.

"P. You mentioned that this man is a member of this FAECT. Do you think that, as a representative of the organization, he would sort of represent their attitude or do you think he is doing this individually?

"O. Oh, the FAECT is quite a big union and has got all sorts of people in it. I'm pretty sure and I don't think it is conceivable that he could be representing the attitude of the union, but it is——

"P. Well, I don't know enough about it to——

"O. I think that at one time—well, I don't know—they had a strong branch up at the Shell Development Research Laboratories, the FAECT—and I believe it is the union which has got organized on the hill.

"J. Yes, it has been around for some time.

"P. This man Eltenton * * * is a scientist.

"O. I don't know, I would guess he was a sort of a chemical engineer.

"P. Would he be in a position to understand the information furnished him?

"O. I don't know that either. It would depend on how well it was furnished. I mean, he has some scientific training and certainly if you sat down with him and took a little time. My view about this whole damn thing, of course, is that the information that we are working on is probably known to all the governments that care to find out. The information about what we are doing is probably of no use because it is so damn complicated. I don't agree that the security problem on this project is a bitter one, because if one means by the security problem preventing information of technical use to another country from escaping. But I do think that the intensity of our effort and our concern with national investment involved—that is information which might alter the course of the other governments and don't think it would have any effect on Russia * * * it might have a very big effect on Germany, and I am convinced about that and that is as everyone else is.

"P. Oh.

"O. To give it roughly what we're after and I think they don't need to know the technical details because if they were going to do it they would do it in a different way. They wouldn't take our methods—they couldn't because of certain geographical differences so I think the kind of thing that would do the greatest damage if it got out, would just be the magnitude of the problem and of the time schedules which we think we have and that kind of thing. To answer your question—Eltenton if you were picking a man which would be an intermediary he wouldn't be a bad choice, I would mention he had some kind of chemical engineering job in Russia. He was trained in England, was in Russia 4 or 5 years and things like that and here——

"P. Does he speak Russian, do you know?

"O. I don't know—I don't know. He speaks with a slight English accent.

"P. If it is necessary would you mind and would it interfere with your work much if I would have to come down and discuss this with you further. Counter assurance—I mean this is—ah——

"O. This is important?

"P. Oh yes, I not only——

"O. If I may express my own opinion as well as my conviction this is not common knowledge.

"P. No, it isn't.

"J. You see a lot of people have reported it to us * * *

"P. That's why Mr. Johnson called me up yesterday it sort of——

"O. Yes. I mentioned this to Colonel Lansdale.

"P. You did.

"O. Yes.

P. Aha, well of course right now I say—ah—it is all new and—it has come to me——

"O. Right now it means absolutely nothing but what you now find out at this——

"P. If—but——

"O. I would like to say that if I think that * * * certain affiliations that were incompatible to the best interests of this country and this business would die * * *.

"P. It may be necessary for us to—to take certain steps in trying to trace this down and so forth—if anything would develop where we would have to or would be interested in either your place down at Los Alamos or other places, you feel it would be all right for me to contact you on it so that——

"O. Oh, certainly * * * certain precautions——

"P. Oh, yeah, yes—what I mean is instead of going out on certain steps which may——

"O. Yeah——

"P. Come to your attention and be a little bit disturbing to you, I would rather discuss those with you first so that you will be aware of it. I think that, that—well that——

"O. Well, I hope that won't * * *. If I had reason to believe * * *. I will if anything ever comes up that I am convinced—I can always say that everything I know is absolutely 100 percent negative.

"P. If we should find any information which would lead us to believe that there still may be some of that going on, and if it would be important for us to then know a little more in detail who the contacts were and everything and we could show you and that is important to us, I hope you will then find it possible to——

"O. I am only trying to define our future and I will try to act reasonably.

"P. Fine.

"O. As I say I am trying to draw the line here between people who took some responsibility and the people who were purely pushed around and since nothing occurred and the responses seem to have been 100 percent negative, I think I am perhaps justified in—in——

"P. I am not persistent (ha ha) but——

"O. You are persistent and it is your duty.

"P. That is, there is one point in there, that you say that the responses were 100 percent negative. Do you feel that you know everyone whom this intermediary contacted?

"O. Well, no, but I think it is practical to say that it is not inconceivable that the people whom he contacted would be—would have come to my attention but I am not sure.

"P. Well, I would like to say——

"O. Well, I think it would be [one word missing] to say that I just don't know.

"P. I would like to leave this thought with you, Dr. Oppenheimer, if you at some time find it possible, we certainly would give a lot of thanks and appreciation for the name of that intermediary because it's going to—I tell you—the only reason why I would want it, is not for his sake but to see who his contacts are——

"O. Yes, I see——

"P. I can see that we are going to have to spend a lot of time and effort which we ordinarily would not in trying to——

"O. Well——

"P. In trying to run him down before we even can get on to these others——

"O. You'd better check up on the consulate because that's the only one that Eltenton contacted and without that contact there wouldn' be anyhing * * *.

"P. You say his man is not employed in the consulate?

"O. Eltenton?

"P. No, no, I mean this man——

"O. I have never been introduced to him * * * or heard his name or anything but I have been given to understand that he is attached to the consulate.

*   *   *   *   *   *

"O. Maybe this guy is a military attaché—I don't know.

"P. You don't know anything about him?

"O. I don't know anything about him and never have. I may have been told the name, but it made no impression.

"P. Is this member of the faculty in any way—does he in any way come in contact with your project? Why would he be contacted? Is it because he has contacted these people?

"O. I think that Eltenton must have said to him * * * I don't know—that would be my impression of the thing * * *.

"P. Well I think that——

"O. Well, I am sorry. I realize that you would like more information but I have been under a little bit of difficulty. The fact that I did not raise this [one word omitted] for a long time——

"P. That's right.

"O. I have difficulty in * * * serious * * * what to do * * * I think my general point of view is that there are some things there which would bear watching.

"P. That's right.

"O. It is doubtful to me if there is anything there which can't be uncovered.

"P. Well, that—I can see where * * *. We will be hot under the collar until we find out what is going on there. I mean—that's the point of view we have to take——

"O. Well, I don't know. * * * Well I would think * * * that it's conceivable— that it wouldn't hurt to have a man in the local of this union FAECT—to see what may happen and what he can pick up.

"P. You feel there could be something—not in the organization itself but some——

"O. Within it.

"P. Within it.

"O. I don't know, I am sure that if they had 20 members, 19 of them might not be involved in it. But I am not sure of the 20th, you see.

"P. Yes.

"O. Forty members correspondingly and—let me put it this way—the bonds that hold them together are very strong you see, and they talk over their problems with their sisters and brothers and it is rather difficult to maintain a complete security in an outfit like that.

"P. Does this union that is up on the hill, do they have members which are not connected with the hill at all?

"O. Oh, yes; they have an international union and has reprepresentatives all over this country.

"P. And the same group then, the same mixture would be of people off and on the project would be in the same——

"O. Oh, I imagine so—I don't know; I don't know about that.

"P. Well, we can——

"O. Ordinarily I think that they would have their own local.

"P. Which would be up there.

"O. Maybe not. Maybe it is all one big local. I'm not sure, but that varies with the union.

"P. Well, that is certainly interesting a—you are going to be here for some time?

"O. Oh, no; I am leaving tonight.

"P. Oh, you are; are you flying?

"O. No; I am not. I have orders not to fly.

"P. At least you get some relaxation in between your project. Well, I think that it may——

"O. I will be very glad to see you there. I have a feeling though, a fellow can be fooled you see. I feel responsible for every detail of this sort of thing down at our place and I will be willing to go quite far in saying that everything is 100 percent in order. That doesn't go for this place up here.

"P. No.

"O. I think that's the truth. If everything weren't being done and if everything weren't proper, I think that I would be perfectly willing to be shot if I had done anything wrong.

"P. Well, ah——

"O. I don't say that about this place. It's a very different situation, a very much harder situation. I don't know the people but it's a hard situation; in particular was put together in a casual way and I think that the problem of being sure that there were no leaks * * * and that pressure can be brought with discretion.

"P. I am then, as I say, I may have the pleasure of visiting your place because it may——

"O. My motto is God bless you.

"P. Well, as I say, if this becomes serious, that is to say, I don't know anything about it, but if it becomes——

"O. My guess is that it wouldn't but if I wern't first absolutely sure that it wouldn't—that it were not serious, I wouldn't——

"P. That's right. Well, if it does become serious I may come down with some of my persistency—I mean I would hate to—I have a responsibility of running things down myself.

"O. I also think the particular way this was—that if there is anything going on it would be very easy to find out. I am not worried about that—we can take care of that ourselves.

"P. No; you wouldn't——

"O. Well, I can handle in a way * * *

"P. But it is a situation which would have to be handled very delicately. That's what makes it so difficult. If it is something that's easy to handle and you don't have to worry about it, why you just sort of bull your way through, but these things one has to be very careful.

"O. That's always the case—wanting to be very careful.

"P. I am not the judge to tell whether they should or should not get the information. My business is to stop it going through illegally.

"O. Well, I think——

"I don't actually know whether, if you were in Washington—asking advice on the question how far should cooperation go. I don't know wherein the right answer lies. I have heard of cases with very strong arguments on both sides.

"P. Yes.

"O. * * * we don't have to worry about * * *

"P. Yes; that's right.

"O. Well, I wish good luck——

"P. We could work a hundred years (I mean) and never get this information. That's where we start you see—I mean—we get this information and we have something to start on—we have something to run down. I certainly appreciate this opportunity to visit you.

"O. I hope it's not a waste of time——

"P. Well, I know it's not a waste of my time and ah——

"O. That's all I meant—perhaps as far as the project is concerned * * * a fair starting point——

"P. Could have——

"O. Why not take an about face?

"P. Do you——

"O. And one could do anything about the attaché—that would be the natural thing to watch.

"P. Do you know anyone—and because we like to eliminate unnecessary work if we have to—do you know anyone who is on the project who is connected with the FAECT, Dr. Oppenheimer?

"O. Who would be willing to——

"P. That's right.

"O. I don't know who is in the union at all. I have heard that a boy called Fox is president of it.

"J. David Fox.

"O. David Fox, but I would feel * * * I hope that the trade union isn't tied up in this—and they would not act like this because I think it would give them a very black eye and it is no love of mine from the start, and it might have consequences beyond the reasonable. I doubt whether anyone mixed with the union in good faith would be very sympathetic.

"P. Yes.

"O. This isn't a suggestion that there is anything wrong. I have no reason at all to believe that there is, except that it is inevitable that any left wingers still interested in left-wing activity would join such a union. I think I can be quite sure of it. And I don't think that is due to unions who are seeking a selected group of people——

"P. Yes.

"O. You might get some—of course, this is just my opinion that there is no harm in discussing it—well, I just don't know.

"P. May I just ask then, Doctor, if you would please not discuss this with anyone—so that they would not be aware of this fact that——

"O. No; I would not have raised the question if it had not seemed to me that it deserved looking into.

"P. Yes.

"O. And if I seem uncooperative I think that you can understand that it is because of my insistence in not getting people into trouble——

"P. I can assure you that if something comes to your attention out there——

"O. Let me dispose of that statement which came over the long-distance phone. Frankly, I got—from that boy a promise to stop all this sort of thing when he came on the job. * * * to that promise [garbled]. * * * I do not know what he was doing it for but I thought there was a possibility. He said he understood that * * * I talked to him yesterday. He said he had no connection * * *

"P. Well, what I mean, if anything does come to your attention in connection with this phase, if you can——

"O. It won't be really necessary——

"P. If, in the first place you will let me know, I will be glad to come down and discuss the matter with you——

"O. Well, I am very glad of that, and we may have other problems which we would like to discuss.

"P. Yes.

"O. But I do not think that there will be any of this nature because really we have * * *

"P. Well, something may come to your attention relating to this place up here. You may get it down there and I would really prefer to——

"O. There is almost no contact. I have official technical letters but really no personal letters from here. I don't know what's going on, and I think the chance of my being useful in that way is very slight. But you ought to be able to find people here who could have their eyes and ears open and who know what's going on. That would be, I would be, I would be fairly sure that there are quite a few here who would be willing to give you—who would realize the importance of it and—I can't advise you any further.

"P. No; O. K.; as a matter of fact I am not formulating any plans, I am just going to have to digest the whole thing.

"P. Well, we appreciate it and the best of luck.

"O. Thank you very much."

Now, having read it, decide how you would cross-examine Oppenheimer. It is not a bad cross-examination, but Oppenheimer's candor made it easy.

Q. When did you first mention your conversation with Chevalier to any security officer?

A. I didn't do it that way. I first mentioned Eltenton.

Q. Yes.

A. On a visit to Berkeley almost immediately after Lansdale's visit to Los Alamos.

Q. Was that to Lieutenant Johnson; do you remember?

A. I don't remember, but it was to a security officer there.

Q. At Berkeley?

A. That is right.

Q. If the record shows that it was to Lieutenant Johnson on August 25, 1943, you would accept that?

A. I would accept that.

Q. You mentioned the Eltenton incident in connection with Lomanitz, didn't you?

A. The context was this. I think Johnson told me that the source of the trouble was the unionization of the radiation laboratory by the Federation of Architects, Engineers, Chemists, and Technicians. Possibly I had heard that from Lansdale. The connection that I made was between Eltenton and this organization.

Q. In your answer at page 22 you say, referring to the Eltenton episode: "It has long been clear to me that I should have reported the incident at once."

A. It is.

Q. "The events that lead me to report it, which I doubt ever would have become known without my report, were unconnected with it."

You have told us that your discussion with Colonel Lansdale encompassed the subject of espionage. Of course, you have told us also that the Eltenton matter involved espionage; is that correct?

A. Let us be careful. The word "espionage" was not mentioned.

Q. No?

A. The word "indiscretion" was mentioned. That is all that Lansdale said. Indiscretion was talking to unauthorized people who in turn would talk to other people. This is all I was told. I got worried when I learned that this union was connected with their troubles.

Q. But, Doctor, you told us this morning, did you not, that you knew that Lansdale was worried about espionage at Berkeley; is that correct?

A. I knew he was worried about the leakage of information.

Q. Isn't that a polite name for espionage?

A. Not necessarily.

Q. I will ask you now, didn't you know that Lansdale was concerned about the possibility of espionage at Berkeley?

A. About the possibility; yes.

Q. Yes.

A. That is right.

Q. So, Doctor, it is not quite correct to say that the Eltenton incident was not connected with your talk with Lansdale, is it?

A. I didn't mean it in that sense. I meant that it had nothing to do with Chevalier or Eltenton with respect to the events that aroused this.

Q. But your talk with Lansdale did have to do with the subject which included Chevalier and Eltenton, didn't it?

A. I have described it as well as I can. Chevalier's name was not mentioned; Eltenton's name was not mentioned; and espionage was not mentioned.

Q. I didn't say that. But it had to do with the subject which involved Chevalier or at least Eltenton?

A. Sure; that is why I brought it up.

Q. What did you tell Lieutenant Johnson about this when you first mentioned Eltenton to him?

A. I had two interviews, and therefore I am not clear as to which was which.

Q. May I help you?

A. Please:

Q. I think your first interview with Johnson was quite brief, was it not?

A. That is right. I think I said little more than that Eltenton was somebody to worry about.

Q. Yes.

A. Then I was asked why did I say this. Then I invented a cock-and-bull story.

Q. Then you were interviewed the next day by Colonel Pash, were you not?

A. That is right.

Q. Who was he?

A. He was another security officer.

Q. That was quite a lengthy interview, was it not?

A. I didn't think it was that long.

Q. For your information, that was August 26, 1943.

A. Right.

Q. Then there came a time when you were interviewed by Colonel Lansdale.

A. I remember that very well.

Q. That was in Washington, wasn't it?

A. That is right.

Q. That was September 12, 1943.

A. Right.

Q. Would you accept that?

A. Surely.

Q. Then you were interviewed again by the FBI in 1946; is that right?

A. In between I think came Groves.

Q. Pardon?

A. In between came Groves.

Q. Yes. But you were interviewed in 1946; is that right?

A. That is right.

Q. Now let us go back to your interview with Colonel Pash. Did you tell Pash the truth about this thing?

A. No.

Q. You lied to him?

A. Yes.

Q. What did you tell Pash that was not true?

A. That Eltenton had attempted to approach members of the project—three members of the project—through intermediaries.

Q. What else did you tell him that wasn't true?

A. That is all I really remember.

Q. That is all? Did you tell Pash that Eltenton had attempted to approach three members of the project——

A. Through intermediaries.

Q. Intermediaries?

A. Through an intermediary.

Q. So that we may be clear, did you discuss with or disclose to Pash the identity of Chevalier?

A. No.

Q. Let us refer, then, for the time being, to Chevalier as X.

A. All right.

Q. Did you tell Pash that X had approached three persons on the project?

A. I am not clear whether I said there were 3 X's or that X approached 3 people.

Q. Didn't you say that X had approached 3 people?

A. Probably.

Q. Why did you do that, Doctor?

A. Because I was an idiot.

Q. Is that your only explanation, Doctor?

A. I was reluctant to mention Chevalier.

Q. Yes.

A. No doubt somewhat reluctant to mention myself.

Q. Yes. But why would you tell him that Chevalier had gone to 3 people?

A. I have no explanation for that except the one already offered.

Q. Didn't that make it all the worse for Chevalier?

A. I didn't mention Chevalier.

Q. No; but X.

A. It would have.

Q. Certainly. In other words, if X had gone to 3 people that would have shown, would it not——

A. That he was deeply involved.

Q. That he was deeply involved. That it was not just a casual conversation.

A. Right.

Q. And you knew that, didn't you?

A. Yes.

Q. Did you tell Colonel Pash that X had spoken to you about the use of microfilm?

A. It seems unlikely. You have a record, and I will abide by it.

Q. Did you?

A. I don't remember.

Q. If X had spoken to you about the use of microfilm, that would have shown definitely that he was not an innocent contact?

A. It certainly would.

Q. Did you tell Colonel Pash that X had told you that the information would be transmitted through someone at the Russian consulate?

(There was no response.)

Q. Did you?

A. I would have said not, but I clearly see that I must have.

Q. If X had said that, that would have shown conclusively that it was a criminal conspiracy, would it not?

A. That is right.

Q. Did Pash ask you for the name of X?

A. I imagine he did.

Q. Don't you know he did?

A. Sure.

Q. Did he tell you why he wanted it?

A. In order to stop the business.

Q. He told you that it was a very serious matter, didn't he?

A. I don't recollect that, but he certainly would have.

Q. You knew that he wanted to investigate it, did you not?

A. That is right.

Q. And didn't you know that your refusal to give the name of X was impeding the investigation?

A. In actual fact I think the only person that needed watching or should have been watched was Eltenton. But as I concocted the story that did not emerge.

Q. That was your judgment?

A. Yes.

Q. But you knew that Pash wanted to investigate this?

A. Yes.

Q. And didn't you know, Doctor, that by refusing to give the name of X you were impeding the investigation?

A. I must have known that.

Q. You know now, don't you?

A. Well, actually——

Q. You must have known it then?

A. Actually the only important thing to investigate was Eltenton.

Q. What did Pash want to investigate?

A. I suppose the 3 people on the project.

Q. You knew, didn't you. Doctor. that Colonel Pash and his organization would move heaven and earth to find out those 3 people, didn't you?

A. It makes sense.

Q. And you knew that they would move heaven and earth to find out the identity of X, didn't you?

A. Yes.

Q. And yet you wouldn't tell them?

A. That is true.

Q. So you knew you were impeding them, didn't you?

A. That is right.

Then, a little later, Robb took it up again:

Q. Doctor, I would like to go back with you, if I may, to your interview with Colonel Pash on August 26, 1943. I will read to you certain extracts from the transcript of that interview.

Colonel Pash said to you:

"Mr. Johnson told me about the little incident or conversation taking place yesterday in which I am very much interested, and had me worried all day yesterday since he called me.

"OPPENHEIMER. I was rather uncertain as to whether I should or should not talk to him, Rossi, when I was here. I was unwilling to do it without authorization. What I wanted to tell this fellow was that he had been indiscreet. I know that is right that he had revealed information. I know that saying that much might in some cases embarrass him. It doesn't seem to have been capable of embarrassing him, to put it bluntly."

Do you recall saying that?

A. Let me say I recognize it.

Q. In substance did you say that?

A. I am sure I did.

Q. So there was no question, Doctor, that this matter of the Eltenton incident came up in connection with your conversation about Lomanitz.

A. That is right.

Q. There is no question, is there, either, that at that time, August 26, 1943, you knew that Lomanitz had revealed certain confidential information?

A. I was told by Lansdale, that he had been indiscreet about information. It was not made clear to me——

Q. This says, "I know that is right that he had revealed information." So wouldn't you agree that you knew he had revealed information?

A. Yes.

Q. Very well. Pash said:

"Well, that is not the particular interest I have. It is something a little more in my opinion that is more serious. Mr. Johnson said that there was a possibility that there may be some other groups interested.

"OPPENHEIMER. I think that is true, but I have no first hand knowledge that it would be for that reason useful. But I think it is true that a man whose name I never heard, who was attached to the Soviet consul, has indicated indirectly through intermediate people concerned with this project that he was in a position to transmit without any danger of a leak or scandal or anything of that kind information which they might supply."

Do you recall saying that in substance?

A. I certainly don't recall it.

Q. Would you deny you said it?

A. No.

Q. Is there any doubt now that you did mention to Pash, a man attached to the Soviet consul?

A. I had completely forgotten it.   I can only rely on the transcript.

Q. Doctor, for your information, I might say we have a record of your voice.

A. Sure.

Q. Do you have any doubt you said that?

A. No.

Q. Was that true.   Had there been a mention of a man connected with the Soviet consul?

A. I am fairly certain not.

Q. You were very certain before lunch that there had not; weren't you?

A. Yes.

Q. You continue in that same answer: "Since I know it to be a fact, I have been particularly concerned about any indiscretions which took place in circles close enough to be in contact with him.   To put it quite frankly, I would feel friendly to the idea of the Commander in Chief of informing the Russians who are working on this problem.   At least I can see there might be some arguments for doing that but I don't like the idea of having it moved out the back door.   I think it might not hurt to be on the lookout for it."

Do you recall saying something like that?

A. I am afraid I am not recalling very well, but this is very much the way I would have talked.

Q. Did you feel friendly to the idea of the Commander in Chief informing the Russians who were working on the problem?

A. I felt very friendly to the attempt to get real cooperation with the Russians, a two-way cooperation, on an official governmental level.   I knew of some of the obstacles to it.

Q. Is this an accurate statement of your sentiments as of August 26, 1943: "I would feel friendly to the idea of the Commander in Chief informing the Russians who are working on this problem"?

A. The Russians who are working on this problem?

Q. Yes, sir.

A. I think that is not an accurate sentence.

Q. That is not the way you felt then?

A. No.   I think I can say that I felt that I hoped that during the war good collaboration all along the line could be established with the Russians through governmental channels but I had no idea that there were any Russians working on the problem.

Q. On the problem, not the project.   On the problem.

A. What problem?

Q. "I would feel quite friendly to the idea of the Commander in Chief informing the Russians who are working on this problem."

If you said that to Colonel Pash; did that express your sentiments?

A. What does it mean?

Q. I am asking you.

A. I don't know.

Q. That language is not intelligible to you?

A. On this problem?   No.

Q. The problem of the atom bomb.   Did you in 1943 feel friendly to the idea of the Commander in Chief of informing the Russians who were working on the problem of the atomic bomb?

A. I don't think there were any Russians working on the problem of the atomic bomb.

Q. Did you feel friendly in 1943 to the idea of the Commander in Chief giving the Russians any information about the work that was being done on the atomic bomb under your supervision?

A. If it had been a completely reciprocal and open affair with their military technology and ours, I would have seen arguments for it; yes, sir.

Q. In other words, you did feel friendly.

A. With these qualifications.

Q. You said here, "At least I can see there might be some arguments for doing that, but I don't like the idea of having it moved out the back door."

A. Right.

Q. Pash then said: "Could you give me a little more specific information as to exactly what information you have? You can readily realize that phase would be to me as interesting pretty near as the whole project is to.

"OPPENHEIMER. Well, I might say the approaches were always made through other people who were troubled by them and sometimes came and discussed them with me and that the approaches were quite indirect. So I feel that to give more perhaps than one name would be to implicate people whose attitudes were one of bewilderment rather than one of cooperation."

Do you recall saying something like that?

A. I don't recall that conversation very well.

Q. But you did, you are sure, tell Colonel Pash there was more than one person involved.

A. Right.

Q. Continuing: "I know of no case, and I am fairly sure in all cases where I have heard of these contacts would not have yielded a single thing. That is as far as I can go on that. There is a man whose name was mentioned to me a couple of times. I don't know of my own knowledge that he was involved as an intermediary. It seems, however, not impossible. If you wanted to watch him it might be the appropriate thing to do. He spent a number of years in the Soviet Union. I think he is a chemical engineer. He was, he may not be here, at the time I was with him here employed by the Shell Development. His name is Eltenton. I would think that there was a small chance—well, let me put it this way. He has probably been asked to do what he can to provide information. Whether he is successful or not, I do not know. But he talked to a friend of his who is also an acquaintance of one of the men on the project and that was one of the channels by which this thing went. Now, I think that to go beyond that would be to put a lot of names down of people who are not only innocent but whose attitude was 100 percent cooperative."

Do you recall saying that to Colonel Pash?

A. This sounds right.

Q. How much of that was not true? Approaching more than one person?

A. More than one person was not true.

Q. He talked to a friend of his, who is also an acquaintance of one of the men on the project. Who was the friend of his that you had in mind?

A. I can only guess, but that would be Chevalier and I would be the man on the project.

Q. Pash said to you: "However, anything we may get which would eliminate a lot of research work on our part would necessarily bring to a closer conclusion anything that we are doing."

In other words, he told you, didn't he, that they were going to have to do a lot of work to investigate this?

You answered, "Well, I am giving you the one name that is or isn't—I mean I don't know the name of the man attached to the consulate. I think I may have been told and I may not have been told. I have at least not purposely, but actually, forgotten. He is and he may not be here now—these incidents occurred in the order of about 5, 6, or 7 months ago."

You did tell Colonel Pash that there was a man from the consulate involved, didn't you?

A. I did.

Q. Was that true?

A. That there was a man in the consulate involved?

Q. Yes.

A. That I read since the end of the war?

Q. No. Did you know then that there was?

A. I am fairly sure not.

Q. Chevalier had not said anything to you about a man from the consulate. had he?

A. I have told you my sharp recollection of it.

Q. Further along you said, "I would feel that the people that they tried to get information from were more or less an accident, and I would be making some harm by saying that."

So you were talking about more than one person always, weren't you?

A. Yes; at that time.

Q. When you said "Well, I will tell you one thing. I have known of 2 or 3 cases, and I think 2 of the men are with me at Los Alamos. They are men who are closely associated with me.

"PASH. Have they told you that either they thought they were contacted for that purpose or they were actually contacted for that purpose?

"OPENHEIMER. They told me they were contacted for that purpose.

"PASH. For that purpose?"

Do you recall saying that to Pash in substance?

A. Yes.

Q. So you told him specifically and circumstantially that there were several people that were contacted.

A. Right.

Q. And your testimony now is that was a lie?

A. Right.

Q. Then you continue: "That is, let me give you the background. The background was, well, you know how difficult it is with relations between these two allies and there are a lot of people that don't feel very friendly towards Russia. So the information, a lot of our secret information, our radar and so on, doesn't get to them, and they are battling for their lives, and they would like to have an idea of what is going on, and this is just to make up in other words for the defects of our official communication. That is the form in which it was presented."

Did you tell Colonel Pash that?

A. I evidently did. This is news to me.

Q. Had the matter been presented to you in that form?

A. No.

Q. Had anyone told you that it had been presented in that form?

A. No.

Q. In other words, this also was a lie?

A. Yes, sir.

Q. Then you continue: "Of course, the actual fact is that since it is not a communication that ought to be taking place, it is treasonable."

Did you say that?

A. Sure. I mean I am not remembering this conversation, but I am accepting it.

Q. You did think it was treasonable anyway, didn't you?

A. Sure.

Q. "But it was not presented in that method. It is a method of carrying out a policy which was more or less a policy of the Government. The form in which it came was that couldn't an interview be arranged with this man Eltenton who had very good contact with a man from the Embassy attached to the consulate who is a very reliable guy and who had a lot of experience in microfilm or whatever,"

Did you tell Colonel Pash that microfilm had been mentioned to you?

A. Evidently.

Q. Was that true?

A. No.

Q. Then Pash said to you: "Well, now, I may be getting back to a little systematic picture. These people whom you mention, two are down with you now. Were they contacted by Eltenton direct?"

You answered, "No."

"PASH. Through another party?"

"OPENHEIMER. Yes."

In other words, you told Pash that X had made these other contacts, didn't you?

A. It seems so.

Q. That wasn't true?

A. That is right. This whole thing was a pure fabrication except for the one name Eltenton.

Q. Pash said to you, "This would not involve the people, but it would indicate to us Eltenton's channel. We would have to know that this is definite on Eltenton."

In other words, Pash wanted to find out the channel, didn't he?

A. Yes.

Q. Pash said again, "The fact is this second contact, the contact that Eltenton had to make with these other people, is that person also a member of the project?"

You said "No." That was correct, wasn't it?

A. Yes.

Q. Again you said to Pash, "As I say, if the guy that was here may by now be in some other town, and then all I would have in mind is this. I understand this man to whom I feel a sense of responsibility, Lomanitz, and I feel it for two reasons. One, he is doing work which he started and which he ought to continue, and second, since I more or less made a stir about it when the question of his induction came up. This man may have been indiscreet in circles which would lead to trouble."

Did you say that to Pash?

A. Yes.

Q. Did you feel some responsibility for Rossi Lomanitz?

A. Evidently.

Q. Why?

A. Well, partly because I had protested his induction. Partly because he was a student of mine. Partly because I tried to persuade him to go into secret work.

Q. And you continue. "That is the only thing I have to say because I don't have any doubt that people often approached him with whom he has contact— I mean whom he sees—might feel it their duty if they got word of something to let it go further and that is the reason I feel quite strongly that association with the Communist movement is not compatible with a job on a secret war project. It is just that the two loyalties cannot go."

Doctor, who were the people that you thought Lomanitz had contact with or whom he saw who might feel it their duty to let the word go further?

A. I had no idea.

Q. You had none then?

A. I don't believe so. I certainly have none now.

Q. You did say that you thought association with the Communist movement was incompatible with work on a secret war project.

A. Right.

Q. Pash said to you again, "Were these two people you mentioned contacted at the same time?"

You answered, "No, they were contacted within a week of each other.

"PASH. They were contacted at two different times?

"OPPENHEIMER. Yes, but not in each other's presence."

Was that part of what you call a cock and bull story, too?

A. It certainly was.

Q. Pash said, "And then from what you first hear, there was somebody else who probably still remains here who was contacted as well?

"OPPENHEIMER. I think that is true."

Do you recall saying something like that?

A. No, but it fits.

Q. "PASH. What I am driving at is that there was a plan at least for some length of time to make these contacts and you may not have known all the contacts?

"OPPENHEIMER. That is certainly true. That is why I mentioned it. If I knew all about it, then I would say forget it. I thought it would be appropriate to call to your attention the fact that these channels at one time existed."

Doctor, is it now your testimony that there was no plan that you knew of?

A. This whole thing, except for the single reference to Eltenton I believe to be pure fabrication.

Q. In other words, your testimony now is that there was no plan that you knew about?

A. Right. I am certain of that.

Mr. GRAY. Excepting the Chevalier incident.

The WITNESS. Yes, yes. The only thing I mentioned here that has any truth to it is Eltenton.

* * *

Q. Doctor, one further item from the Pash interview. You said to Colonel Pash, according to this transcript, or Colonel Pash said to you, "I can see that we are going to have to spend a lot of time and effort which we ordinarily would not in trying to——

"OPPENHEIMER: Well——

"PASH. In trying to run him down before we even go on this.

"OPENHEIMER. You better check up on the consulate because that is the only one that Eltenton contacted and without that contact, he would be inefficient and that would be my——

"PASH. You say this man is not employed in the consulate?

"OPPENHEIMER. Eltenton?

"PASH. No, this man.

"OPPENHEIMER. I have never been introduced to him.

"PASH. Have you ever heard his name mentioned?

"OPPENHEIMER. I have never heard his name mentioned but I have been given to understand that he is attached to the consulate. But isn't it common practice for a consulate or legation to have someone attached to them?

"PASH. Yes. Military attachés are really run efficiently."

Dr. Oppenheimer, assuming that, don't you think you told a story in great detail that was fabricated?

A. I certainly did.

Q. Why did you go into such great circumstantial detail about this thing if you were telling a cock and bull story?

A. I fear that this whole thing is a piece of idiocy. I am afraid I can't explain why there was a consul, why there was microfilm, why there were three people on the project, why two of them were at Los Alamos. All of them seems wholly false to me.

Q. You will agree, would you not, sir, that if the story you told to Colonel Pash was true, it made things look very bad for Mr. Chevalier?

A. For anyone involved in it, yes, sir.

Q. Including you?

A. Right.

Q. Isn't it a fair statement today, Dr. Oppenheimer, that according to your testimony now you told not one lie to Colonel Pash, but a whole fabrication and tissue of lies?

A. Right.

Q. In great circumstantial detail, is that correct?

A. Right.

I think Oppenheimer made it not only easy; I think he made it too easy for Robb. When Robb asked him, "Why did you do that, Doctor?"—almost always an imprudent question for a cross-examiner —Robb could scarcely have expected the success he got. Oppenheimer said, "Because I was an idiot." Of course Robb followed that up, and he got again, "I fear that this whole thing is a piece of idiocy."

How this struck the Board we do not know, but the reader wishes Oppenheimer had been willing to explain. Speaking as a lawyer, I may say that a good witness had better want to be believed. I was not present at either hearing, but I do say that Saint Joan was a better witness than Oppenheimer.

Oppenheimer did better later. Toward the end of the hearings, as you will see, when Gray asked him to "go back to the so-called Chevalier incident," Oppenheimer tried to explain.

Pash had already been suspicious of Oppenheimer. A month or more before this interview, on June 29, 1943, Pash had sent a report on Oppenheimer to Lieutenant Colonel Lansdale in Washington. Pash testified:

Q. Going back for a moment to your interview with Dr. Oppenheimer, you mentioned that he had spoken to you or told you that this unnamed professor had mentioned someone in the Russian consulate, microfilm, the three contacts, two of them having gone to Los Alamos and one being about to leave for Oak Ridge; did you have any opinion as to whether or not Dr. Oppenheimer in those respects was truthfully reporting to you what the unnamed professor had said to him?

A. Yes, I was sure of that.

Q. You were sure of that?

A. Yes.

Q. Why?

A. In the first place, Dr. Oppenheimer spoke to Lyall Johnson, telling him that he had something, as Johnson told me, something important to convey concerning espionage. When I arranged for the interview and Dr. Oppenheimer came in, when I told him that I wanted to discuss the incident, he immediately started discussing Lomanitz with me. When I told him it was the other incident where other parties may be interested in this, he immediately started then relating the information he gave me. I don't think there was any break or adjustment at the time. I felt he was giving something he already had or he knew. Furthermore, as I believe I stated before, and reviewing the situation after a while, I felt that he had this information and he felt that he wanted to give it to us because of the fact that he found out we may be making a rather thorough investigation of the whole project and the activities. Finally, the information given there was rather serious and to a certain extent detailed. It referred to a plan. It included a plan that was supposed to be in existence. It included some details such as the contract, about the availability of contact with the Soviet consulate and the reference to a technical device for purposes of recording what information may be available.

Q. What conclusion did you draw from the fact that the information was in some circumstantial detail? What did that indicate to you?

A. That indicated that it was information already available to a man, and in a field which probably was more operational, and therefore I felt, and feel, that it was transmitted to him rather than made up by him.

Q. Do you still feel that way?

A. Yes, I do.

Q. You had a great deal of experience, have you not, in interrogating witnesses?

A. I have had some experience, yes.

Q. You have been doing it for years, haven't you?

A. For a few years.

Q. You have had a great deal of experience in evaluating statements made by witnesses, have you not, sir?

A. Yes, I have.

Q. Was there then and is there anything now to suggest to you that his statements to you about these details Dr. Oppenheimer was not giving you an accurate report of what he had been told by the unnamed professor?

A. No. I had no reason not to believe they were truthful.

Q. Do you have any now?

A. No, I only know this from newspaper information.

Q. Yes.

A. And whether it is correct, I don't know. But I read in Dr. Oppenheimer's reply to General Nichols he relates this incident. I feel that the information which Dr. Oppenheimer gave me in 1943 was far more damaging to him and to any of his friends than the information as related in the newspaper. If Dr. Oppenheimer was not telling the truth at that time, he was making up a story which would be more damaging to him than it appears the situation was according to the newspaper item. I don't think that that is a normal human reaction. I feel that the story as told then—the story as related in the newspaper probably is in favor of Dr. Oppenheimer. In evaluating that, I felt that the inconsistentcy there in my mind would favor the truth in the preliminary interview, the interview of 1943.

Q. Would you care to elaborate upon your statement that you now consider Dr. Oppenheimer a security risk?

A. As far as I know, Dr. Oppenheimer was affiliated with Communist front activities. I have reason to feel that he was a member of the Communist Party. I have seen no indication which indicates any change from that. I feel that his supposed dropping of the Communist party activities in the early part of the war need not necessarily express his sincere opinions, since that was done by most all members of the Communist party. As a result of that, I feel that the opinion I had back in 1943 probably would stand.

Pash sent the transcript of his interview with Oppenheimer to Lansdale and left a copy for General Groves, who was expected in San Francisco a few days later. Then on September 6, 1943, he sent a memo to Lansdale:

"HEADQUARTERS WESTERN DEFENSE COMMAND AND FOURTH ARMY,
"OFFICE OF THE ASSISTANT CHIEF OF STAFF G–2,
"*Presidio of San Francisco, Calif.*

"In reply refer to: (CIB) September 6, 1943, Subject: J. R. Oppenheimer.

"To: Lt. Col. John Lansdale, Jr., room 2C 654 Pentagon Building, Washington, D. C.

"1. Enclosed is a report on the evaluation of J. R. Oppenheimer, prepared in this office by Capt. Peter deSilva, now engaged in evaluation of the DSM project.

"2. This Office is still of the opinion that Oppenheimer is not to be fully trusted and that his loyalty to a Nation is divided. It is believed that the only undivided loyalty that he can give is to science and it is strongly felt that if in his position the Soviet Government could offer more for the advancement of his scientific cause he would select that Government as the one to which he would express his loyalty.

"3. This Office does not intend to evaluate the importance or worth of Dr. Oppenheimer as a scientist on the project. It is the responsibility of this Office to evaluate him from any possible subversive angle. Because of this the enclosed report is being submitted for your information.

"(Signed)   "Boris T. Pash.
"BORIS T. PASH,
"*Lt. Col. M. I., Chief, Counter Intelligence Branch.*
"For the A C of S. G–2."

The report referred to was prepared by a Captain De Silva. The first two paragraphs are all we need.

"HEADQUARTERS WESTERN DEFENSE COMMAND AND FOURTH ARMY,
"OFFICE OF THE ASSISTANT CHIEF OF STAFF G–2,
"*Presidio of San Francisco, Calif.*

"In reply refer to: (CIB) September 2, 1943, Memorandum for: Lt. Col. B. T. Pash,

"Subject: J. R. Oppenheimer.

"1. With regard to recent developments in the espionage case centering about the DSM project, the part played by J. R. Oppenheimer is believed to take on a more vital significance than has heretofore been apparent. Briefly, it may be said that subject has just recently brought himself to the fore by volunteering scraps of information which are of vital interest to the investigation being conducted by this Office. In conversation with Lt. L. E. Johnson, he had said that he had good reason to suspect that the Soviet Union was attempting to secure information about the project. In a subsequent conversation with Lt. Col. Pash, subject elaborated on the matter and disclosed that about 4 months ago a Shell Development employee, one Eltenton, on behalf of a Soviet consular attaché, had contacted a U. C. professor who in turn had attempted, on at least three occasions, to secure sources of information within the project who would transmit the information to Eltenton, who in turn would supply it to the Soviet consular agent, all to be done informally in order to circumvent a State Department policy of not cooperating with the Soviet Union, which policy is influenced by certain unnamed State Department officials who were supposed to be anti-Soviet and who would not allow such action to be taken openly. Oppenheimer claims he does not condone such methods, and is satisfied that no information was passed by those channels. He did not disclose the name of the professor, as he thought that such an action would be unethical and would merely disturb some of his associates who were in no way guilty of any wrongdoing. Roughly, the above has been the extent of Oppenheimer's most recent activity.

"2. The writer wishes to go on record as saying that J. R. Oppenheimer is playing a key part in the attempts of the Soviet Union to secure, by espionage, highly secret information which is vital to the security of the United States. An attempt will be made to show the reasons for the above statement. It has been known, since March 29, 1943, that an overt act of espionage was committed by the Soviet Union. Subject's statements indicate that another attempt has been made, through Eltenton, Oppenheimer, himself having a rather lengthy record of Communist sympathy and activity, has actively engaged in the development of a secret project. Most of his friends and professional associates are Communists or Communist sympathizers. He himself has gone on record as saying on two occasions, to Lieutenant Colonel Lansdale and to Lieutenant Colonel Pash, that Communist activity on the part of a project employee is not compatible with the security necessary to the project. To quote him, "and that is the reason I feel quite strongly that association with the Communist movement is not compatible with the job on a secret war project, it is just that two loyalties cannot go." To Lieutenant Colonel Lansdale, he said that he knew that two Los Alamos employees had at one time been Communists, but that he was satisfied that they no longer were. Yet during the long period during which he has been in charge of the project, and in spite of the fact that he is perfectly competent to recognize the Communist attitude and philosophy, and further in spite of the fact that he, by choice as well as by professional necessity, is close to his key associates, and again in spite of the fact that he claims, in effect, not to feel confident of the loyalty of a Communist—in spite of all this, Oppenheimer has allowed a tight clique of known Communists or Communist sympathizers to grow up about him within the project, until they comprise a large proportion of the key personnel in whose hands the success and security of the project is entrusted. In the opinion of this officer, Oppenheimer either must be incredibly naive and almost childlike in his sense of reality, or he himself is extremely clever and disloyal. The former possibility is not borne out in the opinion of the officers who have spoken with him at length.

Pash met Oppenheimer only that once, when he interviewed him on August 26, 1943. De Silva was later transferred to Los Alamos and got to know Oppenheimer. In April 1945 he was again transferred, and when he left he wrote Oppenheimer:

"ARMY SERVICE FORCES,
"UNITED STATES ENGINEER OFFICE,
"P. O. Box 1539, Santa Fe, N. Mex., April 11, 1945.

"Dr. J. R. OPPENHEIMER,
"Project Director.

"DEAR OPPIE: Upon my transfer from duty at the project, I want you to know of my sincere appreciation of the support and encouragement which you have personally given me during my services here. In spite of your many more urgent

problems and duties, your consideration and help on matters I have brought
to you have been gratifying and have, in fact, contributed much to whatever
success my office has had in performing its mission.

"I am sure you know that my interests and thoughts will concern themselves
in large measure with the continued progress and ultimate success of the work
which you are directing. My service at the project and my association with
you and your assistants and fellow workers, are matters which I shall remember
with pride.

"I want to wish you and your staff every possible success in your work, upon
which so much depends.

"Sincerely,

"(S) PEER, PEER DE SILVA,
"*Major, Corps of Engineers.*

"cc—Maj. Gen. L. R. Groves."

Lansdale was at that time attached to counterintelligence in G2
in Washington. He was a graduate of V.M.I. and of the Harvard
Law School. After World War II he went back to the practice of
law in Cleveland. He is now a partner of the law firm Squire,
Sanders, and Dempsey.

Lansdale had already come into the story. Robb showed him a
memorandum he had written dated August 12, 1943, and from it
Lansdale testified about a trip he made to Berkeley early in August,
at the request of Dr. Conant, to study the situation there. He said:

> This appears to be when I went out and made
> a trip to quiet people down about Lomanitz. We were having a great deal of
> trouble with Ernest Lawrence about taking Lomanitz away from him. Then
> Dr. Oppenheimer got in the picture, and I just went out to quiet things down.
> Q. Colonel, I detect a slight tendency on your part to blame Lawrence for
> Lomanitz exclusively. Isn't it a fact that Dr. Oppenheimer was also very much
> exercised about Lomanitz?
> A. I don't recall that he was exercised about Lomanitz—yes, he was exer-
> cised about Lomanitz. We got word through Peer de Silva as I recall that
> Oppenheimer was raising a question about us permitting Lomanitz to be in-
> ducted into the Army. I suspect he didn't know we were moving heaven and
> earth to get him inducted. Our main row with Lawrence, we had more trouble
> with Ernest Lawrence about personnel than any four other people put together.

Lansdale had also discussed Oppenheimer with General Groves.
He had received reports, primarily from the F.B.I., concerning Oppenheimer's associations and relatives.

> These caused us, needless to say, a great deal of
> concern. I may be inexact in my dates, but my recollection is that this took
> place about the time that Los Alamos was being established and my recollection
> is that they had not yet moved up on the Hill, but still had the office or laboratory
> down in Santa Fe while we were constructing a road up there.
> I brought up these, because of Dr. Oppenheimer's prominent position as the
> head of the Los Alamos laboratory, to the attention of General Groves and we
> discussed them at some length.
> General Groves' view was (a)—I wonder if I am permitted to say—I don't
> know what his view was, of course, as I only know what he told me.
> Mr. GRAY. You certainly can say what he told you.

The WITNESS. I would like to correct that. Obviously I don't know what was in the man's mind. All I know is what he told me.

General Groves' view, as I recall expressed, was (a) that Dr. Oppenheimer was essential; (b) that in his judgment—and he had gotten to know Dr. Oppenheimer very well by that time—he was loyal; and (c) we would clear him for this work whatever the reports said.

I will confess that I myself at that time had considerable doubts about it. Because of our worry, or my worry, let us say, about Dr. Oppenheimer, we continued to the best of our ability to investigate him. We kept him under surveillance whenever he left the project. We opened his mail. We did all sorts of nasty things that we do or did on the project.

I interviewed him myself a number of times. As I recall, the recommendations of the security organization headed up by Captain Calvert were adverse to Dr. Oppenheimer. They recommended against clearance.

By Mr. GARRISON:

Q. Who was Captain Calvert?
A. I think his official title was District Security Officer. He was on General Nichols', then Colonel Nichols, staff. In any event, I fully concurred with General Groves as our investigation went on with the fact that Dr. Oppenheimer was properly cleared.

Now, you asked to relate our discussions. That is difficult. Our discussions spread over many, many months. They continued when the name——

Mr. GRAY. Excuse me, please. Did you say I asked to relate the discussions?
The WITNESS. No; Mr. Garrison did.

Mr. GRAY. Excuse me. A moment ago I thought when you asked whether you were privileged to say what General Groves said, I said that was all right.

The WITNESS. No. I think that was your question, wasn't it?

Mr. GARRISON. Yes, it was.

The WITNESS. I remember that I asked General Groves early in the game what would he do if it turned out that Dr. Oppenheimer was not loyal and that we could not trust him? His reply was that he would blow the whole thing wide open.

I do not mean to imply by that, that our conclusions as to clearance were necessarily dictated by indispensability. I wish to emphasize it for myself. I reached the conclusion that he was loyal and ought to be cleared.

After Lansdale received De Silva's report from Pash, he interviewed Oppenheimer in Washington on September 12, 1943. He testified:

Q. What do you recall of your interview with Dr. Oppenheimer on what we call here the Chevalier incident, if you know what I have reference to?
A. Yes. That is one of the things which I have had the advantage of reading the transcript of some weeks ago and glancing at one page of it again last night.

I should say that I talked to Dr. Oppenheimer many times. In that particular case the interview was when he was in Washington and I now believe that the interview took place in General Groves' office, although that is a reconstruction. I have no precise recollection of it except that it was in Washington.

Do you wish me to relate the substance of it?
Q. Yes.
A. The substance of it was that Dr. Oppenheimer had advised our people on the west coast that an approach had been made to someone on the project to secure information concerning the project, and that the approach had been made by one Eltenton who was well known to us—from Eltenton to a third person and from the third person to the project.

From reading the transcript and having my attention called to memoranda by Mr. Robb and Mr. Rolander, the information was that the contact was with three persons. It is perfectly obvious that was the story. It is a curious trick of memory but my recollection was one and that the one person was Dr. Oppenheimer's brother, Frank Oppenheimer. I have no explanation as to how I translate it from three into one.

I called General Groves last night and discussed it with him in an attempt

to fathom that and I can't figure it out. But the record shows clearly that
there were three.

My effort was to get Dr. Oppenheimer to tell me the identity of the person
that was later identified as Chevalier. In that I was unsuccessful. Perhaps
I was not as resourceful a questioner as I might have been. In any event I
could not get him to tell me. That is the sum and substance of it.

Here is the transcript of this interview:

"L. Now, I don't want you to feel that any of these questions that I'm going
to ask you—I'm going to ask you some pretty pertinent and direct ones—are made
for any purpose of embarrassing you in any way. It's only that I feel it my
duty to.

"O. I'll answer them as well as I can.

"L. I tried to explain to you my problem, which as you can see is due to
the nature of the kind of espionage we're up against, is extremely difficult.

"O. Because it's so ramified.

"L. It's so ramified, and, after all, we're dealing with an allied nation.

"O. And who are the people in the project at Berkeley, are they my former
students?

"L. I'm not ready yet to tell you. As I say, I'm going to try to——

"O. I'm concerned if they are people for whom I have some kind of responsibility.

"L. Well, I'm not going to try to fence with you or mislead you at all as
I did without success, I feel, to some degree, at Los Alamos.

"O. Well, I felt there was a lot in your mind, and we were talking around,
the conversation was quite clear.

"L. It was perfectly obvious that you did read into it more than was stated.
Well, however, to refer again to this business concerning the party, those reasons
make it clear that the fact that a person says they have severed connection with
the party, the fact that they have at present no apparent interest or contact
in it does not show where they have unquestionably formerly been members that
they are not dangerous to us.

"O. I agree with that.

"L. That again poses a terrific problem because so many of the people * * *
you know as well as I do how difficult it is to prove communism. I'm going
to discuss yourself with you in a few minutes, and that will serve to illustrate
as well as anything some of the difficulties involved. We've got to weigh, we
feel, I believe that the first and primary thing to do is to get the job done.
That is, the project completed. Now, if that involves taking some risks, why,
of course, we'll take the risks. After all, you are risking your lives and everything else to do this, and everything has to be done with a risk so that we don't
want to protect the thing to death. But, therefore, all persons who are essential
to the project in any marked degree, really unless they cease to make themselves
useful there's no use talking about severing their connections while they're there
whether we believe they're Communists, pro-Nazi, pro-Fascist, or what.

"O. I won't agree with that, I mean, I think one has to——

"L. You have to weigh, you never know. I mean if you know it's compara-
tively easy. The only question that remains is whether we shall wait awhile
until we take somebody else or how we shall go about it. Shall we try to prose-
cute him for espionage or shall we just forget about it and weed him out. I
mean, you see that once you've made the decision why then the problem is practical. The difficulty is making the decision. Now, I want to know. In the
first place I think we know now who the man that you referred to as approaching
the other college project was. I wonder if you feel that you're in a position
to tell me.

"O. I think it would be wrong.

"L. I'd like to discuss with you your attitude on that for a minute.

"O. It is primarily this, that this came to me in confidence and the actions
taken were negative, the actions of this intermediary were reported as essentially negative, and although it would have been really negative not to have
touched it, I feel that I would implicate, so to speak, one fellow about whom,
who has initiative, would be persecuted.

"L. You mean Eltenton?

"O. Yes; this is the way it came to me straight.

"L. Well now, you see what you stated that he contacted, I believe it was three persons on the project, and they told him to go to hell in substance.

"O. Although probably more politely.

"L. And how do you know that he hasn't contacted others?

'O. I don't. I can't know that. It would seem obvious that he would have.

"L. If you heard about them they unquestionably were not successful.

"O. Yes.

"L. If you didn't hear about them they might be successful or they might at least be thinking about it, don't you see? Now you can, therefore, see from our point of view the importance of knowing what their channel is.

"O. Yes.

"L. And I was wondering, is this man a friend of yours by any chance?

"O. He's an acquaintance of mine, I've known over many years.

"L. Well do you—I mean there are acquaintances and there are friends. In other words, do you hesitate for fear of implicating a friend?

"O. I hesitate to mention any more names because of the fact that the other names I have do not seem to be people who were guilty of anything or people who I would like to get mixed up in it, and in my own views I know that this is a view which you are in a position to doubt. They are not people who are going to get tied up in it in any other way. That is, I have a feeling that this is an extremely erratic and unsystematic thing.

"L. Here is, I want you to in no derogatory way understand my position again.

"O. Well * * * there is a very strong feeling. Putting my finger on it I did it because of a sense of duty. I feel justified * * *.

"L. Now, here is an instance in which there is an actual attempt of espionage against probably the most important thing we're doing. You tell us about it 3 months later.

"O. More than that, I think.

"L. More than that. When the trail is cold it's stopped, when you have no reason not to suppose that these cases which you hear about are unsuccessful, that another attempt was made in which you didn't hear about because it was successful.

"O. Possibly. I am very, very inclined to doubt that it would have gone through this channel.

"L. Why?

"O. Because I had the feeling that this was a cocktail party channel. A couple of guys who saw each other more or less by accident.

"L. Well, people don't usually do things like that at cocktail parties, I know. All the stuff that we've picked up has certainly not been at cocktail parties.

"O. Well, that's where * * * I don't know, there may be many, many other channels besides Eltenton, and I would assume that there would be, but I have the feeling that Eltenton's suggestion to this fellow was whether he was willing to do this, was really a potential suggestion and not a systematic one.

"L. Well, I don't want to draw this out unduly, but I want to examine that proposition for a few minutes. Why would Eltenton working for the Shell Development Co. be interested on a frolic of his own, as it were, in trying to find out for the Soviet Government what's going on?

"O. I don't think it was a frolic of his own, but my answer is that he worked in Russia for 5 years * * * and had some contacts.

"L. That's right, so what I'm getting at is this—he unquestionably was asked or directed.

"O. Depending upon the point of view.

"L. To see what he could find out?

"O. I would think so.

"L. Which would mitigate against any conclusion that this attempt here was a mere casual thing?

"O. No; I don't think, I mean let me put it this way. The reason I mentioned Eltenton's name was because I thought it was likely that Eltention would persevere in this. But the reason I mention no other names is that I have not felt that those people would. That they were all just accidental.

"L. Now, I don't want these names of the people who were contacted or the person who contacted them. Let's stick to the persons that were contacts. To do anything to them because it's perfectly evident to me that they sure as hell would never come tell you about it if they were going to do it.

"O. Yes, that's right.

"L. Now, while I would like to have those names very much it's not as essential as that we know the contact. Because I think, there's one channel, of course, there's other channels, we know of. We don't know that one. Now we've got no way of knowing whether the ones that we've picked up or the names that I know of are identical with this man. Now, that's a simple reason why I want that name, and I want to ask you pointblank if you'll give it to me. If you won't, well O. K., no hard feelings.

"O. No; I've thought about it a good deal because Pash and Groves both asked me for the name, and I feel that I should not give it. I don't mean that I don't hope that if he's still operating that you will find it. I devoutly do. But I would just bet dollars to doughtnuts that he isn't still operating.

"L. I don't see how you can have any hesitancy in disclosing the name of the man who has actually been engaged in an attempt at espionage to a foreign power in time of war. I mean, my mind just doesn't run along those channels, and——

"O. I know, it's a tough problem, and I'm worried about it a lot.

"L. I can understand personal loyalty, yet you say he's not a close friend of yours. May I ask, do you know him as a Communist?

"O. I know him as a fellow traveler.

"L. You know him as a fellow traveler. Course in our book, membership in the party is not material, it's whether they follow the party line which is a test.

"O. Well, I don't know whether the fellow has or has not in all detail, but he certainly has so far as I know about it in a general way.

"L. He is now at the university?

"O. I don't know that. That is, I think, I don't know the date on this precisely, but I think it was some time maybe before Christmas of last year that this matter was brought to my attention. I don't know how long it is. There was some talk of his trying to get a job elsewhere * * *.

"L. Well, of course, that's the question. Do you now feel you can tell me who it is?

"O. I do not now feel that I ought to tell you.

"L. In what event would you feel that you should?

"O. If I had any evidence or anything came to my attention which was indicative that something was transmitted * * *.

"L. Well I'm telling you it is. Right today, I can't tell you the last time information was passed, but I think it was about a week ago.

"O. I mean something that there is a reasonable chance is the man whose name I don't want to give to you.

"L. Well, of course, I——

"O. There's a very strong feeling on my part that I ought not to.

"L. I have no way, of course, of knowing.

"O. What I want to say is this—I'm not kidding you and I'm not trying to weasel out. It's my overwhelming judgment that this guy isn't involved. That isn't judgment which is based on hope but his character. If I am wrong, then I am making a very serious mistake, but I think that the chances are very, very small.

"L. Let me ask you a personal question—you don't have to answer it if you don't want to. Is part of your feeling based on the fact, don't be insulted please, that you don't consider that it would be such a catastrophe (*sic*) anyway for us if they did find it out?

"O. That is not my feeling. I think it would be a catastrophe (*sic*) and I made this clear when I talked Pash. If Russia found out except through official channels. I do not know whether what we are now doing with the British is the right thing to do. I do not know whether it would be right to include Russia and China in that. I think we are now reopening negotiations with the British, in fact that is why I'm here. I don't know whether that is right. That is a very hard and tough question. I am sure that it is wrong for the Russians to find out about those things in any way except through official channels.

"L. Well, if you won't do it, you won't do it, but don't think I won't ask you again.

Lansdale went back to Los Alamos and told General Groves "that it was up to him, that he just had to get the information for us, which the General undertook to do and later reported back the information."

Before we turn now to General Groves, let us listen to Lansdale's final word on Oppenheimer's veracity. At the end of his testimony, Lansdale summed it up.

Q. I have just one question, Mr. Lansdale.
Referring back to the confused incident of the Chevalier matter, what would you say, on the basis of your total experience with Dr. Oppenheimer, would be your general opinion as to his veracity?
A. There is no question that—I don't believe that he lied to us except about this one incident—my general impression is that his veracity is good. I don't know of any other incident.
Q. Just so there is no possible implication in the record, he had no responsibility for Mr. Greenglass in any way, shape, or form, did he?
A. I don't believe so. I will take full responsibility for that one. That was the outstanding blunder of the century.

CROSS-EXAMINATION

By Mr. ROBB:
Q. Colonel Lansdale, as a lawyer are you familiar with the legal maxim, "Falsus in uno, falsus in omnibus"?
A. Yes; I am. Like all legal maxims, it is a generalization, and not of particular significance when applied to specifics.
Q. When you are trying a jury case and the veracity of a witness is in question, do you request the court to give an instruction on that subject?
A. Oh, certainly; don't you?
Q. Certainly, I want to know what you do.
A. The instruction usually is that the jury may, but does not have to, take that as an indication, and the judgment is to be exercised in the particular case.
Q. And when you are trying a jury case and you examine a witness on the opposite side and you demonstrate that he has lied, don't you argue to the jury from that that they should disregard his evidence?
A. You are speaking now as to what I as an advocate do?
Q. Yes.
A. It depends on circumstances; usually I do.
Q. Sure. Any lawyer worth his salt would.
A. Particularly if it is my belief.

Lansdale, you see, unlike Pash, believed that Oppenheimer had lied to Pash and to himself in these interviews. He believed Oppenheimer was now telling the truth, and, in spite of the lying, Lansdale believed then, and still believed, that Oppenheimer was "completely loyal" and that his continued employment by the A.E.C. "would be clearly consistent with the interests of national security."

Q. Based on your acquaintance with Dr. Oppenheimer, your knowledge that you have of him, what would you say as to his loyalty to the United States?
A. I have never had any question of it. I have no question of it now. He is completely loyal.
Q. Again based on your experience with him and your knowledge of him, would you say that his continued employment as a consultant to the Atomic Energy Commission would be clearly consistent with the interests of national security?
A. So far as I know the situation, I would say yes. I think I would have to qualify that by this fact. While my personal impression, my faith is sound,

it would have to be subject to derogatory evidence that I don't know anything about, which I take it is the purpose of this committee to investigate.

Q. Of course, that goes without saying. I am asking you for your judgment simply based on your own personal feeling about him and knowledge of him.

A. Yes.

Q. As to that, you are clear in your mind.

A. Perfectly clear, yes.

Lansdale had put it up to General Groves to find out from Oppenheimer who the contact was. Early in September the general raised the subject in the course of a trip he and Oppenheimer made to Chicago. Lansdale was with them and he made a memorandum of their "discussion between Cheyenne and Chicago."

"d. Some discussion was had about Dr. Oppenheimer's previous relations to Colonel Pash and Lieutenant Johnson about the Soviet attempt to secure information which had come to Oppenheimer's attention some time ago. Oppenheimer's attitude was that he would give the name of the intermediate contact at the University of California if pressed to do so, and told by General Groves that we had to have it, but that he did not want to do so because he did not believe that any further contacts had been made and was confident that the contacts that had been with the project had not produced any information. He intimated further that it was a question of getting friends of his into difficulties and causing unnecessary troubles when no useful purpose could be served.

It was not until December that the general insisted. Here is Groves's account:

Q. Do you recall your conversation with him about the Chevalier incident?

A. Yes, but I have seen so many versions of it, I don't think I was confused before, but I am certainly starting to become confused today. I recall what I consider the essential history of that affair. As to whether this occurred this time, where I was at the moment, I can't say that I recall it exactly. I think I recall everything that is of vital interest, as far as would be necessary to draw a conclusion as to that affair.

Q. Would you say what your conclusion was?

A. My conclusion was that there was an approach made, that Dr. Oppenheimer knew of this approach, that at some point he was involved in that the approach was made to him—I don't mean involved in the sense that he gave anything—I mean he just knew about it personally from the fact that he was in the chain, and that he didn't report it in its entirety as he should have done. When I learned about it, and throughout, that he was always under the influence of what I termed the typical American schoolboy attitude that there is something wicked about telling on a friend. I was never certain as to just what he was telling me. I did know this: That he was doing what he thought was essential, which was to disclose to me the dangers of this particular attempt to enter the project, namely, it was concerned with the situation out there near Berkeley— I think it was the Shell Laboratory at which Eltenton was supposedly one of the key members—and that was a source of danger to the project and that was the worry. I always had the very definite impression that Dr. Oppenheimer wanted to protect his friends of long standing, possibly his brother. It was always my impression that he wanted to protect his brother, and that his brother might be involved in having been in this chain, and that his brother didn't behave quite as he should have, or if he did, he didn't even want to have the finger of suspicion pointed at his brother, because he always felt a natural loyalty to him, and had a protective attitude toward him.

I felt at the time that what Oppenheimer was trying to tell me and tell our project, once he disclosed this thing at all—as I recall I had the feeling that he didn't disclose it immediately. In other words, he didn't come around the next day or that night and say to our security people, "Listen, some things are going on." I think he thought it over for some time. I am saying what I thought now, and not what we could prove, because we could never prove anything definite on this thing, because it all depended on the testimony of a man who was concerned in it.

I felt that was wrong. If I had not felt it was important not to have any point to protect Chevalier or to protect somebody else who was a friend, whom he felt that the man had made a mistake and he had adequately taken care of that mistake and more or less warned this man off.

I felt tht was wrong. If I had not felt it was important not to have any point of issue on what after all was a minor point with respect to the success of the project, I might have had quite an issue with him right then and there. As he told me very early in my conversation with him, he said, "General, if you order me to tell you this, I will tell you." I said, "No, I am not going to order you."

About 2 months later or some time later, after much discussion in trying to lead him into it, and having then got the situation more or less adjusted, I told him if you don't tell me, I am going to have to order you to do it. Then I got what to me was the final story. I think he made a great mistake in that. I felt so at the time. I didn't think it was great from the standpoint of the project, because I felt that I was getting what I wanted to know which, after all, I did know already, that this group was a source of danger to us. I didn't know that this group had tried to make this direct approach and pinpoint it that way, but I knew they were thoroughly capable of it, and I knew we had sources of danger in the Berkeley project.

I think that really was my impression of it, that he didn't do what he should have done. The reasons why were desire to protect friends and possibly his brother, and that he felt that he had done what was necessary in pinpointing. As far as I was concerned, while I didn't like it, after all it was not my job to like everything my subordinates did, or anybody in the project did. I felt I had gotten what I needed to get out of that, and I was not going to make an issue of it, because I thought it might impair his usefulness on the project.

I think that gives you the general story.

And Groves testified, "I think I was thoroughly familiar with everything that was reported about Dr. Oppenheimer."

This was in the early part of December 1943. In Oppenheimer's cross-examination, the following was brought out:

Q. There came a time at last when you did disclose that Haakon Chevalier was the intermediary.
A. Right.
Q. I find in the file, Doctor, a telegram signed, "Nichols" and addressed to the area engineer, University of California, Berkeley, Calif., attention Lt. Lyle Johnson, reading as follows:
"Lansdale advises that according to Oppenheimer professor contact of Eltenton is Haakon Chevalier. REF, EIDMMI–34. Classified secret. Oppenheimer states in his opinion Chevalier engaged in no further activity other than three original attempts."
That wire is dated December 13, 1943. Would it be about December 13, 1943, that you disclosed the identity of Dr. Chevalier?
A. I thought it was earlier. It could have been that late. I thought it was considerably earlier.
Q. To whom did you make that disclosure?
A. To General Groves.
Q. And under what circumstances?
A. We talked in his room in Los Alamos.
Q. All right.
A. He told me that he simply had to know, and I surely told him that the story I told Pash was a cock and bull story at that time. That there were no

three people.

Q. In other words, you lied to Groves, too?

A. No, I told him that the story I told Pash was a cock and bull story.

Q. You told Groves that you had told Pash a cock and bull story?

A. I am quite certain about that.

Q. You are sure about that?

A. Yes.

Q. You notice in this wire from General Nichols——

A. There are still the three people.

Q. You are still talking about the three people. I notice in the file of the same day General Nichols wired the Commanding Officer, United States Engineer Office, Santa Fe, New Mex., attention, Captain DeSilva. "Haakon Chevalier to be reported by Oppenheimer to be professor at RadLab who made three contacts for Eltenton. Classified secret. Oppenheimer believed Chevalier engaged in no further activity other than three original attempts."

On December 12——

Mr. GARRISON. That last wire was from whom?

Mr. ROBB. Nichols. On December 12, 1943, a wire to Capt. H. K. Calvert, Clinton Engineer Work, Clinton, Tenn. What was that, Oak Ridge?

The WITNESS. Yes.

By Mr. ROBB.

Q. "According to Oppenheimer professor contact of Eltenton is Haakon Chevalier. Oppy states in his opinion beyond original three attempts Chevalier engaged in no further activity. From Lansdale. DeSilva and Johnson to be notified by you."

Does that indicate to you that you told General Groves that there weren't three contacts?

A. Certainly to the contrary. I am fairly clear.

Q. You think General Groves did tell Colonel Nichols and Colonel Lansdale your story was cock and bull?

A. I find that hard to believe.

Q. So do I.

There is an ambiguity here in Oppenheimer's answer. What he found "hard to believe" was not what Robb found hard. It was not that General Groves told Nichols and Lansdale that his story was cock and bull. Oppenheimer had just testified that he told General Groves it was a cock-and-bull story. What Oppenheimer found it hard to believe was that he had failed to tell General Groves "that there weren't three contacts." Oppenheimer testified again at the end of the hearings and brought this matter up again. In a colloquy with Gray Oppenheimer said, "May I add a point. When I did identify Chevalier, which was to General Groves, I told him of course that there were no three people, that this had occurred in our house, that this was me. So that when I made this damaging story, it was clearly with the intention of not revealing who was the intermediary."

Can it be that Pash was right and that Oppenheimer's story to him was the truth? Pash thought and continued to think that Oppenheimer was telling him the truth. You have read Pash's reasons for believing Oppenheimer was telling him the truth. Could it be that Pash found it hard to believe that Oppenheimer could successfully lie to Pash?

The Board did not believe that Oppenheimer was testifying falsely, and the Board was particularly sensitive to any lack of candor on Oppenheimer's part. When Nichols composed his letter of December 23, 1953, he emphasized Oppenheimer's delay in reporting an approach which Chevalier had made on Eltenton's behalf, and his refusal to name Chevalier and himself until he was ordered to do so. There is no suggestion that Oppenheimer was lying to the F.B.I. in 1946, when he told the same story he afterward told the Board. Later, in Nichols' recommendation to the Commission, perhaps persuaded by Pash, Nichols thought it was "a fair inference" that Oppenheimer did tell Pash the truth and so was lying to the Board. The Commission, I think, agreed, although Strauss for the majority said it was not clear. They treated the problem as a dilemma between two equally bad alternatives, which the Commission did not need to solve. Either was derogatory enough to make it unnecessary to decide which was true.

To me it is crassly incredible that Oppenheimer was not now telling the truth. Toward the close of the hearings Oppenheimer went back on the stand, and Gray asked him some final questions. Here is Gray first and then Oppenheimer, summing the matter up before the Board. This was Oppenheimer's final chance to explain.

I want now to go back to the so-called Chevalier incident.
A. Right.
Q. I should like to give you something of a summary of what I believe to have been your testimony before the board. If it is not an accurate summary in your opinion, or your counsel thinks it is not an accurate summary, I would like to know about it. But on the basis of a summary, then, of your testimony, I should like to ask some questions.
The summary would be this: You said that Chevalier was your friend in whom you had confidence, and that you were convinced that his remarks about passing information to the Russians were innocent. For these reasons, you testified, it did not occur to you for a long time that you should report this incident to the security officers, and when you did tell them about it, you declined to name Chevalier, because you were convinced that he was innocent, and in effect wanted to protect him from the harrassment of an investigation because of your belief in his innocence.
You testified on the other hand that the story of the Chevalier incident which you told to Colonel Pash in August 1947, and reaffirmed to Colonel Lansdale in September 1943, was false in certain material respects. Let me repeat, you testified here that that story was false in material respects. I believe you testified that this story was a cock and bull story, and that the whole thing was a pure fabrication except for the name Eltenton, and that this fabrication was in some very considerable circumstanital detail, and your testimony here as to your explanation for this fabrication was that you were an idiot, and that you were reluctant to mention Chevalier and no doubt somewhat reluctant to mention yourself.
However, I believe that your testimony indicated that you agreed that if the story you told Pash had been true, it showed that Chevalier was deeply involved, that it was not just a casual conversation, that it would not under those circumstances just have been an innocent and meaningless contact, and that it was a

criminal conspiracy.

In short, with respect to that portion of your testimony I believe you led the board to believe that you thought that if your story to Colonel Pash had been true it looked like a very unsavory situation, to say the very best about it.

Now, here is my question : If Chevalier was your friend and you believed him to be innocent and wanted to protect him, then why did you tell a complicated false story that on the face of it would show that the individual was not innocent, but on the contrary, was rather deeply involved with several people in what might have been a criminal espionage conspiracy?

Or to put the question in another way, I ask you whether it is not a fair inference from your testimony that your story to Pash and Lansdale as far as it went was a true story, and that the fabrication may have been with respect to the current version.

A. Let me take the second part of your question first.

Q. Yes.

A. The story I told to Pash was not a true story. There were not three or more people involved on the project. There was one person involved. That was me. I was at Los Alamos. There was no one else at Los Alamos involved. There was no one in Berkeley involved. When I heard the microfilm or what the hell, it didn't sound to me as to this were reporting anything that Chevalier had said, or at that time the unknown professor had said. I am certain that was not mentioned. I testified that the Soviet consulate had not been mentioned by Chevalier. That is the very best of my recollection. It is conceivable that I knew of Eltenton's connection with the consulate, but I believe I can do no more than say the story told in circumstantial detail, and which was elicited from me in greater and greater detail during this was a false story. It is not easy to say that.

Now, when you ask for a more persuasive argument as to why I did this than that I was an idiot, I am going to have more trouble being understandable.

I think I was impelled by 2 or 3 concerns at that time. One was the feeling that I must get across the fact that if there was, as Lansdale indicated, trouble at the Radiation Laboratory, Eltenton was the guy that might very well be involved and it was serious. Whether I embroidered the story in order to underline that seriousness or whether I embroidered it to make it more tolerable that I would not tell the simple facts, namely, Chevalier had talked to me about it, I don't know. There were no other people involved, the conversation with Chevalier was brief, it was in the nature of things not utterly casual, but I think the tone of it and his own sense of not wishing to have anything to do with it, I have correctly communicated.

I think I need to say that it was essential that I tell this story, that I should have told it at once and I should have told it completely accurately, but that it was a matter of conflict for me and I found myself, I believe, trying to give a tip to the intelligence people without realizing that when you give a tip you must tell the whole story. When I was asked to elaborate, I started off on a false pattern.

I may add 1 or 2 things. Chevalier was a friend of mine.

Dr. Evans. Did you say is a friend.

The Witness. He was a friend of mine.

Dr. Evans. Today?

The Witness. He was then. We may talk later of our present relations. He was then a friend of mine. As far as I know he had no close relations with anyone else on the project. The notion that he would go to a number of project people to talk to them instead of coming to me and talking it over as we did would have made no sense whatever. He was an unlikely and absurd intermediary for such a task. I think there are circumstances which indicate that there was no—that there would not have been such a conspiracy—but I am in any case solemnly testifying that there was no such conspiracy in what I knew, and what I know of this matter. I wish I could explain to you better why I falsified and fabricated.

I don't think anyone with any understanding of a guilty conscience, or any sympathy for one, can fail to believe Oppenheimer. It was a feeling of guilt which sent Oppenheimer to Johnson and

Pash to volunteer the story he told them, guilt at his concealment of the episode. It was guilt that led Oppenheimer to "embroider the story," in Oppenheimer's phrase. He knew it was a "serious" situation. "Whether I embroidered the story in order to underline that seriousness or whether I embroidered it to make it more tolerable that I would not tell the simple facts, namely, Chevalier had talked to me about it, I don't know." It was the same guilty conscience which led Oppenheimer to agree so readily and so completely with Robb in cross-examination that his story to Pash was a "lie," a "tissue of lies," a "pure fabrication," a "cock and bull story," that he had been "an idiot," again and again.

The fact is, it was a simple lie and, at worst, as General Groves called it, "the typical school boy attitude that there is something wicked about telling on a friend." Oppenheimer was making his wickedness "tolerable" to himself by exaggerating and magnifying the whole episode. He was doing penance to his conscience for his concealment of Chevalier's part in it and his own part in it, and further penance by repeatedly confessing he had lied. His conscience had blinded him to the fact that Chevalier's name must someday come out, and that then his lie would make it as bad for Chevalier as he was making it for himself. Now his conscience was reminding him that this was just what had happened.

Why did Nichols, in his letter of December 23, 1953, stress only Oppenheimer's failure to report the episode for several months and his refusal to identify himself as the one who had been approached or Chevalier as the one who made the approach? Nichols knew all about Oppenheimer's story to Johnson, Pash and Lansdale. He was the security officer for the Manhattan District, and it was he who sent the telegrams announcing that Oppenheimer had at last told Groves that Chevalier was Eltenton's contact and he himself Chevalier's. I think Nichols was then taking the whole affair no more seriously than his then superior officer, General Groves, did at the time and still did at the hearing. Robb, in his cross-examination, decided to accept Oppenheimer's testimony to the Board and make as much of a lie as he could out of his story to Pash.

You have read Groves's account of how Oppenheimer finally told him. You have also read Groves's letter to Oppenheimer on May 18, 1950, from the Remington Rand Laboratory, after Groves had retired. Groves and Lansdale and Nichols were personally and immediately acquainted with all that had happened, as closely as anyone could be, other than Oppenheimer and Chevalier.

Let me now turn to the judgment of a galaxy of men as respectable and responsible as the Board itself, and they too were told all the facts. For they all read a complete summary of Oppenheimer's file in the F.B.I., and it contained the whole Chevalier episode. Smyth removes any doubt about this in his dissenting opinion. "When interviewed by the F.B.I. in 1946, Dr. Oppenheimer recounted the same story of the incident which he has consistently maintained ever since. He stated explicitly in 1946 that the story told to Colonel Pash in 1943 had been a fabrication." I may add that Rolander, in his memorandum to Nichols of October 25, 1954, published in the *U.S. News and World Report* of December 24, 1954, confirms this: "In 1946 Dr. Oppenheimer claimed to the F.B.I. that the story he had given Pash was a 'cock and bull' story." Moreover, "The complete Manhattan Engineering District files concerning J. R. Oppenheimer were sent to the F.B.I. about July or August of 1946, at the time he left employment controlled by the Manhattan Engineering District." So says a memorandum of the staff security officer of the A.E.C. dated March 12, 1946.

These respectable and responsible men were the Atomic Energy Commissioners, and the occasion for their judgment was Oppenheimer's clearance for his appointment to the General Advisory Committee. The Atomic Energy Act of 1946 required a new clearance. These commissioners were: David Lilienthal, the chairman, Dr. Robert F. Bacher, Sumner Pike, Wesley W. Waymack, and Lewis Strauss.

They went to great pains over Oppenheimer's clearance, individually and collectively. As Lilienthal testified, it was "a matter of great interest and importance." Among other things, they all read the summary of Oppenheimer's F.B.I. file, which Hoover sent over on March 8, 1947. Lilienthal testified that there were some items which he accepted as true and some he had doubt about.

> I can't remember which was which, but I have the recollection that some of these things were stronger and more clear than others, but the whole picture was that of derogatory information about the man's post associations, and one episode that was worse than that.
> Q. Which was that?
> A. Involving Chevalier.
> Q. What do you mean, "worse than that," Mr. Lilienthal?
> A. Well, this struck me as being the only thing, the thing in the whole record, that would give the gravest concern, and for that, and the thing that dismissed that concern from my mind was the fact that General Groves and Mr. Lansdale, the security officer, at the time this happened examined this man on the question, and were apparently satisfied that this was not or did not endanger the national security, and the evidence to that was they kept him on. I can't add anything to that. That seemed to me a very conclusive kind of a judgment about whether he was dangerous or not.

Lilienthal testified that he had gone personally to J. Edgar Hoover later to make sure that the Commission had all the information up to date, and Hoover assured him they had. Hoover "had one reservation, which he stated with some emphasis, that he could not feel completely satisfied in view of J. Robert's failure to report promptly and accurately what must have seemed to him an attempt at espionage in Berkeley." This is from a memorandum by T. O. Jones, then the A.E.C. security officer, for the A.E.C. file. So even in Hoover's view, Oppenheimer had been no worse than dilatory and inaccurate. The rub to Hoover was that Oppenheimer had failed to report promptly an unsuccessful attempt at espionage.

I think it is worth our while to go into some detail and see the pains the Commission took in 1947 before they unanimously cleared Oppenheimer for the General Advisory Committee. It was not finally done until August 1947.

We can read an account of all the A.E.C. did in a long memorandum of Carroll L. Wilson, the General Manager.

"March 10, 1947: Summaries of information received on March 8 from the FBI regarding J. Robert Oppenheimer and his brother Frank F. Oppenheimer, were considered by the Commissioners in closed session this morning. This file was accompanied by a letter dated March 8 from Mr. J. Edgar Hoover and the file was delivered to Mr. Jones by the FBI on Saturday morning, March 8.

"The letter from Mr. Hoover transmitted a copy of what was described as a summary of the FBI files concerning J. Robert Oppenheimer and his brother, Frank F. Oppenheimer. The summary consisted of material usually referred to as derogatory.

"The Commission met in closed session and each of the Commissioners read the rather voluminous summary and noted from the incompleteness of the account as contained in the summary that either it did not reflect the results of a full investigation or did not contain all information bearing on the matter. The Commission also noted that the evidence summarized which, as stated in Mr. Hoover's letter, came from confidential sources, could seriously impeach Dr. Oppenheimer and that as a consequence this matter was one in which not only the Commission but also Dr. Bush as chairman of the Joint Research and Development Board and Dr. Conant as chairman of the Atomic Energy Committee of the JRDB were also concerned. Furthermore, in view of the role of both Dr. Bush and Dr. Conant in connection with the Manhattan project during the war, and their association with Dr. Oppenheimer while he was director of the Los Alamos Laboratory of the Manhattan project, it was felt that they should be consulted promptly. Dr. Bush was reached by telephone and it was arranged that he meet the Commission at 3:15 p. m.

At 3:15 p. m. the Commissioners met and were joined by Dr. Bush. The delivery of this file and the fact that it contained derogatory information were reported to Dr. Bush although he was not shown the file. Dr. Bush stated that he was not familiar with Dr. Oppenheimer's background prior to his joining the Manhattan project in 1942, but that he had concurred in the choice of Dr. Oppenheimer by General Groves for the important post of the Los Alamos Bomb Laboratory and that he felt that Dr. Oppenheimer's exceptional performance as director of that laboratory and subsequently in other roles advising the Government on the subject of atomic energy had clearly demonstrated his loyalty as a citizen of the United States and his integrity.

"Inasmuch as Dr. Conant had been closely associated with Dr. Oppenheimer in connection with the Manhattan project, he was invited to sit with the Commission and Dr. Bush for discussion of this matter and he joined the meeting at about 3:45. Dr. Conant stated that his association with Dr. Oppenheimer dated from the beginning of Dr. Oppenheimer's connection with the Manhattan project and that he was not familiar with the contents of any investigative files concerning Dr. Oppenheimer's background. He stated that General Groves had taken full responsibility for selection of Dr. Oppenheimer to head the Los Alamos Laboratory and that it was certainly a matter of public knowledge that this laboratory under Dr. Oppenheimer's brilliant and driving leadership had made an enormous contribution to the war effort.

"Inasmuch as General Groves had made the original selection of Dr. Oppenheimer, the chairman attempted to reach him by telephone but was advised that he was en route by automobile from Florida to Washington and could not be reached.

"Drs. Bush and Conant shared the views of the Commission that the record of Dr. Oppenheimer's contributions to the country in this field during the last 4 or 5 years have been so outstanding that it could leave no doubt as to his loyalty. It was further stated so that, in view of Dr. Oppenheimer's unique position as an authority in this field, if anything were permitted to occur which might cause him to be lost to the Government in connection with atomic energy, it would be a very serious blow to our progress in this field and would have very serious consequences in the attitude of his fellow scientists towards this project. Even if no precipitous action were taken which would affect Dr. Oppenheimer's continuance in his present efforts with respect to this project, any public disclosure, either of the information contained in files or of the fact that such information exists which is the subject of serious concern as to Dr. Oppenheimer's qualifications, the consequences upon the leading scientists engaged in the project would still be serious.

"In view of the interest of the War Department and the role of the War Department in bringing Dr. Oppenheimer originally into this project, Drs. Conant and Bush arranged to see Secretary Patterson later in the afternoon. They did see him and he promptly agreed to contact General Groves.

"March 11, 1947: The Commission met this morning for further consideration of the matters discussed yesterday in connection with Dr. Oppenheimer. The Commission concluded tentatively (1) that on the basis of the——

Mr. GARRISON. What is that?

Mr. ROBB (reading), "The Commission concluded tentatively, (1) that on the basis of the information supplied by Dr. Bush and Dr. Conant concerning Dr. Oppenheimer's outstanding contributions in this project and his consistent concern for the security of this country in connection with his services as a member of the JRDB Committee on Atomic Energy and as an adviser to the Department of State, Dr. Oppenheimer's loyalty was prima facie clear despite material contained in the FBI summary; (2) that as a result of his work for the Government during the last 4 years he is now 1 of the best, if not the best-informed scientist in regard to 'restricted data' concerning atomic energy; (3) that while under these circumstances the questions raised by the summary did not create an issue or any immediate hazard, it was essential to undertake promptly a full and reliable evaluation of the case so that it could be promptly disposed of in one way or another.

"As a first step, it was decided to secure as promptly as possible written expression of views from Dr. Bush, Dr. Conant, and General Groves as to Dr. Oppenheimer's loyalty. As a second step, it was decided that the chairman should confer with Dr. Bush and Mr. Clifford of the White House concerning the establishment of an evaluation board of distinguished jurists to make a thorough review and evaluation of the case. Inasmuch as Dr. Oppenheimer is a Presidential appointee to the General Advisory Committee to the Commission, the case is one in which the White House has a definite interest. In addition, the matter is of interest to the Department of State inasmuch as Dr. Oppenheimer has served as an adviser to the Department of State on many phases of atomic energy, including serving as a member the Board of Consultants to the Department of State in the preparation of a plan for the international control of atomic energy, and subsequently as an adviser to Mr. Baruch and more recently as adviser to Mr. Frederick Osborne.

"At 3 p. m. today Dr. Bush and the chairman"—that was you, wasn't it?

The WITNESS. Yes, sir.

Mr. Robb (reading). "Dr. Bush and the chairman met with Mr. Clifford and advised him of the circumstances in connection with this case and discussed with him the desirability of having a review of this case by a board of distinguished jurists or other citizens. The chairman proposed that there be considered for membership on this board judges of the Supreme Court. Mr. Clifford stated that he was decidedly opposed to any move which would draw members of the court into outside activities and felt that this case did not warrant an exception to that policy. This policy would not preclude selection of other jurists for temporary service on such an evaluation board if it were deemed desirable that such a board be established. Mr. Clifford stated that he would discuss the matter with the President and communicate with the chairman and Dr. Bush on Wednesday.

"The results of the discussion with Mr. Clifford were reported to the Commission at a meeting at 5 p. m. this afternoon. At that meeting the general manager reported that a detailed analysis of the FBI summary was in process of preparation by the Commission's security staff as an aid to evaluation."

Have you any comment on that, Mr. Lilienthal?

The Witness. No. I haven't. It is quite evident that Mr. Clifford in the end did not favor the idea of such a board, or perhaps we changed our minds, but I had forgotten that recommendation.

So much for the way the Commission cleared Oppenheimer for the General Advisory Committee in 1947 and the information on which all the commissioners acted. Strauss is the only one of the five who was still on the Commission in 1954, now the chairman. All the derogatory information which was before the Board and the Commission in these hearings was before the Commission then, except the matter of the attitude and position of Oppenheimer toward the development of the H-bomb in 1949–1951 and except any fresh material which may have come up during the hearings.

You have remarked that I have relied chiefly on contemporaneous memoranda and referred sparingly to Lilienthal's testimony before the Board, though there is also testimony of Dr. Bacher and Sumner Pike. Lilienthal testified from memory without the help of refreshing it from any memoranda, and he forgot some things and was mistaken in some others. He had forgotten his discussion with Clark Clifford about a board of review. He thought Hoover had sent over the F.B.I. file, and not a summary of it only. He thought that the A.E.C. had Oppenheimer's Manhattan District file, when the fact was that the F.B.I. had it.

Lilienthal had not been allowed to refresh his memory before he testified. He had asked to see the documents the day before. He said he understood that the rules of the Commission permitted former commissioners to have access to anything they had had access to during the period of their commissionership. He had been refused. And yet these documents were used to cross-examine him and then declassified to show faults and lapses of memory. I don't

need to comment, because Lilienthal himself and Garrison, Oppenheimer's counsel, made any further comment unnecessary. What
they said, and what Gray said, speaks for itself.

The WITNESS. Mr. Chairman, may I make this comment, that in the great
multiplicity of things that went on at that time, it is not at all impossible that I
should not remember even as important a matter as this, but a simple way to
secure the truth and accuracy would have been to have given me these files
yesterday, when I asked for them, so that when I came here, I could be the
best possible witness and disclose as accurately as possible what went on at
that time. I am a little confused about the technique. The board wants the
facts, and the facts are in the file, and I asked for the file so I could be a better
witness, and it was denied me. So I just have to rely on memory during a very
troubled and difficult time on matters that are obviously important, but they
are not as important as many other things we were concerned with at that time.
It would help me a good deal, and I could be a much better witness if I saw
the files that I helped to contribute to make.

Mr. ROBB. Mr. Chairman, I think Mr. Garrison would agree that it is an entirely
fair comment to make that it is demonstrated that the memory of the witness
was not infallible.

The WITNESS. I would be the first to insist on that.

Mr. ROBB. Since we are depending largely on memory, I think it is a fair test.

Mr. SILVERMAN. Why, when we have documents.

Mr. GARRISON. I thought the notion of an inquiry and not trial was to get at
the truth by the shortest possible route, and it seems to me the attempt to make
a witness seem to be not telling the truth, or his memory is not to be relied on
by this board, by the surprise production of documents, is not the shortest way
to arrive at the truth. It seems to me more like a criminal trial than it does like
an inquiry and I just regret it has to be done here.

Mr. GRAY. Well, the board certainly will take cognizance of the comments of
counsel in respect to this matter, and I think that if counsel is not permitted to
engage in cross examination and simply relies on notes the witnesses may take
from documents in a file, there may be some difficulty in arriving at some evalua-
tions, and now on this particular point, it seems to me pertinent at least against
general and public discussions, with which counsel cannot be unaware, including
the New York Times story, the information for which was furnished by counsel,
it is repeatedly and publicly stated that the Commission and others cleared Dr.
Oppenheimer at the time that these were old charges rehashed, and completely
considered and evaluated at the time. It does seem important to me, at least
as chairman of this board, to find out exactly what did take place at that time.

Mr. GARRISON. I agree with you, Mr. Chairman, in full. I want nothing but
the truth brought out here. And all of the truth about all of the things, and I
want complete cross examination, and I raise only the question of surprising
the witnesses with documents they themselves prepared which are in the file and
which the Government has, and it seems to me a shorter way of arriving at the
truth and a fairer way where a witness has prepared a document which the
Government has in its possession is to ask him if he prepared that document,
and to read it into the record, rather than confuse him first by asking him about
things that he doesn't remember. That is the only point I make, and that limited
point, and I wish in no way to confine this inquiry. But it is an important point
though limited.

Mr. ROBB. May I proceed? I have two more questions.

Mr. GRAY. You are not going to confront the witness with any more documents?

We must not be squeamish about Robb's trial tactics. Cross-
examination is as much a weapon as it is an instrument. It is a
cutlass as well as a scalpel, and its use as either must be encouraged, sometimes the one, sometimes the other. The Board had
permitted Robb to cross-examine Oppenheimer in just the same
way, using the classified recording of Oppenheimer's interview

with Pash to magnify Oppenheimer's fabricated story into "the tissue of lies," and Oppenheimer's guilty conscience had prompted him to co-operate. The recording had been withheld until it had served Robb's purposes. It had been kept classified, not for the security of the country but solely for the purpose of testing Oppenheimer's memory and veracity. Declassification a day or so sooner would not have endangered our security. No doubt this helped Robb score off Oppenheimer. But Oppenheimer was an intelligent and quick-witted witness as well as honest and candid, and the art of cross-examination, to be effective, must needs be brutal.

We may well deplore Robb's tactics, but we must not be squeamish. And yet, to use the same tactics on an ex-chairman of the A.E.C., who could not be suspected of the least intention to deviate from the truth—this was stupid and rude as well as brutal. Robb made Gray's protestations that this was an "inquiry" and not a trial seem sanctimonious. The regulations required the Board to conduct an inquiry, not a trial. The Board would have done better to discipline Robb than to offend the regulations.

You now have all the available facts. You have the opinion of those who were next to the facts, and the judgment of those who had the responsibility of passing on the facts at secondhand. Of equal moment is the opinion of men who know Oppenheimer the man. They may not know the facts so well, but they know the man better. Their knowledge of the man makes up for their lack of first-hand knowledge of the facts. Their long and intimate acquaintance with Oppenheimer the man made up for any shortcomings in the hypothetical questions by which they were given the facts.

Gray, the chairman, put a hypothetical question to Dr. Rabi, and on cross-examination Robb followed it up. Rabi agreed that he had not heard Oppenheimer's testimony and that the Board might be in possession of information which was not available to Rabi. Rabi then explained why he nevertheless had confidence in the validity of his own opinion. He had "a kind of seat of the pants feeling" on which he laid great weight and which he tried to express.

Q. Dr. Rabi, getting back to the hypothetical questions that have been put to you by the Chairman and Dr. Evans about the Chevalier incident, if you had been put in that hypothetical position and had reported the matter to an intelligence officer, you of course would have been told the whole truth about it, wouldn't you?

A. I am naturally a truthful person.

Q. You would not have lied about it?

A. I am telling you what I think now. The Lord alone knows what I would have done at that time. This is what I think now.

Q. Of course, Doctor, as you say, only God knows what is in a man's mind and heart, but give us your best judgment of what you would do.

A. This is what I think now I hope that is what I would have done then. In other words, I do not—I take a serious view of that—I think it is crucial.

Q. You say what?

A. I take a serious view of that incident, but I don't think it is crucial.

Q. Of course, Doctor, you don't know what Dr. Oppenheimer's testimony before this board about that incident may have been, do you?

A. No.

Q. So perhaps in respect of passing judgment on that incident, the board may be in a better position to judge than you?

A. I have the highest respect for the board. I am not going to make any comment about the board. They are working very hard, as I have seen.

Q. Of course, I realize you have complete confidence in the board. But my point is that perhaps the board may be in possession of information which is not now available to you about the incident.

A. It may be. On the other hand, I am in possession of a long experience with this man, going back to 1929, which is 25 years, and there is a kind of seat of the pants feeling which I myself lay great weight. In other words, I might even venture to differ from the judgment of the board without impugning their integrity at all.

Q. I am confining my question to that one incident, Doctor. I think we have agreed that the board may be in possession of information from Dr. Oppenheimer's own lips about that incident which is not now available to you, is that correct?

A. This is a statement?

Q. Yes.

A. I accept your statement.

Q. And therefore it may well be that the board is now in a better position than you, so far as that incident is concerned, to evaluate it?

A. An incident of that sort they may be. I can't say they are not. But on the other hand, I think that any incident in a man's line of something of that sort you have to take it in sum.

Q. Of course.

A. You have to take the whole story.

Q. Of course.

A. That is what novels are about. There is a dramatic moment and the history of the man, what made him act, what he did, and what sort of person he was. That is what you are really doing here. You are writing a man's life.

Q. Of course, but as a scientist, Doctor, and evaluating, we will say, an explosion you perhaps would be in a better position to evaluate an explosion having witnessed it and having first-hand knowledge about it than somebody who had not, is that right?

A. If you put it in that way, I don't know the trend of your question. I am not fencing with you. I really want to know what you are getting at.

Q. I am not fencing with you either.

A. If you are saying that an eyewitness to something can give a better account of it than a historian, that I don't know. Historians would deny it. It is a semantic question, but if you want to be specific about it——

Q. I will put it this way. As a scientist, you would say that one having all the facts about a particular physical manifestation or reaction would be in a better position to evaluate that than somebody who did not have all of the facts or might not know one of the facts?

A. A lot of the things about this are not the sort of things which you term just facts. We have Mr. Morgan here, for example, who has been the head of a big business which he built up. He gets as many facts as possible, but I am sure beyond that there is a lot of experience and color which make his judgment. In a court of law it might be something else. Ultimately you go to a jury who have facts, and then they add a whole lot of things which your heart identifies as facts and their experience in life to a situation. I was afraid your question was tending to put me in the position of a so-called fiction scientist who looks at certain facts and measurements, and we are not talking about such a situation.

Q. Let me get back again to the concrete. Would you agree, Doctor, that in evaluating the Chevalier incident one should consider what Dr. Oppenheimer says happended in that incident, together with the testimony of persons such as yourself?

A. Wait a minute. I didn't testify to that incident because I have only heard about it.

Q. Together with testimony of persons such as yourself about Dr. Oppenheimer.

A. Yes, that is right.

Q. Very well; therefore, one who had heard Dr. Oppenheimer describe the incident and had heard your testimony would be in a better position to evaluate it than one who had not heard Dr. Oppenheimer describe it, is that correct?

A. I will put it this way. I think this committee is going into this and they will be in as good a position as it is humanly possible to be for people who have never met this man before to make a judgment about it. I certainly reserve the right to my own opinion on this, because I am in the possession of a long period of association, with all sorts of minute reactions. I have seen his mind work. I have seen his sentiments develop. For example, I have seen in the last few years something which surprised me, a certain tendency of Dr. Oppenheimer to be inclined toward a preventive war. Nothing went all the way. But talking and thinking about it quite seriously. I have to add everything of that sort. All sorts of color and form my own opinion. But I am not on this board, and I think this board is trying to do what it can in this business of getting testimony, the kind of people to come talk to them, the evaluation of the people and the kind of insight, whether they are just loyal people or whether they have thought about the problem, and so on. It is a tough job. Bpt nevertheless, I say I will still stick to my right to have my own opinion.

Then Dr. Rabi, on a longer and more detailed statement of the episode by Oppenheimer's counsel, gave his opinion and was again cross-examined on it by Robb.

The WITNESS. The only comment I can make on this right off is that it is part and parcel of the kind of foolish behavior that occurred in the early part of the record, that there were very strong personal loyalties there, and I take it in mentioning Eltenton he felt he had discharged his full obligation. My comment is that it was a very foolish action, but I would not put a sinister implication to it. The record is full of actions before Oppenheimer became the sort of statesman he is now of that sort of thing.

By Mr. MARKS:

Q. Are you confident or are you not confident, Dr. Rabi, whichever it is—let me put it this way. Are you confident that Dr. Oppenheimer would not make the kind of mistake again?

A. I certainly am. He is a man who learns with extraordinary rapidity.

Q. Would you agree that incident involved a conflict in loyalties?

A. The question is whether to my mind, whether it involved a conflict of loyalties within his own heart. I don't think it did in his own heart, at least from what you tell me, and taking the sum total. Apparently Chevalier was a man of whom he was very fond personally. They shared a mutual interest, I presume, of French literature. I don't think I have met the gentleman. By pointing the finger at Eltenton I think he felt that he had done the necessary thing for the protection of security. I think if he thought about it more profoundly at the time, and were not so tremendously occupied and burdened by the Los Alamos problems, he might have seen that and this was certainly something that he could not hope to keep quiet. It was a great mistake in judgment and everything else. He should have swallowed that bitter pill at once. But I read no sinister implication in it.

Q. Would you be confident or would you not be confident that today he would resolve the question of his responsibility on the one hand to the country or the public in a way that you would?

A. I think he would be very conscious of his position, not to impair his usefulness to the United States. Even though he might not have shared certain fears, he would not have taken that particular responsibility of withholding that information and have run that particular personal danger of doing it. I think he is just a much more mature person than he was then.

I want you to consider one more such opinion for the same reason. It is John von Neumann's. He is the man whose calculating machines were so essential to the development of a nuclear bomb. He was strongly in favor of going ahead with the H-bomb against Oppenheimer's opinion. We'll come to all that later. Von Neumann has known Oppenheimer since 1926, and he has been his neighbor and his colleague at Princeton since 1947. It was Robb who stated the hypothetical question to Von Neumann, and needless to say Robb brought out all the worst and most derogatory features.

Von Neumann's answer ran this way:

A. Look, you have to view the performance and the character of a man as a whole. This episode, if true, would make me think that the course of the year 1943 or in 1942 and 1943, he was not emotionally and intellectually prepared to handle this kind of a job; that he subsequently learned how to handle it, and handled it very well, I know. I would say that all of us in the war years, and by all of us, I mean all people in scientific technical occupations got suddenly in contact with a universe we had not known before. I mean this peculiar problem of security, the fact that people who looked all right might be conspirators and might be spies. They are all things which do not enter one's normal experience in ordinary times. While we are now most of us quite prepared to discover such things in our entourage, we were not prepared to discover these things in 1943. So I must say that this had on anyone a shock effect, and any one of us may have behaved foolishly and ineffectively and untruthfully, so this condition is something ten years later, I would not consider too serious. This would affect me the same way as if I would suddenly hear about somebody that he has had some extraordinary escapade in his adolescence. I know that neither of us were adolescents at that time, but of course we were all little children with respect to the situation which had developed, namely, that we suddenly were dealing with something with which one could blow up the world. Furthermore, we were involved in a triangular war with two of our enemies had done suddenly the nice thing of fighting each other. But after all, they were still enemies. This was a very peculiar situation. None of us had been educated or conditioned to exist in this situation, and we had to make our rationalization and our code of conduct as we went along.
For some people it took 2 months, for some 2 years, and for some 1 year. I am quite sure that all of us by now have developed the necessary code of ethics and the necessary resistance.
So if this story is true, that would just give me a piece of information on how long it took Dr. Oppenheimer to get adjusted to this Buck Rogers universe, but no more. I have no slightest doubt that he was not adjusted to it in 1944 or 1945.

Von Neumann's explanation, you see, is much the same as General Groves's. To the general, Oppenheimer's attitude was that of "the typical American school boy." To the professor, we were all "little children" at that time, at least "all of us" professors were, toward "this peculiar problem of security" and "this Buck Rogers universe." We were "adolescents," even if we happened to be thirty-nine years old. And, you will notice, that is just what General Groves thought of his scientists, from Niels Bohr, the oldest of them, down; and, the general added, Oppenheimer "was no worse than any of my other leading scientists."

Finally, let us see what the Board thought.

The Board found that Nichols' allegations about this episode were "substantially true." The only mention of the episode in Gray's and Morgan's opinion was this reference to it: "Beginning with the Chevalier incident he [Oppenheimer] has repeatedly exercised an arrogance of his own judgment with respect to the loyalty and reliability of other citizens to an extent which has frustrated and at times impeded the workings of the [security] system."

So I think we may take it that their view of the incident was what Gray stated his own to be in the course of the hearings. He said, during Dr. Rabi's testimony, "This was simply a question of not taking immediate security precautions either in respect to reporting the incident, a later matter of declining to disclose the name of the man who made the approach, and certain other less than frank aspects."

So much for the Chevalier episode.

Just as the episode itself is of greater interest and importance than all the other early derogatory items, so Oppenheimer's continued association with the Chevaliers gave the Board greater concern than his occasional meetings and other associations with his other early associates. I will tell about his continued relations with the Chevaliers first.

One thing should be borne in mind: Oppenheimer was under constant and unremitting surveillance. We can be sure that we know every instance when his former associates crossed his path later. And they were few. Oppenheimer's life and his associations were expanding. He had become one of the leading scientists of the country and as well known abroad as he was here.

Oppenheimer's continued relations with the Chevaliers was a continued friendship. It was also, in the eyes of the Board, "of a high degree of significance." This being the case, I will not undertake to give an account of it myself. I will let Oppenheimer speak for himself, with some additions from the testimony of Mrs. Oppenheimer.

The first time Oppenheimer saw Chevalier again was in June or July 1946, in Berkeley, after he and Eltenton had been interviewed by the F.B.I. Robb cross-examined Oppenheimer.

> Doctor, did Naakon Chevalier tell you he had been interviewed by the FBI about the Eltenton Chevalier incident?
> A. He did.

Q. When did he tell you that?
A. June or July of 1946.
Q. Shortly after he was interviewed?
A. Fairly shortly after.
Q. Did he tell you how long before that he had been interviewed?
A. I don't remember.
Q. Did you get the impression that it had been very recent?
A. I don't recollect the time interval. It was not a year or a month or month or anything—or a half year.
Q. What did he tell you about the interview?
A. He told me that he and Eltenton had been interviewed simultaneously, that they had questioned him about his approach to me.
Q. What else?
A. That they had asked him if he had approached anyone else, and I think—well, that they picked him up at Stimson Beach and had taken him into headquarters.
Q. Anything else?
A. That they pressed him about whether he talked to anyone else.
Q. Did he tell you what he said?
A. Not in any detail.
Q. How did he give you that information—in person or by telephone or by letter, or what?
A. What I recollect is that he came to our home.
Q. In Berkeley?
A. Yes.
Q. Was that before or after you were interviewed by the FBI?
A. It was quite a while before.
Q. So when you were interviewed by the FBI you knew substantially what Chevalier had told them?
A. Not in great detail.
Q. I said substantially.
A. Yes, I think so.
Q. Did you also learn what Eltenton had said?
A. No.
Q. Did you attempt to find out?
A. No.

The next time was in 1950. Chevalier came to Princeton and stayed a couple of days with the Oppenheimers. It was just after Chevalier had been divorced. Oppenheimer testified, cross-examined by Robb:

Q. Doctor, just so the record will be complete, do you recall in 1950 getting a letter from Dr. Chevalier who was then in San Francisco asking you to assist him by telling him what you testified before the House committee about the Chevalier-Eltenton incident?
A. Yes, I remember.
Q. Do you recall answering that letter?
A. I did answer it. I think I did not tell him what I testified, because it was in executive session, but referred him to a press account of what I testified. I am not quite certain on this point.
Q. At that time he was attempting to get a passport to leave the United States, was he?
A. I thought that was later, but I am not sure.
Q. That may have been. You did hear about it when he was attempting to get a passport; did you?
A. Yes.
Q. We will come to that later.
I will read you and ask you if this is the letter that you wrote to him. I am sorry I haven't a copy of it. On the stationery of the Institute for Advanced Study, Princeton, N. J., office of the director, February 25, 1950:

"DR. HAAKON CHEVALIER
    "*3127 Washington Street*
    "*San Francisco, Calif.*

"DEAR HAAKON : Thank you for your good letter of February 21. I can understand that an account of my testimony before the House committee could be helpful to you in seeking a suitable academic position at this time. I cannot send it to you because I have never myself had a transcript, and because the committee ruled at the time that they desired to keep, and would keep, the hearings secret. But I can tell you what I said. I told them that I would like as far as possible to clear the record with regard to your alleged involvement in the atom business. I said that as far as I knew, you knew nothing of the atom bomb until it was announced after Hiroshima; and that most certainly you had never mentioned it or anything that could be connected with it to me. I said that you had never asked me to transmit any kind of information, nor suggested that I could do so, or that I consider doing so. I said that you had told me of a discussion of providing technical information to the U. S. S. R. which disturbed you considerably, and which you thought I ought to know about. There were surely many other points; but these were, I think, the highlights; and if this account can be of use to you, I hope that you will feel free to use it.

"As you know, I have been deeply disturbed by the threat to your career which these ugly stories could constitute. If I can help you in that, you may call on me.'

"Sincerely yours,

                                  "ROBERT OPPENHEIMER."

Did you write that letter?
A. Oh, sure. I didn't recollect it.
Q. Was the account of your testimony which you gave there an accurate one?
A. I think it is fairly accurate.
Q. Dr. Chevalier thereafter used that letter in connection with his passport application.
A. I didn't know that.
Q. Did you talk to him about his passport application?
A. I did. He came to Princeton at the time and I referred him to counsel to help him with it.
Q. To whom did you refer him?
A. Joe Fanelli.
Q. In Washington?
A. Right.
Q. Is that the same Joe Fanelli who represented Mr. Weinberg in his criminal trial?
A. I believe it is.
Q. Was he a friend of yours, Fanelli?
A. No. I had not met him at the time I referred Chevalier to him, but he represented my brother at the time of his appearance before the House Un-American Committee. Wait just a minute——
Mr. ROBB. Mr. Chairman, I am sorry. I don't think counsel should coach the witness.
The WITNESS. You are quite right.
Mr. MARKS. I am very sorry.
Mr. ROBB. Will you resume?
The WITNESS. I did hear the correction.
Mr. ROBB. I hope it won't happen in the future.

Mr. GRAY. I think we should be careful, counsel, if you do not mind. I should repeat I think at this time because Mr. Marks has not been present before, that we consider under the regulations, spirit and letter that this it not a trial but an inquiry. Very considerable latitude, as you have observed and we have all experienced, is certainly allowed, and is to continue, in not trying to conform to rigid court procedures. But as far as the testimony of a witness is concerned, it must be his own testimony.
The WITNESS. I am sorry I did hear it. I was mistaken.
Mr. GRAY. The purpose of the inquiry is not entrapment.
The WITNESS. I understand that. I met Fanelli at one time, but I believe it was after I referred Chevalier to him. I met him first on the train going from Washington to Princeton where I was introduced by a friend, and I met him later in the preparation for the Weinberg case. But he had been recom-

mended to me very highly, and I suggested him to Chevalier.

By Mr. ROBB:

Q. Dr. Chevalier came to Princeton to see you about the matter?

A. He came and stayed a couple of days.   I don't think it would be right to say he came to see me about the passport problem.   He had just been divorced.   He talked of nothing but his divorce.   But he was worried about whether to use an American passport or his French passport.

Q. About when was that, Doctor?

A. Could it have been the spring of 1951?

Q. I don't know.

A. It was immediately at the time he left the country.

Q. You had previously met Mr. Fanelli?

A. I believe I did not meet him until after this.

Q. Who, Doctor, had so highly recommended Fanelli to you?

A. I had heard him warmly spoken of by Mr. Marks.   I think that is what it was.

Q. Who was the friend that was on the train with you?

A. Two, Sumner Pike, and Archie Alexander.

Q. I believe you said that your account of your testimony which you gave to Dr. Chevalier in your letter of February 24, 1950, was substantially accurate to the best of your recollection?

A. It was intended not to be misleading and to be reassuring.

Q. And had your testimony to which this letter referred been true?   Was it the truth?

A. My testimony was certainly true.

The last time was in December 1953. The Oppenheimers had gone to England, where he delivered the Reith Lectures. Then they went to Paris. Robb started with Oppenheimer's awareness of Chevalier's Communistic ties, and then went on:

Q. When did you last see him?

A. On my last trip to Europe.   He is living in Paris, divorced and has been remarried.   We had dinner with them one evening.   The origin of this, or at least part of the origin——

Q. May I interpose?   That was in December 1953?

A. Yes, December.

Q. Go ahead.

A. He wrote me a note saying that he had been at UNESCO and had run into Professor Bohr who told him I was coming to Europe—we were coming to Europe.

Q. Professor who?

A. B-o-h-r.   He asked us to look him up if we got to Paris.   We planned to do so.   My wife called.   He was out of town on a job.   He got back and we had dinner together, the four of us.

The next day he picked us up and drove us out to visit with Malraux, who has had rather major political changes since 1936.   We had a conversation of about an hour and he drove us back to the hotel.

Dr. EVANS. How long was Bohr in this country?

The WITNESS. Bohr?

Dr. EVANS. Yes.

The WITNESS. He has been here many different times.

Dr. EVANS. Just about the time that you began the work.

The WITNESS. He arrived early in 1944 and left about mid-1945; so that would be a year and a half.

Dr. EVANS. Did he go under the name of Bohr here?

The WITNESS. He had the code name of Nicholas Baker.

By Mr. ROBB:

Q. What kind of a code was that?

A. It was meant to conceal from people who should know that he was in this country and working on the atomic project.

Q. I see. Getting back to your visit with Chevalier in December 1953, was Dr. Malraux the gentleman who first introduced you to Chevalier?

A. He did not introduce me. He was the speaker at a meeting at which Chevalier presided. Malraux became a violent supporter of De Gaulle and his great brainman and deserted politics and went into purely philosophic and literary work. Our talk was purely of that.

Q. What was your conversation with Chevalier that you said you had for about an hour?

A. With Malreaux that was.

Q. It was not with Chevalier?

A. Chevalier took us there. We had dinner with him and his new wife the night before. The talk was personal, diffuse, and about how they were living and how we were living.

Q. Did you talk about Chevalier's passport?

A. No.

Q. Did you thereafter go to the American Embassy to assist Dr. Chevalier in getting a passport to come back to this country?

A. No.

Q. Do you know a Dr. Jeoffrey Wyman?

A. Yes, I do.

Q. Who is he?

A. He is the science attaché of the State Department in Paris. He is a man I knew at Harvard when I was a student there and Cambridge. He resigned from Harvard to accept this job.

The first day or so my wife and I were in Paris we called at the Embassy and we called on the Chargé d'Affaires, the Ambassador was ill and away, and Wyman asked us to lunch and we had lunch with him. This was a propriety. We didn't see Wyman again.

Q. Did you discuss with Wyman or anybody else the matter of Chevalier's passport?

A. I did not.

Q. At any time?

A. At no time.

* * *

Q. Is it clear to you that in your visit in the late fall of 1953 to Paris, you did not in any way get involved in Dr. Chevalier's passport problems as of the present time?

A. I don't believe I became involved in them. I am not even sure he discussed them with me.

Q. You say he did discuss them with you?

A. I am not even sure he discussed them with me. I am sure he discussed one point with me at length, which was his continued employment at UNESCO.

Q. You don't remember discussing with him the best possible way to get information on his part about a passport, or the way to obtain a passport?

A. That could well have happened and I would have referred him to the embassy.

Q. Did you in fact do so?

A. If I were sure I would tell you.

Q. I am putting some of the same questions to you now, Dr. Oppenheimer, that Mr. Robb put earlier.

A. Right.

Q. You had luncheon I believe with Mr. Wymans of the embassy?

A. That is right.

Q. I believe you testified on the question of Mr. Robb you did not discuss Mr. Chevalier's passport problem with Mr. Wymans?

A. No, I saw Mr. Wymans long before I saw Mr. Chevalier; not long before, but well a week before.

Q. Have you been in communication with Chevalier since the time you had luncheon with Mr. Wymans?

A. Yes; I saw Chevalier after my lunch with Wymans, but not the other way around.

Q. Have you been in communication with Chevalier since the evening you spent with him?

A. The next day we drove out to visit Malraux.

Q. Yes; you testified about that. Have you been in communication with him since that time?

A. No. Well, we had a card from him, just for my birthday.

Dr. Evans. When did you get that card?

The Witness. Around my birthday, which was during these hearings. I don't recall this. I could have advised Chevalier to consult Wymans with regard to his passport.

By Mr. Gray:

Q. I am sure that you could have, because I believe it to be true that he did, and specifically stated that it was at your suggestion that he do so. I want again to ask you whether you had conversations with anybody else other than Chevalier about his passport problem while you were in Paris in the late fall? I think I am asking you, is it clear to you that you did not?

A. It is quite clear to me. If—I believe I saw no one at the Embassy after seeing Chevalier or no one connected with the Embassy.

Q. Do you have any guess or knowledge as to whether Chevalier today is active in Communist Party affairs?

A. I have a strong, strong guess that he is not. I have no knowledge. His new wife is an extremely sensible, wholly un-Communist girl. The other person we saw together was a man who has become a violent anti-Communist and is now apolitical. I don't have knowledge.

There is not much to add. But Mrs. Oppenheimer testified, and here is what she said:

Q. You saw Dr. Chevalier in France last fall?

A. That is right, in December.

Q. In Paris?

A. In Paris.

Q. How long were you in Paris on that occasion?

A. Well, let's see. We went over—I think we spent 2 days and then went up to Copenhagen and came back, and I think we spent something like a week again. It may have been 5 days or it may have been a little longer than a week; I do not remember.

Q. Was it on the first 2 days that you saw Dr. Chevalier?

A. No.

Q. You mean after you came back from Copenhagen you saw him?

A. I think so, yes.

Q. Do you recall how you happened to get in touch with him?

A. Yes, I do.

Q. Would you tell us that?

A. I called his wife and said we would like to see them. She said that Haakon was in Italy, but she thought he would be back and she would let us know.

Q. Do you remember how you happened to have her telephone number?

A. It was in the book. I think it was in the book. I think I looked it up. On the other hand, I may have had a note from Haakon in my purse with the telephone number on it, which I would have taken along because if we went to Paris we wanted to see them.

Q. Do you recall how you happened to know they were in Paris at all?

A. Yes. I think Haakon wrote us.

Q. How long before you went there?

A. I think he has written us probably 3 or 4 times in the last few years.

Q. I suppose he expressed a hope that if you came there you would look him up?

A. Certainly.

Q. Do you know how he happened to know you might come to Paris?

A. I remember his wife saying to me that they had read in the paper that Robert was giving lectures in England.

Q. This was the occasion of these Reith lectures?

A. R-e-i-t-h.

Q. Do you recall whom else you saw in Paris on that occasion?

A. Yes. Oh, my, now wait. We saw LePrince-Ringuet and we saw a number of physicists. I do not know whether both Auger or Perrin or whether it was just one of them. We went to the apartment of another physicist whose name I can't remember. I will have to ask Robert.

Dr. OPPENHEIMER. May I answer? Goldschmidt.

By Mr. ROBB:

Q. You saw a number of physicists. I don't care about the names.

A. We saw François and Yvonne de Rose.

Q. I believe you had lunch with the Chevaliers or dinner.

A. Dinner. We had dinner at their house.

Q. And then did you take them to lunch or something?

A. Oh, yes, no.

Q. Did they take you to lunch?

A. No. Haakon called for us and we went out to see Malraux.

Q. Do you remember any discussion about Dr. Chevalier's passport difficulties?

A. I do not remember it but it has been recalled to me since.

Q. How was it recalled to you?

A. I think Robert mentioned it to me.

Q. Would you tell us what he had to say about it?

A. He said that he had been asked whether Haakon had spoken to him about it and he did not remember it.

Q. Did Dr. Oppenheimer tell you pretty generally what he had been asked about matters of which you had knowledge?

A. Yes.

Q. Did you meet a Mr. Wymans when you were in Paris on that occasion?

A. Yes, I did.

Q. How did you happen to meet him?

A. He is a—I don't know—a classmate or something of Harvard. He was at the embassies. We had lunch with him.

At the very close of the hearings Robb put in the letters which Chevalier and Jeffries Wyman had exchanged.

"FEBRUARY 23, 1954.

"Mr. JEFFRIES WYMAN,
    "7, Cité Martignac, Paris, 7e.

"DEAR MR. WYMAN: My friend—and yours—Robert Oppenheimer, gave me your name when he was up for dinner here in our apartment early last December, and urged me to get in touch with you if a personal problem of mine which I discussed with him became pressing. He gave me to understand that I could speak to you with the same frankness and fullness as I have with him, and he with me, during the 15 years of our friendship.

"I should not have presumed to follow-up such a suggestion if it had come from anyone else. But as you know, Opje never tosses off such a suggestion lightly.

"If you are in Paris, or will be in the near future, I should, then, like to see you informally and discuss the problem.

"On rereading what I have written, I have a feeling that I have made the thing sound more formidable than it really is. It's just a decision that I have to make, which is fairly important to me, and which Opje in his grandfatherly way suggested that I shouldn't make before consulting you.

"Very sincerely,

"HAAKON CHEVALIER."

There is a signature and then typed name.
The second letter:

"AMERICAN EMBASSY, PARIS, *March 1, 1954.*

"MR. HAAKON CHEVALIER,
    "19, rue du Mont-Cenis, Paris (18e).

"DEAR MR. CHEVALIER: I have just received your letter of February 23. I shall be delighted to see you and talk over your problem with you. Would you care to have lunch with me at my house on Thursday, the 4th of March, at 1 o'clock? The address is 17, rue Casimir Pèrier, Paris (7e), third story. (The telephone is Invalidés 00–10.)

"Time being rather short, will you let me know your answer by telephone either at my house or preferably here at the embassy (Anjou 74–60, extension 249). If the time I suggest is not convenient we will arrange for another.

"You will notice that my address is not that given you by Bob Oppenheimer. I have moved since he was here.

"Yours sincerely,

"JEFFRIES WYMAN, *Science Attaché.*"

What have we got?

When Chevalier is called in by the F.B.I. in 1946 he tells Oppenheimer about it. Then when Oppenheimer testifies before a Congressional committee, Chevalier asks Oppenheimer what he said. Oppenheimer thinks he did not tell Chevalier what he testified, because it was in executive session, but referred him to a press account. "I am not quite certain on this point." Oppenheimer wrote him a discreet letter. Chevalier used Oppenheimer's letter to help get a passport. Why shouldn't he? And why shouldn't Oppenheimer recommend his brother's lawyer to Chevalier, even if he had represented his brother before the House Un-American Activities Committee? As a matter of fact, there was no evidence that Fanelli had represented Frank Oppenheimer before the House Un-American Activities Committee. If you will reread the extract from Oppenheimer's cross-examination, you will see that Oppenheimer was corrected by Marks and said he was mistaken. If you missed it, so did the Board, for the Board made a finding that Fanelli had represented Frank. Nor did it seem to matter to the Board, nor to Gray, who was a lawyer, that Weinberg, whom Fanelli represented in his criminal trial, was acquitted.

After Chevalier's divorce, he came to Princeton and stayed with the Oppenheimers for a couple of days. When Oppenheimer goes abroad to give the Reith Lectures—which were broadcast, by the way, by the BBC and published in this country by Simon and Schuster—the Oppenheimers look up the Chevaliers in Paris. They dine with them. They go out with them to call on André Malraux.

To Gray and Morgan, he is "a Dr. Malraux" who had given a speech at a meeting in California in favor of Spanish relief in 1938 at which Chevalier had presided. Chevalier is the translator of Malraux's novels. Malraux is one of the leading authors of France. But this is not the point. For years Malraux has been one of those who were closest to De Gaulle. Oppenheimer told them this. Obviously he had become one of the stiffest anti-Communists in

France, "a violent anti-Communist," as Oppenheimer told them. Gray and Morgan would not believe him, but the very fact that Malraux had Chevalier as his translator and the further fact that Chevalier was able to take the Oppenheimers to see him testify that Chevalier could no longer be regarded as Communist, whatever and however he may have been.

Gray and Morgan did not know who Malraux was, but they must know who James Burnham is and what his attitude toward Communism is. They should read a dialogue between Burnham and Malraux which Random House published in 1948 under the title *The Case for De Gaulle*. There they would see that Malraux is no less anti-Communist than Burnham. It is also a pity that Janet Flanner's two articles on Malraux in *The New Yorker* in November 1954 were not published in time.

Chevalier is bothered by the question whether he will be cleared to work for UNESCO unless he renounces his American citizenship. So Oppenheimer refers him to an old friend of his at the American Embassy, Professor Jeffries Wyman, whom he knew in college at Harvard. Wyman, by the way, is the son of Jeffries Wyman, a colleague of the great botanist Asa Gray. And, if it is of any importance, he married first a Cabot of Boston and then a Forbes of Milton. Oppenheimer lunches with Wyman and says nothing about Chevalier or his troubles.

The Board makes no mention of the affidavit which Jeffries Wyman gave that "Dr. Oppenheimer did not at that time or later mention or endorse Chevalier." This is the way Smyth stated the substance of Wyman's affidavit in his dissenting opinion. Smyth said it was "in the record." It must have come in after the hearings before the Board closed, for it is not in the transcript. But certainly the Commission had it before them, or Smyth could not have read it. It breaks the candor, if not the veracity, of the remark which Strauss made for the majority of the Commission that Oppenheimer "lent his name to Chevalier's dealings with the United States Embassy in Paris on a problem which, according to Dr. Oppenheimer, involved Chevalier's clearance." What a pity it is to have to scrutinize people's statements!

To see anything derogatory in all this takes a mind overwhelmed by the duty of shifting the burden of proof upon Oppenheimer. Doing your duty seems sometimes to unfit you for doing anything else. Or you can put it another way. It is a question of where discretion ceases and priggishness begins. Guilt by association is bad enough and hard enough to rest a secure judgment on. We must not magnify it and simplify it into contamination, as the Pharisees do.

Yet Gray and Morgan believed that Oppenheimer's "current associations with Dr. Chevalier" were "of a high degree of significance." "It is not important," they said, "to determine that Dr. Oppenheimer discussed with Chevalier matters of concern to the security of the United States." Why not? What mattered was that Oppenheimer had associated at all with Chevalier. As Gray and Morgan went on to say, "What is important is that Chevalier's Communist background and activities were known to Dr. Oppenheimer." Nor does it matter that Oppenheimer believed Chevalier was no longer a Communist. "While he says he believes Chevalier is not now a Communist, his association with him, on what could not be considered a casual basis, is not the kind of thing that our security system permits on the part of one who customarily has access to information of the highest classification." Why not? Gray himself did not know whether Chevalier is a Communist. "I don't know," Gray said, "whether he is a member of the Communist Party or not. It is conceivable that he might have been."

"Loyalty to one's friends," Gray and Morgan said, "is one of the noblest qualities. Being loyal to one's friends above reasonable obligations to the country and to the security system, however, is not clearly consistent with the interests of security." Friendship seems to make it all the worse.

8. OTHER CONTINUED ASSOCIATIONS

For a man with so many and such unimpeachably respectable associations, not to speak of their distinction, consider the other half-dozen continued associations which Nichols regarded as derogatory. As I say, we may be sure that these are all there were; and none of them, you will observe, is a new relation. They are all of them hangovers, some trivial, others unavoidable, from Oppenheimer's salad days. I am going to take only those since the end of the war, 1945. You are familiar with Oppenheimer's earlier associations from reading Nichols' letter and Oppenheimer's reply.

In 1945 Oppenheimer's brother, Frank, and his wife went to the Russian Consulate in San Francisco to attend an informal reception for the Russian scientists who were delegates to the United Nations' Conference. And in 1946 Frank agreed to give a six-week course at the California Labor School, which was later listed by the Attorney General as a Communist organization. On January 1, 1946, Oppenheimer attended a meeting at Frank's house where two members of the Communist Party—David Adelson and Paul Pinsky—were present, and Oppenheimer "analyzed some material which Pinsky hoped to take up with the Legislative Convention in Sacramento, California." Oppenheimer did not know they were members of the Communist Party.

Early in 1946, Oppenheimer was made vice-chairman of an organization which "has been cited by the House Committee on Un-American Activities as a Communist front." It was the Independent Citizens Committee of the Arts, Sciences, and Professions. Oppenheimer soon found that he disagreed with its policies and he resigned in October. What he did not agree with, and the reason he resigned, was the Committee's support of Henry Wallace's proposals for the internationalizing of atomic energy.

Just what is there derogatory about this? Oppenheimer resigned as soon as he saw something wrong, within a few months. I wonder whether any of the other eight vice-chairmen resigned any sooner than Oppenheimer. It was not bad company. They were Joseph E. Davies, then the chairman of the War Relief Control Board, who in that very year received the Medal of Merit; General Carlson of the Marines and Carlson's Raiders; Norman Cousins, who that year received the first Wendell Willkie Award; Reuben G. Gustafson, who was leaving the presidency of the University of Colorado to become Dean of Faculties at the University of Chicago; Fiorello La Guardia, ending his third term as Mayor of New York and then Director General of UNRRA; Paul Robeson; Harlow Shapley, the director of the Harvard Observatory and our foremost astronomer; and Frank Sinatra.

If you are interested in this piece of derogatory information, look up the issue of *Time* for September 9, 1946, a month before Oppenheimer's resignation, where ICCASP is the story of the week. Jo Davidson, the sculptor, is on the cover. He was the president. When Harold Ickes resigned as Secretary of the Interior in February, he became its executive director soon after Oppenheimer became one of its nine vice-presidents. Ickes, too, resigned a month or so after Oppenheimer did. (The New York *Times*, November 12, 1946.)

I still fail to see anything at all derogatory here. New Deal, yes; derogatory, no. Nichols' charge says that ICCASP "has been cited as a Communist-front by the House Committee on Un-American Activities." I do not find that it ever was. I may be wrong, but if I am, the House Committee made no public announcement of it before Oppenheimer's resignation in October 1946. I do find that the Tenney Committee of the California Legislature cited it as a Communist front, but that was five months later, in March 1947. (The New York *Times*, March 25, 1947.) If this were the reason why Oppenheimer and Ickes resigned, they were by so much the more alert. Up to the time of the hearings ICCASP had not been on any of the Attorney General's lists, nor since, through 1954, so far as I can tell from the Federal Register, where the Attorney General officially lists subversive organizations. To be sure, ICCASP may have ceased to exist.

The importance of this item lies not in anything derogatory in it, for there is none, but in the fact that the Board took Oppenheimer's resignation in October 1946 as "the first affirmative action on his part which would indicate complete rejection" of his "sympathetic interests" in communism. The Board said that "it was at this time that he finally realized that he could not collaborate with the Communists, whatever their aims and professed interests. We would prefer to have found an affirmative action at an earlier date."

This last remark should not be misconstrued. Oppenheimer could scarcely have been expected to resign from ICCASP any sooner than he did, but quite aside from this, it would be a mistake to identify his resignation with a rejection of communism, though they came at about the same time. He resigned because he disagreed with ICCASP's foreign policy, particularly in the international problem of the atomic bomb, where ICCASP had adopted Henry Wallace's recommendations, which seemed illusory to Oppenheimer. He made this clear in his letter of resignation.

The Board was referring not to Oppenheimer's resignation but to the date when he ceased to be "a fellow traveler." When Robb asked Oppenheimer if he could "set a date when you were sure you were no longer fellow traveling," Oppenheimer said, "I think I can put it this way. After the war and about the time of . . . my letter to the Independent Citizens Committee, I was clear that I would not collaborate with Communists no matter how much I sympathized with what they pretended to be after. This was absolute. I believe I have not done so since . . . but I think to call me a fellow traveler in 1944 or 1946 would be to distort the meaning of the word as I explained it." This is what the Board was referring to when it said, "We would prefer to have found an affirmative action at an earlier date."

How much earlier? A year earlier? This was October 1946. As soon as Oppenheimer left Los Alamos on October 16, 1945? I do not see how the Board could prefer this earlier date without passing the same judgment on Henry L. Stimson and the opinions he expressed as Secretary of War in a memorandum he wrote the President on September 11, 1945. It was published in McGeorge Bundy's book, *On Active Service* (Harper & Bros., 1948, p. 642 ff.)

Here we step into considerations which are giving us as much concern now as they gave Oppenheimer and Stimson ten years ago, and so I do not hesitate to press the point. Stimson, near the end of his great service as Secretary of War, wrote President Truman:

To put the matter concisely, I consider the problem of our satisfactory relations with Russia as not merely connected with but as virtually dominated by the problem of the atomic bomb. Except for the problem of the control of that bomb, those relations, while vitally important, might not be immediately pressing. The establishment of relations of mutual confidence between her and us could afford to await the slow progress of time. But with the discovery of the bomb, they became immediately emergent. Those relations may be perhaps irretrievably embittered by the way in which we approach the solution of the bomb with Russia. For if we fail to approach them now and merely continue to negotiate with them, having this weapon rather ostentatiously on our hip, their suspicions and their distrust of our purposes and motives will increase. It will inspire them to greater efforts in an all-out effort to solve the problem. If the solution is achieved in that spirit, it is much less likely that we will ever get the kind of covenant we may desperately need in the future. This risk is, I believe, greater than the other, inasmuch as our objective must be to get the best kind of international bargain we can— one that has some chance of being kept and saving civilization not for five or for twenty years, but forever.

The chief lesson I have learned in a long life is that the only way you can make a man trustworthy is to trust him, and the surest way to make him untrustworthy is to distrust him and show your distrust.

If the atomic bomb were merely another though more devastating military weapon to be assimilated into our pattern of international relations, it would be one thing. We could then follow the old custom of secrecy and nationalistic military superiority relying on international caution to prescribe the future use of the weapon as we did with gas. But I think the bomb instead constitutes merely a first step in a new control by man over the forces of nature too revolutionary and dangerous to fit into the old concepts. I think it really caps the climax of the race between man's growing technical power for destructiveness and his psychological power of self-control and group control—his moral power. If so, our method of approach to the Russians is a question of the most vital importance in the evolution of human progress.

Fellow traveling? Wherein does Stimson's advice to the President in September 1945 differ from the attitude toward the Communists which the Board wished Oppenheimer had rejected by some affirmative action earlier than October 1946?

Stimson too changed his opinion and his attitude toward the Communists, but not, I think, as soon as Oppenheimer did. Bundy goes on, after quoting the memorandum, to say:

These opinions, which he urgently expressed again to the President and the Cabinet on the day of his retirement, were the ones with which Stimson left office. As an expression of his views in 1947, they were seriously incomplete. A major point of his September memorandum was that the best way to make a man trustworthy was to trust him. This point he publicly re-emphasized in his last press conference. But what if the man whose trust you sought was a cynical "realist" who did not choose to be your friend? What if Stalin and his lieutenants were in this final and essential test of purpose no different from Hitler? What if the police state were no transitional revolutionary device but a fixed and inevitable accompaniment of nationalistic aggression? Would trust and candor by themselves break down or even modify the menace to the world in such a case?

These questions and others like them acquired for Stimson new and pregnant meaning in the two years that followed his presentation of the September memorandum. The behavior of the Russians during this period filled him with astonishment and regret. Like many other Americans, he had met and talked with Stalin during the years of effective wartime alliance (at Potsdam in July, 1945). Like other Americans, he had received Stalin's cordial acquiescence in his general statement that Russia and the United States were natural friends and allies. But in the two years after Potsdam Russian policy everywhere was based on broken pledges, and the United States replaced Nazi Germany as the target of Communist abuse.

In October 1947 Stimson wrote an article for *Foreign Affairs* in which he said:

We have been very patient with the Soviet Government, and very hopeful of its good intentions. I have been among those who shared in these hopes and counseled this patience. The magnificent and loyal war effort of the Russian people, and the great successful efforts at friendliness made during the war by President Roosevelt, gave us good reason for hope. I have believed—and I still believe—that we must show good faith in all our dealings with the Russians, and that only by so doing can we leave the door open for Russian good faith toward us. I cannot too strongly express my regret that since the early spring of 1945—even before the death of Mr. Roosevelt—the Soviet Government has steadily pursued an obstructive and unfriendly course. It has been our hope that the Russians would choose to be our friends; it was and is our conviction that such a choice would be to their advantage. But, for the time being, at least, those who determine Russian policy have chosen otherwise, and their choice has been slavishly followed by Communists everywhere.

No sensible American can now ignore this fact, and those who now choose to travel in company with American Communists are very clearly either knaves or fools. This is a judgment which I make reluctantly, but there is no help for it. I have often said that the surest way to make a man trustworthy is to trust him. But I must add that this does not always apply to a man who is determined to make you his dupe. Before we can make friends with the Russians, their leaders will have to be convinced that they have nothing to gain, and everything to lose, by acting on the assumption that our society is dying and that our principles are outworn. Americans who think they can make common cause with present-day communism are living in a world that does not exist.

We are far beyond caviling over the date when the Board would have preferred to find Oppenheimer wiser than he had been. We are still wading hip-deep through the same swamp, and still feeling with our feet for some hummocks of understanding.

To go back to Oppenheimer's derogatory associations: In 1946 or 1947, Oppenheimer helped David Bohm get an appointment as Assistant Professor of Physics at Princeton. Later, in 1949, Oppenheimer met Bohm and Lomanitz casually on the street in Princeton and talked briefly with them about the testimony they were about to give before the House Committee on Un-American Activities. Oppenheimer told them to tell the truth. Would he have done better not to have stopped and spoken to them? In 1950 he went to a farewell party which Professor Wigner gave for Bohm at Princeton on the occasion of Bohm's leaving for an academic job in Brazil. Oppenheimer said he would have written a letter of recommendation for Bohm if he had been asked to do so.

The point is, Bohm and Lomanitz had been closely associated with the Communist Party, and before the House Committee they pleaded the Fifth Amendment. What concerns us is the significance which Gray and Morgan attached to Oppenheimer's association with them.

Oppenheimer met them on the street. Gray and Morgan said that while it "may have been a casual one, as he testified, he nevertheless discussed with them their testimony before the Committee." Yes, Oppenheimer testified that he told them "they should tell the truth." He said that he did not discuss "whether they would claim their constitutional privilege." I take it that the F.B.I. has a surveillance report on this meeting on the street. I don't believe the F.B.I. has any reason to question Oppenheimer's testimony about what was said.

As to Oppenheimer recommending Bohm for a position in Brazil, Gray and Morgan said Oppenheimer "testified that today he would give Bohm a letter of recommendation as a physicist and, although not asked whether he would also raise questions about Bohm's security status, he in no way indicated that this was a matter of serious import to him." This is slightly inaccurate. Oppenheimer did not say "today." Oppenheimer testified only that he "would have." Dr. Evans said, "I think I would have recommended Bohm as a physicist. Dr. Oppenheimer was not asked if he would have added that Bohm was a Communist."

One last comment on the relevancy and weight of these associations. It was made by a man of great experience and worldly wisdom, George F. Kennan, in reply to a question by Gray. Kennan has been in the Foreign Service of the State Department for twenty-seven years. From 1947 to 1950 he was Director of the Policy Planning Staff. Then he was Counsellor of the Department of State. In 1952 he was our Ambassador to Moscow.

Mr. GRAY. You in your testimony referred to the possible conflicts of conscience a man might have and you used the expression, I think, pity for friends who perhaps have been misguided. I am not sure those were the words, but the general import.

You perhaps are aware that under the act, one of the criteria imposed by the language of the act seems to be the associations of an individual. I know you feel that past associations must be weighed in the light of more recent conduct and other factors you have stated.

Would you feel continued association with individuals falling in this category for whom one would have pity and with respect to whom one might have had conflicts of conscience, was important at all in the situation?

The WITNESS. I would think, Mr. Chairman, that it is a thing which would have to be explained, but I find great difficulty in accepting the belief that a man must rule out all those associations, whether or not they engage in any way his official responsibilities. I think there are certainly times when they are to be avoided. I suppose most of us have had friends or associates whom we have come to regard as misguided with the course of time, and I don't like to think that people in senior capacity in Government should not be permitted or conceded maturity of judgment to know when they can see such a person or when they can't. If they come to you sometimes, I think it is impossible for you to turn them away abruptly or in a cruel way, simply because you are afraid of association with them, so long as what they are asking of you is nothing that affects your governmental work.

I myself say it is a personal view on the part of Christian charity to try to be at least as decent as you can to them.

I realize that it is not advisable for a man in a position of high security to be seen steadily with people about whose loyalty there is a great doubt, unless they happen to be intimates in his family or something like that.

Mr. GRAY. But when you say intimates of his family, you mean blood relationships?

The WITNESS. Something of that sort.

Mr. GRAY. Or marital relationships and things of that sort.

The WITNESS. Yes.

Mr. GRAY. You said an individual should not decline to see such a person if the approach were made by such other person. Would you think it would be questionable if a person in a high position took the initiative himself in seeing one of his former associates about whom there might be some question?

The WITNESS. It is difficult for me to judge in the absence of the knowledge of the circumstances.

Mr. GRAY. I understand.

The WITNESS. I am aware of this as a very difficult problem of professional ethics. It seems to me once or twice I have had conflicts of this sort myself, but I know that in these cases I would always like to have felt that my superiors in

Government had enough confidence in me to let me handle that problem according to my own best conscience. I do worry about the sort of schoolboy relationship to one's friends and acquaintances which gets involved if you apply too rigid standards of security in that respect.

Mr. GRAY. But you would always feel that in any conflict between loyalty to a friend and obligation to government, it would not be a conflict difficult to resolve?

The WITNESS. No, sir; it would not. There is only one way in which it can be resolved, and that is in favor of the Government. If that is impossible, then I would say a man should resign. He should not permit himself to remain in the Government with any conflict of loyalties of that sort.

Mr. GRAY. One of the hard facts of our times of course is the inevitable conflict of the requirements of what we generally refer to as security and what we like to think of unlimited freedoms of man's mind and conscience. This is maybe a major dilemma of our times, at least in this country.

The WITNESS. May I add one thought to what I said before in reply to your question?

Mr. GRAY. Yes.

The WITNESS. I see as one of the most difficult aspects of this problem the trouble that the individual Government official has in arriving at an assessment of the reliability of his friends. I have continued to accept as friends some people who have been criticized publicly and on whose reliability some suspicion has been thrown publicly in this country, because I myself have never seen yet the proof that those charges were correct, and have not considered myself in a position to arrive at a negative judgment about this. I have felt that until it is demonstrated to me that people who are friends of mine really have been guilty of some genuine derelection of their duty to the Government or their loyalty to the Government, it is not for me to jump to conclusions about it, and out of a timidity lest my name be affected with theirs to cut off social relations with them.

I must say when it is demonstrated to me that anyone has been so derelict, then I have no desire to continue the friendship or the association, and especially if I were in Government service I would consider it quite out of the question. But there have been many instances in which one has been torn between the fact that doubts have been raised, but proof has not been given. There I feel that the burden of proof so far as one's relations with one's friends is concerned is on the accuser. Unless it is demonstrated to me that my friend in some way offended against the law or against his governmental duty, I am slow to drop my friend myself.

Perhaps this is as good advice on this now delicate subject as we have.

9. NEW DEROGATORY MATTER

THE BOARD'S OPINION went on to make findings in the last and new charge in Nichols' letter—Oppenheimer's attitudes and positions toward the development of the hydrogen or nuclear bomb from the time the Russians exploded their atomic bomb in 1949 until the spring of 1951, when Teller came up with his brilliant discovery. This is a separate subject, and we will discuss it at length later, because, although the Commission discarded it and each commissioner stated that he paid no attention to it, what Gray and Morgan found significant and derogatory is of great interest. Before we go into that, I want to discuss the new derogatory items which turned up in the course of the hearings.

Gray and Morgan said:

In the course of the proceedings, there developed other facts which raised questions of such serious import as to give us concern about whether the retention of Dr. Oppenheimer's services would be clearly consistent with the security interests of the United States.

It must be said that Dr. Oppenheimer seems to have had a high degree of discretion reflecting an unusual ability to keep to himself vital secrets. However, we do find suggestions of a tendency to be coerced, or at least influenced in conduct over a period of years.

By his own testimony, Dr. Oppenheimer was led to protest the induction into military service of Giovanni Rossi Lomanitz in 1943 by the outraged intercession of Dr. Condon. It is to be remembered that, at this time Dr. Oppenheimer knew of Lomanitz's connections and of his indiscretions. In 1949, Dr. Oppenheimer appeared in executive session before the House Un-American Activities Committee, and at that time was asked about his friend, Dr. Bernard Peters. Dr. Oppenheimer confirmed the substance of an interview with the security officer which took place during the war years and in which he had characterized Dr. Peters as a dangerous Red and former Communist. This testimony soon appeared in the Rochester, N. Y., newspapers. At this time, Dr. Peters was on the staff of the University of Rochester. Dr. Oppenheimer, as a result of protestations by Dr. Condon, by Dr. Peters himself, and by other scientists, then wrote a letter for publication to the Rochester newspaper, which, in effect, repudiated his testimony given in secret session. His testimony before this Board indicated that he failed to appreciate the great impropriety of making statements of one character in a secret session and of a different character for publication, and that he believed that the important thing was to protect Dr. Peters' professional status. In that episode, Dr. Condon's letter, which has appeared in the press, contained a severe attack on Dr. Oppenheimer. Nevertheless, he now testifies that he is prepared to support Dr. Condon in the loyalty investigation of the latter.

Executive Order 10450 in listing criteria to be taken into account in cases of this sort indicates in part the following:

"Section 8 (a) (1) (i) any behavior, activities, or associations which tend to show that the individual is not reliable or trustworthy.

(v) Any facts which furnish reason to believe that the individual may be subjected to coercion, influence, or pressure which may cause him to act contrary to the best interest of the national security."

Whether the incidents referred to clearly indicate a susceptibility to influence or coercion within the meaning of the criteria or whether they simply reflect very bad judgment, they clearly raise the question of Dr. Oppenheimer's understanding, acceptance, and enthusiastic support of the security system. Beginning with the Chevalier incident, he has repeatedly exercised an arrogance of his own judgment with respect to the loyalty and reliability of other citizens to an extent which has frustrated and at times impeded the workings of the system. In an interview with agents of the FBI in 1946, which in good part concerned itself with questions about Chevalier, when asked about a meeting which Dr. Oppenheimer had attended, at which Communists and Communist sympathizers were in attendance, he declined to discuss it on the ground that it was irrelevant, although the meeting itself was held in Chevalier's home. In a subsequent interview, he declined to discuss people he had known to be Communists.

Indeed, in the course of this proceeding, Dr. Oppenheimer recalled pertinent details with respect to Communist meetings and with respect to individuals with Communist connections, which he had never previously disclosed in the many interviews with Government authorities, in spite of the fact that he had been interviewed regarding such matters.

In 1946 or 1947, he assisted David Bohm in getting a position at Princeton and, at least on a casual basis, continued his associations with Bohm after he had reason to know of Bohm's security status. He testified that today he would give Bohm a letter of recommendation as a physicist, and, although not asked whether he would also raise questions about Bohm's security status, he in no way indicated that this was a matter of serious import to him.

While his meeting with Lomanitz and Bohm immediately prior to their appearance before the House Un-American Activities Committee in 1949, at which time both pleaded the fifth amendment, may have been a casual one as he testified, he nevertheless discussed with them their testimony before that committee.

Moreover, his current associations with Dr. Chevalier, as discussed in detail in item No. 23, are, we believe, of a high degree of significance. It is not important to determine that Dr. Oppenheimer discussed with Chevalier matters of concern to the security of the United States. What is important is that Chevalier's Communist background and activities were known to Dr. Oppenheimer. While he says he believes Chevalier is not now a Communist, his association with him, on what could not be considered a casual basis, is not the kind of thing that our security system permits on the part of one who customarily has access to information of the highest classification.

Loyalty to one's friends is one of the noblest of qualities. Being loyal to one's friends above reasonable obligations to the country and to the security system, however, is not clearly consistent with the interests of security.

We are aware that in these instances Dr. Oppenheimer may have been sincere in his interpretation that the security interests of the country were not disserved; we must, however, take a most serious view of this kind of continuing judgment.

Take the question of a susceptibility to influence first. I find it difficult to understand. Gray and Morgan said, "It must be said that Dr. Oppenheimer seems to have had a high degree of discretion reflecting an unusual ability to keep to himself vital secrets. However, we do find suggestions of a tendency to be coerced, or at least influenced in his conduct over a period of years."

Robb had taken quite a contrary slant. He offered testimony to prove that Oppenheimer was a dominating fellow. You may recall that Borden, in his letter, had referred to Oppenheimer's "potent influence" on the H-bomb program.

Professor Latimer, the associate director of the Radiation Laboratory at Berkeley, testified that General Groves was "very definitely" under Oppenheimer's influence; so too were the members of the General Advisory Committee, Conant and the others, "and that is some influence, I assure you." "I had studied this influence that Dr. Oppenheimer had over men. It was a tremendous thing." He said he was amazed at the G.A.C.'s decision on the H-bomb. "I kept turning over in my mind how they could possibly come to these conclusions, and what was in Oppenheimer that gave him such tremendous power over these men."

Professor Alvarez of the University of California at Berkeley expressed his opinion more moderately. He thought that Oppenheimer "is certainly one of the most persuasive men that has ever lived, and he certainly had influence." Conant, Bush and Groves, he said, "respected his opinions and listened to him."

And finally you will recall that Robb had got Oppenheimer himself to admit that he was "an influential physicist" with "a little more influence than anyone else." Indeed, Gray and Morgan themselves, as you will see when we come to Oppenheimer's opposition to the development of an H-bomb, felt "that Dr. Oppenheimer's influence in the atomic scientific circles with respect to the hydrogen bomb was far greater than he would have led this Board to believe in his testimony before the Board."

Nevertheless, Gray and Morgan suggested three occasions on which it seemed to them that it was Oppenheimer who had been influenced, and, as I think we must take it, unduly influenced, or else there's no point. In all three of these instances, which struck Gray and Morgan as evidence of Oppenheimer's susceptibility to influence, the alleged, or suspected, influence was exerted on Oppenheimer by Dr. Condon. Here they are, one by one.

The first was the fact, in Gray's words, that "Dr. Oppenheimer was led to protest the induction into military service of Giovanni Rossi Lomanitz in 1943 by the outraged intercession of Dr. Condon. It is to be remembered that, at this time, Dr. Oppenheimer knew of Lomanitz's connections and of his indiscretions."

Does this show that Oppenheimer could be coerced or influenced to any undue or dangerous degree?

Here is Oppenheimer's account:

Q. As we have seen, there came a time, did there not, when you learned that Lomanitz was about to be inducted into the Army?
A. That is right.

Q. How did you learn that?
A. I first heard it in a letter from Dr. Condon.
Q. Dr. Who?
A. Condon.
Q. Condon?
A. Yes.
Q. What is his first name?
A. Edward.
Q. Edward Condon?
A. That is right.
Q. How did he happen to write you about it?
A. He had been at Los Alamos as associate director and left after a relatively short time and he transferred to Berkeley where he was involved in getting a transition from the laboratory work to the construction work under Westinghouse. He was director of research or associate director of research for Westinghouse. He was working in Berkeley.

One of the things he was working on was this invention that I mentioned a day or so ago. Why he wrote me about it, I don't know. He wrote me about it in a great sense of outrage.
Q. About when was that?
A. I don't recall.
Q. Do you have a copy of that letter?
A. I don't have a copy of that.
Mr. GARRISON. I don't know. I have not seen it.
The WITNESS. I doubt it.

    By Mr. ROBB:

Q. This would be about when?
A. It would have been at the time the matter came up.
Q. That was about July.
A. That is right. Somewhat earlier, I think.
Q. A little earlier?
A. I think I went to Berkeley in July. I may have my dates mixed up.
Q. You made quite a stir about the matter; didn't you?
A. Apparently I did.
Q. You sent the teletype that we have seen.
A. That is right.
Q. Whom did you talk to about it?
A. Lansdale, when he was in Los Alamos.
Q. That is Colonel Lansdale?
A. That is right.
Q. The security officer of the District?
A. That is right, a security officer whose name I no longer remember in Berkeley.
Q. Would that be Captain Johnson?
A. It is not that you can refresh my memory. I really don't know.
Q. Would it be Colonel Pash?
A. I remember him.
Q. Did you talk to him about it?
A. That I think is possible.
Q. Anybody else?
A. I don't think so.
Q. During that period of time when this matter was under discussion and consideration did you talk to Lomanitz about it?
A. With the approval or the suggestion, I don't remember, of the security officer, I endeavored to persuade Lomanitz to get the thing straight with the security people. He assured me that there was nothing to get straight.
Q. Did you talk to him on the telephone?
A. I don't remember. I thought I talked to him in person.
Q. I think you did, but did you also talk to him on the telephone on several occasions?
A. I have no recollection of that, but you apparently know that I did.

The teletype was to Colonel Marshall, "Manhattan District, New York City." It was dated July 31, 1943, and it read:

"Understand that the deferment of Rossi Lomanitz, left in charge of my end of work for Lawrence project by me, requested by Lawrence and Shane, turned down by your office. Believe understand reasons but feel that very serious mistake is being made. Lomanitz now only man at Berkeley who can take this responsibility. His work for Lawrence preeminently satisfactory. If he is drafted and not returned promptly to project, Lawrence will request that I release 1 or 2 of my men. I shall not be able to accede to this. Therefore, urge you support deferment of Lomanitz or insure by other means his continued availability to project. Have communicated with Fidler and am sending this to you in support of what I regard as urgent request. Lomanitz deferment expires August 2."

On the same day, Oppenheimer wired Lomanitz in Berkeley, "Have requested in proper places reconsideration of support for your deferment. Cannot guarantee outcome but have made strong request. Suggest you ask Fidler for current developments. Good luck. Opje."

When Robb showed this telegram to Oppenheimer, he asked him why it was so important to him that Lomanitz not be drafted. Oppenheimer answered, "I am not sure that it was so important to me. I had this outraged communication from Condon——"

ROBB: "You had what?"

OPPENHEIMER: "An outraged communication from Condon about it. We were very short of people. I doubt whether there was any more to it than that."

ROBB: "Dr. Condon's opinions had a great weight with you?"

OPPENHEIMER: "They had some weight with me."

ROBB: "I beg your pardon?"

OPPENHEIMER: "They had some weight with me. I thought it reflected a sense of trouble in Berkeley."

Dr. Condon was not the only one who wanted Lomanitz's induction deferred. Colonel Lansdale knew about Dr. Oppenheimer's efforts. Lomanitz was one of Lansdale's "top suspects," and Lansdale talked with Oppenheimer about him. Lansdale testified:

ROBB: "Do you recall Dr. Oppenheimer protesting about his [Lomanitz's] induction?"

LANSDALE: "I recall Dr. Oppenheimer raising a question about it. Indeed, if I recall, that was the occasion of at least one of my talks with Dr. Oppenheimer, that is, to ask him 'for goodness sake to lay off Lomanitz and stop raising questions about it.'"

ROBB: "In other words, he had been raising questions about it?"

LANSDALE: "My recollection was that he had. Lomanitz was regarded as a brilliant young man and the people like Ernest Lawrence and Dr. Oppenheimer did not want to lose him. I remember Ernest Lawrence yelled and screamed louder than anybody else about us taking Lomanitz away from him."

The Board was a little hard of hearing here as to what Lansdale was telling it about his other difficulties at that time. At the very time that Lawrence and Oppenheimer were pressing him to leave Lomanitz on his scientific work, Lansdale was being pressed to allow the commissioning of Communists in the Army. "I was being subjected to pressure from military superiors, from the White House and from every other place because I dared to stop the commissioning of a group of fifteen or twenty undoubted Communists. . . . By golly, I stood up in front of General McNarney, then Deputy Chief of Staff of the Army, and had him tell me that I was ruining peoples' careers and doing damage to the Army because I had stopped the commissioning of the political commissar of the Abraham Lincoln Brigade, and the guy was later commissioned on direct orders from the White House."

The second instance which impressed Gray and Morgan with Oppenheimer's susceptibility to influence was his letter to the Rochester papers about the testimony he had given before the House Committee on Un-American Activities against Dr. Bernard Peters. Robb brought it out in cross-examination. It is not in Nichols' letter.

In 1949 Oppenheimer had testified in an executive session of the House Un-American Activities Committee about Dr. Peters, who was then on the staff of the University of Rochester. His testimony, though given in executive session, was published in the Rochester papers. These are the quotations from the newspaper story which Robb showed to Oppenheimer. He thought they were substantially accurate.

"In his testimony, Dr. Oppenheimer said he became 'acquainted' with the existence of a Communist cell at Berkeley 'by disclosure of the intelligence agencies of the Government." The quotes are not closed, but I assume they should be there.

"Concerning Dr. Peters, Dr. Oppenheimer said he had known the scientists as a graduate student in the physics department in the late 1930's.

"Said Dr. Oppenheimer:

" 'Dr. Peters was, I think, a German national. He was a member of the German National Communist Party. He was imprisoned by the Nazis, and escaped by a miracle. He came to this country. I know nothing of his early period in this country. He arrived in California, and violently denounced the Communist Party as being a "do-nothing party." '

"Dr. Oppenheimer said he told Major DeSylva he believed Dr. Peters' background was filled with incidents that would point toward 'direct action.'

"Asked to explain this point, Oppenheimer observed:

" 'Incidents in Germany where he had fought street battles against the National Socialists on account of Communists; being placed in a concentration camp; escaping by guile. It seemed to me those were past incidents not pointing to temperance.'

"Questioned specifically on his reference to 'direct action', Dr. Oppenheimer said of Dr. Peters :

"'I think I suggested his attack on the Communist Party as being too constitutional and conciliatory an organization, not sufficiently dedicated to the overthrow of the Government by force and violence,'

"Asked the source of his information that Dr. Peters had been a member of the Communist Party in Germany, Dr. Oppenheimer replied :

"'It was well known. Among other things, he told me.'

"Dr. Oppenheimer said he could 'affirm that there is no connection between his (Peters') work and any application of atomic energy that falls within the jurisdiction of the (Atomic Energy) Commission. * * * I would believe that if Dr. Peters could teach what he knows to a young man capable of learning it, the country would be better off, because if Dr. Peters cannot be employed by the War Department, at least the young man could be employed by the War Department.' "

Peters, Dr. Hans Bethe, Dr. Condon, Dr. Weiskopf and Oppenheimer's brother, Frank, all protested and told Oppenheimer he should do something about it. Condon wrote a letter to the newspapers. Peters denied that he had ever been a member of the Communist Party.

Oppenheimer consulted Volpe, the General Counsel of the A.E.C., who had accompanied him to the hearing. Then he wrote a letter to the newspapers, and he sent a copy of it to the House Committee.

"EDITOR, *Democrat and Chronicle:*

"Recently the Democrat and Chronicle published an article based on reports of my testimony before an executive session of the House Committee on Un-American Activities, which it seems to me could be damaging to the good name of Dr. Bernard Peters, of the University of Rochester.

"I first knew Dr. Peters about 12 years ago during his student days in California. I knew him, not only as a brilliant student, but as a man of strong moral principles and of high ethical standards. During those years his political views were radical. He expressed them freely, and sometimes, I thought, without temperance. This seemed to me not unnatural in a man who had suffered as he had at Nazi hands. I have never known Dr. Peters to commit a dishonorable act, nor a disloyal one.

"Dr. Peters has recently informed me that I was right in believing that in the early days he had participated in the Communist movement in Germany, but that I was wrong in believing—as the article stated—that he had ever held a membership in the Communist Party. That he has today no regrets for his actions in Nazi Germany he himself made clear in his statement that accompanied the publication of the article.

"From the published article one might conclude that Dr. Peters had advocated the violent overthrow of the constitutional government of the United States. He has given an eloquent denial of this in his published statement. I believe his statement.

"As indicated in the article, the questions which were put to me by the House committee with regard to Dr. Peters arose in part because of reports of discussion between me and the intelligence officers at Los Alamos. These Los Alamos consultations took place in connection with confidential wartime assignments. I wish to make public my profound regret that anything said in the context should have been so misconstrued, and so abused, that it could damage Dr. Peters and threaten his distinguished future career as a scientist.

"Beyond this specific issue, there is ground for another, more general, and even greater concern. Political opinion, no matter how radical or how freely expressed, does not disqualify a scientist for a high career in science ; it does not disqualify him as a teacher of science ; it does not impugn his integrity nor his honor. We have seen in other countries criteria of political orthodoxy applied to ruin scientists, and to put an end to their work. This has brought with it the attrition of science. Even more, it has been part of the destruction of freedom of inquiry, and of political freedom itself. This is no path to follow for a people determined to stay free.

"ROBERT OPPENHEIMER.

"BERKELEY, CALIF., *June 30, 1949.*"

Here now is Robb's cross-examination:

Q. How has your remark or testimony been misconstrued or abused?

A. Well, for one thing they were abused by being made public. This was an executive session. I should not have talked in executive session without thinking what they might do publicly.

Q. How had your testimony been misconstrued?

A. It was being misconstrued to mean that he should not keep his job. I had explicitly said that I thought it was good he keep his job.

Q. The report of your testimony was accurate, wasn't it?

A. Yes.

Q. And you have just told us that this letter was intended at least in part to repudiate that testimony, is that correct?

A. To repudiate is a little strong.

Q. Is it now your testimony, Doctor, that your testimony before the House committee to which we have referred was not true?

A. No, it is certainly not my testimony that it was not true. As to Peters' membership in the Communist Party in Germany, I have only really his word to go on. I am fairly sure of my initial recollection. I am very clear of his later denial. I don't think——

Q. Doctor, when you testified before the House committee, you knew for you to say that Dr. Peters told you that he had been a member of the Communist Party was a matter of great seriousness, didn't you?

A. Right.

Q. You would not have said that, would you, had you not been absolutely sure it was true?

A. I was convinced it was true, or I would not have said it.

Q. Beg pardon?

A. I was convinced it was true.

Q. And yet when Peters came to see you and you received a letter from Dr. Condon, you in effect repudiated that testimony, didn't you?

A. Does it say that I don't believe he was a member of the party?

Q. I have just read it to you.

A. I have forgotten.

Mr. GARRISON. Do you mind if I show it to him?

Mr. ROBB. Not at all.

The WITNESS. I don't say I believe his denial. I just say he denied it.

By Mr. ROBB:

Q. Very well. Isn't the implication of your letter that you were wrong in believing that he had been a member of the party?

A. I think it leaves the matter open.

Q. Was it your intention to convey that impression when you wrote the letter?

A. I think the sum total of my intention was not to get this guy fired from the University of Rochester because of intemperate remarks I made before the House committee.

Q. You thought your remarks were intemperate?

A. I think somewhat.

Q. You thought the truth was intemperate?

A. I think the phrasing of it was intemperate.

Q. Was it intemperate for you to testify, believing it to be true, that Peters had told you he had been a member of the Communist Party?

A. No.

Q. Wasn't it your intention in writing this letter on June 30 to convey to the public the impression that you had been mistaken in saying that he told you he had been a member of the party?

A. I simply gave his own statement.

Q. I know you did. But wasn't it your intention to give the public through the press the impression that you were mistaken?

A. I had no specific intention.

Q. When Dr. Condon wrote you about your own file what do you think he referred to by that?

A. I should think the material before you.

Q. Do you think you were being placed under any pressure by either Peters or Condon to retract what you said?

A. No, the real pressure came from people who were not belligerent at all, but who were regretful.

Q. Who were they?

A. Bethe, Weiskopf, my brother. They wrote very, very nice letters saying, this guy was being put—was suffering for something because I had done it and he should stay on his job.

Q. And you were influenced by that pressure, were you not?

A. Of course, I was.

A little later Gray came back to this episode and compared it to the Chevalier episode. Gray's comparison is interesting.

Mr. GRAY. May I ask you now to turn your mind to an entirely different kind of thing, the Chevalier incident, in which it would appear that at that time and under those circumstances within the framework of loyalty generally—loyalty to an individual, broader loyalty to a country, and I am not talking about espionage—in that case considerations of personal loyalty might have outweighed the broader loyalties.

The WITNESS. I understand that it would appear that way. It is obvious from my behavior that I was in a very great conflict. It is obvious that I decided that with regard to Eltenton the danger was conceivably substantial and that I had an obligation to my country to talk about it. In the case of Chevalier, I would not think that I regarded it as a conflict of loyalties, but that I put too much confidence—put an improper confidence in my own judgment that Chevalier was not a danger.

Mr. GRAY. Another instance which has been discussed in the proceeding, the testimony with respect to Dr. Peters and your subsequent letter to the Rochester newspaper. In writing that letter, which perhaps was motivated by a desire not to hurt the individual, or to make restitution——

The WITNESS. Not to get him fired, anyway.

Mr. GRAY. Not to get him fired—again was this the same kind of conflict that you had with respect to——

The WITNESS. No; I think this was almost wholly a question of public things. Personal things were not involved. He was a good scientist doing according to everyone's account no political work of any kind, doing no harm, whatever his views. It was overwhelming belief of the community in which I lived that a man like that ought not to be fired either for his past or for his views, unless the past is criminal or the views lead him to wicked action. I think my effort was to compose the flap that I had produced in order that he could stay on and that this was not a question of my anguish about what I was doing to him.

Mr. GRAY. As you know, this board is asked to consider present and future circumstances. Do you feel that today where there became a conflict between loyalty to an individual and a desire to protect him and keep his job or have him keep his job—whatever it might be—and a broader obligation, and I consider it to be broader is the reason I put it that way, that you would follow this same kind of pattern with respect to other individuals in the future?

The WITNESS. The Chevalier pattern; no, never. The Peters pattern I do not believe that I violated a broader obligation in writing the letter. It was for the public interest that I wrote it.

Mr. GRAY. You make a distinction between what is said about a man in executive session—we are talking in terms of loyalty—and what is said about a man for public consumption. Do you think on the basis of the same facts it is appropriate to say one thing in executive session, and another thing for public consumption?

The WITNESS. It is very undesirable. I wish I had said more temperate, measured and accurate words in executive session. The it would not have been necessary to say such very different words publicly.

Dr. Evans had one question:

> Dr. Oppenheimer, did the Condon letter have much weight with you in changing your position on that security committee?
> The WITNESS. The Peters thing?
> Dr. EVANS. Yes.
> The WITNESS. No. The letters that had weight with me were from Bethe and Weiskopf. They were written in very moderate and dignified——
> Mr. EVANS. Condon did write a letter about it?
> The WITNESS. He did, and it has been published in the papers. It made me angry.

The third and last instance was Oppenheimer's willingness to testify for Dr. Condon when his loyalty was being attacked. Gray and Morgan said, "In that episode, Dr. Condon's letter, which has appeared in the press, contained a severe attack on Dr. Oppenheimer. Nevertheless, he now testifies that he is prepared to support Dr. Condon in the loyalty investigation of the latter."

I wish I understood the precise significance of Gray's word "Nevertheless." Should we refuse to testify in behalf of people who have attacked us, however severely, or for people who have made us angry?

I will give you the complete testimony on Oppenheimer's willingness to testify on Dr. Condon's behalf. It is not long.

> Q. Have you seen Dr. E. U. Condon since 1951?
> A. Oh, surely.
> Q. Frequently?
> A. No.
> Q. Did you see him in 1952?
> A. I would assume so. He is a member of the visiting committee to the physics department at Harvard of which I am chairman. We see each other at meetings. I would assume I saw him in 1952, but I don't recall.
> Q. 1953?
> A. As to that I am much less sure.
> Q. Have you received any other letters from him other than the letters he wrote you about Peters and the one he wrote you about Lomanitz?
> A. Yes; I have had other letters from him.
> Q. When?
> A. He has recently been having his clearance reviewed.
> Q. His what?
> A. His clearance reviewed, and he wrote me a letter about it.
> Mr. GARRISON. Mr. Chairman, I wonder why we have to go into his relations with Dr. Condon. Are they a part of this case?
> Mr. GRAY. Dr. Condon——
> Mr. GARRISON. I don't know what this is about.
> Mr. GRAY. Dr. Oppenheimer testified earlier——
> The WITNESS. I have no reason not to answer these questions.
> Mr. GARRISON. I withdraw my objection.
> Mr. GRAY. I would like to complete my sentence that it was probably due to Dr. Condon's frantic—I am not sure about the language—at least Dr. Condon's disturbance about Lomanitz that he made the representations on behalf of

Lomanitz. I believe that was your testimony.

Mr. GARRISON. I think the testimony was that was Bethe——

The WITNESS. No, that was a different matter.

By Mr. ROBB:

Q. I think you said that Dr. Condon wrote you about his clearance.

A. Right.

Q. I was about to ask you whether he asked you to testify in his behalf.

A. He did.

Q. How long ago was that?

A. It was shortly after my own case was opened.

Q. I assume you wrote him back you had troubles of your own, is that right?

A. No.

Q. What did you write him?

A. I think he asked me not to testify, but to write him a statement. I wrote him a letter outlining a statement that I could put in the form of an affidavit. In the meantime it seemed only fair for him to know about my situation, or at least for his attorneys to know about. I tried to keep this as quiet as I could. Therefore, my counsel got in touch with Dr. Condon's counsel. I believe that they explained the situation to Dr. Condon's counsel. This is——

Q. Your statement that you submitted to him, I suppose, was favorable to him, was it?

A. I am sure it was.

Is there any other evidence bearing on this suggestion that Dr. Condon had too much influence over Oppenheimer? Yes, one thing. General Groves was talking about the compartmentalization of work at Los Alamos in 1943 in the interests of security, how he wanted more of it and how he never got it.

The absence of compartmentalization on the Los Alamos project, General Groves, would you say that represented on Dr. Oppenheimer's part an honest judgment as to what in his opinion would produce the best operating results among the scientists on the project?

A. I always felt—I can't quite answer that—that Dr. Oppenheimer was led to that breakdown of compartmentalization at Los Alamos by a number of conflicting factors. Here I am just giving my surmise as to what I thought.

First, that he personally felt that was right in view of his background of academic work.

Second, that he felt it was necessary in order to attract the kind of men that he felt he had to have at Los Alamos. I agreed that it was a very decided factor and always thought it was in getting such men. I also felt that he was very much influenced at that time by the influence of Dr. Condon, who was for a very brief time the associate director there, and, as you all know, a very complete disappointment to me in every respect.

I would like to emphasize now before any question is asked that I was not responsible for the exact selection of Dr. Condon, but I was responsible for his selection because I insisted when Dr. Oppenheimer took the directorship that he have as his No. 1 assistant an industrial scientists, and we just made a mistake when we selected Dr. Condon. Who gave his name the first time I don't know, but Dr. Condon turned out to be not an industrial scientist, but an academic scientist with all of the faults and none of the virtues. That was my opinion. He did a tremendous amount of damage at Los Alamos in the initial setup. How much influence he had on Dr. Oppenheimer I don't know. But he was given certain responsibilities with my full approval—in fact, you might say my very insistent suggestion—that Dr. Condon with the industrial background should be the one to establish the working rules and the administrative scientific rules in the establishment, while Dr. Oppenheimer was thinking about how was the actual scientific work to be done.

Dr. Condon did not stay long at Los Alamos. "He left," General

Groves went on to testify, "with, I would say—both Dr. Oppenheimer and myself—we had the utmost distaste for Dr. Condon."

Neither Gray nor Morgan nor any of the commissioners mention this testimony of General Groves. Yet it bears directly on the point, and no one questions the general's veracity. Do you think any the less of Oppenheimer for his willingness to give favorable testimony for a man in spite of his having "the utmost distaste" for him? No, of course you don't. Nor in spite of the fact that he has attacked you and you are angry with him. You think the more of him because he has put his civic duties above prejudices and personalities. This must be so, unless you have good reason to believe that there lurks some malign, almost satanic power which has overwhelmed both the man's decency and his duty. And if you think you see the workings of such a power against all the evidence, you may be having bad dreams.

Is it possible that Gray and Morgan saw something derogatory in Oppenheimer's being influenced at all by Condon? Six years before, the House Un-American Activities Committee had called Condon "one of the weakest links in our atomic security." That was when he was Director of the Bureau of Standards, and the Department of Commerce, of which the Bureau was a part, had cleared him. So too had the Atomic Energy Commission and the military departments. At this very time, in 1954, he was again being cleared by the Eastern Industrial Personnel Security Board for work as director of research for the Corning Glass Works. It made its decision on July 12, 1954. But when this fourth clearance was announced, in October, the Secretary of the Navy asked the board to reconsider it. Condon then resigned from Corning, saying that he was "unwilling to continue a potentially indefinite series of reviews and re-reviews." (The New York *Times*, October 22, 1954; the New York *Times* and the New York *Herald Tribune*, December 14, 1954.) No, I won't agree that Gray and Morgan could have had such a bad dream without mentioning it.

So much, anyhow, for "an over-all common sense judgment" on Oppenheimer's susceptibility to undue influence by Gray and Morgan "as practical men of affairs."

To tell the truth, Gray and Morgan were not so very certain that these episodes did show susceptibility to influence. They said, "Whether the incidents referred to clearly indicate a susceptibility to influence or coercion within the meaning of the criteria or whether they simply reflect very bad judgment, they clearly raise the question of Dr. Oppenheimer's understanding, acceptance, and enthusiastic support of the security system."

"Bad judgment"? Was Oppenheimer's letter to the Rochester newspaper bad judgment? Possibly; but when you try to correct what you are persuaded was an unfair impression which the publication of your testimony in executive session has unexpectedly created, when you wish that your testimony had been more temperate, measured and accurate, is it "bad judgment" to correct it?

This question of Oppenheimer's "understanding, acceptance, and enthusiastic support of the security system" opens one of the most important aspects in the case. It is the first of the four "considerations" which Gray and Morgan said "have been controlling in leading us to our conclusion." "Beginning with the Chevalier incident," they cited half a dozen instances in which they said Oppenheimer had "repeatedly exercised an arrogance of his own judgment with respect to the loyalty and reliability of other citizens to an extent which has frustrated and at times impeded the workings of the system."

We have already gone into the Chevalier incident pretty thoroughly, if not to everyone's satisfaction. "Arrogance" is the wrong term.

Another is Oppenheimer's refusal to tell the F.B.I. in 1946 who was present at some meetings in California in 1940. He said it was irrelevant. Later his wife reminded him that one of the meetings had been at the Chevaliers', and when the F.B.I. questioned him about Chevalier in 1950 he told them about it.

In 1950 he refused to discuss with the F.B.I. Dr. Thomas Addis' or Jean Tatlock's Communist connections on the ground that they were dead and could not defend themselves. He asked the F.B.I. agents if it was important, and they thought not.

We have already covered his continued associations with Bohm and with Lomanitz at Princeton, and his continued and current associaton with Chevalier, which Gray and Morgan are now regarding in a new light. Here it is not that they increase the risk to our security. Here they are evidence that Oppenheimer did not give the security system his "enthusiastic support."

There is something precarious about the reasoning that raises to the dignity of a security risk a failure to give your enthusiastic support to a system. Respect for law has taken the place of law. Enthusiasm for a law has taken the place of obedience to law. All this reaches an apotheosis in Commissioner Murray's opinion, where disregard of the security system is elevated to disloyalty. Smyth called this a "gymnastics of rationalization." Perhaps. But what interests us is its effect on the security system, and on this I have more to say later.

Before we go into the controversy over the H-bomb, here are Nichols' charges, the Board's findings.

24. It was reported that in 1945 you expressed the view that "there is a reasonable possibility that it (the hydrogen bomb) can be made," but that the feasibility of the hydrogen bomb did not appear, on theoretical grounds, as certain as the fission bomb appeared certain, on theoretical grounds, when the Los Alamos Laboratory was started; and that in the autumn of 1949 the General Advisory Committee expressed the view that "an imaginative and concerted attack on the problem has a better than even chance of producing the weapon within 5 years." It was further reported that in the autumn of 1949, and subsequently, you strongly opposed the development of the hydrogen bomb: (1) on moral grounds, (2) by claiming that it was not feasible, (3) by claiming that there were insufficient facilities and scientific personnel to carry on the development, and (4) that it was not politically desirable. It was further reported that even after it was determined, as a matter of national policy, to proceed with development of a hydrogen bomb, you continued to oppose the project and declined to cooperate fully in the project. It was further reported you departed from your proper role as an adviser to the Commission by causing the distribution, separately and in private, to top personnel at Los Alamos of the majority and minority reports of the General Advisory Committee on development of the hydrogen bomb for the purpose of trying to turn such top personnel against the development of the hydrogen bomb. It was further reported that you were instrumental in persuading other outstanding scientists not to work on the hydrogen bomb project, and that the opposition to the hydrogen bomb, of which you are most experienced, most powerful, and most effective member, has definitely slowed down its development.

In order to assess the influence of Dr. Oppenheimer on the thermonuclear program, it has been necessary for the Board not only to consider the testimony but also to examine many documents and records, most of which are classified. Without disclosing the contents of classified documents, the Board makes the following findings, which it believes to be a sufficient reference to this allegation.

The Board confirms that in 1945 Mr. Oppenheimer expressed the view that "'there is reasonable possibility that it (the hydrogen bomb) can be made,' but that the feasibility of the hydrogen bomb did not appear, on theoretical grounds, as certain as the fission bomb appeared certain, on theoretical grounds, when the Los Alamos Laboratory was started; and that in August of 1949, the General Advisory Committee expressed the view that 'an imaginative and concerted attack on the problem has a better than even chance of producing the weapon within 5 years.'"

With respect to Dr. Oppenheimer's attitude and activities in relation to the hydrogen bomb in World War II, the evidence shows that Dr. Oppenheimer during this period had no misgivings about a program looking to thermonuclear development and, indeed, during the latter part of the war, he recorded his support of prompt and vigorous action in this connection. When asked under cross examination whether he would have opposed dropping an H-bomb on Hiroshima, he replied that "It would make no sense," and when asked "Why?" replied, "The target is too small." He testified further under cross examination that he believed he would have opposed the dropping of an H-bomb on Japan because of moral scruples although he did not oppose the dropping of an A-bomb on the same grounds. During the postwar period, Dr. Oppenheimer favored, and in fact urged, continued research in the thermonuclear field and seemed to express considerable interest in results that were from time to time discussed with him. However, he was aware that the efforts being put forth in this endeavor were relatively meager and he knew that if research were continued at the same pace, there would be little likelihood of success for many years. Testimony in this connection indicated that there was a feeling on his part that it was more important to go forward with a program for the pro-duction of a wider range of atomic bombs.

The Board finds further that in the autumn of 1949, and subsequently, Dr. Oppenheimer strongly opposed the development of the hydrogen bomb on moral grounds; on grounds that it was not politically desirable; he expressed the view that there were insufficient facilities and scientific personnel to carry on the development without seriously interfering with the orderly development of the program for fission bombs; and until the late spring of 1951, he questioned the feasibility of the hydrogen bomb efforts then in progress.

Dr. Oppenheimer testified that what he was opposing in the fall of 1949 was only a "crash program" in the development and production of thermo-nuclear weapons. In this connection, Dr. Oppenheimer contended that the main question relating to thermonuclear weapons presented to the GAC at its meeting of October 29, 1949, was whether or not the United States should undertake such a crash program. The Board does not believe that Dr. Oppenheimer was entirely candid with the Board in attempting to establish this impression. The record reflects that Dr. Oppenheimer expressed the opinion in writing that the "super bomb should never be produced," and that the commitment to this effect should be unqualified. Moreover, the alternatives available to the GAC were not a choice between an "all-out effort" and no effort at all; there was a middle course which might have been considered.

The Board further concludes that after it was determined, as a matter of national policy (January 31, 1950) to proceed with development of a hydro-gen bomb, Dr. Oppenheimer did not oppose the project in a positive or open manner, nor did he decline to cooperate in the project. However, Dr. Oppen-heimer is recognized in scientific circles as one of the foremost leaders in the atomic energy field and he has considerable influence on the "policy direction" of the atomic program. The Board finds that his views in opposition to the development of the H-bomb as expressed in 1949 became widely known among scientists, and since he did not make it known that he had abandoned these views, his attitude undoubtedly had an adverse effect on recruitment of scientists and the progress of the scientific effort in this field. In other words, the Board finds, that if Dr. Oppenheimer had enthusiastically supported the thermonuclear program either before or after the determination of national policy, the H-bomb project would have been pursued with considerably more vigor, thus increasing the possibility of earlier success in this field.

The Board finds that Dr. Oppenheimer was not responsible for the distribu-tion, separately and in private, to top personnel at Los Alamos of the majority and minority reports of the General Advisory Committee on development of the hydrogen bomb, but that such distribution was made on the direction of the then general manager of the Atomic Energy Commission, Carroll L. Wilson, apparently in order to prepare the personnel at Los Alamos to discuss the matter with the chairman of the Joint Committee on Atomic Energy of the Congress.

The Board does not find that Dr. Oppenheimer urged other scientists not to work on the program. However, enthusiastic support on his part would perhaps have encouraged other leading scientists to work on the program.

Because of technical questions involved, the Board is unable to make a categorical finding as to whether the opposition of the hydrogen bomb "has definitely slowed down its development." The Board concludes that the opposi-tion to the H-bomb by many persons connected with the atomic energy program, of which Dr. Oppenheimer was the "most experienced, most powerful, and most effective member" did delay the initiation of concerted effort which led to the development of a thermonuclear weapon.

10. THE H-BOMB

ON THE AFTERNOON of the tenth day of hearings the Board was set back on its heels by being abruptly told that it should have refused to sit until Nichols' letter of charges had been redrafted.

Vannevar Bush was testifying. He told the Board about Oppenheimer's appointment to head Los Alamos and about the magnificent piece of work Oppenheimer had done—"one of the most magnificent performances of history." Bush spoke of his own opposition to the explosion of the H-bomb just before the election in 1952, which, he thought, history would show was the turning point "when we entered into the grim world that we are entering into right now." He declined to express an opinion on the controversy in the fall of 1949 over the development of the bomb because he'd had no official part in it. He concluded his direct examination by expressing "his complete confidence in the loyalty, judgment, and integrity of Dr. Oppenheimer," and by saying that he had read Nichols' letter as it appeared in the press. "My faith," he said, "has not in the slightest degree been shaken by that letter or anything else."

Robb had no questions, but Gray wanted to go back to the test of the H-bomb in the fall of 1952. Bush said he was sure that it had been of value to the Russians in their own program. Our proceeding with the H-bomb, he went on to say, had not been a question, as he understood it, of whether we should proceed or not. It was a question of whether we should proceed in a certain manner and on a certain program. "The question of whether we proceeded along a certain path . . ."

Bush interrupted himself. "May I say one more word on that, Mr. Chairman, quite frankly, and I hope you won't misunderstand me, because I have the greatest respect for this Board. Yet I think it is only right that I should give you my opinion."

I feel that this board has made a mistake and that it is a serious one. I feel that the letter of General Nichols which I read, this bill of particulars, is quite capable of being interpreted as placing a man on trial because he held opinions, which is quite contrary to the American system, which is a terrible thing. And as I move about I find that discussed today very energetically, that here is a man who is being pilloried because he had strong opinions, and had the temerity to express them. If this country ever gets to the point where we come that near to the Russian system, we are certainly not in any condition to attempt to lead the free world toward the benefits of democracy.

Now, if I had been on this board, I most certainly would have refused to entertain a set of charges that could possibly be thus interpreted. As things now stand, I am just simply glad I am not in the position of the board.

Mr. GRAY. What is the mistake the board has made?

The WITNESS. I think you should have immediately said before we will enter into this matter, we want a bill of particulars which makes it very clear that this man is not being tried because he expressed opinions.

Mr. GRAY. Are you aware, Dr. Bush, how this got in the press and was spread throughout the world?

The WITNESS. Yes, I know how it was released.

Mr. GRAY. Do you know who released it?

The WITNESS. I believe this gentleman on my right released it.

Mr. GRAY. I don't think you can blame the board. We had quite a discussion about that.

The WITNESS. It was bound to be released sometime when you made your report.

Mr. GRAY. It might have leaked. I don't think it was bound to be released. I assure you, and I am sure that we are all sure that whatever the outcome, this board is going to be very severely criticized.

The WITNESS. I am sure of that, and I regret it sincerely, sir, because I fear that this thing, when your report is released, will be misinterpreted on that very basis whatever you may do.

Dr. EVANS. Dr. Bush, you don't think we sought this job, do you?

The WITNESS. I am sure you didn't, and you have my profound sympathy and respect. I think the fact that a group of men of this sort are willing to do as tough and as difficult a job as this augurs well for the country. It is in stark contrast with some of the things that we have seen going on about us in similar circumstances. Orderly procedure and all of that is good. I merely regret that the thing can be misinterpreted as it stands on the record, and misinterpreted in a way that can do great damage. I know, of course, that the executive branch of the United States Government had no intention whatever of pillorying a man for his opinions. But the situation has not been helped, gentlemen, recently by statements of the Secretary of Defense. I can assure you that the scientific community is deeply stirred today.

The National Academy of Science meets this next week, and the American Physical Society meets, and I hope sincerely that they will do nothing foolish. But they are deeply stirred. The reason they are stirred is because they feel that a professional man who rendered great service to his country, rendered service beyond almost any other man, is now being pilloried and put through an ordeal because he had the temerity to express his honest opinions.

Mr. GRAY. Dr. Bush, are you familiar with the Atomic Energy Act of 1946 at all?

The WITNESS. I have read it.

Mr. GRAY. Are you familiar with the fact that the Commission has a published set of procedures which for these purposes have the effect of law?

The WITNESS. Yes. I am not quarreling with the procedure, Mr. Chairman.

Mr. GRAY. As I understand it, and I can be corrected by counsel, the writing of a letter to Dr. Oppenheimer with specifications is required under these procedures.

The WITNESS. I have been a friend of General Nichols for many years. He wrote the letter. I quite frankly think it was a poorly written letter and should have been written in such a way that it made it absolutely clear that what was being examined here was not the question of whether a man held opinions and whether those were right or wrong, whether history has shown it to be good judgment or poor judgment. I think that should have been made very clear.

Mr. GRAY. I would also point out just in the interest of having a record here,

and I don't consider myself in any argumentation with you, for whom I have
a very high regard, personally and professionally, that there were items of
so-called derogatory information—and that is a term of art—in this letter,
setting aside the allegations about the hydrogen bomb. There were items in
this letter which did not relate to the expression and holding of opinions.

The WITNESS. Quite right, and the case should have tried on those.

Mr. GRAY. This is not a trial.

The WITNESS. If it were a trial, I would not be saying these things to the
judge, you can well imagine that. I feel a very serious situation has been
created, and I think that in all fairness I ought to tell you my frank feeling that
this has gotten into a very bad mess. I wish I could suggest a procedure that
would resolve it.

Mr. GRAY. The proceeding, of course, is taking place in accordance with
procedures, and I am glad to hear you say a few moments ago that you felt
that this was a fair kind of proceeding. I am not sure I am quoting you
correctly.

The WITNESS. You can quote me to that effect. I think some of the things
we have seen have been scandalous affairs. I think in fact the Republic is in
danger today because we have been slipping backward in our maintenance of
the Bill of Rights.

Mr. GRAY. Dr. Evans.

Dr. EVANS. Dr. Bush, I wish you would make clear just what mistake you
think the board made. I did not want this job when I was asked to take it. I
thought I was performing a service to my country.

The WITNESS. I think the moment you were confronted with that letter, you
should have returned the letter, and asked that it be redrafted so that you
would have before you a clearcut issue which would not by implication put you
in the position of trying a man for his opinions.

Dr. EVANS. I was not confronted with that letter, and I don't think it would
have made any difference if I had been. I was simply asked if I would serve on
the board. What mistake did I make when I did that?

Mr. GARRISON. Mr. Chairman, might I make a remark for myself here, speaking
for Dr. Oppenheimer? I have the deepest respect for Dr. Bush's forthright
character, for his lifelong habit of calling a spade a spade as he sees it. I simply
want to leave no misunderstanding on the record here that we share the view
that this board should not have served when asked to serve under the letter
as written.

The WITNESS. I can assure you, Mr. Chairman, that the opinions being
expressed are my own. They usually are.

Mr. GRAY. I have never heard it suggested that you didn't express your own
opinion, Dr. Bush.

Dr. EVANS. Dr. Bush, then your idea is that suppose I was asked to serve
on this board, and I didn't know anything about it—I had not seen any of this
material—after I had agreed to serve, and saw this material, I should have
resigned?

The WITNESS. No, I think you simply should have asked for a revision of the
bill of particulars.

Dr. EVANS. I am just anxious to know what you think my procedure should
have been.

The WITNESS. That is what I think. Now, I don't see how you can get out
of this mess.

Mr. MORGAN. Doctor, on what ground would you ask for a bill of particulars if
you didn't know the record?

The WITNESS. I think that bill of particulars was obviously poorly drawn
on the face of it, because it was most certainly open to the interpretation that
this man is being tried because he expressed strong opinions. The fact that he
expressed strong opinions stands in a single paragraph by itself. It is not
directly connected. It does have in that paragraph, through improper motiva-
tions he expressed these opinions. It merely says he stated opinions, and I think
that is defective drafting and should have been corrected.

Mr. MORGAN. In other words, we want to prejudge the case before we know
anything about it.

The WITNESS. Not at all. But I think this board or no board should ever sit on
a question in this country of whether a man should serve his country or not because he expressed strong opinions. If you want to try that case, you can try me.

I have expressed strong opinions many times, and I intend to do so. They have been unpopular opinions at times. When a man is pilloried for doing that, this country is in a severe state.

Bush's remark that the recent statements of the Secretary of Defense had not helped the situation referred to Secretary Wilson's press conference a week or so before, on April 14, 1954, in which the Secretary had said that a man could be "a bad risk" on account of "his association and his train of thought and his previous activities." Robb had put it in evidence the day before and Gray had said, "I believe there seems to be no question in the minds of any of us that Mr. Wilson in every likelihood was referring to Dr. Oppenheimer."

The Board was plainly taken aback, and with good reason. Bush was then the president of the Carnegie Institution in Washington. He had been the chairman of the National Defense Research Committee from its formation in 1940. He was chairman of the New Weapons Committee of the Joint Chiefs of Staff during the war. After the war he was chairman of the Research and Development Board until 1949. He had been the chairman of the Military Policy Committee, which was in charge of the Manhattan District, to which General Groves reported and with which he took up all his programs and policies.

Bush came back to the witness stand a week later, on May 4, on another matter, and Robb returned to what Bush had said.

> If I might, Dr. Bush, clear up something in the record having to do with your testimony when you came here before. Do you recall you were rather critical of the letter written to Dr. Oppenheimer by Mr. Nichols?
>
> A. Quite right.
> Q. And in particular you were critical of the paragraphing?
> A. No, sir. I don't remember I was critical of the paragraphing. I was critical of one particular statement in there because I said that it could be interpreted readily by the public, and in my opinion was being thus interpreted, as putting a man on trial for his opinions.
> Q. Don't you remember that you made some particular reference to the paragraphing?
> A. I don't remember. Can you give it to me?
> Q. I will read it to you at page 1984. This was in answer to a question by Mr. Morgan:
> "Doctor, on what ground would you ask for a bill of particulars if you didn't know the record?"
> And you answered:
> "I think that bill of particulars was obviously poorly drawn on the face of it, because it was most certainly open to the interpretation that this man is being tried because he expressed strong opinions."
> A. Right.
> Q. (Reading.) "The fact that he expressed strong opinions stands in a single paragraph by itself. It is not directly connected. It does not have in that paragraph, through improper motivations he expressed these opinions. It merely says he stated opinion, and I think that is defective drafting and should have been corrected."

Do you recall that?

A. Yes; I remember that.

Q. You had read that particular paragraph in the New York Times, I take it?

A. Yes; I believe I said so.

Q. Yes; I think you did. I want to show you the New York Times for Tuesday, April 13, 1954, page 16, carrying the text of the letter to Dr. Oppenheimer, and ask you if you will show us the paragraph you were talking about. I think you will find it here some place.

A. Yes, sure; this is it through here.

Q. Which is the one paragraph you had in mind?

A. This is the paragraph I referred to, I think, isn't it?

Q. I don't know, Doctor.

A. Yes.

Q. Would you read us the paragraph you had in mind?

A. Let me be sure I have the right one. "It was further reported"—no, wait a minute. Yes. "It was reported that in 1945 you expressed the view that there was a reasonable possibility—" wait a minute. This is the one. "It was further reported that in the autumn of 1949 and subsequently you strongly opposed the development of the hydrogen bomb on moral grounds, by claiming that it was not feasible, by claiming that there were insufficient facilities and scientific personnel to carry on the development, and four, that it was not politically desirable."

Q. That is the paragraph you had in mind?

A. That is the one I referred to.

Q. And you felt that putting that sentence in a separate paragraph was improper and damaging; is that correct?

A. The fact that it was in a separate paragraph was secondary. I feel that statement as a whole is fully open to the interpretation that a man is being tried for his opinions. That any reasonable man, particularly not a man with legal training, reading that entire statement, would feel that this man is being tried because he had strong opinions and expressed them, which I think is an an entirely un-American procedure.

Q. But the fact of the matter is, Doctor, that you felt that the paragraphing was of sufficient importance that you made a point of it.

A. I think the paragraphing as I read it emphasized the point, but is not necessary to the point that I am making, which is that the statement as a whole, the letter as a whole, was open to that interpretation.

Q. I am directing your attention to your testimony about the paragraph and you concede, Doctor, you gave that testimony, didn't you?

A. I gave the testimony and I referred to that particular paragraph.

Q. And you were not giving testimony before this board about a matter which you thought was trivial?

A. I was giving testimony about a very important matter, indeed.

Q. Yes, sir. Now, Doctor, you took that paragraphing from the New York Times' didn't you?

A. So I said.

Q. Yes, sir. Now, I am going to show you the letter, the actual text of the letter sent to Dr. Oppenheimer, and ask you if you don't see from that that that paragraph which you read was not a separate paragraph in the letter at all, but was part of a much longer paragraph beginning, "It was reported that in 1945 you expressed the view that there was a reasonable possibility" and so forth, and ending "of which you are the most experienced, most powerful and most effective member, had definitely slowed down its development."

In other words, Doctor——

A. But the wording is the same——

Q. May I finish my question, and then you can finish your answer.

In other words, Doctor, the New York Times in its story broke up the paragraph of General Nichols' letter, into four paragraphs.

A. Without changing the wording.

Q. That is right.

A. I don't need to read that, if you tell me that.

(Document handed to witness.)

The WITNESS. This is a separate paragraph [indicating].

By Mr. ROBB:

Q. Where?

A. Here [indicating].

Q. It starts up here, "It was reported in 1945."

A. Oh, yes. Right.

Q. So you agree, Doctor, that the Times no doubt for greater clarity to its readers or for reasons of newspaper technique broke the paragraph in the Nichols letter into four separate paragraphs.

A. I would have expressed exactly the same opinion had I read the thing you later showed to me, namely, that is fully open to the interpretation that a man is being tried for his opinions.

Q. But if you read the original letter, you would not have made your point about the separate paragraphs.

A. No.

Q. Because it was not based on fact, was it?

A. It was based on what facts I cited.

Q. Yes, sir. Wouldn't you conclude from that, Doctor, that before making such statements it is well to know all the facts?

A. Yes; I think you sitting here, if you find me operating on a basis of a published statement, which is not exact, should have called it to my attention at that time.

Q. That is exactly what I am doing now, Doctor. It was not until after you testified that I realized you had been in error. Thank you.

Mr. Gray. Dr. Bush, I think I should say to you that this board was confused about some of your testimony, especially on this particular point. I think that no member of the board was aware that this paragraphing change had been made at the time you were here, so this is not an unimportant matter because we have had another distinguished witness before this board, a man of international distinction, who in milder terms, but in somewhat the same spirit, was critical of the general manager's letter. I don't think he went as far as you did in saying that the board should have refused to serve at the call of the country until——

The Witness. Mr. Chairman, may I interrupt? I don't think I said that.

Mr. Gray. You have interrupted me.

The Witness. Excuse me, sir.

Mr. Gray. You said until the letter had been rewritten.

The Witness. Excuse me.

Mr. Gray. I was in the middle of that sentence.

The Witness. Excuse me.

Mr. Gray. But the other witness to whom I refer made a particular point about the construction of the letter. There was no uncertainty in his views whatsoever, and the thing that concerns me, also, about all of this is public misapprehension of which I am sure there is a great deal. So that if witnesses before this board have testified in such strong terms about the construction of this letter, before the board, they no doubt are testifying in equally strong terms among their associates, perhaps in the scientific community. This is another case of misapprehension or misunderstanding.

I want to make it clear that this discussion which I am conducting with you is for the purpose of emphasizing the seriousness of some of these misapprehensions, and not in defense of or attack upon the letter which was written by the general manager with which this board was not concerned.

I would like to ask you another question which relates now to the Alvarez testimony.

The Witness. I think I might clarify a point if you will let me.

Mr. Gray. You certainly may.

The Witness. I have not discussed the procedure of this board with anyone, of course, while it is going on—scientists or otherwise. I have not given any statement to the press. I have talked over that particular matter which I raised here and which I think is so important with several men, not scientists, as it happens—there was one scientist among them—but men that I have great confidence in, in order to attempt to clarify my own thinking. One of those was a Justice of the Supreme Court. One or two others were men whose names you would recognize.

I realize what an important thing it is that I am calling attention to there. I realize how serious a thing it is in this country if the public gets the impression that a man is being tried for his opinions. Hence, before appearing before you, I talked to a number of men for the purpose of clarifying my own thinking. But otherwise, I have not discussed this matter with scientists, and I certainly

have not done so generally in public.
  Mr. GRAY. All right, sir.

This "other distinguished witness before this Board, a man of international distinction, who in milder terms, but in somewhat the same spirit, was critical of the General Manager's letter," was Conant. Here is what Conant had said:

  Q. You have read the Commission's letter of December 23, 1953, which initiated these proceedings containing the derogatory information about Dr. Oppenheimer?
  A. Yes, I have read it.
  Q. Have you a comment to make on it?
  A. Yes, I have. I would like to comment on it. I would like to comment on one section particularly. Somewhere in the letter it says that the substance of the information which raises the question concerning your eligibility for employment, referring to Dr. Oppenheimer, on atomic energy work, is as follows, and then later it says that it was further reported that in the autumn of 1949 and subsequently you strongly opposed the development of the hydrogen bomb; one, on moral grounds; two, by claiming it was not possible; three, by claiming that there were insufficient facilities and scientific personnel to carry on the development; and four, that it was not politically desirable.
  Well, it seems to me that letter must have been very carelessly drafted, if I may say so, because if you take those two statements together, of course, it would indicate that anybody who opposed the development of the hydrogen bomb was not eligible for employment on atomic energy work later.
  I am sure that no one who drew that letter could have intended that, because such a position would be an impossible position to hold in this country; namely, that a person who expressed views about an important matter before him, as a member of the General Advisory Committee, could then be ineligible because of a security risk for subsequent work in connection with the Government. I am sure that argument would not have been intended. If it did, it would apply to me because I opposed it strongly, as strongly as anybody else on that committee, that is, the development of the hydrogen bomb. Not for the reasons that are given there.
  If I might say so they are a rather caricature of the type of argument which was used in the committee in which I participated. I should say I opposed it as strongly as anybody on a combination of political and strategic and highly technical considerations. I will go into that later to some degree although I don't think this is the place to justify the conclusions of the General Advisory Committee. It would be a long story.
  It seems to me that clearly the question before you here is the question rather, is the implied indictment, I submit, namely, because of the information in the first part of this letter—Dr. Oppenheimer's association with alleged Communist sympathizers in the early days in his youth—that that somehow created a state of mind in Dr. Oppenheimer so that he opposed the development of the hydrogen bomb for what might be said reasons which were detrimental to the best interests of the United States, because they were interests of the Soviet Union which he in one way or another had at heart.
  That, I take it, is the issue which I take it is before you in part in considering this letter. It is to that that I would like to speak for, I think, I have some evidence that convinces me that any such charge is completely ill founded.

The meaning of the charge was plain enough. Nichols stated clearly that Oppenheimer had opposed the development of the hydrogen bomb not only "by claiming that it was not feasible," not only "by claiming that there were insufficient facilities and scientific personnel to carry on the development," which were grounds well within the competence of the General Advisory Committee. Nichols had gone on to say that Oppenheimer had opposed its development "on moral grounds" and by claiming that "it was not politically desirable." The separate paragraphing served only to make what Nichols had written the easier to read and so much the clearer.

It reflects on the firmness of the Board, the susceptibility, if you please, to the influence of counsel, that it accepted Robb's explanation. They said:

We are constrained to make a final comment about General Nichols' letter. Unfortunately, in the press accounts in which the letter was printed in full, Item number 24, which consisted of one paragraph, was broken down into four paragraphs. Many thoughtful people, as a result, felt that the implication of one or more of these paragraphs as they appeared in the press standing alone was that the letter sought to initiate proceedings which would impugn a man on the ground of his holding and forcefully expressing strong opinions. It is regrettable that the language of the letter or the way in which it publicly appeared, might have given any credence to such an interpretation. In any event, the Board wishes strongly to record its profound and positive view that no man should be tried for the expression of his opinions.

This is all very well, but it was not enough. There remained the innuendo that Oppenheimer had opposed the development of the hydrogen bomb out of disloyalty. I have said that Nichols did not use Borden's letter in preparing his charges. Nevertheless, there was a hangover of Borden in this innuendo. There was an implication which had to be disposed of. The Board did just that.

With respect to the second portion of General Nichols' letter, the Board believes that Dr. Oppenheimer's opposition to the hydrogen bomb and his related conduct in the postwar period until April 1951, involved no lack of loyalty to the United States or attachment to the Soviet Union. The Board was impressed by the fact that even those who were critical of Dr. Oppenheimer's judgment and activities or lack of activities, without exception, testified to their belief in his loyalty.

The Board concludes that any possible implications to the contrary which might have been read into the second part of General Nichols' letter are not supported by any material which the Board has seen.

The Board wishes to make clear that in attempting to arrive at its findings and their significance with respect to the hydrogen bomb, it has in no way sought to appraise the technical judgments of those who were concerned with the program.

But Gray and Morgan were not satisfied. They said:

We cannot dismiss the matter of Dr. Oppenheimer's relationship to the

development of the hydrogen bomb simply with the finding that his conduct
was not motivated by disloyalty, because it is our conclusion that, whatever
the motivation, the security interests of the United States were affected.

Three things disturbed them. One was Oppenheimer's failure to
give "enthusiastic support for the program." Another was that he
had been "less than candid" in his testimony on his attitude and
position toward the problem. The third was the intrusion of moral
and political considerations in his convictions, which were "not
necessarily a reflection of technical judgment" nor "necessarily related to the protection of the strongest offensive military interests
of the country."

Take the *lack of enthusiasm* first.
Gray and Morgan said:

We believe that, had Dr. Oppenheimer given his enthusiastic support to the
program, a concerted effort would have been initiated at an earlier date.
Following the President's decision, he did not show the enthusiastic support
for the program which might have been expected of the chief atomic adviser
to the Government under the circumstances. Indeed, a failure to communicate
an abandonment of his earlier position undoubtedly had an effect upon other
scientists. It is our feeling that Dr. Oppenheimer's influence in the atomic
scientific circles with respect to the hydrogen bomb was far greater than he
would have led this Board to believe in his testimony before the Board. The
Board has reluctantly concluded that Dr. Oppenheimer's candor left much to
be desired in his discussions with the Board of his attitude and position in the
entire chronology of the hydrogen-bomb problem.

At another point, the Board said:

The Board further concludes that after it was determined, as a matter
of national policy (January 31, 1950) to proceed with development of a hydrogen bomb, Dr. Oppenheimer did not oppose the project in a positive or open
manner, nor did he decline to cooperate in the project. However, Dr. Oppenheimer is recognized in scientific circles as one of the foremost leaders in the
atomic energy field and he has considerable influence on the "policy direction"
of the atomic program. The Board finds that his views in opposition to the
development of the H-bomb as expressed in 1949 became widely known among
scientists, and since he did not make it known that he had abandoned these
views, his attitude undoubtedly had an adverse effect on recruitment of scientists
and the progress of the scientific effort in this field. In other words, the Board
finds, that if Dr. Oppenheimer had enthusiastically supported the thermonuclear
program either before or after the determination of national policy, the H-bomb
project would have been pursued with considerably more vigor, thus increasing
the possibility of earlier success in this field.

At this point, we have a brief comic interlude, though it is not
very funny. Nichols had been put to it to find anything Oppenheimer had done—besides taking an attitude against the H-bomb—
except for one thing. Nichols had charged: "It was further reported
you departed from your proper role as an adviser to the commission

by causing the distribution, separately and in private, to top personnel at Los Alamos of the majority and minority reports of the General Advisory Committee on development of the hydrogen bomb for the purpose of trying to turn such top personnel against the development of the hydrogen bomb."

Nichols had got the wrong chairman. What had happened was this: it was Senator MacMahon, the chairman of the Joint Congressional Atomic Energy Committee, not Oppenheimer, chairman of the General Advisory Committee, who had distributed those reports. MacMahon was coming to Los Alamos, and Carroll Wilson, the General Manager of the Atomic Energy Commission, telephoned Manley, the associate director of Los Alamos, and asked him to distribute copies of the Committee's report in preparation for a meeting with Chairman MacMahon. Manley called Teller into his office and showed him the reports of the General Advisory Committee. Teller said that Manley "used words which I at least at that time interpreted as meaning that Oppenheimer wanted me to see these reports, which I thought was kind. . . . Manley said something of that kind, that our Chairman, or the Chairman, I don't know which, sends his regards and wants you to see this."

It was an understandable blunder. The trouble was, no one checked it, neither the F.B.I., if they got the story from Teller, nor Nichols, before he made derogatory information against Oppenheimer out of the fact that his own predecessor had distributed the G.A.C. reports. Stupid.

The Board found

> that Dr. Oppenheimer was not responsible for the distribution, separately and in private, to top personnel at Los Alamos of the majority and minority reports of the General Advisory Committee on development of the hydrogen bomb, but that such distribution was made on the direction of the then general manager of the Atomic Energy Commission, Carroll L. Wilson, apparently in order to prepare the personnel at Los Alamos to discuss the matter with the chairman of the Joint Committee on Atomic Energy of the Congress.

To continue with this lack of enthusiasm:

> The Board does not find that Dr. Oppenheimer urged other scientists not to work on the program. However, enthusiastic support on his part would perhaps have encouraged other leading scientists to work on the program.
> Because of technical questions involved, the Board is unable to make a categorical finding as to whether the opposition of the hydrogen bomb "has definitely slowed down its development." The Board concludes that the opposition to the H-bomb by many persons connected with the atomic energy program, of which Dr. Oppenheimer was the "most experienced, most powerful, and most effective member" did delay the initiation of concerted effort which led to the development of a thermonuclear weapon.

I don't see how lack of enthusiasm on the part of an adviser by

any stretch of relevance or reason can make him a security risk. It **may** very well make him less useful as an adviser. It may equally well make him so much the better one. This is for those to decide who want advice. They can always choose another adviser who is more to their liking; or they may think it profitable to have adverse criticism available. Look who was chosen to succeed Oppenheimer as chairman of the General Advisory Committee. It was Dr. Rabi, who had joined with Dr. Fermi in an out-and-out opposition to the hydrogen bomb in 1949. Rabi had come round to support and encourage the development of the H-bomb. So had Oppenheimer. If an adviser has a right to his own opinions—and surely it is his duty to express no other—does he not have an equal right to, and do we not equally want, his own degree of enthusiasm? No, Gray and Morgan would say, he must keep his emotions out of his opinions. But enthusiasm is emotion.

The Board was offering the Commission a reason why Oppenheimer's contract as adviser and consultant should not be renewed. It makes no sense to say that Oppenheimer's lack of enthusiasm made him a security risk.

It makes less than none. It is disturbing to find that Gray and Morgan seem unaware that they are impugning the piety of the "profound and positive view" they expressed "that no man should be tried for the expression of his opinions." They did not question the sincerity of Oppenheimer's opinions. "We are willing to assume that they were motivated by deep moral convictions." What Gray and Morgan held against Oppenheimer, and one of the considerations which led them to regard him as a bad risk, was that he had any convictions at all which did not enthusiastically support the official program of the Government. They reject the charge "which would impugn a man on the ground of his holding and forcefully expressing strong opinions," and they condemn him for holding an opinion which did not enthusiastically support the policy of the Government. They encourage others to have strong opinions one way and condemn Oppenheimer for not having an enthusiastic opinion the other way.

There are, then, only two kinds of persons who do not endanger the common defense and security: those who have no opinions of their own at all and those whose opinions coincide precisely with official policy. No, I am wrong. Those who have no opinions as well as those who agree with the Government—both must enthusiastically support the official policy of the Government. Those who are not with us are against us.

With the seriousness of men who are not aware of the significance of what they are doing, Gray and Morgan were not only impugning their own pious protestations but the very axis of democracy—a toleration of disagreement. Are men turned into tongues? "Here in America we are descended in blood and spirit from revolutionaries and rebels—men and women who dared to dissent from accepted doctrines. As their heirs, may we never confuse honest dissent with disloyal subversion." That was President Eisenhower. (Quoted in the *Listener*, June 10, 1954, by Maurice Latey in the BBC's European Service.)

Now for the *lack of candor*. Gray and Morgan said:

> Dr. Oppenheimer testified that what he was opposing in the fall of 1949 was only a "crash program" in the development and production of thermonuclear weapons. In this connection, Dr. Oppenheimer contended that the main question relating to thermonuclear weapons presented to the GAC at its meeting of October 29, 1949, was whether or not the United States should undertake such a crash program. The Board does not believe that Dr. Oppenheimer was entirely candid with the Board in attempting to establish this impression. The record reflects that Dr. Oppenheimer expressed the opinion in writing that the "super bomb should never be produced," and that the commitment to this effect should be unqualified. Moreover, the alternatives available to the GAC were not a choice between an "all-out effort" and no effort at all; there was a middle course which might have been considered.

I am going to take the paragraph sentence by sentence.

Did Oppenheimer testify that "what he was opposing in the fall of 1949 was only 'a crash program' in the development and production of thermonuclear weapons"? When he was asked if what the G.A.C. opposed at its meeting in October 1949 was "merely a crash program," he said, "Yes. I think it would be a better summary to say we opposed this crash program as the answer to the Soviet atomic bomb."

Was this "the main question" presented to the General Advisory Committee? It was certainly the most immediate, the most pointed and the most discussed. Oppenheimer said it was "the special case" of "the Commission doing what it ought to be doing," which was the general question the Committee was asked. Rabi, then a member of the Committee and now its chairman, succeeding Oppenheimer, testified, "The question came not whether we should make a thermonuclear weapon, but whether there should be a crash program. . . . The question was, should it be a crash program and a technical question: What possibilities lay in that?"

What Strauss was proposing and urging was "an all out program." He had written a memorandum of his own about it on October 5 or 6. It was not put into evidence, but Pike remembered the phrase "crash program." "I would think that phrase arose with Mr. Strauss. At least in my mind it ties in with what he wanted to do." Hartley Rowe, who was a member of the Committee, testified that the Commission asked "the advice of the General Advisory Committee on whether or not we should enter into a crash program looking toward the development of the H-bomb." Fermi recalled that "the committee was confronted with forming an opinion whether it was the right time to start an all out program for developing the hydrogen bomb."

So much seems quite clear. But in the next sentence the Board says, "The Board does not believe that Dr. Oppenheimer was entirely candid with the Board in attempting to establish *this impression*." (The italics are mine.)

What impression?

As I have said, Oppenheimer testified that what the General Advisory Committee opposed was a crash program. "We opposed this crash program as the answer to the Soviet atomic bomb."

As soon as Oppenheimer had said this, Robb quoted to him, out of context, without showing him the text, one sentence from the majority annex of the Committee's report. This sentence, on its face, belied what Oppenheimer had said, for it read, "We believe a super bomb should never be produced." Gray and Morgan were relying on this sentence when they said, "The record reflects that Dr. Oppenheimer expressed the opinion in writing that the 'super bomb should never be produced,' and that the commitment to this effect should be unqualified."

Robb had withheld the next sentence, which read, "Mankind would be far better off not to have a demonstration of the feasibility of such a weapon until the present climate of world opinion changes."

Perhaps Oppenheimer was stupid. The report had been available to him for some time before the hearings, as long ago as Nichols' letter suspending his clearance, but it may be that he had not reread it. On the opening day of the hearings, during a recess, he read some extracts from it which Robb had with him. Presumably they included this whole passage. Anyhow, Oppenheimer forgot that his "never" had been qualified in the next sentence.

Later, several days later, Oppenheimer caught on. Gray was asking the questions.

A. The majority annex I still think never said that we should not have it. I think it said that it would be better if such weapons never existed.

Q. I think this is an important point, and I would like to hold on that.

A. All right. But could we have the context which I also have forgotten?

Q. Yes. I will try not to take it out of context.

Mr. ROBB. Here is the majority annex.

Mr. GARRISON. Mr. Chairman, would it not be helpful if Dr. Oppenheimer could look at the report which he has not seen for some time?

The WITNESS. I saw it the other day.

Mr. GRAY. I will show it to him again. I want to pick out the portions that I think are pertinent here, and let him make any observations about context. The security officer cautioned me that I am really getting on difficult ground.

May I interline this?

Mr. ROLANDER. Yes.

The WITNESS. Does the majority annex contain information which should not be on this record?

Mr. GRAY. I do not know.

(Mr. Rolander handed copy of report to Dr. Oppenheimer.)

The WITNESS. I would like to quote the entire paragraph, if that is permissible. I see something—well, I don't know.

Mr. GRAY. I see no reason why the whole paragraph should not be quoted.

Mr. ROLANDER. It is all right.

The WITNESS. This is the fourth paragraph of a six paragraph annex:

"We believe a super bomb should never be produced. Mankind would be far better off not to have a demonstration of the feasibility of such a weapon until the present climate of world opinion changes."

That is that paragraph in its entirety.

By Mr. GRAY:

Q. That language is pretty clear, isn't it, that "We believe a super bomb should never be produced"?

A. Sure it is.

Q. So that there was not any question that the six people of the majority were saying that we should not take steps to develop and produce.

A. Let me indicate to you——

Mr. GARRISON. Mr. Chairman, could he read it once more, because it is the first we heard it.

The WITNESS. This is one paragraph. The document is full of the word "mankind" and this paragraph reads:

"We believe a super bomb should never be produced. Mankind would be far better off not to have a demonstration of the feasibility of such a weapon until the present climate of world opinion changes."

Let me indicate——

By Mr. GRAY:

Q. The question I would ask which would be related to this paragraph is—I am not attacking the motivation of those who held that belief, I am simply saying that the belief is clearly stated there, that the super bomb should never be produced.

A. That a super bomb should never be produced. But look at what that means. If we had had indication that we could not prevent the enemy from doing it, then it was clear that a super bomb would be produced. Then our arguments would be clearly of no avail. This was an exhortation—I will not comment on its wisdom or its folly—to the Government of the United States to seek to prevent the production of super bombs by anyone.

Q. Again, without reference to its wisdom or its folly, is it unreasonable to think that the Commission, reading this report or hearing it made, whichever form it took, would believe that the majority of the General Advisory Committee recommended that the Government not proceed with steps which would lead to the production of a super bomb?

A. That is completely reasonable. We did discuss this point with the Commission on two subsequent occasions. On one occasion we made it clear that nothing in what we had said was meant to obtain, should it be clear or should it be reasonably probable that the enemy was on this trail.

In another, we made it clear that there was a sharp distinction between theoretical study and experiment and invention and production and development on the other hand. So that the Commission, I think, had a little more than this very bald statement to go on.

And yet the Board kept right on believing that Oppenheimer was unalterably and forever opposed to the development and production of thermonuclear weapons.

Lack of candor? Gray and Morgan had both sentences together before them and quoted only the first. What's more, Dr. Rabi, as well as Oppenheimer himself, had done his best to clear away the consequences of Oppenheimer's hasty answer.

Dr. GRAY. With respect to the development of the H bomb—I don't know how to refer to it exactly, but you know what I am talking about—and the issue of who was for and who was against, was it your impression that Dr. Oppenheimer was unalterably opposed to the development?

The WITNESS. No, I would not say so, because after we had those two statements, which were written by different groups which were put in, I distinctly remember Dr. Oppenheimer saying he would be willing to sign both.

Mr. GRAY. My question was bad, because "unalterably" is a pretty strong word, and you have already testified that subsequent to the President's decision he encouraged the program and assisted in it.

The WITNESS. Yes, sir.

Mr. GRAY. So I think this was a bad question.

The WITNESS. I was really testifying as to that time, that there were two statements of attitudes which differed, and he said he would be ready to sign either or both.

Mr. GRAY. He would have been willing to sign the one which you signed?

The WITNESS. That Fermi and I did, yes.

Mr. GRAY. Would you have considered those two reports absolutely consistent?

The WITNESS. No.

Mr. GRAY. Yourself?

The WITNESS. No. I just answered your question about being unalterably opposed.

Mr. GRAY. There was a real difference?

The WITNESS. Yes, sir, there was a real difference. There was no difference as far as a crash program was concerned. That they thought was not in order.

By Mr. MARKS:

Q. Dr. Rabi, in response to a question of the Chairman, the substance of which I believe was, was Dr. Oppenheimer unalterably opposed to the H-bomb development at the time of the October 1949 GAC meeting, I think you said in substance no. and then you added by way of explanation immediately thereafter the two annexes or whatever they were——

A. During the discussion.

Q. During the discussion he said he would be willing to sign either or both. Can you explain what you meant by that rather paradoxical statement?

A. No, I was just reporting a recollection.

Q. What impression did you have?

A. What it means to me is that he was not unalterably opposed, but on sum, adding up everything, he thought it would have been a mistake at that time to proceed with a crash program with all that entailed with this object that we didn't understand, when we had an awfully good program on hand in the fission field, which we did not wish to jeopardize. At least we did not feel it should be jeopardized. It turned out in the events that both could be done. Los Alamos just simply rose to the occasion and worked miracles, absolute miracles.

The third thing which gave Gray and Morgan concern was that Oppenheimer had allowed *moral considerations* to color his advice.

They did not question his right to his opinions, "shared by other competent and devoted individuals, both in and out of Government. We are willing to assume that they were motivated by deep moral conviction. We are concerned, however, that he may have departed his role as scientific adviser to exercise highly persuasive influence in matters in which his convictions were not necessarily a reflection of technical judgment, and also not necessarily related to the protection of the strongest offensive military interests of the country.".

A little earlier in their opinion they had made their concern a little clearer and more emphatic. "In evaluating advice from a specialist which departs from the area of his speciality, Government officials charged with the military posture of our country must also be certain that underlying any advice is a genuine conviction that this country cannot in the interest of security have less than the strongest possible offensive capabilities in a time of national danger."

You see, Gray and Morgan were not concerned with what Oppenheimer's moral convictions were. They were disturbed by the fact that he had any convictions at all, other than what was technical and what they regarded as patriotic. They were really saying no more than what they had said about his lack of enthusiasm for the thermonuclear program, which they were now calling "the strongest offensive military interests." They did not care what his moral scruples were. It was the fact that he had any at all which was derogatory and which made him a security risk.

This is what made Oppenheimer's examination by Robb and then by Gray on this matter of morals so futile and so hard to understand. They made no attempt to find out what his moral scruples were, and Oppenheimer, I think, saw no need of trying to explain them. What he said is not the less interesting.

Here in answer to Robb:

Q. Doctor, in your work and discussions in 1942, in your work on the thermonuclear weapon at Los Alamos in 1943 to 1945 and in your application for the patent of 1944, and in your advice which you as chairman of the GAC gave to the Commission to get on with the work on this thermonuclear, at all those times and on all of those occasions, were you suffering from or deterred by any moral scruples or qualms about the development of this weapon?
A. Of course.
Q. You were?
A. Of course.
Q. But you still got on with the work, didn't you?
A. Yes, because this was a work of exploration. It was not the preparation of

a weapon.

Q. You mean it was just an academic excursion?

A. It was an attempt at finding out what things could be done.

Q. But you were going to spend millions of dollars of the taxpayers' money on it, weren't you?

A. It goes on all the time.

Q. Were you going to spend millions if not billions of dollars of the taxpayers' money just to find out for yourself satisfaction what was going on?

A. We spent no such sums.

Q. Did you propose to spend any such sums for a mere academic excursion?

A. No. It is not an academic thing whether you can make a hydrogen bomb. It is a matter of life and death.

Q. Beginning in 1942 and running through at least the first year or the first meeting of the GAC, you were actively and consciously pushing the development of the thermonuclear bomb, weren't you? Isn't that your testimony?

A. Pushing is not the right word. Supporting and working on it, yes.

Q. Yes. When did these moral qualms become so strong that you opposed the development of the thermonuclear bomb?

A. When it was suggested that it be the policy of the United States to make these things at all costs, without regard to the balance between these weapons and atomic weapons as a part of our arsenal.

Q. What did moral qualms have to do with that?

A. What did moral qualms have to do with it?

Q. Yes, sir.

A. We freely used the atomic bomb.

Q. In fact, Doctor, you testified, did you not, that you assisted in selecting the target for the drop of the bomb on Japan?

A. Right.

Q. You knew, did you not, that the dropping of that atomic bomb on the target you had selected will kill or injure thousands of civilians, is that correct?

A. Not as many as turned out.

Q. How many were killed or injured?

A. 70,000.

Q. Did you have moral scruples about that?

A. Terrible ones.

Q. But you testified the other day, did you not, sir that the bombing of Hiroshima was very successful?

A. Well, it was technically successful.

Q. Oh, technically.

A. It is also alleged to have helped end the war.

Q. Would you have supported the dropping of a thermonuclear bomb on Hiroshima?

A. It would make no sense at all.

Q. Why.

A. The target is too small.

Q. The target is too small. Supposing there had been a target in Japan big enough for a thermonuclear weapon, would you have opposed dropping it?

A. This was not a problem with which I was confronted.

O. I am confronting you with it now, sir.

A. You are not confronting me with an actual problem. I was very relieved when Mr. Stimson removed from the target list Kyoto, which was the largest city and the most vulnerable target. I think this is the nearest thing that was really to your hypothetical question.

Q. That is correct. Would you have opposed the dropping of a thermonuclear weapon on Japan because of moral scruples?

A. I believe I would, sir.

Q. Did you oppose the dropping of the atom bomb on Hiroshima because of moral scruples?

A. We set forth our——

Q. I am asking you about it, not "we."

A. I set forth my anxieties and the arguments on the other side.

Q. You mean you argued against dropping the bomb?

A. I set forth arguments against dropping it.

Q. Dropping the atom bomb?

A. Yes. But I did not endorse them.

Q. You mean having worked, as you put it, in your answer rather excellently, by night and by day for 3 or 4 years to develop the atom bomb, you then argued it should not be used?

A. No; I didn't argue that it should not be used. I was asked to say by the Secretary of War what the views of scientists were. I gave the views against and the views for.

Q. But you supported the dropping of the atom bomb on Japan, didn't you?

A. What do you mean support?

Q. You helped pick the target, didn't you?

A. I did my job which was the job I was supposed to do. I was not in a policymaking position at Los Alamos. I would have done anything that I was asked to do, including making the bombs in a different shape, if I had thought it was technically feasible.

Q. You would have made the thermonuclear weapon, too, wouldn't you?

A. I couldn't.

Q. I didn't ask you that, Doctor.

A. I would have worked on it.

Q. If you had discovered the thermonuclear weapon at Los Alamos, you would have done so. If you could have discovered it, you would have done so, wouldn't you?

A. Oh, yes.

Q. You were working toward that end, weren't you?

A. Yes. I think I need to point out that to run a laboratory is one thing. To advise the Government is another.

Q. I see.

A. I think I need to point out that a great deal that happened between '45 and '49—I am not supposed to say to what extent—but to a very, very massive extent, we had become armed atomically. The prevailing view was that what we had was too good—too big—for the best military use, rather than too small.

Q. Doctor, would you refer to your answer, please, sir? One further question before we get into that.

Am I to gather from your testimony, sir, that in your opinion your function as a member and chairman of the GAC included giving advice on political policies as well as technical advice?

A. I have testified as to that.

Q. Would you repeat it for me, sir?

A. I will repeat it. Our statutory function was to give technical advice.

Q. Yes, sir.

A. We were often asked questionss which went outside of this narrow frame, sometimes we responded, sometimes we didn't. The reason why the general advice, I would call it, editorializing rather than political advice, contained in our annexes was in the annexes and not in the report because it did not seem a proper function for the General Advisory Committee to respond in these terms to the question that had been put to them.

Here in answer to Gray:

Mr. GRAY. I think I should disclose to you what I am after now. I am pursuing the matter of the moral scruples. Should they not have been as important in 1942 as they might have been in 1946 or 1948 or 1949?

The WITNESS. Yes.

Mr. GRAY. I am trying to get at at what time did your strong moral convictions develop with respect to the hydrogen bomb?

The WITNESS. When it became clear to me that we would tend to use any weapon we had.

Mr. GRAY. Then may I ask this: Do you make a sharp distinction between the development of a weapon and the commitment to use it?

The WITNESS. I think there is a sharp distinction but in fact we have not made it.

Mr. GRAY. I have gathered from what you have said, this was something that underlay your thinking. The record shows that you constantly, with greater intensity at varying times perhaps, encouraged the efforts toward some sort of development, but at the point when it seemed clear that we would use it if we developed it, then you said we should not go ahead with it. I don't want to be unfair, but is that it?

The WITNESS. That is only a small part of it. That is a part of it. The other part of it is, of course, the very great hope that these methods of warfare would never have to be used by anybody, a hope which became vivid in the fall of 1949. The hope that we would find a policy for bringing that about, and going on with bigger and bigger bombs would move in the opposite direction. I think that is apparent in the little majority annex to the GAC report.

Mr. GRAY. Was it your feeling when you were concerned officially and otherwise with a possible disarmament program that the United States and its allies would be in a better bargaining position with respect to the development of some sort of international machinery if it did not have the hydrogen bomb as a weapon in the arsenal, or is that relevant at all?

The WITNESS. The kind of thing we had in mind is what one would do in 1949 and 1950.

Mr. GRAY. This is quite a serious line of questioning as far as I am concerned, because it has been said—I am not sure about the language of the Nichols letter—at least in this proceeding and later on in the press, that you frustrated the development of the hydrogen bomb. That has been said. There have been some implications, I suppose, that there were reasons which were not related to feasible, to cost, et cetera.

The WITNESS. Right. I think I can answer your question.

Mr. GRAY. Very well.

The WITNESS. Clearly we could not do anything about the nonuse or the elimination of atomic weapons unless we had nonatomic military strength to meet whatever threats we were faced with. I think in 1949 when we came to this meeting and talked about it, we thought we were at a parting of the ways, a parting of the ways in which either the reliance upon atomic weapons would increase further and further or in which it would be reduced. We hoped it would be reduced because without that there was no chance of not having them in combat.

Mr. GRAY. Your deep concern about the use of the hydrogen bomb, if it were developed, and therefore your own views at the time as to whether we should proceed in a crash program to develop it—your concern about this—became greater, did it not, as the practicabilities became more clear? Is that an unfair statement?

The WITNESS. I think it is the opposite of true. Let us not say about use. But my feeling about development became quite different when the practicabilities became clear. When I saw how to do it, it was clear to me that one had to at least make the thing. Then the only problem was what would one do about them when one had them. The program we had in 1949 was a tortured thing that you could well argue did not make a great deal of technical sense. It was therefore possible to argue also that you did not want it even if you could have it. The program in 1951 was technically so sweet that you could not argue about that. It was purely the military, the political and the humane problem of what you were going to do about it once you had it.

Why did Oppenheimer's moral scruples against the hydogen bomb disappear as soon as Teller, in 1951, showed that it could be made? Partly, I think, because they were overwhelmed by the deep conviction of the scientist that whatever can be done must be explored. Oppenheimer had said earlier, "However, it is my judgment in these things that when you see something that is technically sweet, you go ahead and do it and you argue about what to do about it only after you have had your technical success. That is the way it was with the atomic bomb." Partly too because then the ways had parted and the opportunity, as Fermi put it, "to outlaw the thing before it was born" had gone. "I sort of had the view at that time," Fermi said, "that perhaps it would be easier to outlaw by some kind of international agreement something that did not exist. My opinion was that one should try to do that, and failing that, one should with considerable regret go ahead."

This was why Bush had so strongly opposed the test of the hydrogen bomb in the fall of 1952, just before the election. He went to Dean Acheson, the Secretary of State, and tried to persuade him that the test should be postponed.

> There were two primary reasons why I took action at that time, and went directly to the Secretary of State. There was scheduled a test which was evidently going to occur early in November. I felt that it was utterly improper—and I still think so—for that test to be put off just before election, to confront an incoming President with an accomplished test for which he would carry the full responsibility thereafter. For that test marked our entry into a very disagreeable type of world.
>
> In the second place, I felt strongly that that test ended the possibility of the only type of agreement that I thought was possible with Russia at that time, namely, an agreement to make no more tests. For that kind of an agreement would have been self-policing in the sense that if it was violated the violation would be immediately known. I still think that we made a grave error in conducting that test at that time, and not attempting to make that type of simple agreement with Russia. I think history will show that was a turning point that when we entered into the grim world that we are entering right now, that those who pushed that thing through to a conclusion without making that attempt have a great deal to answer for.
>
> That is what moved me, sir. I was very much moved at the time.

None of this, however, was the concern of the Board. Oppenheimer had moral scruples. He could not, therefore, be genuinely convinced "that this country cannot, in the interests of security, have less than the strongest possible offensive capabilities."

I can well understand how moral scruples of one kind or another may make a man less fit for a particular job, but when we find that there is something derogatory about moral scruples and when it is also derogatory not to be enthusiastic about what we have moral scruples against doing, then we know that the very axis of our moral world is tumbling.

Is it possible to put ourselves back through the millennium of the last half-dozen years to the time when it seemed that the hydrogen bomb might well be no greater a menace than "a contradiction of the laws of physics"? For, to Rabi, this is what it seemed it might be—and he hoped it would be. We'd be going back to a Golden Age, when men could be killed only thousands at a time. I suppose it is now as impossible to go back as it was in our youth to go back to the age when men killed other men only a few at a time. For in our sight the last half-dozen years have been an eternity. And yet in the eyes of our children they may be the Golden Age.

At the meeting of the British Association for the Advancement of

Science in the fall of 1954, its president, Dr. E. D. Adrian, told its members—and us—how close to the end we were. I give you a shortened version, broadcast by the BBC and printed in the *Listener* on September 2, 1954. The full text was in the *Bulletin of the Atomic Scientists* for November 1954.

. . . We all know where our curiosity has now landed us; with advances in atomic physics which might be applied to devastate half the world. And the immense explosions and ruined cities are not the only dangers, for even if we survive them we must face the possibility that repeated atomic explosion might produce a degree of general radio activity which no one could escape.

This is a real danger, though the level would not rise rapidly and there is a large margin in hand. When atomic energy is used to supply power for industry the risk of contamination can be avoided. But in a major war precautions would soon be set aside. A few hundred large bombs might destroy most of Britain without world-wide risk. A few thousand would pass the danger line. A war bound to end in wholesale destruction can appeal only to people who are desperate. But they can be made desperate; controls and conventions are not fool-proof, and in future if ever the world is split in two opposing groups with large stores of atomic weapons it must face this added risk of catastrophe.

Yet we have surely no right to feel that our troubles are so much worse than those of earlier generations. Our grandfathers could do nothing to ward off the danger which seemed to face their dearest beliefs, but our fate is in our own hands. Our predicament is the inevitable result of our curiosity and of the physical nature of the world we live in. Yet if we can make our behaviour worthy of our increased knowledge we can live safely.

So the scientist has a double responsibility. He must apply his science to the study of human nature to prevent its failures, but he cannot wait for the discoveries which might make us act more wisely; he must make it abundantly clear now that the human race cannot stand more than a few thousand major atomic explosions, whether they hit their target or miss it. If we can make this known universally our meeting will not have failed.

Fermi and Rabi had forebodings six years ago, in 1949. They put the following words into their annex to the General Advisory Committee's Report: "The fact that no limits exist to the destructiveness of this weapon makes its very existence and the knowledge of its constuction a danger to humanity as a whole. It is necessarily an evil thing considered in any light. For these reasons we believe it important for the President of the United States to tell the American public and the world that we think it wrong on fundamental ethical principles to initiate the development of such a weapon."

Churchill told the House of Commons in November 1954 that an undue number of atomic- and hydrogen-bomb explosives might have serious effects on the earth's atmosphere for five thousand years. For that long, then, they are cumulative. It would be the great, and final, irony if mankind were to exterminate itself, not in the catastrophe and holocaust of war but slowly and painstakingly by tests and experiments; not by manfully killing one another but boastfully, by way of demonstrating to themselves how easily and efficiently it can be done.

11. OPPENHEIMER'S OPPOSITION
TO THE H-BOMB IN 1949

I AM NOT going to undertake to present the case for the development of the H-bomb. I find it too hard to believe that it was adequately presented in the testimony before the Board. What else the Board had before it, of course, I do not know. It would be idle for me, and impertinent to you, if I were to rely on current scuttlebut. Anyhow, the case for the H-bomb won.

The Commission called seven witnesses on this issue. Borden I will ignore. Teller, who wanted to develop the H-bomb and told us how to do it, simply disagreed with Oppenheimer's judgment, which is fair enough. Professors Latimer, Pitzer and Alvarez from Berkeley agreed with Teller and could not understand anyone who did not. Latimer gives me the impression that he smells brimstone. He seems to regard Oppenheimer as a sort of Faust who has made a pact with Satan. Unfortunately the Board did not have the testimony of Ernest Lawrence. He was sick. He started East, got as far as Oak Ridge, but had to return to Berkeley. This leaves the two witnesses from and for the Air Force, General Roscoe C. Wilson and David T. Griggs, who had been chief scientist for the Air Force in 1951–1952. I am going to give you only the testimony of General Wilson.

General Wilson told the Board, "I am a dedicated airman," and added, "I am first of all a big-bomb man." He was a candid, careful witness. He wanted it "clearly understood" that he was not raising any question of Oppenheimer's loyalty. He testified that he was "worried" by a number of things. They gave him "concern." Not enough to bring them to the Provost Marshal, but enough to go to the Chief of Air Force Intelligence. There were four things which gave him enough concern to testify about them.

One was "the fact that Dr. Oppenheimer was interested in what I call the internationalizing of atomic energy, this at a time when the United States had a monopoly." Certainly Oppenheimer was interested in internationalizing atomic energy. In 1946 he was a member of the board of consultants who prepared the Acheson-Lilienthal report. The other members were Chester I. Barnard, Charles A. Thomas, Harry A. Winne and David Lilienthal. Then he helped Bernard Baruch with his plan and in his negotiations with the Soviets that summer. General Wilson said that Oppenheimer's interest in internationalizing atomic energy was the first of "these things that worried me," and when he was asked whether "perhaps it might be better to internationalize it while there was a chance to do so"—that is, before the Russians got it—the general said, "I have never heard that argument."

Another concern of Wilson's was the fact that Oppenheimer was "not enthusiastic" about two of the three devices in the long-range-detection program of the Air Force, because of "the then state of development of those devices," though he admitted that "the one that appeared to be most immediately promising, the one that perhaps we had the most information on was the one that Dr. Oppenheimer supported to the greater degree."

Wilson's third particular concern was Oppenheimer's "lack of confidence in the timely success" of nuclear-powered flight over nuclear-powered ships. "I don't challenge his technical judgment, but at the same time he felt less strongly opposed to the nuclear-powered ships."

Finally and generally, General Wilson was worried because Oppenheimer approached thermonuclear weapons with "more conservatism than the Air Force would have liked." Every word General Wilson said is to be taken seriously and given full weight, for he was an honest and candid witness. But I do not see that his testimony added up to enough to be taken seriously as a whole.

It is possible that this is not all that worried Wilson. There are two rows of stars in the transcript of his testimony here, one after his worry about "the internationalizing of atomic energy," the other after he spoke about nuclear-powered aircraft. These stars indicate the deletion of something that was classified, but I see no reason to think it was more than secret details. If it were, Wilson would scarcely have gone on to say, as he did, "The sum total of this, to my mind, was adding up that we were not exploiting the full military potential in this field. Once again it was a matter of judgment. I would like to say that the fact that I admire Dr. Oppenheimer so much, the fact that he is such a brilliant man, the fact that he has such a command of the English language, has such national prestige, and such power of persuasion, only made me nervous, because I felt if this was so it would not be to the interest of the United States, in my judgment. It was for that reason that I went to the Director of Intelligence to say that I felt unhappy."

Why did Oppenheimer oppose the development of a hydrogen bomb in the fall of 1949? What were his reasons? What were the reasons of the other members of the General Advisory Committee, of which he was the chairman? They too opposed it, all of them except Dr. Seaborg, who was away in Sweden and who preferred not to take a position one way or the other when he returned, too late for the meeting of October 29, 1949, but in time for the next meeting and before President Truman had made his decision.

The obvious answer to these questions lies in the General Advisory Committee's report, which eight of its nine members signed, and in its two annexes. There were two annexes containing the more general views of the members on the great issues of policy. One of them was signed by Conant, DuBridge, Rowe, Buckley, Smyth and Oppenheimer himself. The other was signed by Fermi and Rabi. The Board, of course, had these before it, and Oppenheimer was permitted to reread them before he testified, but they were still classified. So neither you nor I nor Oppenheimer's counsel can read more than the few passages which were read into the record. I will give you Oppenheimer's testimony, and also Conant's, DuBridge's, Rowe's, Buckley's, Fermi's and Rabi's. You will then have all but Smyth's, who had become a commissioner and did not testify, and Seaborg's, who was away but wished to express no opinion anyway.

We are near the end of October 1949. The Russians had exploded their first atomic bomb a month before. Our own atomic-bomb program was progressing. Our stock of atomic bombs was already large, and it was increasing. No one yet knew how to make a thermonuclear bomb, although we were trying. We were not trying so hard as some thought we should. We had other things to do. We had only so many people who were up to trying. People were as necessary as money. Moreover, at that time, in the fall of 1949, the question was not so much whether we ought to develop a thermonuclear bomb as it was whether we should make more of an effort to discover how to.

Bethe testified, "I was hoping that it might be possible to prove that thermonuclear reactions were not feasible at all. I would have thought that the greatest security for the United States would have lain in the conclusive proof of the impossibility of a thermonuclear bomb. I must confess that this was the main motive which made me start work on thermonuclear reactions in the summer of 1950."

Rabi testified, "I just want to give my own impression that it was a field where we really did not know what we were talking about, except on the basis of general experience. We didn't even know whether this thing contradicted the laws of physics." "You didn't know what?" "Whether it contradicted the laws of physics." "In other words, it could have been altogether impossible?" "It could have been altogether impossible. The thing we are talking about. I want to be specific."

Here is Oppenheimer's testimony. I will interrupt it for the testimony of others to whom he refers or wherever else it seems appropriate:

During October or late September, I think October, a good many people came to see me or called me or wrote me letters about the super program. I remember three things. Dr. Teller arrived. He told me that he thought this was the moment to go all out on the hydrogen-bomb program.

Mr. GRAY. May I interrupt? I am sorry. This is following——

The WITNESS. Following the GAC meeting of September and prior to the meeting in October.

Mr. GRAY. Yes.

The WITNESS. Dr. Bethe arrived. I think they were there together or their visits partly overlapped, although I am not sure. He was very worried about it. He will testify.

By Mr. GARRISON:

Q. About what?

A. About the thermonuclear program, whether it was right or wrong; what his relations to it should be. I assume he will testify to that better than I can. It was not clear to me what the right thing to do was.

Mr. ROBB. You say to you or to him?

The WITNESS. To me.

Teller testified:

Q. Will you tell the board whether or not shortly thereafter you had a conversation with Dr. Oppenheimer about the thermonuclear or about what activity should be undertaken to meet the Russian advance?

A. I remember two such conversations. One was in the fall and necessarily superficial. That was just a very few hours after I heard, returning from a trip abroad, that the Russians had exploded an A-bomb. I called up Oppenheimer who happened to be in Washington, as I was at that time, and I asked him for advice, and this time I remember his advice literally. It was, "Keep your shirt on."

Perhaps I might mention that my mind did not immediately turn in the direction of working on the thermonuclear bomb. I had by that time quite thoroughly accepted the idea that with the reduced personnel it was much too difficult an undertaking. I perhaps should mention, and I think it will clear the picture, that a few months before the Russian explosion I agreed to rejoin Los Alamos for the period of 1 year on leave of absence from the University of Chicago.

I should also mention that prior to that Oppenheimer had talked to me and encouraged me to go back to Los Alamos, and help in the work there. I also went back to Los Alamos with the understanding and with the expectation that I shall just help along in their normal program in which some very incipient phases of the thermonuclear work was included, but nothing on a very serious scale.

I was quite prepared to contribute mostly in the direction of the fission weapons. At the time when I returned from this short trip abroad, and was very much disturbed about the Russian bomb, I was looking around for ways in which we could more successfully speed up our work and only after several weeks of discussion did I come to the conclusion that no matter what the odds seemed to be, we must at this time—I at least must at this time put my full attention to the thermonuclear program.

I also felt that this was much too big an undertaking and I was just very scared of it. I was looking around for some of the old crew to come out and participate in this work. Actually if anyone wanted to head this enterprise, one of the people whom I went to visit, in fact the only one where I had very strong hopes, was Hans Bethe.

Q. About when was this, Doctor?

A. To the best of my recollection it was the end of October.

Q. 1949?

A. Right. Again I am not absolutely certain of my dates, but that is the best of my memory. I can tie it down a little bit better with respect to other dates. It was a short time before the GAC meeting in which that committee made a decision against the thermonuclear program.

After a somewhat strenuous discussion, Bethe, to the best of my understanding, decided that he would come to Los Alamos and help us. During this discussion, Oppenheimer called up and invited Bethe and me to come and discuss this matter wih him in Princeton. This we did do, and visited Oppenheimer in his office.

When we arrived, I remember that Oppenheimer showed us a letter on his desk which he said he had just received. This letter was from Conant. I do not know whether he showed us the whole letter or whether he showed us a short section of it, or whether he only read to us a short section. Whichever it was, and I cannot say which it was, one phrase of Conant's sticks in my mind, and that phrase was "over my dead body," referring to a decision to go ahead with a crash program on the thermonuclear bomb.

Apart from showing us this letter, or reading it to us, whichever it was, Oppenheimer to the best of my recollection did not argue against any crash program. We did talk for quite awhile and could not possibly reproduce the whole argument but at least one important trend in this discussion—and I do not know how relevant this is—was that Oppenheimer argued that some phases of exaggerated secrecy in connection with the A-bomb was perhaps not to the best interests of the country, and that if he undertook the thermonuclear development, this should be done right from the first and should be done more openly.

Oppenheimer went on:

I had a communication. I can't find it as a letter, and I don't know whether it was a letter or phone call. It was from Dr. Conant. He said that this would be a very great mistake.

By Mr. GARRISON:

Q. What would be a great mistake?

A. To go all out with the super. Presumably he also will testify to this. He did not go into detail, but said if it ever came before the General Advisory Committee, he would certainly oppose it as folly.

No letter ever showed up. It was probably a phone call. There was, however, a letter from Oppenheimer to Conant on October 21, 1949, a week before the meeting. It was addressed to "Uncle Jim," as Conant had been known in Los Alamos. Oppenheimer said it expressed his views "as measured and honest as any record could be."

"Dear Uncle Jim:

"We are exploring the possibilities for our talk with the President on October 30th. All members of the advisory committee will come to the meeting Saturday except Seaborg, who must be in Sweden, and whose general views we have in written form. Many of us will do some preliminary palavering on the 28th.

"There is one bit of background which I would like you to have before we meet. When we last spoke, you thought perhaps the reactor program offered the most decisive example of the need for policy clarification. I was inclined to think that the super might also be relevant. On the technical side, as far as I can tell, the super is not very different from what it was when we first spoke of it more than 7 years ago: a weapon of unknown design, cost, deliberability and military value. But a very great change has taken place in the climate of opinion. On the one hand, two experienced promoters have been at work, i. e., Ernest Lawrence and Edward Teller. The project has long been dear to Teller's heart; and Ernest has convinced himself that we must learn from Operation Joe that the Russians will soon do the super, and that we had better beat them to it."

"On the technical side, he proposes to get some neutron producing heavy water reactors built; and to this, for a variety of reasons, I think we must say amen since"

"* * * and many other things will all profit by the availability of neutrons.

"But the real development has not been of a technical nature. Ernest spoke to Knowland and McMahon, and to some at least of the joint chiefs. The joint congressional committee, having tried to find something tangible to chew on ever since September 23d, has at least found its answer. We must have a super, and we must have it fast. A subcommittee is heading west to investigate this problem at Los Alamos, and in Berkeley. The joint chiefs appear informally to have decided to give the development of the super overriding priority, though no formal request has come through. The climate of opinion among the competent physicists also shows signs of shifting. Bethe, for instance, is seriously considering return on a full time basis; and so surely are some others. I have had long talks with Bradbury and Manley, and with Von Neumann. Bethe, Teller, McCormack, and LeBaron are all scheduled to turn up within the next 36 hours. I have agreed that if there is a conference on the super program at Los Alamos, I will make it my business to attend.

"What concerns me is really not the technical problem. I am not sure the miserable thing will work, nor that it can be gotten to a target except by ox cart. It seems likely to me even further to worsen the unbalance of our present war plans. What does worry me is that this thing appears to have caught the imagination, both of the congressional and of military people, as the answer to the problem posed by the Russian advance. It would be folly to oppose the exploration of this weapon. We have always known it had to be done; and it does have to be done, though it appears to be singularly proof against any form of experimental approach. But that we become committed to it as the way to save the country and the peace appears to me full of dangers.

"We will be faced with all this at our meeting; and anything that we do or do not say to the President, will have to take it into consideration. I shall feel far more secure if you have had an opportunity to think about it.

"I still remember my visit with gratitude and affection.

"ROBERT OPPENHEIMER.

"Dr. JAMES B. CONANT,
"President, Harvard University, Cambridge 38, Mass."

Conant gave the Board his views:

Q. There was put in evidence here, Dr. Conant, a letter which Dr. Oppenheimer identified as one written to you shortly before the meeting of the General Advisory Committee in October 1949, in which he addressed you as "Uncle Jim" and talked about the question of the hydrogen bomb and the forthcoming meeting.

When I showed you that letter, as I did ——
A. Yes, you showed me that last night.

Q. A copy of it, I mean. Did you have any recollection of having received it?
A. No, I had not. I did not remember it. I couldn't say that when I saw it. I suppose it was delivered. It must have been a classified document. I was very fussy about not taking classified documents when they came to the office. If I received it, I must have taken it right down to Washington. I don't say I didn't see it, but I have no remembrance of it. I would not have known about it if you had not called it to my attention.

Q. Do you remember any discussion with Dr. Oppenheimer one way or another before the October meeting?
A. No, I am afraid my detailed recollection of that period is very hazy. I think there were two meetings at least of the General Advisory Committee.

Q. One in October and one in December?
A. Yes. There was certainly plenty of discussion in those meetings. Those I remember pretty well, but when and where I first discussed this matter, where I first heard of it, is not clear in my mind. Whether I walked into it, or whether, as implied by that letter, it was before, or whether it was some other source of information, I am sorry I just don't remember.

Q. How did Dr. Oppenheimer as chairman of the General Advisory Committee conduct the meetings?
A. He was an excellent chairman, but I hope he won't take it amiss if I say he ran them like a faculty meeting. There was a great deal of discussion and a great deal of talk. They were the most lengthy meetings I ever sat in on in my life. They consumed an un-Godly amount of time, but they covered the ground from A to Z.

Q. Coming now to the meeting of October 29, 1949, when you first discussed the hydrogen bomb, upon whose technical advice did you rely?
A. I can't be sure of that meeting because, as I say, my memory of that period is not accurate enough to spot the meeting and the discussions, and so on. As I said, in my comment here a minute ago, I was moved in my opposition to this in signing the statement of the General Advisory Committee, which I have not seen since, by a mixture of political, strategic, and technical considerations. Those technical considerations are extremely detailed, but judging from some things I have read in general in the press, completely misunderstood.

Of course they concerned the question of what kind of large weapon to make and what was the cost and what were the opportunities of doing it, and what were the probabilities.

When it came to a question of the nuclear physics in which I am by no means an expert, I always counted on Dr. Fermi's judgment. With all due respect to all the other members of the committee, I felt he was both experimentally and theoretically the man whose judgment was to be relied on. Indeed his record during the development of the atomic bomb I consider one of the most extraordinary pieces of scientific correct calculations I can image. The story is a perfectly amazing one.

Q. Would you state very briefly for the board the reasons which lead you to make the recommendation which you did make on the subject of the hydrogen bomb?
A. It is a very complicated thing. I think it would take a long time to do a detailed inquiry into that. Some day if the Government wants to set that up, I should be glad to take the time, but I would have to go back into the record.

Therefore, what I shall do is only a general sketch. With all due respect to Dr. Gray and his colleagues, this would take a board, which included a nuclear physics expert, to assess the questions of whether the technical part of this decision was right or wrong.

On the general strategic and political grounds there were some of the same reasons which we subsequently brought to a head on the committee on the present danger, namely, this was supposed to be an answer to the fact that the Russians had exploded an atomic bomb.

Some of us felt then, and I felt more strongly as time went on, that the real answer was to do a job and revamp our whole defense establishment, put in something like Universal Military Service, get Europe strong on the ground, so that Churchill's view about the atomic bomb would not be canceled out.

One of the considerations was that this was sort of a Maginot Line psychology being pushed on us. On the technical ground the question was the investment in preparing certain materials which I am not going into, which are restricted, which seemed at that time necessary; the use of materials which I don't want to mention, which would be used up.

The question was when you expended a certain amount of manpower and energy and material, would you actually from the point of view of delivering blows against a potential enemy be very much better off even if this line worked?

Oppenheimer continued:

The General Advisory Committee was called to meet in Washington, and met on two questions which were obviously related. The first was, was the Commission doing what it ought to be doing. Were there other things which it should now be undertaking in the light of the Soviet explosion.

The second was the special case of this; was it crash development, the most rapid possible development and construction of a super among the things that the Commission ought to be doing.

There was ample confirmation that this is what the Commission asked the G.A.C. It came from two members of the Commission, Lilienthal and Pike, and from three other members of the Committee, Rowe, Rabi and Fermi.

Oppenheimer went on:

Now I have reviewed for you in other connections some of the earlier hydrogen-bomb tale. The work on it in the summer of 1942, when we were quite enthusiastic about the possibility, my report on this work to Bush, the wartime work in which there were 2 discoveries. 1 was very much casting doubt on the feasibility, and 1 which had a more encouraging quality with regard to the feasibility. Of the talks with General Groves in which he had indicated that this was not something to rush into after the war. Of the early postwar work, prior to the establishment of the Commission. Of our encouragement to the Commission and thus to Los Alamos and also directly to Los Alamos to study the problem and get on with it in 1947 and 1948.

The GAC record shows I think that there were some thermonuclear devices that we felt were feasible and sensible and encouraged. I believe this was in 1948. But that we made a technically disparaging remark about the super in 1948. This was the judgment we then had. I remember that before 1949 and the bomb, Dr. Teller had discussed with me the desirability of his going to Los Alamos and devoting himself to this problem. I encouraged him to do this. In fact, he later reminded me of that, that I encouraged him in strong terms to do it.

Now, the meetings on——

By Mr. GARRISON:

Q. The meeting of October 19?
A. The meeting of October 19, 1949. Have we the date right?
Mr. ROBB. October 29.
The WITNESS. October 29. I think what we did was the following. We had a first meeting with the Commission at which they explained to us the double problem: What should they do and should they do this? We then consulted a number of people. * * *
We had consultations not with the Secretary of State, but with the head of the policy planning staff, who represented him, George Kennan, as to what he

thought the Russians might be up to, and where our principal problems lay from the point of view of assessment of Russian behavior and Russian motives. We had consultations with the Military Establishment, General Bradley was there, Admiral Parsons, I think General Hull or General Kyes, head of the Weapons Systems Evaluation Committee, General Nichols, probably. I won't try to recall all. Also Mr. LeBarron.

We have Kennan's testimony:

A. I can only give my recollection here, and I must say my recollection of all these official matters at that time are somewhat telescoped and entirely capable of being in error with regard to details. But the recollection is simply this. When it was first made known to the Secreaty of State that there was a technical possibility of going ahead with the development of this weapon, at least to the extent the Government now had before it a decision as to whether to develop the weapon or not——

Q. The question of making it.

A. The question of making a decision as to whether to attempt to develop the weapon or not. When that state of affairs was first brought to the attention of the Secretary of State, he at a very early stage there asked me into his office. My recollection is that Dr. Oppenheimer was there, and there may possibly have been one or two other people, but I do not remember who they were. We spoke about this and the only thing I can remember, I think, of that conversation is that we were all agreed that regardless of how the decision might fall, it was important that this Government should reexamine its position with respect to the international control of atomic energy to make sure that nothing had been left undone from our side to get international agreement about these weapons, before we proceeded with this program of the hydrogen bomb.

In other words, we wanted to make absolutely certain that before launching on this new phase of the atomic weapons race, our position in the United Nations on the international control of atomic energy was the best position that we could devise, and most hopeful one.

The Secretary of State asked me to reexamine this question, to have another look at our international negotiation position as we had exposed it in the United Nations bodies with regard to the international control of atomic energy, and to see whether that was still sound, whether anything had happened in the circumstances of the preceding 2 or 3 years since we had advanced it to change the assumptions on which it rested, whether there was anything more that we could now propose which might have a chance of putting an end to the atomic weapons race instead of facing us with the necessity of going ahead with this.

I did look at this problem in the course of the ensuing weeks and my recollection is that I gave my opinion to the Secretary of State in January 1950 on that subject.

Q. I take it that on at least one or perhaps more occasions in the course of carrying out this assignment or at least the initiation of it you heard Dr. Oppenheimer express his views.

A. I recall going to Princeton in the fall of 1949 on one occasion. I had several things to do there. I called on Dr. Oppenheimer at the Institute if my memory is correct, and we discussed it then. I was also once at some time in that period—I don't know exactly when—asked to appear before the General Advisory Committee of the Atomic Energy Commission, simply as a consultant. They wanted to hear my views. They asked me questions. The questions related primarily to the present state of our relations with the Soviet Union, the state of what we called the cold war. I replied as frankly as I could to them.

Q. What impression did you get, if your remember it, of Dr. Oppenheimer's views?

A. I would not be able to quote his views in memory or in any detail or in any great accuracy. I can only say that the general impression I carried with me was the impression of a man who was greatly troubled by what he felt to be the extremely solemn implications of this decision.

Q. That is the pending decision?

A. The pending decision. Who realized that it was one the implications of which might carry very far. That it was almost impossible to predict where we might end up if this sort of a race with weapons of mass destruction were to go on indefinitely, and therefore was greatly troubled and concerned to arrive at the most enlightened and sound decision that could be made.

Q. Did he try to sell you on any view?

A. It is not my recollection that he did. I fear that I talked more about my own views here than he did about his with regard to this subject. But I do not have the recollection that he endeavored to persuade me that any answer to this problem was the right one or the wrong one. To me, then, we were still at a preliminary stage in it. The entire effort really on the part of both of us then was to try to identify the considerations that were relevant to the problem to see what we had that we could really hang onto in approaching the decision.

Q. When it came time for you to give the Secretary of State your views or your analysis of the problem, what did you report to him, and when was it approximately?

A. I reported to him approximately in the month of January, I would think around the middle of the month or shortly after.

Mr. Robb. 1950?

The Witness. 1950, yes. The gist of my own views was simply this: I felt that this Government was in no way in good position to make any great decisions with regard to either the international control of atomic energy or actually with regard to its own weapons program before it gained greater clarity in its own mind as to the purposes for which it was holding what were sometimes called the A, B, C, weapons in general. By that I am thinking of the weapons of mass destruction, the atomic, chemical, and so forth. It seemed to me that there was unclarity in the councils of our Government as to the reasons why we were cultivating and holding these weapons. The unclarity revolved around this question. Were we holding them only as a means of deterring other people from using them against us and retaliating against any such use of these weapons against us, or were we building them into our military establishment in such a way that we would indicate that we were going to be dependent upon them in any future war, and would have to use them, regardless of whether they were used against us first.

By Mr. Marks:

Q. Have we not taken the position that we would only use them for purposes of retaliation?

A. It is not my impression that we have, and it was not my impression at that time that there was any such determination in the councils of the United States Government.

On the other hand, if I remember correctly, I was able to cite statements that had been made by some of our high military leaders—I think both in the councils of this Government and in the NATO councils of Europe—which indicated very strongly that we were getting ourselves into a position where we would have to use these weapons as forward military weapons, regardless of whether they were used against us.

The point that I tried to emphasize to the Secretary of State related, of course, directly to the question of international control about which I had been asked. I told him that I thought we ought first to face this problem. It was my belief that we should hold these weapons only for purposes of retaliation and as a deterrent to their use against us. That anything else would get us into a race with these mass destruction weapons to which I could see no end, which I was afraid would distort the thinking of the public mind about problems of foreign policy and military policy in this country if it were permitted to proceed. So as I say, I favored the holding of these weapons only for purposes of retaliation and as a deterrent.

Whether that came out clearly in my report to the Secretary of State, I do not know, because that was not actually the question that was asked me. But I am sure it was implicit in what I said to the Secretary, and by the same token I think it was implicit that we ought really to make this other decision before we made decisions about the hydrogen bomb.

Q. Mr. Kennan, you will have to explain a little more to me at least what you conceived to be the relevance of clarification of this question to the question of whether or not we ought to proceed with making hydrogen bombs.

A. Yes. As I saw it, the relevance was this. If you were asked, should we or should we not proceed to the development of a whole new range of more powerful atomic weapons which was involved in the hydrogen bomb decision, you had to ask yourself how much do we need the weapons of mass destruction in general. That is the first question that had to be faced, because if you already had enough, perhaps you didn't need the hydrogen bomb at all. I could not see how you could answer the question of how much do we need until you had answered the question of why are we holding these weapons anyway, and what do we expect to accomplish with them.

If you were holding them as deterrents and for purposes of retaliation, really for purposes in order that they might not be used against you, then what you needed was merely enough to make it an unprofitable and unpromising undertaking on the part of anyone else, the Russians in particular, to use these weapons against us.

If on the other hand you were going to regard them as an integral part of forward American military planning and something on which we would be dependent in a future war, regardless of the circumstances of the origin of that war, then you came up with a different answer or you might come up with a different one in regard to the hydrogen bomb.

Q. So the point you are making is not that you were opposed to the hydrogen bomb necessarily, but only it seemed to you that it was essential first that this other subsidiary question should be clarified?

A. That is correct. I must say that personally while I was not competent to form a finished opinion on this and was never called upon to do so, I had not at that time seen the evidence that what we already held in the old and regular atomic bomb, I may speak of it that way, was not enough to make it a fruitless undertaking from the standpoint of Soviet policy to launch a war on us with these weapons.

In other words, I considered the burden of proof to rest on that point. It seemed to me you would have to prove that we could not do the job with the weapons we already had, and to my knowledge that was never demonstrated to me at the time. Perhaps the answer might have been one thing or the other, but I had never seen the proof.

Oppenheimer went on:

Prior to this meeting there had been no great expression of interest on the part of the military in more powerful weapons. The atomic bomb had of course been stepped up some, but we had not been pressed to push that development as fast as possible. There had been no suggestion that very large weapons would be very useful. The pressure was all the other way; get as many as you can.

We discussed General Bradley's analysis of the effects of the Russian explosion, and what problems he faced and with the staff, of course.

Then we went into executive session. I believe I opened the session by asking Fermi to give an account of the technical state of affairs. He has always been interested in this possibility. I think it occurred to him very early that the high temperatures of a fission bomb might be usable in igniting lighter materials. He has also an extremely critical and clear head. I asked others to add to this. Then we went around the table and everybody said what he thought the issues were that were involved. There was a surprising unanimity—to me very surprising—that the United States ought not to take the initiative at that time in an all out program for the development of thermonuclear weapons.

Different people spoke in different ways. I don't know how available to you the actual record of this conversation is or even whether it fully exists. But there was not any difference of opinion in the final finding. I don't know whether this is the first thing we considered or whether we considered the Commission's other question first. I imagine we went back and forth between the two of them.

To the Commission's other question, were they doing enough, we answered no. Have you read this report, because if you have, my testimony about it will add nothing.

Mr. GRAY. I believe that the report with two——

The WITNESS. Annexes.

Mr. GRAY. I don't know whether they are actually annexes, but two supplementary statements, I don't know whether that is in one page signed by two people or two separate sheets.

The WITNESS. The report itself you have.

Mr. Gray. The report is available.

By Mr. Garrison:

Q. I think you better say what you recollect of it.

A. I recollect of it that the first part of the report contained a series of affirmative recommendations about what the Commission should do. I believe all of them were directed toward weapons expansion, weapons improvement and weapons diversification. Some of them involved the building of new types of plant which would give a freedom of choice with regard to weapons. Some of them involved just a stepping up of the amount. I don't think that this expressed satisfaction with the current level of the Commission effort.

On the super program itself, I attempted to give a description of what this weapon was, of what would have to go into it, and what we thought the design would be. I explained that the uncertainties in this game were very great, that one would not know whether one had it or not unless one had built it and tested it, and that realistically one would have to expect not one test, but perhaps more than one test. That this would have to be a program of design and testing.

We had in mind, but I don't think we had clearly enough in mind, that we were talking about a single design which was in its essence frozen, and that the possibility did not occur to us very strongly that there might be quite other ways of going about it. Our report had a single structure in mind—or almost a single structure—whose characteristics in terms of blast, of damage, of explosive force, of course, and certainly we tried in the report to describe as faithfully as we knew how. I think in the report itself we were unanimous in hoping that the United States would not have to take the initiative in the development of this weapon.

There were two annexes, neither of which I drafted. There is nothing of restricted data in those I believe, but perhaps we can't read them into the record anyway. Are there any restricted data?

Mr. Rolander. I think the question raised is whether other security information might be divulged.

The Witness. How many bombs we have and so on?

Mr. Rolander. Yes.

Mr. Robb. Perhaps Dr. Oppenheimer could give us his summary.

The Witness. It is a long time since I read them. This ought to be in the record, ought it not? Could you let me read them?

Mr. Robb. They have been available to Dr. Oppenheimer ever since the letter was sent to him. I think that was clearly understood, was it not, Doctor?

The Witness. I was told by counsel that I would be allowed——

Mr. Robb. Any reports that you had prepared?

The Witness. That is right.

Mr. Robb. So far you have not come down to avail yourself of it.

The Witness. I see. They are not here?

Mr. Robb. We have extracts of them, yes, sir.

The Witness. I would think I might read the two annexes and paraphrase them.

Mr. Gray. I think I am going to ask that we recess now, because there is not another matter to bring up not related to the testimony. I think in the meantime, Mr. Robb, the chairman would like to be advised about this.

Mr. Robb. The security aspect?

Mr. Gray. Yes. So we will recess now until two o'clock.

(Thereupon, at 12:25 p. m., a recess was taken until 2 p. m., the same day.)

AFTERNOON SESSION

Mr. Gray. Gentlemen, shall we proceed.

(Thereupon, Albert J. Gasdor, the reporter, was duly sworn by the chairman.)

Whereupon, J. Robert Oppenheimer, the witness on the stand at the time of taking the recess, resumed the stand, and testified further as follows:

DIRECT EXAMINATION (Continued)

By Mr. Garrison:

Q. You were in the course of commenting on the 1949 Report when we recessed.

A. Yes.

I find that the report has a letter of transmittal, that it has a section on affirmative actions to be taken, that it has a section on super bombs and that it has these two annexes of which you have heard.

As far as length is concerned, the section on affirmative actions and the section on super bombs are about equal, and I guess I can't tell you what is in the one on affirmative actions except in the very general terms I used before.

The first page of the page-and-a-half of the report on the super bomb is an account of what it is supposed to be, what has to be done in order to bring it about, and some semiquantitative notions of what it would take, what kind of damage it would do, and what kind of a program would be required. The essential point there is that as we then saw it, it was a weapon that you could not be sure of until you tried it out, and it is a problem of calculation and study, and then you went out in the proper place in the Pacific and found out whether it went bang and found out to what extent your ideas had been right and to what extent they had been wrong.

It is on the second page that we start talking about the extent of damage and the first paragraph is just a factual account of the kind of damage, the kind of carrier, and I believe I should not give it—I believe it is classified, even if it is not possibly entirely accurate.

I would like to state one conclusion which is that for anything but very large targets, this was not economical in terms of damage per dollar, and then even for large targets it was uncertain whether it would be economical in terms of damage per dollar. I am not claiming that this was good foresight, but I am just telling you what it says in here.

I am going to read two sentences:

"We all hope that by one means or another, the development of these weapons can be avoided. We are all reluctant to see the United States take the initiative in precipitating this development. We are all agreed that it would be wrong at the present moment to commit ourselves to an all-out effort towards its development."

This is the crux of it and it is a strong negative statement. We added to this some comments as to what might be declassified and what ought not to be declassified and held secret if any sort of a public statement were contemplated. If the President were going to say anything about it, there were some things we thought obvious and there would be no harm in mentioning them. Actually, the secret ones were out in the press before very long.

The phrase that you heard this morning, "We believe that the imaginative and concerted attack on the problem has a better than even chance of producing the weapon * * *"—I find that in this report, and in this report there is, therefore, no statement that it is unfeasible. There is a statement of uncertainty which I believed at the time was a good assessment. You would have found people who would have said this was too conservative, it could be done faster and more certainly, and you would find other people who would say that it could not be done at all; but the statement as read here, no member of the General Advisory Committee objected to, and I have heard very little objection to that as an assessment of the feasibility at that time.

This is the report itself, and there are parts of it which I think you should read but, for the record, there are parts that I cannot get into here.

Mr. ROBB. Mr. Chairman, I think it might be well for the record to show at this point that the board has read the entire report.

The WITNESS. I see. Then, what am I doing that for?

Mr. ROBB. Doctor, that is up to you.

Mr. GARRISON. I thought, Mr. Chairman, there was expressed a little doubt on the part of the board this morning as to just how completely it was recalled at this time, and I think also for that reason it is quite appropriate for Dr. Oppenheimer to perhaps tell the board in his own way what was in it.

Mr. GRAY. That is what I understood was the purpose of addressing his remarks as he is doing.

Mr. GARRISON. I am sure counsel was not mentioning that in the form of an objection.

Mr. ROBB. No, not at all. I was not offering that as an objection, and I do not object to anything. In fact, I might say that later on we might want to come back to this report.

The WITNESS. One important point to make is that lack of feasibility is not the ground on which we made our recommendations.

Another point I ought to make is that lack of economy, although alleged is not the primary or only ground, the competition with fission weapons is obviously in our minds. The real reason, the weight, behind the report is, in my opinion, a failing of the existence of these weapons would be a disadvantageous thing. It says this over and over again.

I may read, which I am sure has no security value, from the so-called minority report, Fermi and Rabi.

"The fact that no limits exist to the destructiveness of this weapon makes it very existence and the knowledge of its construction a danger to humanity as a whole. It is necessarily an evil thing considered in any light. For these reasons, we believe it important for the President of the United States to tell the American public and the world that we think is wrong on fundamental ethical principles to initiate the development of such a weapon."

Fermi testified:

Q. You participated then in the deliberations of that committee concerning the advice to the Commission on the thermonuclear program in the fall of 1949?

A. I did.

Q. Would you tell the board briefly what you can in an unclassified way about those deliberations, the positions taken, the reasons for them?

A. Yes. I should perhaps mention the matter goes back to about 5 years, and my recollection is partly vivid, partly a little bit uncertain, but I think I remember the essentials, which are about this way: That the committee was confronted with forming an opinion whether it was the right time to start an all out program for developing the hydrogen bomb.

Q. This would have been the meeting of October 29, 1949?

A. That I understand is the date, although I don't remember it on my own. So we were confronted with this decision. I can testify naturally to my feelings in this matter better than I can to those of other people. As far as I could see the situation, I had the concern that the pressure for this development was extremely inordinate, or at least so it seemed to me. I was concerned that it might weaken the development of conventional atomic weapons which was then picking up and essentially set it back for what seemed to me at the time a not quite decided advantage on the other side. For that reason, and I believe that these views must have been shared more or less by everybody in our group, because a decision that it was not the right time to go in an absolutely overriding way in that direction was, as far as I remember, unanimous.

There was a subsequent point on which some difference of opinion arose, and I found myself in this connection in the minority together with Rabi. Again I have no absolutely clear recollection. I have no doubt that the board has available the records of those meetings presumably where things are spelled out in full detail. My recollection is that this divergence of opinion was on whether to essentially declare or establish the policy not to go ahead with the program or whether some circumstances could make us go ahead.

My opinion at that time was that one should try to outlaw the thing before it was born. I sort of had the view at that time that perhaps it would be easier to outlaw by some kind of international agreement something that did not exist. My opinion was that one should try to do that, and failing that, one should with considerable regret go ahead.

Q. Do you remember, Dr. Fermi, whether or not there was opportunity at those meetings late in October 1949 with the freest and fullest discussion among you—consistent with the rather brief time, few days?

A. Yes, I think so. I think everybody had a right to his own opinion and to defend his own opinion.

Q. Was there a great deal of discussion and debate?

A. No doubt there was. I think we had some trouble and some soul searching, all of us.

Rabi testified:

A. As I recollect it now—it is 5 years ago—the chairman, Dr. Oppenheimer, started very solemnly and as I recall we had to consider this question. The question came not whether we should make a thermonuclear weapon, but whether there should be a crash program. There were some people, and I myself was of that opinion for a time, who thought that the concentration on the crash program to go ahead with this was the answer to the Russian thermonuclear weapon. The question was, should it be a crash program and a technical question: What possibilities lay in that? What would be the cost of initiating a crash program in terms of the strength of the United States because of the weakening of the effort on which something which we had in hand, namely, the fission weapons, and the uncompleted designs of different varieties, to have a really flexible weapon, the question of interchangeability of parts, all sorts of things which could be used in different military circumstances.

Then there was the question of the military value of this weapon. One of the things which we talked about a great deal was that this weapon as promised which didn't exist and which we didn't know how to make, what sort of military weapon was it anyway? What sort of target it was good for. And what would be the general political effect.

In other words, we felt—and I am talking chiefly about myself—that this was not just a weapon. But by its very nature, if you attacked a target, it took in very much more. We felt it was really essential and we discussed a great deal what were you buying if you got this thing. That was the general nature of the discussion.

Technical, military, and the combination of military political.

Q. Does the attitude that you have described on the subject of continental defense mean that you are opposed to a powerful strategic air policy?

A. As far as I am concerned, I certainly am not.

Q. Am not what?

A. Opposed to it. I am very much in favor of it. I would like to see it more effective than it is. * * *

Q. Are the two things compatible, the continental defense you are talking about, and the strategic?

A. Absolutely. These are the 2 arms. One is the punching arm and the other the guard. You have to have both, in my opinion.

Q. Do you know whether Dr. Oppenheimer's views are materially different from yours on the subject?

A. I don't think they are. I think his emphasis might be somewhat different. I don't think the views are different. I think the emphasis might be different.

Q. In what way?

A. Now we are getting into things which I would prefer not to answer.

Q. Why?

A. Because it comes into questions of actual strategy and tactics of which we have special knowledge and I don't want to go into any details of that sort.

Q. All right. Just so that I will understand what you are saying, I take it that you strongly favor, and to your knowledge Oppenheimer strongly favors, a powerful strategic air policy.

A. Yes.

Q. And that you also favor an effective continental defense.

A. That is right.

Q. And that you regard the two things as not incompatible?

A. No, no. I think they are just absolutely complementary. They both have to be there. To put it in a word, a strategic air arm unless you are going to prevent a war is a psychological weapon, a deterrent. But the other fellow may not be the same and you have to have some kind of defense before he does you irreparable damage, and furthermore, your plans may not go as you expect. They may miscarry. Unless you have a defense, you are not getting another chance.

Oppenheimer then turned to the other annex which Conant had written and which DuBridge, Buckley and Oppenheimer had signed:

In the report which got to be known as the majority report, which Conant wrote, DuBridge, Buckley and I signed, things are not quite so ethical and fundamental, but it says in the final paragraph: "In determining not to proceed to develop the super bomb, we see a unique opportunity of providing by example some limitations on the totality of war and thus of eliminating the fear and arousing the hope of mankind."

I think it is very clear that the objection was that we did not like the weapon, not that it couldn't be made.

Now, it is a matter of speculation whether, if we had before us at that time, if we had had the technical knowledge and inventiveness which we did have somewhat later, we would have taken a view of this kind. These are total views where you try to take into account how good the thing is, what the enemy is likely to do, what you can do with it, what the competition is, and the extent to which this is an inevitable step anyway.

My feeling about the delay in the hydrogen bomb, and I imagine you want to question me about it, is that if we had had good ideas in 1945, and had we wanted to, this object might have been in existence in 1947 or 1948, perhaps 1948. If we had had all of the good ideas in 1949, I suppose some little time might have been shaved off the development as it actually occurred. If we had not had good ideas in 1951, I do not think we would have it today. In other words, the question of delay is keyed in this case to the question of invention, and I think the record should show—it is known to you—that the principal inventor in all of this business was Teller, with many important contributions * * * other people, * * * It has not been quite a one-man show, but he has had some very, very good ideas, and they have kept coming. It is probably true that an idea of mine is embodied in all of these things. It is not very ingenious but it turned out to be very useful, and it was not enough to establish feasibility or have a decisive bearing on their feasibility.

The notion that the thermonuclear arms race was something that was in the interests of this country to avoid if it could was very clear to us in 1949. We may have been wrong. We thought it was something to avoid even if we could jump the gun by a couple of years, or even if we could outproduce the enemy, because we were infinitely more vulnerable and infinitely less likely to initiate the use of these weapons, and because the world in which great destruction has been done in all civilized parts of the world is a harder world for America to live with than it is for the Communists to live with. This is an idea which I believe is still right, but I think what was not clear to us then and what is clearer to me now is that it probably lay wholly beyond our power to prevent the Russians somehow from getting ahead with it. I think if we could have taken any action at that time which would have precluded their development of this weapon, it would have been a very good bet to take that, I am sure. I do not know enough about contemporary intelligence to say whether or not our actions have had any effect on theirs but you have ways of finding out about that.

I believe that their atomic effort was quite imitative and that made it quite natural for us to think that their thermonuclear work would be quite imitative and that we should not set the pace in this development. I am trying to explain what I thought and what I believe my friends thought. I am not arguing that this is right, but I am clear about one thing: if this affair could have been averted on the part of the Russians, I am quite clear that we would be in a safer world today by far.

Mr. GRAY. Would you repeat that last sentence. I didn't quite get it.

The WITNESS. If the development by the enemy as well as by us of thermonuclear weapons could have been averted, I think we would be in a somewhat safer world today than we are. God knows, not entirely safe because atomic bombs are not jolly either.

A few days later four of them—Conant, Buckley, Rabi and Oppenheimer—were called in by the Commission; and not long after that Oppenheimer appeared before the Joint Committee on Atomic Energy. This was just before the President announced his decision.

Oppenheimer called the period between the President's announcement in January 1950 and the day in the spring of 1951 when Teller produced his brilliant discovery the "doldrums." He said:

The WITNESS. I think it would be fair to say that between the first of 1950 and early 1951, my attitude toward this object was that we didn't know how to make it, and it was going to be very hard to make, but we had been told to dot it and we must try.

In the spring of 1951, there were some inventions made. * * * and from then on it became clear that this was a program which was bound to succeed. * * * Why none of us had them earlier, I cannot explain, except that invention is a somewhat erratic thing.

Teller had been working on this from 1942 on, his heart was in it, but it wasn't until 1951 that he thought about how to do it right.

Now, I have a few matters here which came in between. During the doldrums of the H-bomb, the war in Korea broke out, and a large part of GAC's and other committee's attention was, as I say, devoted to the very immediate and the very obvious, and, I would say, to using an atomic explosive not merely in a strategic campaign but also in a defensive or tactical campaign, and I think the record will bear out that that is what we were spending most of our time worrying about. That is the origin of the panel Kelly talked about this morning, the origin of the exercises which led to the development of a tactical capability in Europe, the origin of one at least of the threads, one at least of the reasons for the very great expansion in the atomic energy enterprise to support a much more diversified use of weapons, even leading some people to suggest—I think this was Gordon Dean—that maybe the atomic weapons on the battlefield would be so effective that it would not be necessary to use them strategically. I have never really believed that that was possible or believed that a sharp distinction between the two could be maintained or made intelligible.

Meanwhile, Oppenheimer was trying to resign as chairman.

In the late summer and autumn of 1950, I had an obvious personal worry. I had made as chairman, and had participated in, the recommendation against the development of the super. The super was a big item on the program. It wasn't going very well, and I wondered whether another man might not make a better chairman for the General Advisory Committee. This was particularly true since there were three new members added to the committee—Whitman, Murphree and Libby—and I felt a little uncomfortable about continuing in that office. I discussed it with several physicists. I remember discussing it with Teller and Bacher. Teller says that he does not remember discussing it with me. The general advice was: Let's all stick together as well as we can and don't resign and don't change your position.

Mr. ROBB. What was that date?

The WITNESS. In the summer of 1950.

When I got back in the autumn of 1950, the first meeting, I went to see Mr. Dean, who was Chairman of the Commission, and Commissioner Smyth and told them about my problem, and they said that obviously the chairman should be someone who would be comfortable with them—what would be their suggestions? They protested in very forceful terms that I should not quit as chairman, and that they would be very unhappy if I did, that I ought to carry on.

I also took the thing up with our committee, but our committee was not a very responsive group when it came to electing other chairmen, and I got no place. I did not feel that I ought to resign as chairman or refuse to serve. I thought I ought to do what was comfortable for the Commission and the committee, and I tried to ascertain what that was.

Then in the spring of 1951 came the momentous meeting at Princeton.

In the spring of 1951, I called—I am not sure whether I suggested it or whether Commissioner Smyth suggested it but we consulted about it—a rather large gathering for a couple of days at the institute in Princeton, and we had there, I think, all five Commissioners, the general manager and his deputy, the head of the Division of Military Applications, Bradbury and his assistants, Teller, Von Neumann, Bethe, Bacher, Fermi who was no longer a member of the committee, and Wheeler and one of his assistants, the people who were working on the program, and we had a couple of days of exposition and debate. I chaired the meeting, and I suppose I did the summarizing. It was not the full General Advisory Committee—the Weapons Subcommittee, essentially; the secretary of the committee was there and he took some notes but he did not write up an official report. At that time, I think we did three things. We agreed that the new ideas took top place and that although the old ones should be kept on the back burner, the new ones should be pushed. I believe there was no dissent from this; there was no articulated dissent. But later Commisisoner Murray asked if this wasn't a violation of the Presidential directive, and I could only respond that I didn't know as to what, but I thought it was a good course and, if it was, maybe the President would modify his directive.

At that meeting, I remember no dissent from that but there was a great deal of surprise at how things were changed. Fermi knew nothing of these developments and was quite amazed, and I think for the Commission it was quite an education to see what had happened in the meantime. At least that was the purpose, to get everybody together so that there was a common understanding.

The second thing was to recognize that some materials * * * might be handy to have, and the Commission was urged to get started on producing some of these materials. This was something that there was a little bit of objection to on the ground that everything changed so often in the past and maybe change in the future, and why get committed to a cumbersome operation on the basis of the then-existing state of knowledge, but I believe the prevailing opinion, and I know mine, was that the prevailing state of opinion was that it was a lot solider than anything that had occurred before and that they ought to go ahead and even at the risk of wasting a small amount of money.

The third thing we did was to talk about the construction and test schedules for these things, and there there were differences of opinions, having to do with whether the schedule should be aimed at a completed, large-scale explosion, or whether one should be aimed at componentry testing which presumably was supposed to have happened earlier and therefore might be illuminating with regard to the large-scale explosion.

As I say, there was not agreement, but the consensus was that unless the studies of the summer passed out on the feasibility of it, one should aim directly at the large-scale explosion, and the time scale of that operation from mid-1951 to late 1952 was, I think, a miracle of speed. I know there may be people who disagree, and I think it might have been done faster, but I can only reminisce and say that in the first days of Los Alamos, and in the fall of 1943, Bethe and Teller, two of the most brilliant theorists in this game and in their way most responsible men, said to me: "If we had the material now, we could have a bomb in 3 weeks." Actually, we were ready for the material just about when it arrived, which was not quite 2 years later, and the laboratory had doubled every 9 months in the interval and everybody was busy; and I think that the estimate of the theorists on how quickly you could do things that involve engineering and involve new chemistry and involve new metallurgy was likely to be a little optimistic.

I am continually impressed by the speed, sureness, certainty, skill and quality of the work that went into the preparation of this first large explosion and the subsequent work to exploit the development there established.

The next thing on which I had notes is that in the autumn of 1951——

Mr. GARRISON. That was at Princeton?

The WITNESS. This was the Princeton meeting that I have described. I think it was a very useful meeting. It might have been useful to me if we had made a record of it.

It was largely that it was not a formal type of GAC meeting and our secretary did not want to keep a record, but I believe a fairly good account of the substantive findings exist, and I believe Commissioner Smyth knows where to get hold of it. I don't know how to get hold of it.

In the autumn of 1951, there was an international conference in Chicago, and I attended it even though I was called away to testify for money for the National Science Foundation.

While there, I talked at some length with Teller and the summer's work had only made things look tied together. Teller expressed dissatisfaction with the arrangements made at Los Alamos. He didn't think the man whom Bradbury had put in charge of this development was the right man for the job, and he expressed to me the view that Fermi or Bethe or I would be the only people that he would be happy to work with. I don't know whether he meant me, but I said, "Well, that is fine," and he said that Bethe and Fermi wouldn't; "Would you be willing to?" I won't quote myself verbatim, but I remarked that that would depend on whether I would be welcomed by Bradbury. I had not planned to go back to Los Alamos. It seemed to me a bad thing for an ex-director to return. I was content with my job and work at Princeton, but I would communicate with Bradbury, and I called him and told him of the conversation and he gave no signs of wanting to have the ex-director back, and said that he had full confidence in the present man, and that was the end of that.

I don't believe that it would have been practical. I think you can't make an anomolous rise twice. I think I could create and guide Los Alamos during the war, but I think if I had returned there the situation would have been so different; I would have been ancient and not on my toes anymore, and I doubt if I would have felt appropriate, but, in any case, the success of this would have decisively depended on its being something that was actively in the desires and interests of the director, and it was not so.

The hydrogen bomb was not done, and during the winter of 1951–52 Los Alamos was working on it, and we kept in quite close touch. Bradbury came in quite frequently. He sent Froman and other people in to report to us, and I want to make it clear that I was not actually calculating out and working on it. I was merely trying to understand where the difficulties lay, if any, what the alternatives were, and to form a reasonable judgment so that I might give reasonable advice.

At that time, Teller's unhappiness with the arrangements became quite generally known, and we were frequently asked by the Commission, "Should there be a second laboratory?" We were asked, "Should this work be split off in some way from Los Alamos?" I don't know how many times that came up during the winter of 1951–52 as an item before the General Advisory Committee.

I think, on this point, we were not unanimous. I think Dr. Libby thought it would be a good idea to have a second laboratory at any time. The laboratory, the purpose of which would be to house Teller and bring you people into the program who were not now working on it, even though this might take some people away from Los Alamos, even though it might interfere with the work then going on. The rest of us, I think, were fairly clear that the things were really going along marvelously well, and that if it was too difficult for Los Alamos to do the whole job, then steps should be taken to get some of their more routine operations moved to Sandia. We talked at great length about the rearrangement of the workload between the two places. Some of the suggestions we made were adopted.

We also talked to Bradbury about making within the framework of Los Alamos an advanced development section in which really radical ideas and wild ideas could be thought up and tried out. The Director thought it was feasible if he could get the right man. He tried very hard to get one man for it and, after some delay, this man turned him down, and I don't believe such a reform was undertaken then.

I believe that with the Commission's reluctance to establish a second weapons laboratory, there was some thought that the Air Force might directly establish one, and I think the Commission protested that but this is hearsay.

In any case, during the winter, our recommendations were to fix up Los Alamos so that it could do the job rather than start a separate establishment. Later, in the spring, perhaps in April, we learned that there had been some preliminary talks toward the converting of the laboratory at Livermore which had been engaged in an enterprise related to atomic energy, of which we the members of the GAC took a rather sour view of converting this, in part, so that it could get more weapons testing work with a special eye to the thermonuclear program. This we liked and this we endorsed.

The laboratory at Berkeley had often been involved in the instrumentation of weapons tests, and it seemed that this was a healthy growth which wouldn't weaken Los Alamos, which would bring new people into it where there was an existing managerial framework and where the thing could occur gradually, and, therefore, constructively, the notation of setting out into the desert and building a second site like Los Alamos and building a laboratory around Teller had always seemed to us to be something that was not going to work, given the conditions and given the enormous availability to Los Alamos of the talent that was needed for this problem.

In any case, the Livermore Laboratory was established sometimes perhaps in the summer of 1952, and has played its part in the subsequent work at the time when my clearance was suspended, the major and the practical, and the real parts of the program were still pretty much Los Alamos doing, but it was my hope, all our hope, that both institutions would begin pulling great weight. There had also been no serious friction between them.

Mr. GARRISON. Did you tell the board that Dr. Teller was in charge of the Livermore Laboratory?

The WITNESS. My understanding is that the director is Herbert York, but that this part of the laboratory's work was under the scientific direction of Teller. I think the board probably knows that better than I do at this point.

The super also—well, it was no longer the super—I forgot one thing, and it may be of some slight importance. This goes back—and I am sorry to have a bad chronology here——

Mr. GRAY. I think the record should show that Dr. Evans has just stepped out of the room.

Mr. ROBB. Dr. Evans has just stepped back into the room.

The WITNESS. At the time that the H-bomb problem first came up—I forgot to say two things.

I spoke of my later feeling that I should perhaps not be the chairman of the General Advisory Committee myself—but two things happened much earlier. I had some talks with the Secretary of State, too, I think, and so had Dr. Conant. Dr. Conant brought back, and so did Mr. Lilienthal, from the Secretary of State 2 messages; 1 was a message to Conant and me, for heck's sake not to resign or make any public statements to upset the applecart but accept this decision as the best to be made and not to make any kind of conflict about it. That was not hard for us to do because we hardly would have seen any way of making a public conflict, and the second part of the message was to be sure to stay on the General Advisory Committee; and that is what both of us did.

There was another item. He recognized, as has Mr. Lilienthal and as would any other sane man, whether or not a hydrogen bomb could be made, how soon we made it, the Russian possession of an atomic bomb raised a lot of other problems, military and political and upset a great many things.

The Government had been saying we had been expecting it, but now here it was—with regard to the defense of Europe; with regard to the usefulness of atomic retaliation in special conflicts, and I was called in to help in the preparation of the Security Council paper which was prepared that spring on the subject of which essentially was rearmament and the subject of which was how to solidify our alliances and increase the overall military power of the United States.

Mr. GRAY. This was the spring of 1950?

The WITNESS. This was the spring of 1950, in NSC 68 or 69, and you probably remember the number better than I do * * *.

In any case, it needs to be testified by me that I was very aware of the fact that you couldn't, within the atomic energy field alone, find a complete or even a very adequate answer to the Russian breaking of our monopoly. I don't think I had a major part in this paper. It took months of staff work to do it. I wouldn't be surprised if—I don't know whether I had any part—but, in any case, I approved and helped with some parts of that and its purpose was the buildup which started some months later after Korea.

Mr. GRAY. Is that a good breaking point? Shall we take a 5-minute recess?

The WITNESS. It is fine since that is out of order and I apologize for putting it that way.

(Brief recess.)

Mr. GRAY. Shall we proceed?

The WITNESS. I have a few more words on the hydrogen bomb which are not very major. The hydrogen bomb once it looked like it got in Dr. Kelly's province, of course, came out in the Research and Development Board committee on which I served. * * *

Oppenheimer summed it all up in this way:

I would like to summarize a little bit this long story I think you will hear from people who believed at the time, and believe now that the advice we gave in 1949 was wrong. You will hear from people who believed at the time and who even believe now that the advice we gave in 1949 was right. I myself would not take either of these extreme views.

I think we were right in believing that any method available consistent with honor and security for keeping these objects out of the arsenals of the enemy would have been a good course to follow. I don't believe we were very clear and I don't believe we were ever very agreed as to what such course might be, or whether such a course existed. I think that if we had had at that time the technical insight that I now have, we would have concluded that it was almost hopeless to keep this resource out of the enemy hands and maybe we would have given up even suggesting that it be tried. I think if we had had that technical knowledge, then we should have recommended that we go ahead full steam, and then or in 1948 or 1946 or 1945.

I don't want to conceal from you, and I have said it in public speeches so it would not make much sense to conceal from you the dual nature of the hopes which we entertained about the development of bigger and bigger weapons, first the atomic bomb, and then its amplified version, and then these new things.

On the one hand, as we said at the time, and as I now firmly believe, this stuff is going to put an end to major total wars. I don't know whether it will do so in our lifetime. On the other hand, the notion that this will have to come about by the employment of these weapons on a massive scale against civilizations and cities has always bothered me. I suppose that bother is part of the freight I took into the General Advisory Committee, and into the meetings that discussed the hydrogen bomb. No other person may share that view, but I do.

I believe that comes almost to the end except for one thing. I know of no case where I misrepresented or distorted the technical situation in reporting it to my superiors or those to whom I was bound to give advice and counsel. The nearest thing to it that I know is that in the public version of the Acheson-Lilienthal report, we somewhat overstated what could be accomplished by denaturing. I believe this was not anything else than in translating from a technical and therefore secret statement into a public and therefore codified statement, we lost some of the precision which should have gone into it, and some of the caution which should have gone into it.

I am now through with this.

By now you are thinking that we have been a long way on an errand just around the corner. You are quite right. It has been too far to go simply to find nothing derogatory in Oppenheimer's failure to give enthusiastic support to the development of a bomb which these men—statesmen and businessmen as well as scientists —opposed. And we must not forget that what they opposed in 1949 was quite a different creature from the bomb Teller discovered and came up with two years later in 1951.

There were two bombs, the one as different from the other as either from the atomic bomb. The one Oppenheimer wrote Uncle Jim about in 1949 was something which no one knew how to make, which was never made and which, if made, would have had to be delivered by oxcart. The other is the one we may call Teller's. Oppenheimer's fault and the fault of these gentlemen is that their failure to give their enthusiastic support to the first may possibly have delayed the discovery of the second. Dr. Evans said that there was no delay. I suppose it could plausibly be argued that opposition to the first may in fact have hastened the discovery of the second by keeping us from going down a blind alley. I won't try to argue this, because I don't know anything about it. Few of us do. However, it seems clear that the dispute was over something which did not exist and might never exist, and here, I think, lies what we had to go such a long way to fetch.

This is the right attitude we should take toward the next weapon, whether it should be the attitude that Oppenheimer and these others took or the attitude of those who smelled something derogatory, even disloyal, in that attitude. You and I are interested in Oppenheimer's attitude toward the development of the H-bomb because you and I are going to be confronted by the same problem, unless this thermonuclear bomb is the last word, the final weapon. If it is not, if it is only the next to the last, or the next but one to the last, unless indeed there is to be a last, then we are going to have to meet the same problem. The weapon will be different, but the problem will be the same.

It will not be a simple problem. It will be simple only to the simple-minded. It is even nonsense to think that it can simply be reasoned out. There is no use pretending that we can be wholly rational about a matter of life and death, our own as well as others'. We are dealing, and we may be dealing again, with weapons which are drawing homicide and suicide nearer together. It's a mad world, my masters! And all the madder if we treat its most complicated problem as if it were simple.

There will be no simple answer. There will be no single approach to an answer. The problem will have as many aspects and points of view as there are human talents, political, scientific, moral, religious and military. None may safely be neglected or ignored, and all must be presided over by that sense which in ourselves we dignify by calling common and which in our leaders we call statesmanship. Again and again we must recite the remark of Whitehead: "There are no whole truths; all truths are half-truths. It is trying to treat them as whole truths that plays the devil." (*Dialogues of Alfred North Whitehead*, Lucien Price, Atlantic Monthly Press, 1954, p. 16.)

Whitehead's comment is particularly pertinent to our government. "Republics," Machiavelli said, "have a longer life and enjoy better fortune than principalities, because they can profit by their greater internal diversity. They are the better able to meet emergencies." I think this is not in *The Prince*, but in Machiavelli's *Discourse on Livy*. Anyhow, it speaks for itself. The same thing has been said by others in different ways. Oppenheimer, on Edward R. Murrow's TV show "See It Now" in January 1955, said:

The trouble with secrecy is that it denies to the government itself the wisdom and the resources of the whole community, of the whole country, and the only way you can do this is to let almost anyone say what he thinks—to try to give the best synopses, the best popularizations, the best mediations of technical things that you can, and to let men deny what they think is false—argue what they think is false, you have to have a free and uncorrupted communication.

And this is—this is so the heart of living in a complicated technological world—it is so the heart of freedom that that is why we are all the time saying, "Does this really have to be secret?" "Couldn't you say more about that?" "Are we really acting in a wise way?" Not because we enjoy chattering—not because we are not aware of the dangers of the world we live in, but because these dangers cannot be met in any other way.

The fact is, our government cannot do without us—all of us.

12. THE BOARD'S OPINION

WHERE ARE WE when we come out? Where are we left?

Oppenheimer was loyal. No doubt about that. The Board said, "On the one hand; we find no evidence of disloyalty. Indeed, we have before us much responsible and positive evidence of the loyalty and love of country of the individual concerned."

They said, "For example, Dr. Oppenheimer served his Government because it sought him. The impact of his influence was felt immediately and increased progressively as his services were used. The Nation owes these scientists, we believe, a great debt of gratitude for loyal and magnificent service. This is particularly true with respect to Dr. Oppenheimer."

Again they said, "The Board had before it eloquent and convincing testimony of Dr. Oppenheimer's deep devotion to his country in recent years and a multitude of evidence with respect to active service in all sorts of government undertakings to which he was repeatedly called as a participant and as a consultant. We feel that Dr. Oppenheimer is convinced that the earlier involvements were serious errors and today would consider them an indication of disloyalty. The conclusion of this Board is that Dr. Oppenheimer is a loyal citizen."

And again they said, ". . . We have given particular attention to the question of his loyalty, and we have come to a clear conclusion, which should be reassuring to the people of this country, that he is a loyal citizen."

There was, of course, the letter which Borden wrote to the F.B.I. on November 7, 1953. Borden stood by it in his testimony. He said he thought that Oppenheimer, "more probably than not," was an espionage agent. We may pay him the courtesy of ignoring him.

There was also the somewhat feverish testimony of Dave Griggs: "I want to say, and I can't emphasize too strongly, that Dr. Oppenheimer is the only one of my scientific acquaintances about whom I have ever felt there was a serious question as to their loyalty."

Griggs is both honest and candid. He added, "I feel I have no adequate basis for judging Dr. Oppenheimer's loyalty or disloyalty." And he said, "I have been involved in a great many—not a great many, but a number of pretty strong controversies in the military, and I think it is a fair general observation that when you get involved in a hot enough controversy, it is awfully hard not to question the motives of people who oppose you. This, I am sure, could not but have colored my views on the subject." And there is Griggs's more than candid conversation with Oppenheimer on May 23, 1952, of which he made the following memorandum:

"4. After he had showed me the GAC recommendation of December 1949 that the United States not intensify H-bomb development, but publicly renounce its development, and when I was pressing the point that such a course of action could well be disastrous to this country, Oppenheimer asked if I thought he were pro-Russian or just confused. After a moment I replied frankly that I wish I knew. He then asked if I had 'impugned his loyalty.' I replied I had." In my testimony this morning I expanded that. "He then said he thought I was paranoid. After a few more pleasantries our conversation came to an end."

Griggs testified that he still wished he knew, "and I hope that all of us who have question will be reassured by the proceedings of this Board one way or the other."

Oppenheimer was not only loyal. He was discreet. No one—barring the conscientiously credulous Borden—even suggested that any of our secrets, from the most secret to the least restricted, had escaped through Oppenheimer, and Borden never named one. The Board said, "It must be said that Dr. Oppenheimer seems to have had a high degree of discretion reflecting an unusual ability to keep to himself vital secrets."

Why, then, wasn't this completely loyal and highly discreet citizen fit to serve his country?

In arriving at our recommendation' we have sought to address ourselves to the whole question before us and not to consider the problem as a fragmented one either in terms of specific criteria or in terms of any period in Dr. Oppenheimer's life, or to consider loyalty, character, and associations separately.

However, of course, the most serious finding which this Board could make as a result of these proceedings would be that of disloyalty on the part of Dr. Oppenheimer to his country. For that reason, we have given particular attention to the question of his loyalty, and we have come to a clear conclusion, which should be reassuring to the people of this country, that he is a loyal citizen. If this were the only consideration, therefore, we would recommend that the reinstatement of his clearance would not be a danger to the common defense and security.

We have, however, been unable to arrive at the conclusion that it would be clearly consistent with the security interests of the United States to reinstate Dr. Oppenheimer's clearance and, therefore, do not so recommend.

The following considerations have been controlling in leading us to our conclusion:

1. We find that Dr. Oppenheimer's continuing conduct and associations have reflected a serious disregard for the requirements of the security system.

2. We have found a susceptibility to influence which could have serious implications for the security interests of the country.

3. We find his conduct in the hydrogen-bomb program sufficiently disturbing as to raise a doubt as to whether his future participation, if characterized by the same attitudes in a Government program relating to the national defense, would be clearly consistent with the best interests of security.

4. We have regretfully concluded that Dr. Oppenheimer has been less than candid in several instances in his testimony before this Board.

Respectfully submitted.

GORDON GRAY, *Chairman.*
THOMAS A. MORGAN.

Let me sum up and assess the four considerations which Gray and Morgan said they regarded as "controlling" and "leading us to our conclusion."

The *first* is "that Dr. Oppenheimer's continuing conduct and associations have reflected a serious disregard for the requirements of the security system."

They did not mean that Oppenheimer had violated it. They made that clear.

There remains also an aspect of the security system which perhaps has had insufficient public attention. This is the protection and support of the entire system itself. It must include an understanding and an acceptance of security measures adopted by responsible Government agencies. It must include an active cooperation with all agencies of Government properly and reasonably concerned with the security of our country. It must involve a subordination of personal judgment as to the security status of an individual as against a professional judgment in the light of standards and procedures when they have been clearly established by appropriate process. It must entail a wholehearted commitment to the preservation of the security system and the avoidance of conduct tending to confuse or obstruct.

The Board would assert the right of any citizen to be in disagreement with security measures and any other expressed policies of Government. This is all a part of the right of dissent which must be preserved for our people. But the question arises whether an individual who does not accept and abide by the security system should be a part of it.

This is the Board's gloss on one item in section 8(a) of the President's Executive Order 10450 of April 27, 1953: "6. Intentional, unauthorized disclosure to any person of security information, or of other information disclosure of which is prohibited by law, or willful violation *or disregard of* security regulations"; and on the similar phrase in the A.E.C. Criteria: "6. Violated *or disregarded* security regulations to a degree which would endanger the common defense or national security."

There is no special emphasis on these words other than I have given them. A disregard, as well as a violation, of security regulations is one item of derogatory information, to be treated as such and no more. But here Gray and Morgan are calling for "the pro-

tection and support of the entire system itself." They are expecting
every government employee to give his "active cooperation" and
make "a wholehearted commitment to the preservation of the security system." More than this. They are finding fault with Oppenheimer for not giving it "enthusiastic support."

I will remind you that they used the same words when they were
finding fault with Oppenheimer's attitude toward the development
of a hydrogen bomb. As you recall, they then said, ". . . if Dr.
Oppenheimer had enthusiastically supported the thermonuclear
program . . ." and they said, "However, enthusiastic support on
his part would perhaps have encouraged other leading scientists to
work in the program." There they were concerned with his failure
to support "the strongest military interests of the country." Here
they are concerned about his failure to support the security system.
In both they expected and required his support to be "enthusiastic."

Gray and Morgan are coming perilously close to sacrificing other
considerations on the altar of "the entire system itself." So too, as
we shall see, Commissioner Murray set every other consideration
aside in his belief that a disregard of the security system was simple
disloyalty. Love me, love my dog. To me there is something
mysterious in the emergence of this one item of derogatory information and the way it threatens to swallow up the whole. Suspend
your judgment until you have read Murray's opinion, for there the
security system receives its apotheosis and its most eloquent expression.

But did Oppenheimer continue to disregard the security system,
however "fantastic," however "idiotic" he had once regarded it in
Los Alamos?

We have been all through the Board's instances of Oppenheimer's "disregard," and there is no point summing them up—the
Chevalier incident, what and why Oppenheimer would not tell the
F.B.I., helping Bohm get a position at Princeton and casually meeting him on the street, being willing to give him a letter of recommendation as a physicist for a job in Brazil, telling Bohm and
Lomanitz to tell the truth to the House Un-American Activities
Committee, having supper with the Chevaliers in Paris in 1953, and
allowing the Chevaliers to take him and his wife to see André Malraux. I don't know whether you take, as Gray and Morgan took, "a
most serious view of this kind of continuing association." I don't.

The *second* consideration which controlled Gray and Morgan
was "a susceptibility to influence which could have serious implica-

tions for the security interests of the country."

The legal basis for this is a paragraph in the Executive Order: "Any facts which furnish reason to believe that the individual may be subjected to coercion, influence, or pressure which may cause him to act contrary to the best interests of the national security."

I take it that this paragraph in the Executive Order was aimed at people who have relatives in Russia. I recognize that the words go farther. Do they, however, go so far as to unfit a man regarded by the Board as one whose "influence in the atomic scientific circles with respect to the hydrogen bomb was far greater than he would have led this Board to believe in his testimony before the Board"?

It does seem a little ridiculous with one breath to call Oppenheimer a man whose influence in one field was far greater than he was willing to admit, and then in another breath to say that he was so susceptible to influence that it could raise serious implications for our security.

We have examined each of the three instances which Gray and Morgan cite on Oppenheimer's susceptibility—Oppenheimer's letter to the Rochester newspapers about Dr. Peters, his protest against the induction into the Army of the scientist Lomanitz, and the fact that he would be willing to testify for Dr. Condon in his loyalty investigation.

Their *third* controlling consideration was Oppenheimer's "conduct in the hydrogen bomb program."

Let us first assess the consequences of his conduct.

In Gray's and Morgan's own words, if Oppenheimer had enthusiastically supported the program, "the *possibility* of earlier success in this field" would have been increased; "enthusiastic support on his part would *perhaps* have encouraged other leading scientists to work on the program"; and "the opposition to the H-bomb *by many persons* connected with the atomic energy program, of which Dr. Oppenheimer was the "most experienced, most powerful and most effective member, did delay *the initiation* of concerted effort which led to the development of a thermonuclear weapon." I have done the emphasizing.

Gray and Morgan said, "We find his conduct in the hydrogen bomb program sufficiently disturbing as to raise a doubt as to whether his future participation, if characterized by the same attitudes in a government program relating to the national defense, would be clearly consistent with the best interests of security."

I cannot believe that either Gray or Morgan was aware of the significance of the doubt which disturbed them. It was a doubt as to whether Oppenheimer would be enthusiastic about the future programs of the A.E.C. In other words, it was a doubt as to whether the Commission might not prefer the advice of someone who would agree with the Commission's programs, whatever they might be. Can a lack of enthusiasm be inconsistent with anything else?

Gray's and Morgan's *fourth* and final controlling consideration was their regretful conclusion that Oppenheimer "has been less than candid in several instances in his testimony before this Board."

I have already said enough about this. I think Oppenheimer may have been too candid. He was sometimes ingenuous. Was there anything misleading in his manner? Dr. Evans thought him "still naïve, but extremely honest." Did Gray and Morgan expect him to be penitent about his opposition to the hydrogen bomb? When he thought he had done wrong, you have seen how he was all too penitent. Did they think he should have made it simpler and easier for them to understand? He couldn't, in good conscience, have made it any simpler. Anyhow, when conscientious candor, mistaken for too little, renders a man unfit to serve his country, who shall escape calumny?

13. THE BOARD'S "GENERAL CONSIDERATIONS"

It is not quite right to try to deal strictly with Gray's and Morgan's controlling considerations. Sympathy for their sincerity dogs your understanding. They were as troubled over their decision in this proceeding as Oppenheimer was over his attitude toward the thermonuclear bomb; and Gray's and Morgan's troubles are, perhaps, of equal importance. If there is any validity, any importance, anything praiseworthy in moral principles, the declaration that a man is unfit to serve his country is as momentous—one way or the other, to the country as well as to him—as the destruction or the survival of a city, the fall of a sparrow or an injustice to an individual. In morals there is no difference, even no distinction. It is a tribute to all of us and to our civilized society that Oppenheimer, Gray and Morgan were all equally troubled by the necessity of making the decisions which confronted them.

Gray and Morgan were indeed troubled. They did not quite dare grasp or reject the nettle that was thrust into their hands. Conscience, which can sometimes be a bad adviser, made cowards of them both. The struggle and the resulting confusion between their sense of duty and their good sense came out in the part of their opinion which they called "General Considerations." I say Gray and Morgan and I do not include Evans, for I take it that Evans did not join in this part of the opinion. After agreeing to the "findings" up to a point—page 32 of the typewritten document, which is through the seventh paragraph on page 19 of the printed volume—Evans said, "I do not, however, think it necessary to go into any philosophical discussion to prove points not found in Mr. Nichols' letter."

Gray and Morgan say that "one of the important issues presented in cases of this sort is that of rehabilitation," which they "firmly believe" is possible. They are "conscious of the atmosphere of the time in which Dr. Oppenheimer's clear-cut Communist affiliations occurred." They refer to "the pervasive disillusionment" and "the perhaps normal tendency of a humanitarian to turn to an organization which seemed to him to be espousing primarily humanitarian causes." They are "aware that the fact that the Soviet Union was an ally during some of those years cannot be overlooked." They recognize that "1943 conduct cannot be judged solely in the light of 1954 conditions. At the same time, it must be remembered that standards and procedures of 1943 should not be controlling today."

But is our danger greater now than it was then? Farther on in their opinion they think not. "We acknowledge that the national necessity may at times require the taking of a calculated risk." Such a risk was taken, they say, when Oppenheimer was employed and retained as Director of Los Alamos in 1943. "Again, wartime experiences demanded the use of Nazi scientists before the issues with Germany were settled." But not now. "What we have learned in this inquiry makes the present application of this principle inappropriate in the instant case." Yet they learned nothing since about Oppenheimer that was worse than his conduct and associations had been then.

The Army took a calculated risk on Oppenheimer in 1943. Out of this nettle, danger, the Army plucked this flower, safety. The A.E.C. Criteria expressly require that "a determination must be reached . . . which balances the cost to the program of not having his services against any possible risks involved." The Criteria required the Board to take just such a calculated risk in 1954.

I wonder whether the word *security* has not been insensibly changing its meaning, without our becoming fully aware of the transition, from "safety" to "peace of mind." In this sort of an emergency we are our own enemy, for "the wound of peace is surety, surety secure." Benjamin Franklin went farther than Shakespeare: Poor Richard said, "The way to be safe is never to be secure."

There is, or at least there used to be, a sign hung in sleeping cars from which we may take warning: "Better be Safe than Lucky." And on the knob of your hotel bedroom you can hang a placard, "Please Do Not Disturb." When you ride in a taxi, sometimes you are confronted with "Sit Back, Relax, and Enjoy Your Ride." But the government of the United States is not a Pullman, nor a hotel bedroom, nor a taxicab.

We are driving our own car, and the only complete security we can ever get is to pull off the road and park. It's a pity, but it's true, that our national security, like the security of each of us, has to keep on the highway. It is a continuous calculation of chances.

What do we stand to lose? What are the odds? What do we stand to win?

What is the stake? Some of our secrets can be counted on to remain secrets until they become historical. Such is the number of our atomic and nuclear bombs in stock. Such too are our strategic intentions. But our technical secrets are as perishable as ripe fruit. "Ideas won't keep," Professor Whitehead told Lucien Price (*Dialogues of Alfred North Whitehead*, p. 100). They spoil by independent discovery. Fermi once spoke of the "relatively short time that will elapse before the 'secrets' will naturally become open knowledge by rediscovery on the part of scientists and engineers of other countries." This was in 1946 at the George Westinghouse Centennial Forum. Such secrets can be preserved only by being constantly refreshed and replenished. The security regulations don't speak of these considerations. They either take them for granted or they ignore them. I don't know which.

Just before the Board convened, James G. Beckerly, then Director of Classsification of the A.E.C., spoke before the Atomic Industrial Forum on March 16, 1954. I will ask you to read as much of his remarks as were later printed in *Harper's* in its November 1954 issue:

In historical perspective, secrecy in atomic energy matters has been based at least in part on wishful thinking. . . . We can only surmise why the U.S.S.R. became armed so soon. Personally, I believe it was primarily through the efforts of Soviet scientists and engineers, backed up by a ruthless totalitarian resolve to dominate the world, that the U.S.S.R. became armed with fission weapons as early as 1949. . . .

Espionage assisted the Soviet project but only in a secondary way. Ascribing Soviet achievement primarily to espionage is tantamount to grossly underestimating the technical strength of this enemy of free nations. . . . We must stop kidding ourselves with the dangerous fiction that we are just naturally better than the U.S.S.R. in technical matters. The Russians have the skills and the plants to make fissionable materials and bombs. . . . No matter how much we conceal, they will go ahead in proportion to the effort they expend. . . .

On the other hand, there are the winnings. What may we expect this man to do for us if we clear him and keep him? Here we have a person appearing before us. What he himself may do for us may be all we can expect of him, or it may be the least. A man is a manifold of services. There is what a man does and there is what a man helps others to do. We must look beyond a man's own achievements to get the true measure of his value. "You can either get something done or get credit for doing it," Zacharias told the Board. He added, "And not both."

Here Gray and Morgan were suprisingly unimaginative, as you will see when we come to read Commissioner Zuckert's opinion. They were content not to take a calculated risk as soon as they were told that Oppenheimer's "services as a consultant were used by the Atomic Energy Commission during the entire year of 1953 for a period approximating only 2½ days' time." We shall learn from Zuckert what Oppenheimer's other services amounted to. Indeed, the fact they were in such demand was the reason for these proceedings.

Gray and Morgan spoke of government service as a privilege. For this they had the authority of the preamble of the Executive Order of 1953. I wonder whether it is the right attitude. Is it not sounder to regard government service as a duty? I think so, despite the Executive Order. However, Gray and Morgan are making the point that neither Oppenheimer's "previous contributions" nor "his brilliant capabilities" gives him a right to be employed by the Government. Of course, no one has a right to public office on the ground of either his merits or his deserts. Congress may give our public employees such a right and thereby create a civil service, and Congress may qualify the right, as it did in the Summary Dismissal Act of 1950. But there is no need of taking the attitude that government service is a privilege to prove that it is not a right. Anyhow, Oppenheimer's employment, by the terms of his contract as consultant, could be terminated on seven days' notice. This was the simple answer here.

Gray and Morgan were properly worried over the effect of their decision on "scientists and intellectuals," and they did their best to make it clear that their decision was not "an attack upon scientists and intellectuals generally." These proceedings, they said, were no more than a "prudent study of an individual's conduct and character within the necessary demands of the national security." Yet they had already, near the start of their opinion, expressed the belief that "the Government can search its own soul and the soul of an individual whose relationship to his Government is in question with full protection of the rights and interests of both." Its own soul, surely. The soul of an individual, query. Scientists and intellectuals may well be apprehensive. The Government cannot expect to eat its soul and have it too. Or, as Emerson not so gently put it, we must not "castrate the benefactors." (*Journal*, June 1863.)

Gray and Morgan said, "We know that scientists, with their un-usual talents, are loyal citizens, and, for every pertinent purpose, normal human beings. We must believe that they, the young and the old and all between, will understand that a responsible Government must make repsonsible decisions." Yes, almost all scientists are normal human beings, and one of the pertinent purposes of a normal human being is to be guided by what a responsible Government does to one of the most distinguished, loyal and discreet among them. The Board was as reassuring as the Wolf was to Little Red Riding Hood.

This, at any rate, is no exaggeration of the immediate effect their decision had on our scientists. In June, after the publication of the Board's decision and before the announcement of the Commission's decision, John von Neumann and Vannevar Bush testified before a subcommittee of the House Committee on Government Operations. What they said shows us what we have to worry about. Bush testified:

> I don't need to bore you, certainly, with a detailed recital. I feel that the way in which our security system is working at the present time is driving a wedge between the military and the scientific people of the country, and is doing great harm.
>
> During the war there was developed a partnership between military men and scientific men. It was not brought about automatically; it is not a thing that occurs readily. These men come from different backgrounds, and it is hard for each group to understand the other; but nevertheless, by the end of the war an excellent situation had developed in which there was mutual respect between the two groups and they operated to-gether well. It must be remembered that one cannot plan modern war merely from the military standpoint or merely from the scientific stand-point. It takes both types of thinking to produce success. That partner-ship, which was a healthy one at the end of the war, is, in my opinion, now almost destroyed, and one of the primary reasons is the security system.

Bush had said the same thing the Sunday before in an article in the New York *Times*. Congressman John W. McCormack asked Von Neumann what he thought about Bush's article.

Mr. McCormack: "Did you notice in there that he went to the extent of saying that the relationship has been gravely damaged and is in danger of being gradually destroyed? Did you see that?"

Dr. von Neumann: "Yes, I saw that."

Mr. McCormack: "What are your views on that?"

Dr. von Neumann: "I wouldn't say it is being destroyed. It is certainly being damaged. There is no doubt about it."

Mr. McCormack: "His language was that it is being gravely damaged."

Dr. von Neumann: "I wouldn't say its relationship to the military, but its relationship to the Government."

McCormack then read two paragraphs from Bush's article and again asked Von Neumann what his views were. Dr. von Neumann replied, "I wouldn't be quite so pessimistic. In other words, I wouldn't use the words that it is being gradually destroyed. I would certainly say that it is now being damaged and endangered."

Another "important consideration brought into focus by this case," Gray and Morgan said, "is the role of scientists as advisers in the formulation of Government policy." Indeed, yes, and perhaps the most important.

"We must take notice," Gray and Morgan said, "of the current and inevitable amplification of influence which attaches to those giving advice under these circumstances. These specialists have an exponential amplification of influence which is vastly greater than that of the individual citizen. . . . The impact of his [Dr. Oppenheimer's] influence was felt immediately and increased progressively as his services were used." Who, we may ask parenthetically, is susceptible to whose influence now?

"It is vitally important," they went on four paragraphs later, "that Government and scientists alike understand the need for and the value of the advice of competent technicians. This need is a present and continuing one. Yet those officials in Government who are responsible for the security of the country must be certain that the advice which they seriously seek appropriately reflects special competence on the one hand, and soundly based convictions on the other, uncolored and uninfluenced by considerations of an emotional character."

There is, surely, a danger in our susceptibility to the advice of our experts. Their deeper knowledge may seem to us to be as broad as it is deep, which is not necessarily so, and we may well make the mistake of yielding our better judgment to it. Gray and Morgan are saying that, beyond a scientist's special and technical competence, all he really has to offer us is emotional. And so it may be. We must be on our guard. We must not be awed into accepting their emotions instead of what we seek, which is their technical judgment. We must be careful not to let our cult of the expert turn into an ecstasy of admiration.

But it is our own emotions that we must chiefly guard against, our own sometimes almost religious admiration of their deeper knowledge. We must not forget that we have our own special competence, we who are neither experts nor specialists, to appraise and assess other men's opinions about what they know and we do not. Our responsibility is quite as great as theirs, and we do better when we leave them free to mingle their emotions with their technical opinions and to trust our own special ability to disentangle one from the other. We'd be unwise to distract ourselves so far as to force them to stick to their last. They will be the better shoe-makers for their freedom, and we shall get the better advice, much better than if we insist on their being nothing more than technicians. Mayhem on the man will mutilate the scientist.

Scientists know this if we do not.

Dr. Norris Bradbury, the Director of Los Alamos, testified:

The WITNESS. Scientists are human beings. I think as a class, because their basic task is concerned with the exploration of the facts of nature, understanding, this is a quality of mind philosophy—a scientist wants to know. He wants to know correctly and truthfully and precisely. By this token it seems to me he is more likely than not to be interested in a number of fields, but to be interested in them from the point of view of exploration. What is in them? What do they have to offer. What is their truth. I think this degree of flexibility of approach, of interest, of curiosity about facts, about systems, about life, is an essential ingredient to a man who is going to be a successful research scientist. If he does not have this underlying curiosity, willingness to look into things, wish and desire to look into things, I do not think he will be either a good or not certainly a great scientist.

Therefore, I think you are likely to find among people who have imaginative minds in the scientific field, individuals who are also willing, eager to look at a number of other fields with the same type of interest, willingness to examine, to be convinced and without a priori convictions as to rightness or wrongness, that this constant or this or that curve or this or that function is fatal.

I think the same sort of willingness to explore other areas of human activity is probably characteristic. If this makes them peculiar, I think it is probably a desirable peculiarity.

Another scientist, Erwin Schrödinger, an atomic physicist, had said in 1950:

It seems plain and self-evident, yet it needs to be said: the isolated knowledge obtained by a group of specialists in a narrow field has in itself no value whatsoever, but only in its synthesis with all the rest of knowledge and only inasmuch as it really contributes in this synthesis something toward answering the demand, "who are we?"

Schrödinger here quotes the Greek, which I'll skip. He goes on:

Not that we can avoid specialization altogether; that is impossible if we want to get on. Yet the awareness that specialization is not a virtue but an unavoidable evil is gaining ground, the awareness that all specialized research has real value only in the context of the integrated totality of knowledge. The voices become fainter and fainter that accuse a man of dilettantism who dares to think and speak and write on topics that require more than the special training for which he is "licensed" or "qualified." And any loud barking at such attempts comes from very special quarters of two types—either very scientific or very unscientific quarters—and the reasons for the barking are in both cases translucent. . . .

I should formulate the demand thus:

Never lose sight of the role your particular subject has within the great performance of the tragi-comedy of human life; keep in touch with life—not so much with practical life as with the ideal background of life, which is ever so much more important; and, *keep life in touch with you.* If you cannot—in the long run—tell everyone what you have been doing, your doing has been worthless.*

The decision on the hydrogen bomb, like all deliberate decisions, came out of a welter of technical insight and emotion, a clash and confusion of opinion. The advice of the General Advisory Committee to the contrary was a valuable, perhaps a necessary, ingredient of the final judgment, the judgment of the statesmen. Had the scientists offered nothing but technical opinions, the decision of the statesmen would have been impoverished and the less secure. As they were unable to understand the technicalities, a "soundly based conviction" would have reflected only their own ignorant convictions. For Gray and Morgan made it quite clear that this was what they meant by a "soundly based conviction." They said, "In evaluating advice from a specialist which departs from the area of his specialty, Government officials charged with the military posture of our country must also be certain that underlying any advice is a genuine conviction that this country cannot in the interest of security have less than the strongest possible offensive capabilities in a time of national danger."

They said this twice. Two pages later they repeated it. They said they were concerned that Oppenheimer "may have departed his role as scientific adviser to exercise highly persuasive influence

* Erwin Schrödinger, *Science and Humanism*, Cambridge University Press, 1951, pp. 5, 7, and 8.

in matters in which his convictions were not necessarily a reflection of technical judgment, and also not necessarily related to the protection of the strongest offensive military interests of the country."

I do not know whether our policy was then or is now as sole and simple as that "the strongest offensive military interests of the country." Gray and Morgan certainly knew more about it than I do, but if our national policy be a simple-minded monomania, which ignores or is ignorant of the manifold of other considerations, political, diplomatic, economic, financial, and which leaves moral considerations to find their own way in, then so much the more need of advice, even from a scientist transcending his special and technical limitations.

It is hard to believe that Gray and Morgan think much of scientists, or even of technicians. A few pages back from where I have just been quoting, they rejected the idea of applying "one test to an individual, however brilliant his capacities and however magnificent his contributions, and another test to an individual with more mundane capabilities and lesser contributions." "Can a different test for security purposes," they asked, "be justified in the case of the brilliant technical consultant than in the case of the stenographer or clerk?"

This is sound equalitarian doctrine, to be sure; but it is not what the Atomic Energy Commission required of them. Let me quote it again. "A determination must be reached . . . which balances the cost to the program of not having his services against any possible risks involved." You must be a strict equalitarian to equate the services of a brilliant consultant with those of a stenographer or a clerk, and a very bad mathematician to assume that the cost to your program is the same.

However, Gray's and Morgan's disregard of the Atomic Energy Commission's Criteria is not the point. What Gray and Morgan failed to perceive is the great difference between the technician, however talented, and the genius, the explorer, the discoverer, the illuminator and the catalyzer. Oppenheimer tried to tell them. Teller was a living incarnation who stood and talked there before them. Difficult, capricious, unhandy, unconformable, naïve, anything you wish. The scientific genius may be all these, almost anything except dispensable. It is destructive to ignore the difference between competence and talent. It is catastrophic to be blind to the difference between competence and genius, between a clerk and an Oppenheimer, between a stenographer and a Teller.

14. THE MAN HIMSELF

THE CRITERIA of the Atomic Energy Commission say, "The judgment of responsible persons as to the integrity of the individuals should be considered. The decision as to security clearance is an over-all common-sense judgment. . . ." The Commission had itself made just such a decision in 1948 in the case of Dr. Frank Graham, and it had emphasized that this was what it wanted done by taking the unusual step of publishing its opinion in which it declared that this was what it was doing. Garrison quoted it to the Board:

"The five members * * * are fully satisfied that Dr. Graham is a man of upright character and thoroughgoing loyalty to the United States. His career as a leading educator and prominent public figure in the South has, it appears, been marked by controversy, engendered in part by his role in championing freedom of speech and other basic civil or economic rights.

"6. In the course of his vigorous advocacy of the principles in which he believes, Dr. Graham has allied himself, by sponsorship or participation, with large numbers of people and organizations all over the country. In this way he has been associated at times with individuals or organizations influenced by motives or views of Communist derivation. These associations, which in substance are described in various published material, are all referred to in the security file.

"7. 'Associations,' of course, have a probative value in determining whether an individual is a good or bad security risk. But it must be recognized that it is the man himself the Commission is actually concerned with, that the associations are only evidentiary, and that commonsense must be exercised in judging their significance. It does not appear that Dr. Graham ever associated with any such individuals or organizations for improper purposes; on the contrary, the specific purposes for which he had these associations were in keeping with American traditions and principles. Moreover, from the entire record it is clear in Dr. Graham's case that such associations have neither impaired his integrity nor arouse in him the slightest sympathy for Communist or other antidemocratic or subversive doctrines. His record on controversial issues has made this abundantly clear, and his course of conduct during the past two decades leaves no doubt as to his opposition to communism and his attachment to the principles of the Constitution.

"8. All five members of the Commission agree with the conclusion of the General Manager that, in the words of the Atomic Energy Act of 1946, it 'will not endanger the common defense or security' for Dr. Graham to be given security clearance, and·that it is very much to the advantage of the country that Dr. Graham continue his participation in the atomic-energy program. Our long-range success in the field of atomic energy depends in large part on our ability to·attract into the program men of character and vision with a wide variety of talents and viewpoints."

So I say to you, Mr. Chairman and members of the board, that in the Commission's own view of the matter it is the man himself that is to be considered, commonsense to be exercised in judging the evidence, and that it is appropriate to consider in the final reckoning the fact that our long-range success in the field of atomic energy depends in large part on our ability to attract into the program men of character and vision with a wide variety of talents and viewpoints.

The Board, indeed, went further. It went so far as to say that it had to "search the soul" of Oppenheimer. A precarious undertaking at best. The London *Economist* called it "a shocking claim to make on behalf of the State—a claim of divine prescience which even the totalitarians do not bother to put forward." (*The Economist* for June 12, 1954.) Well, maybe; but in one way or another, even without the help of such prescience, some sort of total judgment must be made when what you undertake to determine is what a man is likely to do and not merely what he has done.

Dr. Rabi put it more mundanely than *The Economist*. When Robb suggested that the Board might be in possession of information about the Chevalier incident which was not available to him, he said, "It may be. On the other hand, I am in possession of a long experience with this man, going back to 1929, which is 25 years, and there is a kind of seat of the pants feeling [on] which I myself lay great weight."

At any rate, the Board, in its quest of Oppenheimer's soul, listened to a great number of judgments of highly responsible persons. I don't suppose any man in our time whose character has been doubted has had it endorsed by so many of the great and responsible. The witnesses to Oppenheimer's character have good enough credit to allow him to discount it in heaven. I don't know quite how many of them or which of them I should ask to tell you what they told the Board. Some I should like almost to insist on your hearing. Others I should like simply to offer. You will make your own choice.

Let me pick first those who knew Oppenheimer best. Start with Conant and Bush. They had watched Oppenheimer direct Los Alamos and had worked with him ever since.

Conant had written a letter to the A.E.C. about Oppenheimer in 1947. It was shown to him. He testified:

May I, with the board's permission, just read you the last two paragraphs. The first four of the letter have to do with a recital of your acquaintance with Dr. Oppenheimer and the circmumstances of your writing the letter. Then you went on to say: "I can say without hesitation that there can be absolutely no question of Dr. Oppenheimer's loyalty. Furthermore, I can state categorically that, in my opinion, his attitude about the future course of the United States Government in matters of high policy is in accordance with the soundest American tradition. He is not sympathetic with the totalitarian regime in Russia and his attitude towards that nation is, from my point of view, thoroughly sound and hard headed. Therefore, any rumor that Dr. Oppenheimer is sympathetically inclined towards the Communists or towards Russia is an absurdity. As I wrote above, I base this statement on what I consider intimate knowledge of the workings of his mind. [Reading:]

"At the time of Dr. Oppenheimer's entering the work on atomic energy, I heard that there was some question of his clearance by the security agencies. I understand that was based on his associations prior to 1939 and his 'left-wing' sympathies at that time. I have no knowledge of Dr. Oppenheimer previous to the summer of 1941, but I say unhesitatingly that whatever the record might show as to his political sympathies at that time or his associations, I would not deviate from my present opinion, namely, that a more loyal and sound American citizen cannot be found in the whole United States."

You wrote that?

A. Yes, I wrote that. I have every reason to believe I wrote it.

Q. Dr. Conant, you formed your judgment at that time on your appraisal of Dr. Oppenheimer as a total man?

A. Yes. That was based clearly on my acquaintance with him during the Los Alamos project and this other period which I mentioned in which we discussed the whole question of the control of the bomb, which gave me a chance to explore many political problems which we would not have explored at Los Alamos.

Q. Having in mind the Commission's letter of December 23, 1953, to which we have referred on the one hand, and what Dr. Oppenheimer has done since March 1947 when this letter was written, do you have reason to modify or alter the view which you expressed about him in March 1947?

A. No. I would think on the contrary the actions and decisions which I put on the record here seem to me to make quite clear that he was party to many actions on the part of the General Advisory Committee which were strongly opposed to any Soviet policy. It makes more certain the statements I then made based on what was after all a shorter acquaintance with him.

Bush had also written a letter to the A.E.C. about Oppenheimer in 1947. He testified:

The WITNESS I could not find a copy anywhere, but my stenographer had his old notebooks and that is where I got it from. Isn't is quicker for me to read it?

Mr. GRAY. Why don't you read it?

The WITNESS. "At our conference yesterday you asked me to comment concerning Dr. J. Robert Oppenheimer, and I am very glad to do so. Dr. Oppenheimer is one of the great physicists of this country or of the world for that matter. Prior to the war he was on the staff of the University of California, and was regarded as the leader of theoretical aspects of atomistics and similar subjects of physics. Shortly after the Army entered into the development of atomic energy he was given a very important appointment by General Groves. This appointment made him director of the laboratory at Los Alamos, which was in all probability the most important post held by any civilian scientist in connection with the entire effort. General Groves undoubtedly made this appointment after a very careful study of the entire affair from all angles, as this was his custom on important appointments. Subsequent developments made it very clear that no error had been made in this connection, for Dr. Oppenheimer proved himself to be not only a great physicist, but also a man of excellent judgment and a real leader in the entire effort. In fact, it was due to the extraordinary accomplishments of Oppenheimer and his asociates that the job was completed on time. Subsequent to the end of the war Dr. Oppenheimer has had a number of important appointments. He was invited by Secretary Stimson as one of the scientists consulted by the Secretaries of War and Navy in connection with the work of the Interim Committee. He was appointed by the State Department as a member of the board which drew up the plan on which Mr. Baruch based his program. He has recently been appointed by the President as a member of the General Advisory Committee of your organization. I have appointed him a member of the Committee on Atomic Energy of the Joint Research and Development Board. All of this has followed from his extraordinary war record in which he made a unique and exceedingly important contribution to the success of the war effort of this country.

"I know him very well indeed and I have personally great confidence in his judgment and integrity."

Mr. ROBB. I have the original now.

By Mr. Garrison:

Q. At the time you wrote that letter, had you been through Dr. Oppenheimer's personnel file, the FBI reports?

A. I don't think I ever went through Dr. Oppenheimer's FBI file. If I did, I certainly do not remember.

Q. Did you understand at the time that you wrote that letter that he had left wing associations?

A. I understood that at the time of his first appointment was made at Los Alamos. I had an exposition of the entire affair from General Groves.

Q. You read the letter of General Nichols dated December 23, 1953, to Dr. Oppenheimer, containing the items of derogatory information?

A. Yes, I read that as it appeared in the press.

Q. Is there anything in that letter which would cause you to want to qualify the letter which you wrote to Mr. Lilienthal that you have just read?

A. Now, let me answer that in two parts. I had at the time of the Los Alamos appointment complete confidence in the loyalty, judgment, and integrity of Dr. Oppenheimer. I have certainly no reason to change that opinion in the meantime. I have had plenty of reason to confirm it, for I worked with him on many occasions on very difficult matters. I know that his motivation was exactly the same as mine, namely, first, to make this country strong, to resist attack, and second, if possible, to fend off from the world the kind of mess we are now getting into.

On the second part of that, would I on the basis of that document, if those allegations were proved, change my judgment. That is what I understand this board is to decide. I don't think I ought to try to prejudge what they might find out.

Q. I would not want to ask you to do that, and my question is not designed to do that.

A. My faith has not in the slightest degree been shaken by that letter or anything else.

General Groves worked with Oppenheimer at Los Alamos, and you may be sure that the general's opinion of Oppenheimer stands on its own feet. General Groves told the Board:

Q. How would you rate the quality of his achievement as you look back on it?

A. Naturally I am prejudiced, because I selected him for the job, but I think he did a magnificent job as far as the war effort was concerned. In other words, while he was under my control—and you must remember that he left my control shortly after the war was over.

Q. If you had to make the decision again, would you make it in the same way with respect to the selection of Dr. Oppenheimer and devolving the responsibilities on him which you did?

A. I know of no reason why not. Assuming all the conditions are the same, I think I would do it.

Q. You saw him very closely during those years?

A. I saw him on the average, I would say, of anywhere from once a week to once a month. I talked to him on the phone about anywhere from 4 to 5 times a day to once in 3 or 4 days. I talked on all possible subjects of all varieties. During the time I spent a number of days, for example, on trains traveling where we might be together for 6 or 8 or 12 hours at a time.

Q. You were aware of his leftwing associations at the time—his earlier leftwing associations?

A. Was I or am I?

Q. Were you at the time you appointed him?

A. At the time I appointed him to the project, I was aware that there were suspicions about him, nothing like what were contained—and I might say I read the New York Times, the letter of General Nichols and Dr. Oppenheimer's letter. I was not aware of all the things that were brought out in General Nichols' letter at the time of the appointment, but I was aware that he was or that he had, you might say, a very extreme liberal background.

I was also aware of another thing that I think must be mentioned, that he was already in the project, that he had been in charge of this particular type of work, that is, the bomb computations, and that he knew all that there was to know about that. In general, my policy was to consider the fact that the man was already in the project, and that made it very questionable whether I should separate him and also whether I should separate him under what might be termed unpleasant conditions, because then you never know what you are going to do to him. Are you going to drive him over to the other side or not? As far as what I knew at the time of his actual selection, I knew enough to tell me that I would have considered him an extreme liberal with a very liberal background. Just how many of the details I knew at the time I don't know. I did know them all later.

Q. Based on your total acquaintance with him and your experience with him and your knowledge of him, would you say that in your opinion he would ever consciously commit a disloyel act?

A. I would be amazed if he did.

Von Neumann was Oppenheimer's neighbor and colleague at Princeton and a member of the G.A.C. He was one of his opponents over the H-bomb. He said:

Q. You have known Dr. Oppenheimer, I think you said, substantially continuously since 1943 to the present date?

A. Yes.

Q. With the exception of the period from 1945, the end of the Los Alamos days, until 1947, when Dr. Oppenheimer came to the institute as director.

A. That is correct.

Q. During that period you have really lived in the same small town?

A. Yes.

Q. And been friends and known each other quite well during all that time?

A. Yes.

Q. Both professionally and socially?

A. Yes, that is correct.

Q. Do you have an opinion about Dr. Oppenheimer's loyalty to the United States, his integrity?

A. I have no doubts about it whatever.

Q. Your opinion I take it is quite clear and firm?

A. Yes, yes.

Q. Do you have an opinion as to Dr. Oppenheimer's discretion in the handling of classified materials and classified information?

A. Absolutely. I have personally every confidence. Furthermore I am not aware that anybody has questioned that.

Q. There seems to be some question among my associates whether I asked this. Do you have an opinion about Dr. Oppenheimer's loyalty?

A. Yes.

Q. What is that?

A. I would say he is loyal.

Q. Do you have any doubt on that subject at all?

A. No.

Listen to the two chairmen of the A.E.C. before Strauss.

David Lilienthal said:

Q. As a result of your experience with Dr. Oppenheimer and your knowledge of him, have you formed an opinion as to his loyalty, his integrity, his character, all the other factors that go into forming a judgment as to his loyalty, security?

A. Yes, I have.

Q. What is your opinion?

A. I have no shadow of a doubt in my mind that here is a man of good character, integrity and of loyalty to his country.

Q. How would you assess him as a security risk?

A. I did not regard him up until the time my knowledge of the program ceased, and had no occasion to regard him as a security risk.

Q. I think you already indicated that in March 1947 you consciously assayed the situation and came to the conclusion that he was not a security risk?

A. Yes. At that time we had this file before us and that was my conclusion, that in the light of the overall picture, taking everything into account, the minus signs were very few indeed, and the plus signs very great indeed, and I thought he was a contribution to the security of the country. I have had no occasion since that time to change that view.

Q. Has your experience with him confirmed that view?

A. My experience from that time did confirm that view. I am sure that it is clear that he has made great contributions to the security of the country.

Gordon Dean said:

Q. Summing up your convictions about Dr. Oppenheimer, you have testified to his loyalty and to his integrity and character with full knowledge of what you told us about your reading of his personnel file. I take it, also, that it goes without saying that you have read the Commission's letter which initiated this proceeding?

A. The charges? Yes, I have.

Q. The Commission refers to them as items of derogatory information, and not as charges.

A. That is right. I read that letter.

Q. On the basis of that knowledge and your experience with him, in your opinion is he or is he not a security risk?

A. He is not a security risk in my opinion. If I had so considered him a security risk, I would have initiated such a hearing long, long ago. I think his usefulness has been impaired by all this. I don't know how much he can contribute further to his country, but I would hope we would get the maximum out of him. I am certain that he is devoted to his country and if given an opportunity to serve, will serve and effectively as always.

Take some others, not scientists. These are businessmen.

Sumner Pike, a former member of the A.E.C., said:

Q. On the basis of your knowledge of Dr. Oppenheimer and your experiences with him, what is your opinion as to his loyalty?

A. I never had any question about his loyalty. I think he is a man of essential integrity. I think he has been a fool several times, but there was nothing in there that shook my feeling. As a matter of fact, it was a pretty good summary, it seemed to me, of the material that was turned over to us early in 1947 by the FBI, all except the last thing about the hydrogen bomb. Of course, that was not in then.

Q. The letter and, I assume, the file contained data about past associations of his.

A. Yes.

Q. In your judgment is his character and the associations of the past and his loyalty such that if he were to continue to have access to restricted data, he would not endanger the common defense or security?

A. No, I don't think he would endanger the common defense or security the least bit.

Hartley Rowe of the United Fruit Company and a former member of the G.A.C. said:

A. I can only speak from my acquaintance with Dr. Oppenheimer during these years that I have outlined to you. So far as I am personally concerned, and so far as my own observations go, Dr. Oppenheimer is no greater risk than any other American citizen except for one thing, and that is he has a greater knowledge of atomic fission than anyone else that I know of in the country. If you are put in a position of knowing secret and top secret information, the more you know, the greater risk you become, if you are ever in circumstances where you, as our boys have been in Korea—I don't know how I would react, and I don't know how Dr. Oppenheimer would react to brutal treatment. But in the course of his associations in the United States, I would have no reservation whatever.

Q. Are you saying that you have no question as to the loyalty, character or associations?

A. None whatever, based on my association with him.

* * *

Mr. GRAY. Do you feel that your present conviction about Dr. Oppenheimer's character, loyalty and associations, would be the same if you knew that the information contained in the Nichols letter by early associations was true? Would your reply still be the same?

Let me repeat, Mr. Rowe, I am not saying that it is or is not true. Can you assume that derogatory information and still arrive at the answer you gave to Mr. Marks' question?

The WITNESS. I think my answer to that would be I would make it just that much stronger because people make mistakes and people in the climate of public opinion in those days which was quite different than it is now—we know a great deal more than we did then—I think a man of Dr. Oppenheimer's character is not going to make the same mistake twice. I would say he was all the more trustworthy for the mistakes he made.

John J. McCloy, who had been our High Commissioner in Germany before Conant and was now the chairman of the board of the Chase National Bank in New York, said:

A. In the first place, just to get it out of the way, let me say that there is nothing that occurred during the entire period of my contact with Dr. Oppenheimer which gave me any reason to feel that he was in any sense disloyal to the United States. But I would want to put it more positively than that, and also add that throughout my contacts with him, I got the impression, as one who has had a good bit of contact and experience with defense matters, that he was very sensitive to all aspects of the security of the United States.

I gathered the impression that he was deeply concerned about the consequences of this awful force that we had released, anxious to do what he could toward seeing that it was not used or did not become a destroyer of civilization. He was somewhat puzzled as to what form that would take and still be consistent with the interests of the United States. That perhaps more than a number of others who were, so to speak, laymen in this field, who were members of that study group, was aware of the techniques of the defense of the United States. He was a little more aware than those who had not been really associated with the Defense Department of the military position of the United States somewhat apart from the atomic situation. So much for loyalty.

I can't be too emphatic as to my impression of Dr. Oppenheimer in this regard. I have the impression of his being a loyal, patriotic citizen, aware of his responsibilities and that I want to accent.

As to his security risk—to use the current phrase—I again can state that negatively certainly. I know of nothing myself which would make me feel that he was a security risk. I don't know just exactly what you mean by a security risk. I know that I am a security risk and I think every individual is a security risk. You can always talk in your sleep. You can always drop a paper that you should not drop, or you can speak to your wife about something, and to that extent no human being is an absolutely secure person. I don't suppose we are talking about that.

I never heard of any of Dr. Oppenheimer's early background until very recently, and so that has never been an element in my thinking. I have only thought of him as being a figure whom I feel I know, and I feel I am somewhat knowledgeable in this field, and one I feel I know is as much responsible as anybody else if perhaps not more than anybody else in this particular field of the weapon for our preeminence in that field. Too many reports came in to us as to the work that he was doing, the difficulties under which he was laboring, and they were difficulties because there had to be very great security precautions and a lot of barbed wire and what not which introduced serious human problems in connection with the plants where he was operating, and the reports all were that in spite of all this, and in spite of the little squabbles that took place among this confined group of scientists, there was a certain inspiration to their work and enthusiasm and a vigor and energy that many ascribed to Dr. Oppenheimer, and which I am quite clear played a major part in bringing about the achievement of the weapon at the critical point, and time that it was achieved.

George F. Kennan, for twenty-five years a career diplomat and recently our Ambassador to Moscow, said:

A. I formed the conviction that he was an immensely useful person in the councils of our Government, and I felt a great sense of gratitude that we had his help. I am able to say that in the course of all these contacts and deliberations within the Government I never observed anything in his conduct or his words that could possibly, it seemed to me, have indicated that he was animated by any other motives than a devotion to the interests of this country.

Q. Did you ever observe anything that would possibly have suggested to you that he was taking positions that the Russians would have liked?

A. No. I cannot say that I did in any way. After all, the whole purpose of these exercises was to do things which were in the interest of this country, not in the interests of the Soviet Union, at least not in the interests of the Soviet Union as their leaders saw it at that time. Anyone who collaborated sincerely and enthusiastically in the attempt to reach our objectives, which Dr. Oppenheimer did, obviously was not serving Soviet purposes in any way.

Q. Have you said that he contributed significantly to the results?

A. I have, sir.

Q. Mr. Kennan, is there any possibility in your mind that he was dissembling?

A. There is in my mind no possibility that Dr. Oppenheimer was dissembling.

Q. How do you know that? How can anybody know that?

A. I realize that is not an assertion that one could make with confidence about everyone. If I make it with regard to Dr. Oppenheimer it is because I feel and believe that after years of seeing him in various ways, not only there in Government, but later as an associate and a neighbor, and a friend at Princeton, I know his intellectual makeup and something of his personal makeup and I consider it really out of the question that any man could have participated as he did in these discussions, could have bared his thoughts to us time after time in the way that he did, could have thought those thoughts, so to speak, in our presence, and have been at the same time dissembling.

I realize that is still not wholly the answer. The reason I feel it is out of the question that could have happened is that I believed him to have an intellect of such a nature that it would be impossible for him to speak dishonestly about any subject to which he had given his deliberate and careful and professional attention.

That is the view I hold of him. I have the greatest respect for Dr. Oppenheimer's mind. I think it is one of the great minds of this generation of Americans. A mind like that is not without its implications.

Q. Without its what?

A. Implications for a man's general personality. I think it would be actually the one thing probably in life that Dr. Oppenheimer could never do, that is to speak dishonestly about a subject which had really engaged the responsible attention of his intellect. My whole impression of him is that he is a man who when he turns his mind to something in an orderly and responsible way, examines it with the most extraordinary scrupulousness and fastidiousness of intellectual process.

I must say that I cannot conceive that in these deliberations in Government he could have been speaking disingenuously to us about these matters. I would suppose that you might just as well have asked Leonardo da Vinci to distort an anatomical drawing as that you should ask Robert Oppenheimer to speak responsibly to the sort of questions we were talking about, and speak dishonestly.

Teller was Oppenheimer's leading opponent in the H-bomb wrangle. Asked if Oppenheimer was disloyal, he said:

A. I do not want to suggest anything of the kind. I know Oppenheimer as an intellectually most alert and a very complicated person, and I think it would be presumptuous and wrong on my part if I would try in any way to analyze his motives. But I have always assumed, and I now assume that he is loyal to the United States. I believe this, and I shall believe it until I see very conclusive proof to the opposite.

Q. Now, a question which is the corollary of that. Do you or do you not believe that Dr. Oppenheimer is a security risk?

A. In a great number of cases I have seen Dr. Oppenheimer act—I understood that Dr. Oppenheimer acted—in a way which for me was exceedingly hard to understand. I thoroughly disagreed with him in numerous issues and his actions frankly appeared to me confused and complicated. To this extent I feel that I would like to see the vital interests of this country in hands which I understand better, and therefore trust more.

In this very limited sense I would like to express a feeling that I would feel personally more secure if public matters would rest in other hands.

Mr. GRAY. Dr. Teller, you are familiar with the question which this board is called upon to answer, I assume.

The WITNESS. Yes, I believe so.

Mr. GRAY. Let me tell you what it is and invite counsel to help me out if I misstate it. We are asked to make a finding in the alternative, that it will or will not endanger the common defense and security to grant security clearance to Dr. Oppenheimer.

I believe you testified earlier when Rr. Robb was putting questions to you that because of your knowledge of the whole situation and by reason of many factors about which you have testified in very considerable detail, you would feel safer if the security of the country were in other hands.

The WITNESS. Right.

Mr. GRAY. That is substantially what you said?

The WITNESS. Yes.

Mr. GRAY. I think you have explained why you feel that way. I would then like to ask you this question: Do you feel that it would endanger the common defense and security to grant clearance to Dr. Oppenheimer?

The WITNESS. I believe, and that is merely a question of belief and there is no real information behind it, that Dr. Oppenheimer's character is such that he would not knowingly and willingly do anything that is designed to endanger the safety of this country. To the extent, therefore, that your question is directed toward intent, I would say I do not see any reason to deny clearance.

If it is a question of wisdom and judgment, as demonstrated by actions since 1945, then I would say one would be wiser not to grant clearance. I must say that I am myself a little bit confused on this issue, particularly as it refers to a person of Oppenheimer's prestige and influence. May I limit myself to these comments?

Mr. GRAY. Yes.

The WITNESS. I will be glad to answer more questions about it to you or to counsel.

Mr. GRAY. No, I think that you have answered my question.

Here is a general in the Air Force. Major General James Mc-Cormack said:

Q. In the course of your meeting and acquaintanceship with Dr. Oppenheimer, did you feel you came to know him quite well?

A. Oh, yes.

Q. Do you have an opinion as to Dr. Oppenheimer's loyalty to the United States?

A. I never had a question as to it.

Q. Do you have an opinion as to whether he is a security risk, as to his discretion in the use of classified materials, whether it is safe to trust him with such?

A. Nothing in my associations with him would raise the question with me.

You have heard me quote Dr. Rabi before. He is the chairman

of the G.A.C. Let me quote him again.

Do you feel that you know Dr. Oppenheimer well enough to comment on the bearing of his character, loyalty and associations on this issue?

A. I think Dr. Oppenheimer is a man of upstanding character, that he is a loyal individual, not only to the United States, which of course goes without saying in my mind, but also to his friends and his organizations to which he is attached, let us say, to the institutions, and work very hard for his loyalties; an upright character, very upright character, very thoughtful, sensitive feeling in that respect.

With regard to the question of association, I might say that I have seen the brief form of what would you call it, the report of Dr. Oppenheimer?

Q. What is that?

A. It is some document about 40 pages which is a summary.

Q. When did you see it?

A. Some time in January.

Q. How did you happen to see it?

A. The Chairman of the Commission asked me to take a look at it.

Mr. GARRISON. What year?

The WITNESS. This year. I would say that in spite of the associations in there, I do not believe that Dr. Oppenheimer is a security risk, and that these associations in the past should bar him from access to security information for the Atomic Energy Commission.

By Mr. MARKS.

Q. The report you speak of, is that in amplification of the letter of allegations or derogatory information which you have read of General Nichols to Dr. Oppenheimer?

A. I don't know whether it was made as an amplification.

Q. I am just trying to get some sense of what it is.

A. I don't know. I understood it to be a digest of a very big file.

Q. I didn't understand clearly, Dr. Rabi. You used the phrase "bar him." Would you mind repeating what you had in mind?

A. I will put it this way. If I had to make the determination, after having read this and knowing Dr. Oppenheimer for all the years I would know him, I would have continued him in his position as consultant to the Atomic Energy Commission, which he was before.

This is an invidious selection. Let me make amends. Here are a dozen more. Listen to them.

Mervin J. Kelly, the president of the Bell Telephone Laboratories, had served on the Atomic Energy Standing Committee of the Research and Development Board under Oppenheimer's chairmanship since late 1949. He said:

He was an unusually able chairman. I have been on lots of committees and chairman of some, and I would put him right at the top in his patience in developing views and getting the views of everyone, and promoting full discussion, and yet giving the minimum of waste time for busy people that goes with committees of that size.

We came up, after much discussion, with very common views because it was in an area where, excepting for the enemy situation, there was generally a background of factual knowledge to work on.

After we had gotten to where we had a commonness of view as to what we should say the program should be in scope and emphasis, Dr. Oppenheimer undertook the job of preparing our report, which was an aid to all of us. I remember his staying on in Washington between meetings and beyond meetings for drafting the report. He drafted a report which with very minor modifications, I would say, all of us could sign as representing fully our own views as to what the military emphasis in research and development should be.

This was just at the threshold of the time where atomic basic knowledge had reached the point that it was possible to consider versatility. By that I mean extending the range of weapons well beyond that of the large free falling bombs. So this was rather a critical time.

Q. What would you say as to Dr. Oppenheimer's reputation for straightforwardness, directness, veracity?

A. Among his peers, he is, first, known and recognized for his accuracy of thought and cleanness of expression. His words are considered generally well-weighed and meaningful because of their accuracy and temperate. I would know of no one that knew him as well as I that would feel that he overstated his position.

As to his veracity and dedication, I know of no one in the program, with the high clearances that he has had, and that I have, Q and top secret, everything he has done and said gives a full appearance to a great dedication, as full an appearance as any of us that are in and still cleared.

Q. Would you say that as chairman of this panel he made a contribution to the national welfare?

A. I am sure that he did. In the form that he writes all of his things, getting the views of the full committee that he shared, as to what the forward looking program should be, getting it clean, orderly, and well placed was a great contribution, as anyone working in the atmosphere of the Pentagon knows the great need for, that is, of getting direction and aim and purpose well spelled out. It was in this report of the panel which was his fine, clean writing, but which was the views of all of us which he shared.

Q. What have you to say as to his reputation for integrity and patriotism and your own personal feeling about that?

A. Among his peers, those who know him and know his work, I would say his reputation is the highest. As to my own personal belief, I know of no one in the program that I would have any more confidence in their integrity and dedication than I would of Dr. Oppenheimer.

Karl T. Compton, the president of the Massachusetts Institute of Technology from 1930 to 1948, said:

A. I have never had any question of it. I have no question of it now. He is completely loyal.

Q. Again based on your experience with him and your knowledge of him, would you say that his continued employment as a consultant to the Atomic Energy Commission would be clearly consistent with the interests of national security?

A. So far as I know the situation, I would say yes. I think I would have to qualify that by this fact. While my personal impression, my faith is sound, it would have to be subject to derogatory evidence that I don't know anything about, which I take it is the purpose of this committee to investigate.

Q. Of course, that goes without saying. I am asking you for your judgment simply based on your own personal feeling about him and knowledge of him.

A. Yes.

Q. As to that, you are clear in your mind.

A. Perfectly clear, yes.

Q. What in your judgment would be the effect, if any, on the scientific community if Dr. Oppenheimer's clearance were to be revoked?

A. I believe—and I feel very certain of this—that there would be a shock, there would be a discouragement, there would be confusion. I think the result would be very bad.

Q. Bad for the country?

A. For the country.

General Frederick Osborn was the Deputy Representative of the United States on the United Nations Atomic Energy Commission from 1947 to 1950, where he worked with Oppenheimer on the Baruch plan. He said:

Q. From these contacts with Dr. Oppenheimer during these 2 years, 3 years actually, did you form an impression of his character and his quality as an American citizen?

A. I formed the impression of a man most consistent and determined in his desire to protect the United States against what he considered a very dangerous situation, a great number of dangers in these negotiations, and willing to take infinite pains to see that we didn't fall into any of these traps.

Hence I considered him a man of real patriotism and very consistent character and great loyalty because, after all, the very first thing I did, knowing nothing about this situation—when 2 weeks after he had taken the trouble to fly out from California—I had gone against his advice without telling him what I was doing. This made no difference. He just stuck at what he considered his job of seeing that we didn't fall into any pitfalls on this thing.

Q. By going against his advice, you have reference to your testimony that, after consulting with the British, French, and Canadians, you favored continuing negotiations with the Russians?

A. Yes. He remained intensely loyal. It has always struck me. I have been in a good many jobs, and this is not always the case when you cross a man at the beginning.

Here is another scientist, Hans Bethe, a professor at Cornell and a consultant at Los Alamos. He had known Oppenheimer since 1929.

Q. On the basis of your association with him, your knowledge of him over these many years, would you care to express an opinion about Dr. Oppenheimer's loyalty to the United States, about his character, about his discretion in regard to matters of security?

A. I am certainly happy to do this. I have absolute faith in Dr. Oppenheimer's loyalty. I have always found that he had the best interests of the United States at heart. I have always found that if he differed from other people in his judgment, that it was because of a deeper thinking about the possible consequences of our action than the other people had. I believe that it is an expression of loyalty—of particular loyalty—if a person tries to go beyond the obvious and tries to make available his deeper insight, even in making unpopular suggestions, even in making suggestions which are not the obvious ones to make, are not those which a normal intellect might be led to make.

I have absolutely no question that he has served this country very long and very well. I think everybody agrees that his service in Los Alamos was one of the greatest services that were given to this country. I believe he has served equally well in the GAC in reestablishing the strength of our atomic weapons program in 1947. I have faith in him quite generally.

Q. You and he are good friends?

A. Yes.

Q. Would you expect him to place his loyalty to his country even above his loyalty to a friend?

A. I suppose so.

James B. Fisk was vice-president in charge of research at the Bell Telephone Laboratories and a member of the General Advisory Committee.

Q. Have you formed an opinion as a result of your contact with Dr. Oppenheimer, and your knowledge of Dr. Oppenheimer with respect to his integrity, his loyalty and any other factors that might bear on his being a security risk?

A. Yes, I have. I have a very high opinion of all of these factors and I would go on to say that I know of no more devoted citizen in this country.

Norris E. Bradbury was then, and is now, the director at Los Alamos. He succeeded Oppenheimer in 1945. He said:

Q. How long have you known Dr. Oppenheimer?

A. I knew him as an instructor when I was a graduate student at Berkeley in 1932–31, probably, somewhere through there. I knew him as director of Los Alamos Scientific Laboratory from June of 1944 until October 1945. I knew him thereafter as chairman of the General Advisory Committee and saw him regularly, I would say, several times a year, in that capacity. He visited Los Alamos, I would again say, at least once a year or perhaps twice, in connecton with his responsibilities as chairman of the General Advisory Committee.

Q. How well do you think you know him as a man, his character, and so on, the kind of person he is?

A. I would think I would know him as well as one knows any individual with whom one has had friendly and professional contact over quite a long number of years, and perhaps better than the average having seen him in his capacity as director of the laboratory, in which I then had an assisting subordinate position.

Q. Do you have an opinion as to Dr. Oppenheimer's loyalty to the country, and as to whether he would be a security risk?

A. I do have such an opinion and it is a very strong one.

Q. Would you state it, please?

A. I would regard him from my observation as completely loyal to this country. In fact, I would make a statement of this sort, I think, that while loyalty is a very difficult thing to demonstrate in an objective fashion, if a man could demonstrate loyalty in an objective way, that Dr. Oppenheimer in his direction of Los Alamos Laboratory during the war years did demonstrate such loyalty. I myself feel that his devotion to that task, the nature of the decisions which he was called upon to make, the manner in which he made them, were as objective a demontration of personal loyalty to this country as I myself can imagine.

Q. As to this business of a security risk, which I take it is perhaps a little different from loyalty, do you have an opinion on that?

A. I do not regard him as a security risk.

Lee A. DuBridge was a member of the General Advisory Committee for the six years, 1946 through 1952, with Oppenheimer. He said:

A. Even if Dr. Oppenheimer had not been officially elected Chairman each year, and if I may say so, he resigned or attempted to resign each year, feeling that a new Chairman should be elected, the Committee unanimously rejected his recommendation every year, and asked him to continue to serve as Chairman. He was so naturally a leader of our group that it was impossible to imagine that he should not be in the chair. He was the leader of our group first because his knowledge of the atomic energy work was far more intimate than that of any other member of the Committee. He had obviously been more intimately involved in the actual scientific work of the Manhattan project than any other person on our Committee. He was a natural leader because we respected his intelligence, his judgment, his personal attitude toward the work of the Commission, and the Committee. Of course, without saying we had not the faintest doubt of his loyalty. More than that, we felt, and I feel that there is no one who has exhibited his loyalty to this country more spectacularly than Dr. Oppenheimer. He was a natural and respected and at all times a loved leader of that group.

At the same time I should emphasize that at no time did he dominate the group or did he suppress opinions that did not agree with his own. In fact, he encouraged a full and free and frank exchange of ideas throughout the full history of the Committee. That is the reason we liked him as a leader, because though he did lead and stimulate and inform us and help us in our decisions, he never dominated nor suppressed contrary or different opinions. There was a free, full, frank exchange, and it was one of the finest Committees that I ever had the privilege to serve on for that reason.

It is almost monotonous, but none the less impressive.

Harry Alonzo Winne, of General Electric, and from 1945 in

charge of its engineering policy until he retired in 1953, said:

Q. In the course of these working relations and other relations you had with Dr. Oppenheimer, did you form any opinion about his loyalty to the United States, and his character?

A. Yes: very definitely. I have no question at all as to his loyalty to the United States. I think he is a man of high character. I have great respect and admiration for him.

Q. What led you to this opinion?

A. I can't cite specific instances, but his discussion, his remarks during the deliberations of first the board of consultants in 1946, and at later meetings of the Committee on Atomic Energy. As I say, I can't specify remarks, specify comments, but there just developed within me a conviction as to his great concern for our country and his loyalty to it, his great concern for the safety of our country.

Q. What, if any, attitude did you observe with respect to Russia?

A. The feeling that Russia is the country which we have to guard against, a country maybe certainly our enemy and maybe the one to start a war against us, and one against which we must be on our guard at all times.

Q. When did you first form this impression?

A. I can't cite any particular date or time. It gradually developed.

Q. 1946, 1947?

A. It developed in the days of our board of consultants meetings in 1946, Mr. Marks, and, has, if anything, been strengthening since that time.

Charles C. Lauritsen, professor of physics at Cal Tech, worked on rockets in 1941 until he went to Los Alamos in 1945 to assist Oppenheimer, and shared Oppenheimer's office. He had known Oppenheimer since 1928 or 1929, "as well as I have known any member of our faculty." He said:

Q. Dr. Lauritsen, what opinion do you have about Dr. Oppenheimer's loyalty and character? By loyalty I mean loyalty to the United States.

A. I have never had any reason to doubt it.

Q. Do you think you could be mistaken about this?

A. I suppose one can always be mistaken, but I have less doubt than any other case I know of.

Q. Less doubt than in any other case?

A. Than in any other person that I know as well.

Q. Do you know many people better?

A. Not many. I suppose I know my own son better, but I don't trust him any more.

Jerrold R. Zacharias is professor of physics at M.I.T. He knew Oppenheimer since the summer of 1926 when they met as students in Leyden. His close association with Oppenheimer began at Los Alamos. He said.

Q. As a result of your association with Dr. Oppenheimer have you formed an opinion or conviction as to his character and his loyalty to the United States?

A. I am completely convinced of his loyalty to the United States. Can I add a little way of saying it?

When you are gathered in a group of men who are discussing the details on how to combat the Russians, how to contain the Russians, how to keep them from overrunning the rest of the world, and so on, the loyalties come out very, very clearly. There just is not any question in my mind that Dr. Oppenheimer's loyalty is for this country and in no way or shape by anything other than hostility toward the U. S. S. R.

Q. What about his character?

A. His character? Ethical, moral is first rate.

Q. Do you have any views as to his capacity to exercise discretion in dealing with classified and restricted data and military secrets?

A. In my opinion, he is always discreet and careful and has regarded the handling of secret documents and secret ideas and so on with discretion and understanding. You might thnk it is not the easiest thing in the world to carry around a head full of secrets and go about in public, too, and talk about burning questions of the day. It is difficult. I believe that Dr. Oppenheimer has showed in every instance to my knowledge that he can do this kind of thing.

Then at the close of his testimony:

A. There are very few people who have Dr. Oppenheimer's ability to synthesize the additions of others along with the ideas of himself. He has that wonderful ability. Meetings that have gone on without Dr. Oppenheimer, in my opinion, have suffered somewhat from this lack. Mind you, there are people on that Committee who have a real gift for summary, but they are not the equal of Robert Oppenheimer. In particular, DuBridge and Killian, two college presidents. Maybe that is part of the equipment of a college president, but neither one of them will focus the ideas quite as well as Robert Oppenheimer.

Dr. EVANS. I did not get what you said about the equipment of college presidents.

The WITNESS. The ability to bring ideas into a clear focus. I am afraid it sounded——

Dr. EVANS. You say that is the ability or is not the ability?

The WITNESS. It is the ability.

Dr. GRAY. He said it may be.

Oliver E. Buckley had been for ten years the president of the Bell Telephone Laboratories. In 1948 he had been appointed to the General Advisory Committee, and his term of six years was coming to an end. He said:

Q. Do you feel that your associations with Dr. Oppenheimer in the years that you served with him on GAC and your service with him on the Science Advisory Committee were sufficiently close to enable you to form a judgment as to his character and loyalty to the United States?

A. The question never arose in my mind as to whether he was loyal to the United States. I believed and believe that he was loyal to the United States. I just don't recall any event that even raised that issue in my mind.

Q. Would you have any comment as to the quality of his service in those years to the country?

A. This is in the postwar years you are speaking of?

Q. Yes.

A. I think it was extraordinary service to the country. The job of being chairman of the GAC is a very heavy and time consuming job. He was our unanimous chairman during the period that my service overlapped his and he was so outstandingly good in that position that if you give value to the services of the GAC you must also give great value to the service of its chairman who was an excellent chairman.

Q. What would you say as to his discretion or lack of discretion, particularly with reference to his knowledge of classified material of a very secret character?

A. I assumed and believed him to be discreet with reference to such material.

Q. You read the Commission's letter of December 23, 1953, to Dr. Oppenheimer which initiated these proceedings.

A. I read it in the newspaper.

Q. Do you have the same confidence in him today that you had when you served with him in the postwar years?

A. Yes.

Robert F. Bacher is the chairman of the Division of Physics at Cal Tech. He had known Oppenheimer since 1929 or 1930. Their close association began at Los Alamos. He was a member of the A.E.C. from 1946 to 1949. Bacher said:

Q. How well do you feel that you know Dr. Oppenheimer?

A. I feel I know him very well. I have worked very closely with him during the war, have seen him frequently since the war, and feel I know him really very well. I just don't think it would be possible to work with a man as closely as I worked with Dr. Oppenheimer during the war without knowing him very well.

Q. What is your opinion as to his loyalty to the United States?

A. I have no question at all of his loyalty.

Q. On what do you base that? Is that purely a subjective judgment?

A. I think opinions of that sort are always subjective judgments. In this case I put great credence in my own judgment, naturally, because I know him very well. But this is essentially an assessment on my part based on knowing him for a great many years. I have the greatest confidence in his loyalty.

Q. What would you say as to his sense of discretion in the use that he would make of the knowledge that has come to him and will continue to come to him assuming that he continues in Government work?

A. I found Dr. Oppenheimer to very discreet. I can remember during the war once when we had to go out on a trip together and it was essential that he carry a memorandum, that even in note form was classified, and he was so careful and he pinned it in his hip pocket. I thought here is a man who really is very careful about these things. But to say more generally as to his discretion, I have always found Dr. Oppenheimer to be very discreet in his handling of classified information.

Q. Is there anything else you care to say to this board about his character as a man and as a citizen?

A. I have the highest confidence in Dr. Oppenheimer. I consider him to be a person of high character. I consider him to be a man of discretion, a good security risk and a person of full loyalty to the country.

Monotonous? It is tedious. Is Oppenheimer that good? Stop to consider the meager offering Robb made in derogation of Oppenheimer's integrity and loyalty. We may confidently lean back on the adversary process, of which Robb was an admirable exponent. We may say, If none could be called, or ordered, to testify against Oppenheimer's loyalty, there was none. This has weight with me. It may have weight with you. It did not have weight enough with the Board. It had no weight at all, as we shall see, with the Commission. The more's the pity.

15. THE CONDUCT
OF THE HEARINGS

THE BOARD looked back on their conduct of the hearings with some degree of complacency. Oppenheimer had thanked them for the "patient and courteous consideration" which he had received at the hands of the Board. His counsel had referred to the "fairness which the members of the Board had displayed in the conduct of these hearings." You and I cannot be complacent and we need not be polite. Let us see how fair the hearings were, how fairly they were conducted, and whether they were conducted as fairly as they could be.

We may begin by seeing how fair the Board thought they were:

The Board approached its task in the spirit of inquiry, not that of a trial. The Board worked long and arduously. It has heard 40 witnesses including Dr. J. Robert Oppenheimer and compiled over 3,000 pages of testimony in addition to having read the same amount of file material.

Dr. Oppenheimer has been represented by counsel, usually four in number, at all times in the course of the proceedings. He has confronted every witness appearing before the Board, with the privilege of cross-examination. He is familiar with the contents of every relevant document, which was made available to the Board, except those which under governmental necessity cannot be disclosed, such as reports of the Federal Bureau of Investigation. He has, in his own words, received patient and courteous consideration at the hands of the Board. The Board has, in the words of his chief counsel, displayed fairness in the conduct of the hearings. And, finally, perhaps it should be said that the investigation has been conducted under the auspices of the responsible agency which has the obligation of decision.

As it considered substance, the Board has allowed sympathetic consideration for the individual to go hand in hand with an understanding of the necessities for a clear, realistic, and rugged attitude toward subversion, possible subversion, or indeed broader implications of security.

It was quite impossible for the Board to be wholly fair. For the hearings before our loyalty and security boards must be conducted —and it may be they'd better be—with only the board and the attorney for the Government knowing what is in the F.B.I. files and what is classified in the files of the department—here the A.E.C. But necessity can justify only itself. It cannot make the hearings any the more fair.

The rub comes in the jar between our security and our justice. No, those words are too high and mighty—between our sense of safety and our sense of fair play. We have both. We want to keep both. We can't do without either, but the more we keep of one the less we have of the other. The tighter the secrecy the greater may be our sense of safety, but the more we offend our sense of fair play. We are continually asked, and we have to go on answering, the question of whether the disclosure of this or that paper or report or letter, or the confrontation or even the identity of this or that witness, will endanger the nation enough to persuade us to swallow the pride we take in our sense of fair play.

About the files of the F.B.I., we have made an absolute rule. They are not to be disclosed. Here we have another reason, another danger to guard against than security. We want to prevent their political use. Here we are willing to sacrifice justice, not for the sake of security but in the cause of democracy and decency. We are afraid of our own government, and the danger has been thrust under our noses. Even our Attorney General, a year or so ago, used an F.B.I. file to attack a dead man, Harry Dexter White, and an ex-President, Harry Truman. And in the fall of 1954 we watched our Vice-President use an F.B.I. report in campaigning against the re-election of a congressman, Robert L. Condon, in California. (The New York *Times*, October 27, 1954.) Nothing like this happened in these proceedings. The Board conscientiously applied the absolute prohibition, at what cost in justice we do not know and cannot know. I should say none. At any rate, I saw no indication of any.

What I found disquieting here was the doubt as to whether more of the three thousand pages which the Board said it had examined could not have been declassified and produced without endangering our security. It was quite plain that much that was produced could have been produced sooner without endangering anything but Robb's zest for cross-examination, as you will soon see. It is what more could have been produced, or at least declassified in time to show to counsel before the hearings, that gives me pause. Were there so many things so sacredly secret that they could not go into the record? Consider the hazard. It is whether the gravity of their contents, discounted by the improbability of further disclosure, justified such an invasion of justice as was necessary to avoid the danger. (A paraphrase of Learned Hand's words in the

Dennis case, 183 Fed. 2d at 212, which were adopted by the Supreme Court, 341 U. S. at 510.)

The Board laid great stress on the requirement by the A.E.C. that "the proceeding is an inquiry and not a trial." (Rules and Regulations, s. 4.15a.) Gray opened the hearings with the announcement, "At this point, I should like to remind everyone concerned that this proceeding is an inquiry and not in the nature of a trial. We shall approach our duties in that atmosphere and in that spirit." And later: "I should repeat I think at this time, because Mr. Marks has not been present before, that we consider under the regulations, spirit and letter, that this is not a trial but an inquiry. Very considerable latitude, as you have observed and we have all experienced, is certainly allowed, and is to continue, in not trying to conform to rigid court procedures."

Robb, counsel for the A.E.C., did not allow the proceedings to remain an inquiry for very long. As soon as Gray had finished saying this to Marks, Robb resumed his cross-examination of Oppenheimer, asking him whether he had not made certain statements. Robb was reading from the transcript of Oppenheimer's interview with Colonel Pash in 1943. The extracts Robb read were designed to show that some of Oppenheimer's testimony that morning and earlier that afternoon was not true. They showed clearly enough, as we know, that Oppenheimer's memory had been at fault in a number of respects, and he confessed, as he had confessed before to General Groves and to the F.B.I., that part of what he had told Pash had been a lie.

Garrison interrupted:

Mr. GARRISON. Mr. Chairman, could I just make a short request at this point?
Mr. GRAY. Yes.
Mr. GARRISON. I appreciate the existence of the rule under which we cannot ask for access to the file and I am not going to protest that rule. I wonder, however, if it would not be within the proprieties of this kind of proceeding when counsel reads from a transcript for us to be furnished with a copy of the transcript as he reads from it. This, of course, is orthodox in a court of law. I don't pretend that this is a court of law, but I do make the request because I don't know what else is in the transcript, and if parts of it are read from, it would seem to me that it would be proper for us to see what parts are not read from and to look at it as a whole. I don't want to make an argument. I put the question to you.
Mr. ROBB. Mr. Chairman, I don't know of any rule in the court of law that you must furnish counsel with the copy of the transcript you are reading of at the time. I might say that my thought would be at the conclusion of this examination to make the entire transcript a part of the record and let Mr. Garrison read it and see it, and then if he wants to ask anything about it on redirect, he can do so.
Mr. GRAY. I think that would be appropriate. I would like to indicate a caution—I don't know about this particular transcript—but I am not sure that in any case you could be able to make the whole thing a part of the record.

Mr. ROBB. I don't know, sir; this is presently marked "Secret" so I could not make it available to Mr. Garrison at this time.

The WITNESS. But it is being read into the record.

Mr. ROBB. That is right.

Robb continued in the same way the rest of the afternoon. The next day Oppenheimer's cross-examination was interrupted to let General Groves testify. When it was resumed, Robb took up the transcript of Oppenheimer's interview with Colonel Lansdale.

Garrison interrupted again:

Mr. GARRISON. Mr. Chairman, what troubles me about this whole method of examination is that counsel is reading from a transcript bits and parts without the full course of the conversation which took place to a witness whose memory at best, as anyone of ours would be, is very, very hazy upon all these things, and picking here a sentence and there a sentence out of context, and then holding him to the answer. I do think that this is a method of questioning that seems to me to be very unfair.

Mr. ROBB. Mr. Chairman, I don't mean to make any argument about the matter, but I assume that this Board is following this transcript. If the Board feels I am being unfair at any point, I suppose the Board will interpose.

Mr. GARRISON. Why shouldn't counsel be allowed to follow as any court of law, and this is not even a trial?

Mr. ROBB. As you no doubt know, I have tried a good many cases, and I don't think it would be in the ordinary course of a trial.

Mr. GARRISON. I disagree with you.

Mr. ROBB. I resent counsel's statement that I am trying to be unfair with this witness, because I assure you that I have made every attempt to be fair with him. In fact, were I trying to be unfair, I would not ask this witness any of these questions, but would leave it in the file for the Board to read. I am giving this witness a chance to make whatever explanation he wishes to make.

Mr. GARRISON. I still think that the fair thing would be to read the whole conversation and ask him what parts you want, instead of to pick isolated questions.

Mr. GRAY. On the point of picking isolated questions, without trying to look at this whole question at this moment, I think it is clear that this interview concerned itself with matters which are involved in the questions Mr. Robb has been putting to the witness, and which are generally, I think, not new material. General Nichols' letter of December 23, and Mr. Oppenheimer's reply of March 4, I think both address themselves in one way or another to these individuals, Lomanitz, Weinberg, Bohm, which have been the subject of these questions.

I would say, Mr. Garrison, that I don't think it would be helpful to you at this point to have the transcript. I have said, however, that Dr. Oppenheimer and his counsel will be entitled to examine it and certainly after examination if you wish to reopen any of this testimony, you will be given every opportunity to do so. I think it is the feeling of the chairman of the board that things are not taken here out of context in a way which is prejudicial. I think also that the board has heard Dr. Oppenheimer say that with respect to some of these matters he has no recollection, which at least to me is perfectly understandable, many of these things having taken place many years ago. I do not think that it is the purpose of counsel to develop anything beyond what the facts are in this case. At least that is my interpretation.

Mr. ROBB. That is my endeavor, Mr. Chairman.

And again:

Mr. GARRISON. Mr. Chairman, forgive me for coming back to the same point, but during the recess I discussed this problem with my partner, Mr. Silverman, who has spent his life trying cases in the State of New York—I am not a trial lawyer, sir—our practice I am informed up there universally is that when counsel is cross examining a witness on a transcript he has never seen, counsel for the other side, if he asks the court for a copy, so he may read along with it, that request is granted. So if nothing else—I would not think of impugning this to Mr. Robb, and I hope he won't misunderstand me—I think it is the basis of the rule. That is the only reason I mention it. In other words, to make sure that the questions are in fact being read accurately from the transcript, and there are no interlineations or marks or matters of that sort that might perhaps raise a question as to the accuracy of what is there quite apart from the method by which the transcript was arrived at, and also to understand what the thread and continuity of the matter is. I merely report that to the Chairman. I don't want to put this on the basis of rules of law, because God knows, it is the rule here that this not a trial,, but an inquiry, and I should suppose that a fortiori, what is proper in court of law would be accorded to us here in an inquiry. I do not labor the point. I present it to you and I will rest upon it.

You will note that Garrison asked only that Oppenheimer's counsels be shown the transcript while Oppenheimer was being cross-examined. He did not ask that it be shown to the witness. If he had done so, he would have raised a question of law on which judicial opinion is divided. This is the rule known to lawyers as the Rule in the Queen's Case, where an English court held that the whole document must be shown to the witness (2 B. and B., 286). It is still the law in New York (*see* Wigmore, section 1263, p. 521), but it is not the law in the U.S. Courts (see *U.S. v. Dilliard,* 101 Fed. 2d 829, 1938; per Learned Hand). Nor is it the better rule. The Model Code of Evidence of the American Law Institute rejects the Queen's Case (Rule 106). So too does Wigmore, very energetically; and with examples well worth anyone's reading (sections 1259– 1263). The better procedure is not to require the whole document to be shown to the witness while he is being cross-examined; but it must be produced and shown before he leaves the stand so that his counsel may examine him on it (Wigmore, section 1861).

During the rest of Robb's cross-examination of Oppenheimer his counsel were allowed to follow the text of the transcript. Later, both he and his counsel were allowed to read the whole transcript of the Pash interview and to listen to the recordings of both his and Lansdale's.

I think that not much harm, perhaps no harm, was done by Robb's tactics of not declassifying these recordings until they had served the purpose of his cross-examination. Oppenheimer did not have to be pressed to admit that he had lied to Pash. It would have been fairer, and certainly more in the spirit of an inquiry, if the complete transcripts had been declassified a few hours sooner. The security of the nation would not have suffered during those hours.

Then there was the way Robb used the letter Oppenheimer had

received from Dr. Seaborg, a member of the General Advisory Committee at the time of the discussion on the development of the hydrogen bomb. Oppenheimer did not remember this letter and testified that he did not know how Dr. Seaborg felt about the question, that there had been no communication from him. The fact was that Oppenheimer had received this letter from him. It was also a fact that the letter was inconclusive, and later, when Dr. Seaborg returned and attended the next meeting, he preferred not to say anything one way or the other on the hydrogen-bomb issue.

I don't think the Board held Oppenheimer's failure to remember the letter against him. After all, Conant had forgotten that Oppenheimer had written a letter to him on the same subject at about the same time. Dr. Evans, however, made his view clear in his dissent. "He said on one occasion that he had not heard from Dr. Seaborg, when in fact he had a letter from Dr. Seaborg. In my opinion he had forgotten about the letter or he would never have made this statement, for he would have known that the Government had the letter. I do not consider that he lied in this case."

Robb persisted in this practice. You will recall that he did the same thing to Lilienthal, an ex-chairman of the A.E.C. Lilienthal was called as a witness for Oppenheimer. Much of his testimony concerned Oppenheimer's clearance by the Commission in 1947 for his appointment as chairman of the G.A.C. Garrison had asked for copies of the relevant documents two months before. He was informed that they were not available. Then Lilienthal himself, the day before he testified, asked to be allowed to read over his own file. He was refused. He testified as best he could from memory, and he too, like Oppenheimer, forgot a number of things. I don't need to repeat Lilienthal's comment.

The memoranda and papers were finally produced, and no harm was done, aside from a great discourtesy to an ex-chairman of the Commission and some injury to the Board's complacency.

I don't want to stress these adversary tactics of the counsel for the Commission. I think there is no need of saying anything more, except, perhaps, to mention that Robb refused, and the Board allowed him to refuse, to tell Oppenheimer's counsel ahead of time the names of the witnesses he was going to call.

On the whole, in spite of Robb the hearings were more of an inquiry than a trial. They were less fairly conducted than they could have been. They were less fairly conducted than a good judge would have conducted a trial. The Board was always cour-

teous and always dignified, but dignity and courtesy are no substitute for fair dealing. They do not cure but only palliate unfair
practices.

Nor should the Board, as I see it, have been satisfied with only
the rudiments of fair procedure. Perhaps I am asking too much.
Yet an inquiry can be made fairer than a trial, just as it can
fearfully easily be made so much worse. A trial at law has certain
minimum standards which the judge insists on. An inquiry can
reach a maximum of fairness, and such a good Board could very
easily have done better than it did. There was no excuse for not
declassifying and producing documents until they had served
Robb's purposes in cross-examination. There was no reason why
the Board should not have required Robb to give the names of the
witnesses he proposed to call. Robb's only excuse was that their
names would leak out and that if they were scientists they would
be subject to pressure.

As I say, I don't see that the adversary tactics which the Board
permitted Robb to use affected the upshot. What I deplore is that
the Board fell short of what we had a right to expect of such respectable and distinguished people.

One last word about all this. Inquiries, which are necessarily
conducted by the inquisitorial process, have become part of our
political life, and a new part. We are familiar with the adversary
process, where neither side is seeking the truth but where we
believe the truth arises out of the conflict. We are not versed in
the inquisitorial process, where everyone must join in seeking the
truth. We have a lot to learn about it. The Board here, for all its
shortcomings, has given us a start. After the indignities and the
indecencies of so many Congressional committees, the Board did
us the service of showing us how much better an inquiry can be. It
was not because Robb's attempt to turn this inquiry into a trial did
Oppenheimer any harm that I wanted to emphasize it. It was because I wanted to show you how easy it would have been for the
Board to make it a better inquiry.

However, since we may now have to teach this new process—
new, that is, to us—this bastard child in our law, how to behave, let
us get one thing clear in our minds. The adversary process and the
inquisitorial process are not only incompatible; they are contra-
dictory. They don't mix. If you do mix them, each destroys the
other. You can't half turn one into the other. The adversary process
is contrapuntal. It calls for two performers. If one is lacking, the

other, still acting as an adversary, becomes in the best of good faith savagely unjust. So too, if one of the participants in an inquiry turns into an adversary, the affair ceases to be an inquiry until he is either disciplined or suppressed; and if the other participant counters, the inquiry at once turns into a trial by an instant and immediate metamorphosis. There is no intermediate stage. The proceedings must be pure-bred from either blood line.

Robb's trial tactics very nearly turned the proceedings into a criminal trial. The Board could have prevented it, but the Board owes its survival as an inquiry to Garrison, who patiently and persistently, as the extracts from the transcript show you, continued to perform his part in an inquiry of the whole truth of the derogatory information. When your client is an Oppenheimer it is the whole truth which best serves your cause. As every lawyer knows, some clients fare better with only half of it. In my judgment, Garrison's unswerving service to an inquiry helped rather than hurt his client's cause: It was good strategy against Robb's bad tactics. When Robb tried to make Oppenheimer's failure to recollect a letter or a meeting look like a lie, the Board was not impressed. Robb's rudeness to Lilienthal did not prevent Garrison from bringing out the complete and detailed account of the facts of Oppenheimer's clearance by the Commission in 1947. I think it served only to emphasize the pains which Lilienthal and each of the other commissioners had taken, and their confidence in the conclusion to which each came when they cleared him.

If Garrison had preferred to let the inquiry turn into a trial and fought out his client's fate on his adversary's terms, would he have succeeded? Would he have done any better? I think not. I think he would simply have exasperated the Board. After starting off, quite rightly I think, by calling Robb counsel for the Board, the Board slipped into regarding him and treating him as counsel for the Commission. The Board seemed to me to defer to his conduct of the proceedings to an extent scarcely in keeping with the Board's function and authority. This was a pity. It certainly gave Garrison no reason to expect that the Board would be indulgent if he should treat the spirit of an inquiry equally insolently.

16. "AN OVER-ALL
COMMON-SENSE JUDGMENT"

GARRISON, summing up the case, told the Board that the standards set by the A.E.C. Personnel Security Clearance Criteria were all to be considered. He said:

> I think that it is both sensible and logical and clearly intended by section 4.16 (a) that you, in making your recommendations to the General Manager, would take into account the things which he has to take into account in arriving at the decision.
>
> Mr. GRAY. May I interrupt?
>
> Mr. GARRISON. Yes.
>
> Mr. GRAY. I am very much interested in this point, Mr. Garrison. You earlier, I believe, suggested that the usefulness of a man to the program of the Commission was something that the general manager had to consider. Does this most recent observation you made mean that this board must take into account that kind of thing also, because if you say that this board takes into account everything the general manager takes into account, then it seems to me that is inconsistent with an earlier portion of your argument.
>
> Please don't misunderstand me. I am not arguing with you but I want to have your views clearly on this point because it may be an important one.

A little earlier Garrison had said that it was "up to the Atomic Energy Commission as to when and where and under what circumstances they shall seek his advice. That, of course, is not a question that this board is concerned with. The basic question is whether in the handling of restricted data he is to be trusted." I do not myself see any inconsistency. This was the basic question, and although it was up to the Commission to decide whether or not to consult Oppenheimer, just as it was up to it to decide whether to employ him at all, the A.E.C. Criteria expressly enjoined the Board to balance his usefulness against possible security risks.

Garrison had already drawn this to the Board's attention when McCloy made his observations about there being a positive as well as a negative security; Garrison pointed out that this had a place within the framework of the A.E.C. Criteria by quoting the sentence, "Cases must be carefully weighed in the light of all the information and a determination must be reached which gives due recognition to the favorable as well as unfavorable information concerning the individual *and which balances the cost to the program of not having his services against any possible risks involved.*" I have emphasized the last clause because Robb had at once remarked that this sentence "applies to the decision which is to be made by the General Manager as an administrative matter in determining whether the subject is to be kept on." "It does not refer to this board," Robb said.

This was, indeed, as Gray suggested, an important point, and it is worth laboring, for Gray's question shows that he was muddled and that Robb was quite wrong.

Both the Board and the General Manager are bound by the A.E.C.'s Criteria. The Criteria, it is true, say that they are "intended to serve as aids to the General Manager in resolving his responsibility in the determination of an individual's eligibility for security clearance. . . ." Yes, but the A.E.C. Rules in the section which Garrison cited, Section 4.16(a), say, "The Board shall carefully consider all material before it, including reports of the F.B.I., the testimony of all witnesses, the evidence presented by the individual, and"—I emphasize—"*the standards set forth in the A.E.C. Personnel Security Clearance Criteria for Determining Eligibility.*" (14 F.R. 42.)

Moreover, the Rules go on to lay the same general injunction on the Board as the Criteria do. The Rules say, "In considering the material before the board, the members of the board, as practical men of affairs, should be guided by the same consideration that would guide them in making a sound decision in the administration of their own lives." The Criteria, as you will recall from Garrison's quotation during Dr. Winne's cross-examination, say that "the decision as to security clearance is an over-all common-sense judgment, made after consideration of all the relevant information as to whether or not there is risk that the granting of security clearance would endanger the common defense or security."

The Board as well as the General Manager is bound to make an over-all common-sense judgment, as practical men of affairs making a sound decision in their own lives. The Board as well as the General Manager is to balance the cost to the program of not having the man's services against any possible risks involved. The Board made its recommendations to the General Manager. He in turn made his recommendation to the Commission. There is no conflict, no difference of function here on the question of the man's eligibility for employment. Here the functions of the Board and the General Manager overlap.

Gray was confusing the problem of eligibility, which the Board shared with the General Manager, with the larger problem which was the one the General Manager and the Commission had to decide, whether they wanted to continue to employ Oppenheimer as adviser. Gray was confusing a common-sense approach to the question of eligibility with the managerial problem of employment. He saw no reason why the Board should be called on to decide whether Oppenheimer's contract was to be renewed. Nor do I. Nor, I think, do you.

But the Board had not been asked that question. The Board was asked, and the Board was to answer, only the question whether Oppenheimer was to be eligible. These are "Criteria for Determining Eligibility." Certainly common sense is equally applicable to each question. Common sense does not require you to answer more than you are asked, but it ought to be bold enough to do as it is told. The fact that the Board as well as the General Manager was required to give "an over-all common-sense judgment" "as practical men of affairs" who were to take into account "the cost to the program of not having his services against any possible risks involved," the fact that the Board had to act in this sensible way did not saddle it with the responsibility of answering the further and larger question: Shall the A.E.C. continue to employ Oppenheimer as an adviser? The answer of the Board might be decisive, but it was only preliminary.

It is a pity that Gray and Morgan failed to follow these plain and explicit instructions. For if they had, they might have come to a different conclusion. They as much as said so. They said:

It seemed to us that an alternative recommendation would be possible, if we were allowed to exercise mature practical judgment without the rigid circumscription of regulations and criteria established for us.

In good sense, it could be recommended that Dr. Oppenheimer simply not be used as a consultant, and that therefore there exists no need for a categorical answer to the difficult question posed by the regulations, since there would be no need for access to classified material.

The Board would prefer to report a finding of this nature. We have had a desire to reconcile the hard requirements of security with the compelling urge to avoid harm to a talented citizen.

It was a blind blunder. "If we were allowed to exercise mature practical judgment . . ." Why, the Criteria required them to do just that, to act "as practical men of affairs." "In good sense . . ." The Rules expressly called for "an over-all common-sense judgment." They could very well have balanced the cost to our security program of no longer having available the services of this "talented citizen." Indeed, they were told they must do just that.

Is there any excuse for Gray's and Morgan's retreat behind the security of what they thought was "the rigid circumscription of the regulations and criteria"? How can they defend themselves for their disregard of these important provisions in our security system? Are we to blame them, or are we to blame the system?

We can't very well excuse them on the ground that the new Executive Order 10450, which President Eisenhower made on April 27, 1953, does not mention common sense or practical judgment or balancing the cost to the program of the loss of services against the risk. The Commission had not thought it necessary to change its rules or its criteria, and they were binding on the Board.

But, at the same time, it is only fair to add that this new Executive Order had made a very great change in the approach to security generally. The very axis had been changed from loyalty to security. Dismissal no longer turned on disloyalty but on security. Both words are incommensurably vague, too vague to say that one has a larger meaning than the other. Anyway, you can't compare them. Loyalty is a state of heart and mind, a matter of devotion, an orientation of the whole man. Security is, or ought to be, a matter of fact. But both call for a diagnosis of what a man may do in the future, not just a finding of what he has done in the past, and this may lead into some searching of his soul as well as an examination of his conduct. Nevertheless, there is no doubt that a man can be a security risk without being disloyal. The Board was wholly certain that Oppenheimer was loyal. It did not necessarily follow that he was not a security risk, though how he could be both loyal and discreet—both of which the Board found him to be—and at the same time a security risk I do not see.

At any rate, if you recall the campaign of 1952 and the boasts of some Republicans in the campaign of 1954, you need no demonstration of the fact that the Republican administration expanded the grounds of ineligibility for office. If you don't, I shall have to ask you to compare what was regarded as derogatory under President Truman's Order 9835 in 1947 with what became derogatory in

1953 under President Eisenhower's Order 10450. Eligibility was edging over into suitability, and this in turn came very close to becoming desirability. Executive and administrative officers were tempted to shirk their responsibilities, wash their hands and turn their power of appointment over to a personnel security board.

Gray and Morgan, quite understandably and equally conscientiously, shrank from accepting a responsibility which they thought belonged to the General Manager or to the Commission, if not indeed to the President himself. Here before them stood a man as high as any in the services he might render, and just as momentous were the secrets we were therefore to entrust to him. Who short of the President could properly be asked to take the responsibility? Surely we can understand why Gray and Morgan looked askance at the instructions which they had misread. But this is no excuse for not applying the practical judgment of men of affairs which they were so eminently qualified to do.

There is better than this to say in behalf of Gray and Morgan, and a harsher judgment to be passed on the security system.

President Truman's Executive Order 9835 of March 21, 1947, in which the question turned on a man's loyalty, prescribed that the standard for the refusal of employment or the removal from employment "shall be that, on all the evidence, reasonable grounds exist for the belief that the person involved is disloyal to the Government of the United States." In other words, the evidence had to be strong enough to raise a reasonable belief that the man was disloyal.

In 1951 President Truman reversed this. By his Order 10241 of April 28, 1951, he struck out the words "that, on all the evidence, reasonable grounds exist for belief that the person involved is disloyal" and substituted "that, on all the evidence, there is reasonable doubt as to the loyalty of the person involved." The loyalty and security boards no longer had to reach a belief. All that was needed to drop a man out of Government service was a doubt.

When, in 1953, President Eisenhower shifted the axis from loyalty to security, he left the burden of proof on the individual. In the words of his Order 10450, the question was "whether the employment or retention in employment in the Federal Service of the person being investigated is clearly consistent with the interests of the national security."

Why doesn't this make nonsense out of the requirement that the Board must exercise "an over-all common-sense judgment," "as practical men of affairs," "guided by the same consideration that would guide them in making a sound decision in the administration of their own lives"? You can balance a man's value to the program against a doubt of his security. That's a calculated risk. But how can you expect a man to give you an over-all common-sense judgment as a practical man of affairs if you tell him to stop short at a doubt?

This is not the way Gray and Morgan naturally behave. It is not the way they make their own decisions in their own lives as the practical men of affairs they eminently are. They were quite aware of the dilemma. "These Criteria," they said, "which, of course, are binding on this Board . . ." No wonder it went against their grain. To exercise a "mature practical judgment," as they wished they could, requires courage more often than caution. Courage is an integral and inseparable part of wisdom, even of prudence. And we tell them to find danger in a doubt!

Look what this did to General Groves's judgment. You have not forgotten what the atomic program owes to him in Los Alamos, nor his opinion of Oppenheimer then and since. But he would not clear Oppenheimer now. And why? For a sole reason:

> It is not a case of proving that the man is a danger. It is a case of thinking, well, he might be a danger, and it is perfectly logical to presume that he would be, and that there is no consideration whatsoever to be given to any of his past performances or his general usefulness or, you might say, the imperative usefulness. I don't care how important the man is, if there is any possibility other than a tortured one that his associations or his loyalty or his character might endanger.

This injunction to abide by a doubt had the same effect on Gray and Morgan, men of equal vigor and strength of judgment. "We could," they said, "in good conscience, we believe, conclude our difficult undertaking by a brief, clear, and conclusive recommendation" against clearance, because, as they said, "any doubts whatsoever must be resolved in favor of the national security. The material and evidence presented to this Board leave reasonable doubts with respect to the individual concerned."

Imagine Gray administering the War Department or the University of North Carolina in any such fashion! Imagine Morgan running the Sperry Company on any such basis! They went on, as I have already quoted them, to say, "It seemed to us that an alternative recommendation would be possible, if we were allowed to exercise mature practical judgment without the rigid circumscription of regulations and criteria established for us."

No wonder the only reasons they could give for their decision were slight and meager. So long as they believed they could not be themselves, there were no better. They would have done better to reject the responsibility which was thrust upon them on these terms. They should either have insisted on making "an over-all common-sense judgment" "as practical men of affairs" or none at all.

Had this been a trial in the adversary system of law in which we were brought up and to which we are accustomed, this contradiction would not have bothered the Board. I don't think it would have existed. In the adversary process, the question for adjudication is: Which is the more right, the plaintiff or the defendant, the Government or the man who is charged? A court is asked only to choose between alternatives. The burden of proof may shift from one side to the other, and when the court's mind is evenly divided, the burden of proof or a presumption allows the court to decide one way or the other. If it is a presumption of innocence, it gives the Government a harder case to win. Its proof must be the stronger to overcome the presumption. Justice tempered by mercy.

But in an inquiry the burden of proof in the sense we are used to is either out of place or something quite different. Here a presumption tampers with wisdom. The tribunal, here the Board, is seeking to learn the degree of truth in a given particular proposition—in this case, the danger to our national security of employing Oppenheimer and trusting him with our secrets. The Board was asked to conduct this inquiry as practically as it was capable of doing, limited only by the amount of evidence it could collect and by the urgency of time. Its problem was not who was right, Garrison or Robb. It was whether, or how much, Oppenheimer was a security risk. So when the Board was told that Oppenheimer had the burden of proof and that he was a security risk if the Board had any doubt about it, they were told to substitute a doubt for a belief, and stop short of such a conclusion as they would make as practical men of affairs. It was as if a scientist were told that he must conduct his research and his experiments on a certain dogmatic hypothesis, as if a business executive were told he must set aside his best judgment in favor of a theory of economics. Gray and Morgan were equally frustrated and equally stultified.

To start with a presumption is useful and necessary. Scientists call it an hypothesis. But to act on a presumption is to act as if it existed, and if it does not exist you are simply pretending that it does. It is a fictitious motive, not simply a refuge from a doubt which might stop you from acting at all. It may even become a creed. Now, no one has yet devised a way of measuring the intensity of belief or the degree of a doubt. Nevertheless, there are degrees of doubt as there are degrees of persuasion. We tell the jury in a criminal case that they must be persuaded of the defendant's guilt "beyond a reasonable doubt," which is, as Learned Hand has said, "the required degree of satisfaction" (in *Becher v. U. S.*, 5 Fed. 2d 45). It is, as Chief Justice Lemuel Shaw told the jury who hanged a Harvard professor for murder back in 1850 (*Commonwealth v. Webster*, 5 Cushing 295 at 320), not "a probability, though a strong one arising from the doctrine of chances," but rather "a certainty that convinces and directs the understanding, and satisfies the reason and judgment." It is, Shaw called it, "an abiding conviction, to a moral certainty." This is the classical statement. It has been repeated to countless juries since. It is no less authoritative because Lemuel Shaw was the father-in-law of Herman Melville. The point of all this is not by any means that we should allow any presumption of innocence to creep out of our criminal code into our security system, but that Gray and Morgan felt compelled to do just the contrary, to be content with a degree of dissatisfaction and moral uncertainty and indeed of improbability. They were told to make indecision itself decisive.

Let me give you a small example here in the evidence for and against one of the charges against Oppenheimer. Reread Item 17, on page 50, that "in the latter part of July or early August 1941" he attended a closed meeting of the Communist Party in his house in Berkeley. Oppenheimer denied this, categorically and specifically, as you may see in his letter of reply to Nichols of March 4, 1954. He said, you may recall, that he had searched his memory and that he was "quite certain" that no such meeting had occurred. Then, later, he was "able to establish that my wife and I left Berkeley within a few days after July 4, 1941, and did not return until toward the end of the first week in August."

Now Gray and Morgan were "of the opinion that the evidence with respect to this meeting is inconclusive." In other words, they had doubts. What was their doubt based on? What was the evidence which made them doubt Oppenheimer's denial and his testimony that he did not attend any such meeting? It must have been the testimony which Paul Crouch and his wife had given before the California State Committee on Un-American Activities in 1950, many years later.

Of course it is possible, but it is scarcely more than possible, that Gray and Morgan had other evidence to justify their doubt. None was produced, and neither Crouch nor his wife was called as a witness, though he was "a special consultant" for the Department of Justice and certainly was available. Robb's brief cross-examination did not even imply that there was any more; and it got nowhere. There was, on the other hand, substantial evidence to confirm Oppenheimer. Crouch had fixed the date of the alleged meeting in Berkeley at July 23, 1941. Hans Bethe, a professor at Cornell, a consultant to the A.E.C., testified that he saw the Oppenheimers at their ranch in New Mexico on July 24, where Oppenheimer had testified he had been since shortly after July 4 and into the first week in August.

I am sure that the F.B.I. files must have contained a good deal of evidence which bore directly on Crouch's credibility, and documentary at that. The *Nation* ran an account of much of this evidence in its April 10, 1954, number, just about the time Gray and Morgan were spending a week going over the F.B.I. files. And if the *Nation* had it, the F.B.I. must already have had it, especially because Crouch had been a "special consultant" of the Department of Justice since 1951. This documentary evidence showed a startling number of inconsistencies and contradictions in the testimony which Crouch had given in a number of trials in which he had appeared for the Government and identified people as Communists. Gray and Morgan may or may not read the *Nation*, but they had the F.B.I. files and the F.B.I. is not ill-informed.

There's no need of going into this evidence about Crouch. You may have seen a brief account of it in *Time* for July 19, 1954. There was enough to give Gray and Morgan pause. There was enough to lead the Attorney General to announce, as *Time* reported, that he was going to investigate Crouch. The New York *Times* reported, on July 9, 1954, that the credibility of some of Crouch's testimony had been challenged and that as a result the Attorney General had promised on June 30 to investigate. Crouch's reaction to this is interesting and significant. The New York *Times* reported, "Mr. Crouch asserted this decision of the Justice Department officials might force the reopening of about sixty hearings and trials in which he had been a principal witness." A pretty reason for not investigating him! Crouch felt so strongly about it that he formally demanded a Congressional investigation of Attorney General Brownell and of his deputy, William P. Rogers.

Enough about Crouch; and enough, I think, to demonstrate to you how little and what shoddy evidence sufficed to raise a doubt in the minds of Gray and Morgan. I am not saying that they knew all this about Crouch before they sent their decision to Nichols on May 27, 1954, but I think they must have been given some idea that Crouch's testimony was not reliable or else their inquiry in this respect was less than thorough and certainly unsuccessful.

However, no wonder they felt frustrated when they were expected to satisfy their understanding, and content their better judgment, with such a meager doubt. The presumption of guilt makes a black mass of the ritual of the presumption of innocence.

Like the practical men they were, they looked for a way out. "In good sense," they said, "it could be recommended that Dr. Oppenheimer simply not be used as a consultant, and that therefore there exists no need for a categorical answer to the difficult question posed by the regulations, since there would be no need for access to classified material." "The Board would prefer," they said, "to report a finding of this nature."

17. THE NECESSITY
OF THESE PROCEEDINGS

So THE Board asked the Commission why it had not simply declined to make use of Oppenheimer's services instead of revoking his clearance. The Commission's answer, as the Board stated it, ran like this:

> The Board questioned why the Commission chose to revoke Dr. Oppenheimer's clearance and did not follow the alternative course of declining to make use of his services, assuming it had serious questions in the area of security. To many, this would seem the preferable line of action. We think that the answer of the Commission to this question is pertinent to this recital. It seemed clear that other agencies of Government were extending clearance to Dr. Oppenheimer on the strength of AEC clearance, which in many quarters is supposed to be an approval of the highest order. Furthermore, it was explained that without the positive act of withdrawal of access, he would continue to receive classified reports on Atomic Energy activities as a consultant, even though his services were not specifically and currently engaged. Finally it is said that were his clearance continued, his services would be available to, and probably would be used by, AEC contractors. It is noted that most AEC work is carried on by contractors. Withdrawal of clearance and Dr. Oppenheimer's request for a hearing precipitated this proceeding.

It strikes me that there is here either a lack of candor or a misunderstanding. Of course Oppenheimer "would continue to receive classified reports on Atomic Energy activities *as a consultant*"—I am emphasizing these words—"even though his services were not specifically and currently engaged." So long, that is, as he continued to be a consultant. But he was not then receiving such reports because his clearance had been suspended, and he would not continue to receive them, we must take it, after he ceased to be a consultant; and this would be on June 30, a little more than a month hence.

Perhaps the Board asked the wrong question. Perhaps the Board misunderstood the Commission's reply. Only if the Commission were to renew Oppenheimer's contract, when it expired on June 30, would he continue to have access to classified data and again receive the reports which he had ceased to receive when his clearance was suspended the previous December. But it needed no security board and no decision by the Commission to keep Oppenheimer from having access to restricted data—not after June 30, unless his contract were renewed.

Otherwise, why should Strauss have been willing to have Oppenheimer resign? On December 21, 1953, two days before his clearance was suspended and these proceedings started, Strauss put up to Oppenheimer "as a possibly desirable alternative" that he request the termination of his contract. Oppenheimer refused, but I do not believe Strauss would have offered him this alternative unless it would have terminated his access to restricted data as effectively as would the Commission's termination of his contract or its expiration on June 30.

Gray and Morgan, however, were convinced that they could not escape the dilemma into which the provisions of our security system had put them, and they proceeded to make what seems to me an unfortunate choice. They gave up trying to make a mature practical judgment and chose to rest their decision on a doubt. This made it possible for them to reach their decision "in good conscience," for they were enabled to content their conscience with a doubt. But I think you will agree that it made good reasons for their decisions impossibly hard to find and "an over-all common-sense judgment" "as practical men of affairs" impossible to make.

Dr. Evans made the other choice, and now I ask you to read his brief opinion.

18. DR. EVANS' DISSENT

WHAT A refreshing thing good English is—the direct, simple, immediate language which we lovingly call our mother tongue! It is as different and distinguished as fresh vegetables in the market. So here. After the opinion we have been examining, often so painfully and at times so tediously, it is a relief to read an opinion which all but reads itself. Whether or not you agree with Dr. Evans, you will assuredly agree with me that the chemist writes better than the college president. Or perhaps it is because practical good sense is easier to express.

MINORITY REPORT OF DR. WARD V. EVANS

I have reached the conclusion that Dr. J. Robert Oppenheimer's clearance should be reinstated and am submitting a minority report in accordance with AEC procedure.

The Board, appointed by the Commission, has worked long and arduously on the Oppenheimer case. We have heard 40 witnesses and have taken some 3,000 pages of testimony in addition to having read a similar number of pages of file material. We have examined carefully the notification letter to Dr. Oppenheimer from Mr. Nichols of December 23, 1953, and all other relevant material.

I am in perfect agreement with the majority report of its "findings" with respect to the allegations in Mr. Nichols' letter and I am in agreement with the statement of the Board concerning the significance of its "findings" to the end of page 32.* I also agree with the last paragraph of this section in which the Board makes a final comment on Mr. Nichols' letter. I do not, however, think it necessary to go into any philosophical discussion to prove points not found in Mr. Nichols' letter.

The derogatory information in this letter consisting of 24 items has all been substantiated except for one item. This refers to a Communist meeting held in Dr. Oppenheimer's home, which he is supposed to have attended.

On the basis of this finding, the Board would have to say that Dr. Oppenheimer should not be cleared.

But this is not all.

Most of this derogatory information was in the hands of the Commission when Dr. Oppenheimer was cleared in 1947. They apparently were aware of his associations and his left-wing policies; yet they cleared him. They took a chance on him because of his special talents and he continued to do a good job. Now when the job is done, we are asked to investigate him for practically the same derogatory information. He did his job in a thorough and painstaking

---

*The reference is to p. 32 of the typewritten document. In this reproduction the material referred to is to the end of the seventh full paragraph on p. 19.

manner. There is not the slightest vestige of information before this Board that would indicate that Dr. Oppenheimer is not a loyal citizen of his country. He hates Russia. He had communistic friends, it is true. He still has some. However, the evidence indicates that he has fewer of them than he had in 1947. He is not as naive as he was then. He has more judgment; no one on the Board doubts his loyalty—even the witnesses adverse to him admit that—and he is certainly less of a security risk than he was in 1947, when he was cleared. To deny him clearance now for what he was cleared for in 1947, when we must know he is less of a security risk now than he was then, seems to be hardly the procedure to be adopted in a free country.

We don't have to go out of our way and invent something to prove that the principle of "double jeopardy" does not apply here. This is not our function, and it is not our function to rewrite any clearance rules. The fact remains he is being investigated twice for the same things. Furthermore, we don't have to dig deeply to find other ways that he may be a security risk outside of loyalty, character, and association. He is loyal, we agree on that. There is, in my estimation, nothing wrong with his character. During the early years of his life, Dr. Oppenheimer devoted himself to study and did not vote or become interested in political matters until he was almost 30. Then, in his ignorance, he embraced many subversive organizations.

His judgment was bad in some cases, and most excellent in others but, in my estimation, it is better now than it was in 1947 and to damn him now and ruin his career and his service, I cannot do it.

His statements in cross examination show him to be still naive, but extremely honest and such statements work to his benefit in my estimation. All people are somewhat of a security risk. I don't think we have to go out of our way to point out how this man might be a security risk.

Dr. Oppenheimer in one place in his testimony said that he had told "a tissue of lies." What he had said was not a tissue of lies; there was one lie. He said on one occasion that he had not heard from Dr. Seaborg, when in fact he had a letter from Dr. Seaborg. In my opinion he had forgotten about the letter or he would never have made this statement for he would have known that the Government had the letter. I do not consider that he lied in this case. He stated that he would have recommended David Bohm as a physicist to Brazil, if asked. I think I would have recommended Bohm as a physicist. Dr. Oppenheimer was not asked if he would have added that Bohm was a Communist. In recent years he went to see Chevalier in Paris. I don't like this, but I cannot condemn him on this ground. I don't like his about face in the matter of Dr. Peters, but I don't think it subversive or disloyal.

He did not hinder the development of the H-bomb and there is absolutely nothing in the testimony to show that he did.

First he was in favor of it in 1944. There is no indication that this opinion changed until 1945. After 1945 he did not favor it for some years perhaps on moral, political or technical grounds. Only time will prove whether he was wrong on the moral and political grounds. After the Presidential directive of January 31, 1950, he worked on this project. If his opposition to the H-bomb caused any people not to work on it, it was because of his intellectual prominence and influence over scientific people and not because of any subversive tendencies.

I personally think that our failure to clear Dr. Oppenheimer will be a black mark on the escutcheon of our country. His witnesses are a considerable segment of the scientific backbone of our Nation and they endorse him. I am worried about the effect an improper decision may have on the scientific development in our country. Nuclear physics is new in our country. Most of our authorities in this field came from overseas. They are with us now. Dr. Oppenheimer got most of his education abroad. We have taken hold of this new development in a very great way. There is no predicting where and how far it may go and what its future potentialities may be. I would very much regret any action to retard or hinder this new scientific development.

I would like to add that this opinion was written before the Bulletin of the Atomic Scientists came out with its statement concerning the Oppenheimer case.

This is my opinion as a citizen of a free country.

I suggest that Dr. Oppenheimer's clearance be restored.

WARD V. EVANS.

19. UP TO THE COMMISSION

AFTER THE hearings concluded, with the Board's adverse recommendation, Oppenheimer and his counsel waived his right to review by a Personnel Security Review Board and requested the immediate consideration of the case by the A.E.C. itself. Time was running short. Oppenheimer had received a copy of the Board's Findings and Recommendations on May 28. It was now June 1. There were only thirty days of Oppenheimer's contract left. As soon as it expired there would be no need for the Commission to do anything more than accept the General Manager's recommendation not to renew it. Just as Oppenheimer had preferred the proceedings to resigning, so now he preferred to complete the proceedings rather than quit. The Commission had started this. The Commission should finish it. To the Commission's credit, it did not delay. It acted promptly and accepted the responsibility of denying a clearance which after June 30 would have expired of itself.

Let me, before we leave the Board and go up to the Commission, ask you to take with you what Dr. Rabi, the present chairman of the General Advisory Committee, told Strauss, the chairman of the A.E.C. The asterisks show an omission for security reasons. Dr. Rabi said:

> I never hid my opinion from Mr. Strauss that I thought that this whole proceeding was a most unfortunate one.
> Dr. EVANS. What was that?
> The WITNESS. That the suspension of the clearance of Dr. Oppenheimer was a very unfortunate thing and should not have been done. In other words, there he was; he is a consultant, and if you don't want to consult the guy, you don't consult him, period. Why you have to then proceed to suspend clearance and go through all this sort of thing, he is only there when called, and that is all there was to it. So it didn't seem to me the sort of thing that called for this kind of proceeding at all against a man who had accomplished what Dr. Oppenheimer has accomplished. There is a real positive record, the way I expressed it to a friend of mine. We have an A-bomb and a whole series of it, * * * and what more do you want, mermaids? This is just a tremendous achievement. If the end of that road is this kind of hearing, which can't help but be humiliating, I thought it was a pretty bad show. I still think so.

20. THE COMMISSION'S DECISION

THE HEARINGS before the Board had run three weeks, from April 12 through May 6, 1954. The Board gave Oppenheimer's counsel a week to file a brief. On May 27 the Board submitted to the General Manager, General Nichols, its recommendation against reinstating Oppenheimer's clearance.

Oppenheimer, as I have said, waived his right to appeal to an intermediate review board. He preferred to take the case directly to the Commission. Garrison asked leave to make an oral argument. This was not a part of the official procedure, and it was denied; he was allowed to file a written brief, in which John W. Davis now joined him. It was filed on June 7.

Five days later, on June 12, General Nichols made his recommendation to the Commission. He agreed with the Board that Oppenheimer's clearance should not be reinstated. Neither Oppenheimer nor his counsel was allowed to see Nichols' report until the Commission had made its decision. It would have been as easy as appropriate to let them see it and to ask them to argue it orally. I can think of nothing but awe for official procedure to prevent the Commission's doing this. The Commission had the power to make exceptions. The written brief was an exception, as Campbell pointed out in his opinion. He objected to any departure from the regular official procedure. There was much that was new in Nichols' report, and the Commission plainly relied on Nichols' considerations, the new as well as the old. It was less than fair and it was quite unnecessary not to let Garrison and Davis see it and argue it. An appellate court would have demanded argument.

Nichols gave the Commission a brief account of Oppenheimer's contribution to the atomic-energy program and of his clearance in 1943 to direct Los Alamos:

Dr. Oppenheimer has been intimately associated with the atomic energy program virtually from its inception. He participated in early weapons research and was selected as the wartime Director of the Los Alamos Laboratory. As district engineer of the wartime Manhattan Engineer District, I was keenly aware of the contribution he made to the initial development of the atomic bomb. His leadership and direction of the Los Alamos weapons program were outstanding; his contributions leading to a successful atomic weapon have properly received worldwide acknowledgment and acclaim.

As deputy district engineer of the Manhattan District, I was also aware of the circumstances, which have been brought out in the record, surrounding Dr. Oppenheimer's appointment as head of the Los Alamos Laboratory, and his subsequent clearance. He was selected in spite of the fact that he was considered a "calculated risk." He would not have been chosen had he not been considered virtually indispensable to the atomic bomb program. After he was chosen, as General Groves testified before the Board, Dr. Oppenheimer probably would not have been cleared had he not already been thoroughly steeped in knowledge of weapons research and had he not been considered absolutely essential.

Security officers opposed the clearance of Dr. Oppenheimer and it was not until July of 1943, after he had participated in the program for many months, that the decision to clear him was made by General Groves. I personally signed the directive advising the commanding officer at Los Alamos that there was no objection to Dr. Oppenheimer's employment.

The Manhattan District had one mandate—to build an atomic bomb as quickly as possible. Fears that Germany would build an atomic weapon first and possibly win the war thereby spurred the Manhattan District in what was felt to be a race against the German effort. Communist Russia was also fighting Germany at that time.

General Groves testified before the Board that he did not regret having made the decision to clear Dr. Oppenheimer in consideration of all of the circumstances which confronted him in 1943 but that under the present requirements of the Atomic Energy Act, as he interprets them, he would not clear Dr. Oppenheimer today.

Nor would Nichols now, under the Atomic Energy Act and Executive Order 10450. He concurred with the findings and the recommendations of the majority of the Board, and he referred in particular to a number of considerations relating to Oppenheimer's character and associations on which he found that Oppenheimer was a security risk. If I were to go into Nichols' considerations, it would only anticipate some of the reasons which led the majority of the Commission to the same conclusion. I will refer to them where necessary in our discussion of the Commission's opinion.

Nichols then turned to "the effect which denial of security clearance would have upon the atomic energy or related programs."

In addition to determining whether or not Dr. Oppenheimer is a security risk, the General Manager should determine the effect which denial of security clearance would have upon the atomic energy or related programs. In regard to Dr. Oppenheimer's net worth to atomic energy projects, I believe, first, that through World War II he was of tremendous value and absolutely essential. Secondly, I believe that since World War II his value to the Atomic Energy Commission as a scientist or as a consultant has declined because of the rise in competence and skill of other scientists and because of his loss of scientific objectivity probably resulting from the diversion of his efforts to political fields and matters not purely scientific in nature. Further, it should be pointed out that in the past 2 years since he has ceased to be a member of the General Advisory Committee, his services have been utilized by the Atomic Energy Commission on the following occasions only:

> October 16 and 17, 1952.
> September 1 and 2, 1953.
> September 21 and 22,.1953.

I doubt that the Atomic Energy Commission, even if the question of his security clearance had not arisen, would have utilized his services to a markedly greater extent during the next few years. I find, however, that another agency, the Science Advisory Committee, Office of Defense Mobilization, has stated in a letter dated June 4, 1954, signed by Dr. L. A. DuBridge, Chairman, and addressed to Chairman Strauss, that:

"* * * It is, therefore, of great importance to us that Dr. Oppenheimer's 'Q' clearance be restored. This is especially true since our Committee is planning to undertake during the coming months an intensive study of important items related to national security on which Dr. Oppenheimer's knowledge and counsel will be of very critical importance."

Dr. DuBridge further stated that:

"* * * His value is, it seems to me, so enormous as to completely overbalance and override the relatively trivial risks* which the Personnel Security Board reports. In other words, the net benefits to national security will be far greater if Dr. Oppenheimer's clearance is restored than if it is terminated. Even though he served the Government in no other capacity than as a member of the Science Advisory Committee of the Office of Defense Mobilization, the above statements will, I am confident, be true beyond question."

Other Government agencies may also desire to use Dr. Oppenheimer's services if he were to be cleared. In addition, contractors and study groups involved in atomic power activities undoubtedly will from time to time, as one or two have already indicated, desire to clear Dr. Oppenheimer for consulting work.

Dr. Oppenheimer could of course make contributions in all these fields, but he is far from being indispensable.

Nichols put a footnote to the phrase in Dr. DuBridge's letter, "the relatively trivial risks": "It should be noted that Dr. DuBridge to my knowledge has never had access to the complete file or the transcript of the hearing." Let me point out that this letter from the Science Advisory Committee was written on June 4, after the Board had announced its findings. The Committee was referring to the security risks which Gray and Morgan had thought serious enough to warrant their decision. The Committee regarded them as "relatively trivial."

DuBridge himself had testified:

Q. May I just for a moment remind you that the Atomic Energy Act requires the board to consider character, associations, and loyalty. Having this frame of reference that the board here must consider, the character, associations and loyalty of Dr. Oppenheimer, in determining whether or not his continuance of his clearance would endanger the national safety, having in mind the past associations set forth in the letter, having in mind what you know about Dr. Oppenheimer's character, having in mind what you say that the continuance of his clearance would to any degree endanger the national safety?

A. In no degree whatsoever.

Q. On what do you base this judgment?

A. In the first place, these associations that are mentioned were those of many, many years ago. As I understand it, they have largely long since been terminated, in at least one case by death. In the second place, these were rather natural associations of a person who had strong human interests, interests in human rights and human liberties and human welfare, who had strong revulsions against the growth of dictatorship in Germany, Spain, and Italy, and who wanted to express his opposition to such violations of human liberty as he regarded these dictatorships. He therefore found himself among others of like minds, some of whom it turned out were possible members of the Communist Party. But this was only a natural exhibition of his deep interest in human beings and in human liberty and had nothing to do with his devotion to this country, or nothing adverse to do with this country.

In the second place, it seems to me that to question the integrity and loyalty of a person who has worked hard and devotedly for his country as Dr. Oppenheimer has on such trivial grounds is against all principles of human justice. It seems to me whatever his ideas and associations were in 1935, is quite irrelevant in view of the last years since 1941–42, during which he has shown such a devoted interest to the welfare, security and strength of the United States. Whatever mistakes, if they were mistakes, and I do not suggest that they were, that were made in the thirties have well been washed out and the value of a man like Dr. Oppenheimer to his country has been adequately and repeatedly proved.

It would be in my opinion against all principles of justice to now not recognize the way in which his loyalty has been proved in a positive way through positive contributions. Furthermore, this country needs men of that kind, and should not deprive itself of their services.

Nichols concluded his memorandum to the Commission:

I have conscientiously weighed the record of Dr. Oppenheimer's whole life, his past contributions, and his potential future contributions to the Nation against the security risk that is involved in his continued clearance. In addition, I have given consideration to the nature of the cold war in which we are engaged with communism and Communist Russia and the horrible prospects of hydrogen bomb warfare if all-out war should be forced upon us. From these things a need results to eliminate from classified work any individuals who might endanger the common defense or security or whose retention is not clearly consistent with the interests of national security.

Dr. Oppenheimer's clearance should not be reinstated.

On June 16 the Commission published the transcript and Garrison and Davis their written brief. Otherwise, we'd not know what we were talking about.

On June 28, the question of the clearance of Dr. Oppenheimer was formally presented to the Commission, and it was voted, four to one, to deny him clearance. The next day its decision and the five opinions of the commissioners—each one wrote an opinion— were released to the press. The day after that, June 30, Oppenheimer's contract ran out.

The opinion of three of the commissioners—Murray concurred in the decision for reasons of his own, and Smyth dissented—was written by Chairman Strauss.

As you read it, I think you will find a number of questions rising in your mind. One will be, What was it that made Strauss, who was one of the commissioners who cleared Oppenheimer seven years before, in 1947, change his mind? Not that consistency was either necessary or imperative. Times change and no doctrine of *stare decisis* was staring him in the face. But a change of mind or of heart calls for explanation. What new derogatory information did he have to rely on, either newly discovered or given new derogatory significance by the Executive Order of 1953 or by the A.E.C. Criteria of 1950?

I think you will also find yourself comparing the way the Commission went about the same problem in 1947 under Lilienthal with the way it went about it in 1954 under Strauss. Garrison finally succeeded, by persistent inquiry, in getting before the Board—and so now before you—a detailed account of what the Commission did then. You will recall how informally the commissioners handled the problem in 1947. They handled it themselves. They had to, for there was no security system then. Was it better that they did have to? You have an opportunity to wonder whether a case like this, of such dimensions and such difficulty, concerning a man of such importance, is better handled formally by a board of inquiry, as we have watched it being done in 1954, or informally and immediately by the commissioners themselves.

You will recall Lilienthal's examination. Robb asked him who was present at the meeting of the commissioners he called on March 10, 1947, to consider the information Hoover had sent over. They were Dr. Bacher, Sumner T. Pike, Lewis L. Strauss, Wesley W. Waymack, and Lilienthal himself. "Will you tell us," Robb asked, "what happened at that Commission meeting?" Lilienthal said:

A. Commission conference would be the best description because it continued for some time. It was very informal. We had this file which I requested all the commissioners to read. It was not necessary to request them to because it was obviously a matter of great interest and importance. Instead of delegating this to someone else, it seemed clear that we should do the evaluating, since the responsibility of deciding what should be done, if anything, was ours.

Let me not speak slightingly or disparagingly of delegating duties. There are duties which never get done unless you delegate them. There are other duties which are better done by delegation. There remain some which you would do better not to delegate, though here the commissioners had no choice. In 1947 they had no one to delegate their duties to, for the security system had not yet been set up, and Lilienthal got nowhere when he asked Clark Clifford if President Truman wanted to set up a special board. And in 1954 the commissioners' duties in this respect were delegated by law to these security proceedings. My question is academic, and yet I remember what Justice Brandeis told Judge Wyzanski when Wyzanski first went into public service. "The reason the public thinks so much of the Justices of the Supreme Court is that they are almost the only people in Washington who do their own work." (Judge Charles E. Wyzanski's Brandeis Lecture at Brandeis University on March 4, 1954.)

You will be impressed also by the distance we have come from Borden's charges. It is a long way from espionage and treason down to . . . You will judge for yourself.

You will bear in mind that the members of the Commission were quite as distinguished and respectable as the members of the Board.

Lewis Strauss had served on the Commission before, from 1946 to 1950. He was back now as chairman. A West Virginian, fifty-eight years old, he had been educated in the public schools in Richmond and the Medical College of Virginia. After the First World War, in which he had worked with Hoover, he went to New York, entered investment banking and worked up through Kuhn Loeb to the top. In the Second World War he was in the Naval Reserve and rose to the rank of rear admiral, earning the Legion of Merit with a gold star.

Eugene M. Zuckert was forty-three, a New Yorker, a Yale man, and a graduate of the Yale Law School in 1937. He devoted the next fifteen years, before his appointment to the Commission in 1952, about equally, at first to legal work for the Securities and Exchange Commission, then to an assistant deanship at the Harvard Business School, and after that to his duties as Assistant Secretary of the Air Force.

Joseph Campbell was fifty-four, a New Yorker, and a graduate of Columbia. After a successful career as an accountant and work in the Manhattan District with the A-bomb, he had become treasurer of Columbia University until he was appointed to the Commission in 1953.

These are the three commissioners for whom Strauss wrote the majority report. The other two, who each went his own way, were Murray, who agreed with the decision of the majority for his own reasons, and Smyth, who dissented.

Thomas E. Murray was sixty-three, a highly successful engineer in the electrical and welding fields, a graduate of the Sheffield

Scientific School at Yale when he was only twenty. He has honorary degrees from Fordham, Georgetown, St. Johns, Marquette, and Boston College. He was a trustee of the United Mine Workers Welfare Fund, and a director of Chrysler, the Bank of New York, and the Fifth Avenue Bank.

Henry DeWolf Smyth, a few years older, was a distinguished physicist. After graduating from Lawrenceville and then from Princeton University, A.B., A.M., and Ph.D., Smyth went to Cambridge University as a National Research Fellow and came back to teach at Princeton, where he became a professor in 1936. He had worked with the Manhattan District, and he was the author of the official War Department report on the A-bomb, the Smyth Report. He had been on the Commission since 1949.

Below is Strauss's opinion for himself, Zuckert and Campbell. I will interrupt it for discussion.

After stating the issue of whether the security of the United States warranted Oppenheimer's continued access to restricted data of the Atomic Energy Commission and their conclusion that it did not, Strauss quoted the Atomic Energy Act of 1946. It requires the Commission, he said, to reach a determination on three points—Oppenheimer's character, his associations and his loyalty. Strauss put loyalty aside, but he refrained from assuring us that Oppenheimer was loyal, as the Board had. Strauss, Zuckert and Campbell reached their decision on "the proof of fundamental defects" in Oppenheimer's "character" and a finding that "his associations with persons known to him to be Communists have extended far beyond the tolerable limits of prudence and self-restraint. . . ."

Strauss said:

On the basis of the record before the Commission, comprising the transcript of the hearing before the Gray Board as well as reports of Military Intelligence and the Federal Bureau of Investigation, we find Dr. Oppenheimer is not entitled to the continued confidence of the Government and of this Commission because of the proof of fundamental defects in his "character."

This is the first time that I recall any mention of the use of reports of military intelligence as evidence, though the Board made it pretty clear that the F.B.I. reports were not the only files it had read in the week before the hearings opened. We do not, of course, know anything at all about these military intelligence reports which were before the Commission. Possibly they contained no more than such as General Wilson had brought to the

Director of Intelligence about which he testified, but what bearing that had on Oppenheimer's "character" I don't see. It is disturbing to find the Commission using undisclosed military intelligence reports. Particularly disturbing is the idea that they were used to judge a man's character.

In respect to the criterion of "associations," we find that his associations with persons known to him to be Communists have extended far beyond the tolerable limits of prudence and self-restraint which are to be expected of one holding the high positions that the Government has continuously entrusted to him since 1942. These associations have lasted too long to be justified as merely the intermittent and accidental revival of earlier friendships.

Neither in the deliberations by the full Commission nor in the review of the Gray Board was importance attached to the opinions of Dr. Oppenheimer as they bore upon the 1949 debate within the Government on the question of whether the United States should proceed with the thermonuclear weapon program. In this debate, Dr. Oppenheimer was, of course, entitled to his opinion.

All the commissioners, equally explicitly, said the same thing. The charge to which Bush and Conant had taken such strong exception was not to play any part in their deliberations. Nichols, in his letter to the Commission, had said that he had not intended to question Oppenheimer's right to an honest opinion. He had meant only to raise the question of Oppenheimer's good faith. He had written:

It should be emphasized that at no time has there been any intention on my part or the Board's to draw in question any honest opinion expressed by Dr. Oppenheimer. Technical opinions have no security implications unless they are reflections of sinister motives. However, in view of Dr. Oppenheimer's record coupled with the preceding allegation concerning him, it was necessary to submit this matter for the consideration of the Personnel Security Board in order that the good faith of his technnical opinions might be determined. The Board found that, following the President's decision, Dr. Oppenheimer did not show the enthusiastic support for the program which might have been expected of the chief atomic adviser to the Government under the circumstances; that, had he given his enthusiastic support to the program, a concerted effort would have been initiated at an earlier date, and that, whatever the motivation, the security interests of the United States were affected. In reviewing the record I find that the evidence establishes no sinister motives on the part of Dr. Oppenheimer in his attitude on the hydrogen bomb, either before or after the President's decision. I have considered the testimony and the record on this subject only as evidence bearing upon Dr. Oppenheimer's veracity. In this context I find that such evidence is disturbing.

Strauss gave a brief account of the course of the proceedings:

The fundamental issues here are apart from and beyond this episode. The history of their development is as follows:

On December 23, 1953, Dr. Oppenheimer was notified that his security clearance had been suspended, and he was provided with the allegations which had brought his trustworthiness into question. He was also furnished with a copy of the Atomic Energy Commission's security clearance procedures, and was informed of his right to a hearing under those procedures. By telegram dated

January 29, 1954, Dr. Oppenheimer requested a hearing. On March 4, 1954, after requesting and receiving three extensions of time, he submitted his answer to the letter of December 23, 1953. On March 15, 1954, Dr. Oppenheimer was informed that Mr. Gordon Gray, Mr. Thomas A. Morgan, and Dr. Ward V. Evans would conduct the hearing.

The hearing before the Gray Board commenced on April 12, 1954, and continued through May 6, 1954. Dr. Oppenheimer was represented by four lawyers. He was present to confront all witnesses; he had the opportunity to cross-examine all witnesses; his counsel made both oral and written argument to the Board.

The Board submitted its findings and recommendation to the General Manager of the Commission on May 27, 1954. A majority of the Board recommended against reinstatement of clearance, Dr. Evans dissenting.

Dr. Oppenheimer had full advantage of the security procedures of the Commission. In our opinion he had a just hearing.

On May 28, 1954, the General Manager notified Dr. Oppenheimer of the adverse recommendation of the Personnel Security Board and forwarded to him a copy of the Board's findings and recommendation. The General Manager informed Dr. Oppenheimer of his right to request review of his case by the Personnel Security Review Board. Dr. Oppenheimer was also informed that upon consideration of the record in the case—including the recommendation of the Personnel Security Review Board in the event review by that Board was requested—the General Manager would submit to the Commission his own recommendation as to whether or not clearance should be reinstated and that the Commission would thereafter make the final determination.

By letter of June 1, 1954, Dr. Oppenheimer waived his right to a review of his case by the Personnel Security Review Board. He requested immediate consideration of his case by the Commission. On June 7, 1954, his counsel submitted a written brief to the Commission. The General Manager reviewed the testimony and the findings and recommendation of the Gray Board and the briefs; his conclusion that Dr. Oppenheimer's clearance should not be reinstated was submitted to the Commission on June 12, 1954.

Prior to these proceedings, the derogatory information in Government files concerning Dr. Oppenheimer had never been weighed by any board on the basis of sworn testimony.

The important result of these hearings was to bring out significant information bearing upon Dr. Oppenheimer's character and associations hitherto unknown to the Commission and presumably unknown also to those who testified as character witnesses on his behalf. These hearings additionally established as fact many matters which previously had been only allegations.

Strauss said that they had taken into account Oppenheimer's "past contributions to the atomic energy program." At the same time Strauss declared that Oppenheimer's position of high trust carried commensurately high obligations and that "access to the most sensitive areas" calls for "exemplary standards of reliability, self-discipline, and trustworthiness." Oppenheimer "has fallen far short of acceptable standards."

In weighing the matter at issue, we have taken into account Dr. Oppenheimer's past contributions to the atomic energy program. At the same time, we have been mindful of the fact that the positions of high trust and responsibility which Dr. Oppenheimer has occupied carried with them a commensurately high obligation of unequivocal character and conduct on his part. A Government official having access to the most sensitive areas of restricted data and to the innermost details of national war plans and weapons must measure up to exemplary standards of reliability, self-discipline, and trustworthiness. Dr. Oppenheimer has fallen far short of acceptable standards.

The record shows that Dr. Oppenheimer has consistently placed himself outside the rules which govern others. He has falsified in matters wherein he was charged with grave responsibilities in the national interest. In his associations he has repeatedly exhibited a willful disregard of the normal and proper obligations of security.

Strauss then turned to Oppenheimer's "character." He does not mention the opinions of the highly respectable persons who testified to Oppenheimer's integrity of character. I cannot believe he did not read their testimony. His own A.E.C. Criteria required him to do that. "The judgment of responsible persons as to the integrity of the individual should be considered." And yet, for all we know, the Commission ignored the freely offered and strongly expressed judgments of its last two ex-chairmen, Lilienthal and Dean; of three former members, Sumner Pike, Dr. Bacher and Dr. Glennan; of the chairman of its General Advisory Committee, Dr. Rabi, and of five former members; of the Director of the Los Alamos Laboratory, Dr. Bradbury; of Conant, the High Commissioner of Germany, and of McCloy, his predecessor; of Dr. Vannevar Bush, Karl Compton, George F. Kennan, and Mervin Kelly, vice-president of the Bell Telephone Laboratories. These and others testified to the integrity of Oppenheimer's character, and for all that appears, the Commission ignored them. Arrogance?

Let us see what the Commission preferred to rely on. Strauss gave six incidents from which the Commission inferred its conclusion that there were "fundamental defects" in Oppenheimer's "character." All but one, the third, about Lambert, were instances on which Nichols had relied.

Strauss said:

The catalog does not end with these six examples. The work of Military Intelligence, the Federal Bureau of Investigation, and the Atomic Energy Commission—all, at one time or another have felt the effect of his falsehoods, evasions, and misrepresentations.

Yet he offered no others. I do not have access to the F.B.I. files and I am in no position to say that there were no others; but Smyth was, and he said, in his dissenting opinion, that these six "constitute the whole of the evidence extracted from a lengthy record. . . . Any implication that these are illustrations only and that further substantial evidence exists in the investigation files to support these charges is unfounded."

So we may examine Strauss's six examples with the assurance that these are all he had. Any others must have been so less derogatory that they were not derogatory.

The *first* is the Chevalier incident. Strauss did not regard it, as the Board did, solely as a derogatory episode in 1943. Strauss says it presents a dilemma. Either Oppenheimer lied to the security officers in 1943 or Oppenheimer perjured himself before the Board. So far as Strauss was concerned, it did not matter which. He said:

> (1) Dr. Oppenheimer has now admitted under oath that while in charge of the Los Alamos Laboratory and working on the most secret weapon development for the Government, he told Colonel Pash a fabrication of lies. Colonel Pash was an officer of Military Intelligence charged with the duty of protecting the atomic-weapons project against spies. Dr. Oppenheimer told Colonel Pash in circumstantial detail of an attempt by a Soviet agent to obtain from him information about the work on the atom bomb. This was the Haakon Chevalier incident. In the hearings recently concluded, Dr. Oppenheimer under oath swears that the story he told Colonel Pash was a "whole fabrication and tissue of lies"
>
> It is not clear today whether the account Dr. Oppenheimer gave to Colonel Pash in 1943 concerning the Chevalier incident or the story he told the Gray Board last month is the true version.
>
> If Dr. Oppenheimer lied in 1943, as he now says he did, he committed the crime of knowingly making false and material statements to a Federal officer. If he lied to the Board, he committed perjury in 1954.

We have discussed the Chevalier incident. We found that the only person on the spot who believed that Oppenheimer's "fabrication and tissues of lies" were the truth was Pash, to whom they were told and who may have found it hard to believe that anyone could lie to him successfully. Now we find that a majority of the Commission do not know which story to believe.

Nichols, in his report to the Commission on June 12, had taken a different view of the Chevalier incident than he had in his letter of December 23, 1953. There, you will recall, Nichols had said nothing about any false statements. He had stressed Oppenheimer's failure to report the episode and his refusal to identify Chevalier as the man who had approached him until he was ordered to do so. Robb, in his cross-examination, pressed the fact that Oppenheimer had lied to Pash and Lansdale. Now, Nichols, in his June report to the Commission, takes the contrary view. He now thinks it "a fair inference" that Oppenheimer's story to Pash was true and his testimony to the Board false. Nichols reported:

> 2. *The Chevalier incident.*—Dr. Oppenheimer's involvement in the Chevalier incident, and his subsequent conduct with respect to it, raise grave questions of security import.
>
> If in 1943, as he now claims to have done, he knowingly and willfully made false statements to Colonel Pash, a Federal officer, Dr. Oppenheimer violated what was then section 80, title 18, of the United States Code; in other words if his present story is true then he admits he committed a felony in 1943. On

the other hand, as Dr. Oppenheimer admitted on cross-examination, if the story Dr. Oppenheimer told Colonel Pash was true, it not only showed that Chevalier was involved in a criminal espionage conspiracy, but also reflected seriously on Dr. Oppenheimer himself.

After reviewing both the 16-page transcript (as accepted by the Board) of the interview between Dr. Oppenheimer and Colonel Pash on August 26, 1943, and recent testimony before the Board, it is difficult to conclude that the detailed and circumstantial account given by Dr. Oppenheimer to Colonel Pash was false and that the story now told by Dr. Oppenheimer is an honest one. Dr. Oppenheimer's story in 1943 was most damaging to Chevalier. If Chevalier was Dr. Oppenheimer's friend and Dr. Oppenheimer, as he now says, believed Chevalier to be innocent and wanted to protect him, why then would he tell such a complicated false story to Colonel Pash? This story showed that Chevalier was not innocent, but on the contrary was deeply involved in an espionage conspiracy By the same token, why would Dr. Oppenheimer tell a false story to Colonel Pash which showed that he himself was not blameless? Is it reasonable to believe a man will deliberately tell a lie that seriously reflects upon himself and his friend, when he knows that the truth will show them both to be innocent?

It is important to remember also that Dr. Oppenheimer did not give his present version of the story until 1946, shortly after he had learned from Chevalier what Chevalier himself had told the FBI about the incident in question. After learning of this from Chevalier, Dr. Oppenheimer changed his story to conform to that given to the FBI by Chevalier.

From all of these facts and circumstances, it is a fair inference that Dr. Oppenheimer's story to Colonel Pash and other Manhattan District officials was substantially true and that his later statement on the subject to the FBI, and his recent testimony before the Personnel Security Board, were false.

Of course it is "a fair inference" that the "tissue of lies" to Pash was true, just as Pash's belief in its truth was understandable. The reason both Nichols and Pash give—that the more damaging and derogatory a story is, the more likely it is to be true—makes sense. The question Nichols asks is as fair as the inference he draws: "Is it reasonable to believe a man will deliberately tell a lie that seriously reflects upon himself and his friend, when he knows that the truth will show them both to be innocent?"

But what Nichols tells us "it is important to remember" is not true. Oppenheimer had told General Groves in 1943 that his story to Pash and Lansdale was false. This was three years before 1946 when the F.B.I. called Chevalier in to question him. You have read what General Groves testified. Doesn't Nichols believe him?

The *second* instance turns on the question of whether Oppenheimer knew that Rossi Lomanitz was "an active Communist" or that Lomanitz had disclosed information to an unauthorized person when Oppenheimer tried to get his induction into the Army deferred and keep him on his work in the atomic program in Berkeley. Dr. Ernest Lawrence was the one who wanted this done. Colonel Lansdale said, "I remember Ernest Lawrence yelled and screamed louder than anybody else about us taking Lomanitz away from him." You will recall Lansdale's saying that induction into the Army was the way security officers got rid of security risks.

Strauss said:

(2) Dr. Oppenheimer testified to the Gray Board that if he had known Giovanni Rossi Lomanitz was an active Communist or that Lomanitz had disclosed information about the atomic project to an unauthorized person, he would not have written to Colonel Lansdale of the Manhattan District the letter of October 19, 1943, in which Dr. Oppenheimer supported the desire of Lomanitz to return to the atomic project.

The record shows, however, that on August 26, 1943, Dr. Oppenheimer told Colonel Pash that he (Oppenheimer) knew that Lomanitz had revealed information about the project. Furthermore, on September 12, 1943, Dr. Oppenheimer told Colonel Lansdale that he (Oppenheimer) had previously learned for a fact that Lomanitz was a Communist Party member

Oppenheimer testified flatly that he did not know, when he wrote the letter, that Lomanitz was an active Communist. He testified: "In any event, you didn't know then, did you?" "No." And when he was asked whether he would have written the letter if he had known that Lomanitz had disclosed confidential information, he said, "Of course not."

Did Oppenheimer know, when he wrote the letter on October 19, 1943, that Lomanitz was a member of the Communist party? Robb read an extract from the transcript of his interview with Colonel Lansdale on September 12, 1943.

LANSDALE: "Who do you know on the project in Berkeley who are now—that's probably a hypothetical question—or have been members of the Communist Party?"

OPPENHEIMER: "I will try to answer that question. The answer will, however, be incomplete. I know for a fact, I know, I learned in my last visit to Berkeley that both Lomanitz and Weinberg were members. I suggested that before, but was not sure. I never had any way of knowing."

Then Robb asked Oppenheimer whether he would now concede that he knew at that time that both Lomanitz and Weinberg had been members of the Party. Oppenheimer answered, "Evidently. Was I told by the security officers?" Robb replied, "I don't know. I have just read what you said," and repeated his question. "So it appears," Oppenheimer answered.

So it does appear from so much of the transcript as Robb read. But a little later in the interview Lansdale brought the subject back to Lomanitz and wanted to know whether a discussion Oppenheimer had had with him "had any relation to his work in the Party."

OPPENHEIMER: "None whatsoever. I did not know he was a member of the Party."

LANSDALE: "Until just recently . . ."

OPPENHEIMER: "Yes, and I knew he was extremely Red, but frankly I thought he was a member of the Trotskyite faction."

LANSDALE: "Which would ipso facto prevent him from . . ."

OPPENHEIMER: "Being a member of the Party. That's what I thought at that time."

Strauss cited the first passage in the interview. He did not mention this later passage. It leaves me uncertain enough of what Oppenheimer meant to be quite certain I cannot pass judgment.

Did Oppenheimer know, when he wrote the letter, that Lomanitz had revealed information? Robb read to Oppenheimer a passage from the beginning of his interview with Colonel Pash on August 26, 1943, in which it appeared that Oppenheimer had said, "What I wanted to tell this fellow [Lomanitz] was that he had been indiscreet. I know that is right that he had revealed information."

ROBB: "There is no question, is there, either, that at that time, August 26, 1943, you knew that Lomanitz had revealed certain confidential information?"

OPPENHEIMER: "I was told by Lansdale, that he had been indiscreet about information. It was not made clear to me . . ."

ROBB: "This says, 'I know that is right that he had revealed information.' So wouldn't you agree that you knew he had revealed information?"

OPPENHEIMER: "Yes."

Isn't it pretty clear that Oppenheimer was only accepting what Lansdale told him?

The *third* instance was new. The Board had not mentioned it, nor had Nichols. Strauss wrote:

(3) In 1943, Dr. Oppenheimer indicated to Colonel Lansdale that he did not know Rudy Lambert, a Communist Party functionary. In fact, Dr. Oppenheimer asked Colonel Lansdale what Lambert looked like. Now, however, Dr. Oppenheimer under oath has admitted that he knew and had seen Lambert at least half a dozen times prior to 1943; he supplied a detailed description of Lambert; he said that once or twice he had lunch with Lambert and Isaac Folkoff, another Communist Party functionary, to discuss his (Oppenheimer's) contributions to the Communist Party; and that he knew at the time that Lambert was an official in the Communist Party

There is no doubt that Oppenheimer knew Lambert, though not well. In his reply Oppenheimer referred to him and said, "Our association never became close," and he testified in substance just as Strauss says he did.

The passage in his interview with Colonel Lansdale to which Strauss refers and on which he relies to show that Oppenheimer "indicated to Colonel Lansdale" in 1943 that Oppenheimer did not know Lambert runs as follows:

LANSDALE: "Do you know a fellow named Rudy Lambert?"

OPPENHEIMER: "I'm not sure. Do you know what he looks like?"

LANSDALE: "No, I've never seen him. He's a member of the Party."

After Robb quoted this from the interview with Lansdale, Robb asked, "You knew what Rudy Lambert looked like, didn't you?"

Oppenheimer said, "Sure."

"Why did you ask Lansdale what he looked like?"

"I don't know that I did."

"If you did, Doctor, would it mean that you were ducking the question?"

"I would think so."

This may amount to an "indication" that Oppenheimer did not know Lambert. It may also indicate that Oppenheimer thought he did know Lambert. Smyth thought it was "dependent on a garbled transcript."

The *fourth* instance is the letter to the Rochester papers about Oppenheimer's testimony on Dr. Peters before the Congressional committee.

(4) In 1949 Dr. Oppenheimer testified before a closed session of the House Un-American Activities Committee about the Communist Party membership and activities of Dr. Bernard Peters. A summary of Dr. Oppenheimer's testimony subsequently appeared in a newspaper, the Rochester Times Union. Dr. Oppenheimer then wrote a letter to that newspaper. The effect of that letter was to contradict the testimony he had given a congressional committee

There is no need of going over this episode again. The Board thought that it suggested "a tendenecy to be coerced, or at least influenced in conduct over a period of years." Strauss took quite a different view of it. He regarded it as one more proof of a "fundamental defect" in Oppenheimer's character. I find this hard to understand.

Oppenheimer had testified at an executive session of the House Committee on Un-American Activities. His testimony had been made public. Dr. Bethe, Dr. Weiskopf, Dr. Condon, and his brother, Frank Oppenheimer, as well as Dr. Peters himself, all protested. Dr. Condon wrote a letter to the papers about it. Oppenheimer talked with Dr. Peters and came to the conclusion that his testimony, at any rate the way he had phrased his testimony, had been "intemperate." He consulted Volpe, the General Counsel of the A.E.C., who had accompanied him to the executive session. Oppenheimer then wrote his letter to the papers, and sent a copy to the committee (Smyth). He testified that he did not want "to get this guy fired from the University of Rochester because of intemperate remarks I made before the House Committee." "I should not have talked in executive session without thinking what they might do publicly. . . . It was being misconstrued to mean that he should not keep his job. I had explicitly said that I thought it was good he keep his job."

Would you think better of Oppenheimer if, all things considered, he had not written the letter? It is certainly not a defect in your character to be persuaded that what you told a Congressional committee was not quite accurate or not quite right. Does it show a defect that when the committee allows what you told them to be made public you make your correction public too and send a copy to the committee? It is clear now that it would have been more prudent to have done nothing. Which way would you have thought better of yourself?

The *fifth* instance is the letter Oppenheimer got from Dr. Seaborg and forgot. Strauss said:

(5) In connection with the meeting of the General Advisory Committee on October 29, 1949, at which the thermonuclear weapon program was considered, Dr. Oppenheimer testified before the Gray Board that the General Advisory Committee was "surprisingly unanimous" in its recommendation that the United States ought not to take the initiative at that time in a thermonuclear program. Now, however, under cross-examination, Dr. Oppenheimer testifies that he did not know how Dr. Seaborg (1 of the 9 members of Dr. Oppenheimer's committee) then felt about the program because Dr. Seaborg "was in Sweden, and there was no communication with him." On being confronted with a letter from Dr. Seaborg to him dated October 14, 1949—a letter which had been in Dr. Oppenheimer's files—Dr. Oppenheimer admitted having received the letter prior to the General Advisory Committee meeting in 1949. In that letter Dr. Seaborg said: "Although I deplore the prospects of our country putting a tremendous effort into this, I must confess that I have been unable to come to the conclusion that we should not." Yet Dr. Seaborg's view was not mentioned in Dr. Oppenheimer's report for the General Advisory Committee to the Commission in October 1949. In fact the existence of this letter remained unknown to the Commission until it was disclosed during the hearings

Let me, to begin with, speak a little meticulously about this last sentence that "the existence of this letter remained unknown to the Commission until it was disclosed during the hearings." The letter was produced by Robb, counsel for the Commission, in the course of his cross-examination of Oppenheimer on April 16, 1954. It had been in the possession of the Commission for something more than three months. For it was in one of the files which the Commission took from Oppenheimer in the week between Christmas and New Year's Day. As to the fact of its existence, the Commission had had in its files for some five years a letter from Oppenheimer to its chairman, Lilienthal, dated October 14, 1949, which, after saying that Seaborg could not be at the meeting on October 29, said, "I have, however, made arrangements to obtain from him in writing, and, if necessary, consultation, his views on the subject of the meeting." And in Oppenheimer's letter to Conant of October 21, which you have read and which the Commission found in Oppenheimer's files, Oppenheimer referred to this letter from Seaborg as having been received, saying, "except Seaborg, who must be in Sweden, and whose general views we have in written form." This is a small point I am making, but is it any smaller and is it not sounder than the point which the Commission is trying to make against Oppenheimer?

Oppenheimer, in his direct testimony and also in his reply, spoke of the surprising—"to me very surprising"—unanimity of the General Advisory Committee in October 1949. Oppenheimer made it clear that he was referring to the unanimity of those present, "around the table." He had already said in his reply of March 4, 1954, that Dr. Seaborg was abroad, and he had also made it clear that only eight members of the Committee had joined in the report.

On cross-examination, Robb asked Oppenheimer if he knew how Dr. Seaborg "felt about it." Oppenheimer said that Dr. Seaborg "was in Sweden, and there was no communication with him." Robb went on to ask Oppenheimer if he had testified to the Joint Committee on Atomic Energy "that there was unanimity but that Dr. Seaborg was not heard there; is that right?" "It is true," Oppenheimer answered, "and I suppose I was asked."

Three pages later in the transcript Robb went back to Oppenheimer's statement that there had been "no communication with him" and showed Oppenheimer Dr. Seaborg's letter to him of October 14, 1949. It had come from Oppenheimer's files in Princeton.

Oppenheimer at once said, "I am going to say before I see that that I had no recollection of it." "Why did you tell the Joint Congressional Committee on Atomic Energy when you testified on January 29, 1950, that Dr. Seaborg had not expressed himself on the subject prior to the meeting?" "I am sure because it was my recollection." "But weren't you asked, or didn't you tell the Joint Committee that Dr. Seaborg had not expressed himself on this subject prior to the meeting of October 29, 1949?" "I would have to see the transcript. I don't remember that question and the answer."

And then it turns out, after a recess, that Oppenheimer's testimony before the Joint Committee had been three months after the October meeting of the General Advisory Committee and after its next meeting. He had told the Joint Committee that Seaborg "was away when the matter was discussed and that he had not expressed himself on it." He did not tell the Joint Committee that Dr. Seaborg had not expressed himself prior to the October meeting. He told them Dr. Seaborg had not expressed himself, and this was the simple truth. For Seaborg had returned in time before the next meeting, just before Oppenheimer testified to the Joint Committee, and at this next meeting after his return Seaborg had preferred "not to say anything one way or the other on the hydrogen bomb issue."

Some months later, Strauss dropped a possibly cryptic remark in the course of an interview he gave to the *U.S. News and World Report* which was published on December 17, 1954. He said that the General Advisory Committee was opposed to the hydrogen bomb in 1949, "with the exception of one member who was abroad and whose opinion subsequently became known." To whom? Not to the Board in 1954, so far as appears; nor to the Commission, so far as appears. Oppenheimer's testimony that Seaborg preferred "not to say anything one way or the other on the hydrogen bomb issue" was not contradicted. Strauss must have meant that Seaborg expresssed his opinion in favor of the hydrogen bomb, as they all did, after Teller's invention in the spring of 1951, which was two years later.

There are two points to be made in this fifth instance. Did Oppenheimer try to suppress or had he simply forgotten Dr. Seaborg's letter? The answer to this seems to me obvious. There is no reason that I can see to believe he tried to suppress it. The other point is what I have just said about Oppenheimer's testimony before the Joint Committee. This Strauss does not mention.

The *sixth and last* instance was a contradiction between what Oppenheimer told the F.B.I. in 1950 and what he had told Colonel

Lansdale in 1943 about one Joseph Weinberg. Strauss said:

(6) In 1950, Dr. Oppenheimer told an agent of the Federal Bureau of Investigation that he had not known Joseph Weinberg to be a member of the Communist Party until that fact become public knowledge. Yet on September 12, 1943, Dr. Oppenheimer told Colonel Lansdale that Weinberg was a Communist Party member

Did Oppenheimer tell the F.B.I. in 1950 "that he had not known Joseph Weinberg to be a member of the Communist Party until that fact became public knowledge?" You and I have not got the F.B.I. report. Here is Oppenheimer's testimony:

A. I may have said I was not certain. My own recollection of it is contrary to this interview with Lansdale which is that the first time I was alerted to it was by the FBI in 1946. But it is clear that I learned something about it or it may be clear that I learned something about it during the war.
Q. Didn't you tell the FBI agent on that occasion that you did not know that Weinberg was a Communist until it became a matter of public knowledge?
A. I don't remember.
Q. You don't remember whether you told them that or not?
A. No.
Q. When did it become a matter of public knowledge?
A. It is still not.
Q. Long after 1943, wasn't it?
A. He still denied it and I don't quite know what this refers to.

Here, now, is Oppenheimer's testimony about what had been said in the 1946 interview:

Q. When did you first hear that Weinberg had been a Communist?
A. At the time of the 1946 interview with the FBI, the agents told me—they questioned me about Weinberg, Lomanitz and so on—and I said, "What is wrong with them?" He said, "There is a question of their membership in the Communist Party."
Q. Were you surprised to hear that?
A. A little bit but not much in the case of Weinberg.
Q. You are quite sure that is the first time you ever heard or had been told he was a Communist?
A. No. I had heard an earlier rumor.
Q. When?
A. When he came to Berkeley that he had been a member of the YCL, the Young Communist League in Madison, but it was hearsay.
Q. Who told you that?
A. I don't remember.
Q. Did you hear anything more about him at that time?
A. No.

Did Dr. Oppenheimer tell Colonel Lansdale on September 12, 1943, that Weinberg was a Communist Party member?

From the transcript of Oppenheimer's interview with Colonel Lansdale on page 875 which Strauss refers to it would appear that he did; and when Oppenheimer was cross-examined on this passage he said, "So it appears."

But a little later on in the interview, on page 882 of the transcript, comes a passage which Robb did not quote to Oppenheimer and which Strauss did not mention. Here it is:

"L. Of course, you now know that Weinberg and Lomanitz are both members of the party and members of the union.
"O. I didn't know Weinberg was a member.
"L. Well, as a matter of fact, I don't either.
"O. I had a feeling of surprise * * *
"L. He's probably mixed up. He's close to Lomanitz who unquestionably is a member.

It is not clear whether Weinberg was a member of the Party or only of the Union or of both. The asterisks in this passage indicate a security omission, not my interruption.

Smyth says this contradiction is "dependent on a garbled transcript." Garbled or not in the transcript, it was certainly garbled by Strauss when he cited only the passage on page 875 and not also this passage which followed almost immediately on page 882.

There was good reason why the Commission would have done well to let Garrison and Davis argue the case to them. As soon as they saw General Nichols' report, they knew very well that it had raised new points and new charges against Oppenheimer. New, at any rate, in that they had not been thought "derogatory" enough to be included in Nichols' letter of December 23, 1953, which summed up all the information Nichols then had about Oppenheimer which seemed to him to warrant the Board's consideration. New, moreover, in that the Board had thought none of them worth mentioning. New enough to make it perilous to pass an *ex parte*, as the lawyers say, judgment on them.

Let Garrison and Davis argue them? The Commission should have shown them the report at once and asked them to argue at least these new charges. Of these six instances of "fundamental defects" in Oppenheimer's character only two had been presented and argued to the Board—the letter about Dr. Peters and the letter from Dr. Seaborg. The Chevalier incident had been given a new and different aspect. Nichols had raised the question of whether Oppenheimer had perjured himself. The three instances of conflicting testimony about Lomanitz, Lambert and Weinberg were all new. Two of them—the one about Lomanitz and the one about Weinberg—had been raised by Nichols as matters of "veracity." The third, about Lambert, was newly raised by the Commission itself.

Campbell, in his opinion, said that the brief submitted by Oppenheimer's counsel "contains no new evidence." No, it did not. What was new was contained in General Nichols' report, on which the Commission leaned so heavily. Indeed, Campbell remarked that General Nichols had "even strengthened the findings of the Personnel Security Board." Yet Campbell, though he was stickling for procedure, announced that he had opposed giving Garrison permission to file even a brief.

It is joking at justice to say that a man has been represented by counsel when a case is decided on charges which his counsel is not allowed to argue.

Dr. Oppenheimer's persistent and willful disregard for the obligations of security is evidenced by his obstruction of inquiries by security officials. In the Chevalier incident, Dr. Oppenheimer was questioned in 1943 by Colonel Pash, Colonel Lansdale, and General Groves about the attempt to obtain information from him on the atomic bomb project in the interest of the Soviet Government. He had waited 8 months before mentioning the occurrence to the proper authorities. Thereafter for almost 4 months Dr. Oppenheimer refused to name the individual who had approached him. Under oath he now admits that his refusal to name the individual impeded the Government's investigation of espionage. The record shows other instances where Dr. Oppenheimer has refused to answer inquiries of Federal officials on security matters or has been deliberately misleading.

So much for what Strauss and with him a majority of the Commission believed enough to show a "fundamental defect" in Oppenheimer's character.

The other leg on which the Commission stood was Oppenheimer's "associations."

"Associations" is a factor which, under the law, must be considered by the Commission. Dr. Oppenheimer's close association with Communists is another part of the pattern of his disregard of the obligations of security.

Dr. Oppenheimer, under oath, admitted to the Gray Board that from 1937 to at least 1942 he made regular and substantial contributions in cash to the Communist Party. He has admitted that he was a "fellow traveler" at least until 1942. He admits that he attended small evening meetings at private homes at which most, if not all, of the others present were Communist Party members. He was in contact with officials of the Communist Party, some of whom had been engaged in espionage. His activities were of such a nature that these Communists looked upon him as one of their number.

However, Dr. Oppenheimer's early Communist associations are not in themselves a controlling reason for our decision.

They take on importance in the context of his persistent and continuing association with Communists, including his admitted meetings with Haakon Chevalier in Paris as recently as last December—the same individual who had been intermediary for the Soviet Consulate in 1943.

This remark, that Chevalier was "the same individual who had been intermediary for the Soviet Consulate in 1943," belies what

Strauss had said a few paragraphs back: "It is not clear today whether the account Dr. Oppenheimer gave to Colonel Pash . . . is the true version." Or else it shows that what Strauss really meant was that they thought it was the true version, though they did not say so. For what Oppenheimer told Pash is the only basis for Strauss's assertion that Chevalier was "intermediary for the Soviet Consulate." Oppenheimer, as we know, declared it was a lie. It was part of the "tissue of lies" he had told Pash. Nichols thought it was "a fair inference" that it was the truth. At first Strauss wouldn't say. Now he shows that he thinks it was true. It would have been more candid to have said so to begin with.

Oppenheimer's continuing association with Chevalier is the only one the Commission speaks about specifically. We are therefore justified in taking it, at any rate, as the most important and and the most derogatory. Strauss said:

> On February 25, 1950, Dr. Oppenheimer wrote a letter to Chevalier attempting "to clear the record with regard to your alleged involvement in the atom business." Chevalier used this letter in connection with his application to the State Department for a United States passport. Later that year Chevalier came and stayed with Dr. Oppenheimer for several days at the latter's home. In December 1953, Dr. Oppenheimer visited with Chevalier privately on two occasions in Paris, and lent his name to Chevalier's dealings with the United States Embassy in Paris on a problem which, according to Dr. Oppenheimer, involved Chevalier's clearance. Dr. Oppenheimer admitted that today he has only a "strong guess" that Chevalier is not active in Communist Party affairs.
>
> These episodes separately and together present a serious picture. It is clear that for one who has had access for so long to the most vital defense secrets of the Government and who would retain such access if his clearance were continued, Dr. Oppenheimer has defaulted not once but many times upon the obligations that should and must be willingly borne by citizens in the national service.
>
> Concern for the defense and security of the United States requires that Dr. Oppenheimer's clearance should not be reinstated.
>
> Dr. J. Robert Oppenheimer is hereby denied access to restricted data.

You and I have gone pretty thoroughly into these three renewals or continuations of Oppenheimer's old friendship with Chevalier. We know all we can now expect to know about them. I think we shall agree that there is nothing even faintly derogatory about any of them, unless Chevalier is still Communistic. I am assuming that he once was, back in Oppenheimer's California days. But Strauss is taking it for granted that Chevalier still is.

Yet the only evidence Strauss gives that Chevalier still is a Communist, which is the only thing that would make these meetings "a serious picture," is "that today Oppenheimer has only a 'strong guess' that Chevalier is not active in Communist party affairs."

To be precise and complete, what Oppenheimer said under

questioning by Gray was this:

Q. Do you have any guess or knowledge as to whether Chevalier today is active in Communist Party affairs?
A. I have a strong, strong guess that he is not. I have no knowledge. His new wife is an extremely sensible, wholly un-Communist girl. The other person we saw together was a man who has become a violent anti-Communist and is now apolitical. I don't have knowledge.

Even if this were not Oppenheimer's way of making as strong an assertion as his scientific candor allowed him to make, it is no warrant at all for the A.E.C. to regard Chevalier as still Communistic or to regard Oppenheimer's meeting and seeing him as a derogatory association. It is, of course, possible that the F.B.I. files, to which Strauss had access and we have not, contain evidence which may support Strauss; and if so, the security regulations would prevent him from citing it. At any rate, there is no evidence that Chevalier is a member of the Party. Gray had equal access to the F.B.I. files, and Gray said distinctly to Dr. Rabi, "I don't know whether he [Chevalier] is a member of the Communist Party or not. It is conceivable that he might have been."

Oppenheimer's "early Communist associations are not in themselves a controlling reason for our decision," Strauss says. Their importance lies "in the context of his persistent and continuing association with Communists." But the only "continuing association with Communists" which the Commission cites is with Chevalier, and now it appears that the only reason to think Chevalier is still a Communist is that Oppenheimer cannot say of his own knowledge that he is not. Oppenheimer gave good reason for his belief that Chevalier is not. I don't see why this is not enough for Strauss, Zuckert and Campbell. It strikes me that they are as hard to convince one way as they are easy to convince the other way. What was it Swift said? "The most positive men are the most credulous." These three manage to be both credulous and incredulous at the same time on the same subject.

So much for the majority opinion, except for one thing. Strauss says, at the end of his opinion for the majority of the Commission, "It is clear that for one who has had access for so long to the most vital defense secrets of the Government and *who would retain such access if his clearance were continued . . .*" What I have italicized was strictly but only temporarily true. It was true when Strauss wrote it. It was true on June 29 when he released it for publication. It remained true for another two days. It would not have continued to be true after June 30 unless Oppenheimer's contract as adviser were then renewed. For Oppenheimer's access "to the most vital secrets" of the A.E.C. would then have ceased, unless his clearance were continued, which the Commission obviously did not intend to do. Strauss, Zuckert and Campbell are being no more candid with you and me than the Commission was in its reply to the Board's question of why the Commission did not use Oppenheimer simply as a consultant. Don't forget that Strauss would have been content if Oppenheimer had terminated his contract himself.

21. THE INDIVIDUAL OPINIONS

I WANT NOW to go on to the opinions of the individual commissioners, Zuckert's, Campbell's, Murray's independent opinions, and finally Smyth's dissent.

Zuckert joined in Strauss's opinion and he also wrote one of his own, as they all did. It begins:

1. BASIS OF AGREEING TO DENY ACCESS

In subscribing to the majority decision and the substance of the Commission opinion, I have considered the evidence as a whole and no single factor as decisive. For example, Dr. Oppenheimer's early Communist associations by themselves would not have led me to my conclusion. The more recent connections, such as those with Lomanitz and Bohm, would not have been decisive. The serious 1943 incident involving Chevalier would not have been conclusive, although most disturbing and certainly aggravated by the continuation of the relationship between Chevalier and Dr. Oppenheimer. Individual instances of lack of veracity, conscious disregard of security considerations, and obstruction of proper security inquiries would not have been decisive.

But when I see such a combination of seriously disturbing actions and events as are present in this case, then I believe the risk to security passes acceptable bounds. All these actions and events and the relation between them make no other conclusion possible, in my opinion, than to deny clearance to Dr. Oppenheimer.

There follow some additional observations of my own which I believe are pertinent in the consideration of this case and the problems underlying it.

It is a source of real sadness to me that my last act as a public official should be participation in the determination of this matter, involving as it does, an individual who has made a substantial contribution to the United States. This matter certainly reflects the difficult times in which we live.

2. "SECURITY" IN 1954

The fact is that this country is faced with a real menace to our national security which manifests itself in a great variety of ways. We are under the necessity of defending ourselves against a competent and ruthless force possessed of the great advantage that accompanies the initiative. There is no opportunity which this force would not exploit to weaken our courage and confuse our strength.

The degree of attention which Dr. Oppenheimer's status has evoked is indication of the extent to which this force has imposed upon us a new degree of intensity of concern with security. There has always been a recognition of the need for security precautions when war threatened or was actually in progress. It is new and disquieting that security must concern us so much in times that have so many of the outward indications of peace. Security must indeed become a daily concern in our lives as far as we can see ahead.

In this Nation, I believe we have really commenced to understand this only within the past 10 years. It would be unrealistic to imagine that in that brief period of time we could have acquired a well-rounded understanding, much less an acceptance, of the implications of such a change in our way of life. It will not prove easy to harmonize the requirements of security with such basic concepts as personal freedom. It will be a long and difficult process to construct a thoroughly articulated security system that will be effective in protecting strength and yet maintain the basic fabric of our liberties.

It is clear that one essential requirement of the struggle in which this Nation is engaged is that we be decisive and yet maintain a difficult balance in our actions. For example, we must maintain a positive armed strength, yet in such a manner that we do not impair our ability to support that strength. We must be vigilant to the dangers and deceits of militant communism without the hysteria that breeds witch hunts. We must strive to maintain that measure of discipline required by real and present-day danger without destroying such freedoms as the freedom of honest thought. Our Nation's problem is more difficult because of a fundamental characteristic of a democratic system: We seek to be a positive force without a dominated uniformity in thought and action dictated by a small group in power.

The decision in this particular matter before us must be made not in 1920 or 1930 or 1940. It has to be made in the year 1954 in the light of the necessities of today and, inevitably, with whatever limitations of viewpoint 1954 creates. One fact that gives me reassurance is that this decision was reached only after the most intensive and concerned study following a course of procedure which gave the most scrupulous attention to our ideas of justice and fair treatment.

The problem before this Commission is whether Dr. Oppenheimer's status as a consultant to the Atomic Energy Commission constitutes a security risk.

3. THE CONCEPT OF "SECURITY RISK"

One of the difficulties in the development of a healthy security system is the achievement of public understanding of the phrase "security risk." It has unfortunately acquired in many minds the connotation of active disloyalty. As a result, it is not realized that the determination of "security risk" must be applied to individuals where the circumstances may be considerably less derogatory than disloyalty. In the case of Dr. Oppenheimer, the evidence which convinced me that his employment was not warranted on security grounds did not justify an accusation of disloyalty.

The "security risk" concept has evolved in recent years as a part of our search for a security system which will add to the protection of the country. In that quest, certain limited guidelines have emerged. With respect to eligibility of people for sensitive positions in our Government we have said, in effect, that there must be a convincing showing that their employment in such positions will not constitute a risk to our security. Except in the clearest of cases, such as present Communist membership, for example, the determination may not be an easy one. In many cases, like the one before us, a complex qualitative determination is required. One inherent difficulty is that every human being is to some degree a security risk. So long as there are normal human feelings like pain, or emotions like love of family, everyone is to some degree vulnerable to influence, and thus a potential risk in some degree to our security.

Under our security system it is our duty to determine how much of a risk is involved in respect to any particular individual and then to determine whether that risk is worth taking in view of what is at stake and the job to be done. It is not possible, except in obvious cases, to determine in what precise manner our security might be endangered. The determination is rather an evaluation of the factors which tend to increase the chance that security might be endangered. Our experience has convinced us that certain types of association and defects of character can materially increase the risk to security.

Those factors—many of which are set forth in the majority opinion—are present in Dr. Oppenheimer's case to such an extent that I agree he is a security risk.

To me the most interesting part of Zuckert's opinion is what he said about the necessity of the proceedings. His reasons why Oppenheimer's contract as consultant was not "merely allowed to lapse when it expires on June 30th, and thereafter not use his services" are illuminating and important. They deserve grave consideration: Here they are:

4. POSSIBILITY OF AN ALTERNATIVE ACTION

There have been suggestions that there may be a possible alternative short of finding Dr. Oppenheimer a security risk. One possibility suggested was that the Commission might merely allow Dr. Oppenheimer's consultant's contract to lapse when it expires on June 30, 1954, and thereafter not use his services. I have given the most serious consideration to this possibility and have concluded that it is not practical.

The unique place that Dr. Oppenheimer has built for himself in the scientific world and as a top Government adviser make it necessary that there be a clear-cut determination whether he is to be given access to the security information within the jurisdiction of the Commission.

As a scientist, Dr. Oppenheimer's greatest usefulness has been as a scientific administrator and a scientific critic. He has been looked to for scientific judgment by people within the profession. He is a personality in whom students place particular reliance for leadership and inspiration. These qualities, coupled with a nature that enables him to keep in active touch with great numbers of people in the scientific professions, have given him a unique place in the scientific community.

The Commission's clearance has permitted Dr. Oppenheimer to carry out his role as an active consultant of scientists. For example, Los Alamos Laboratory reports on the most intimate details of the progress of the thermonuclear and fission programs have continued to flow to him. I would gather that these reports were sent to Dr. Oppenheimer because his leadership and scientific judgment were recognized, and it was felt that he should be kept intensively abreast of the development of the weapon art.

I think the Commission is clearly obligated to determine whether Dr. Oppenheimer may continue to carry out this function and whether scientists may continue to call upon him as they have in the past in regard to highly classified material.

In addition, the scope of Dr. Oppenheimer's activities as a top adviser to various agencies of Government on national security policies make imperative a determination of his security status.

After the development of the atomic bomb and the end of World War II, Dr. Oppenheimer was quite suddenly projected into a far more important capacity than he had held as a scientist and laboratory director at Los Alamos. He was given responsibilities for the formulation of international controls of atomic energy. His post as chairman of the General Advisory Committee and a host of other committees in the Defense Establishment made him an adviser on national security problems at the top level of Government. His advice was sought on many matters in which science or technical aspects of atomic energy were important, but important as incidentals and background. With his unique experience, his intellect, his breadth of interests and his articulateness it was almost inevitable that he was consulted on a growing number of national security policy matters. As a result, his degree of access to the detailed essentials of our most secret information was, in my opinion, among the greatest of any individuals in our Government. I doubt that there have been contemporaneously more than a handful of people at the highest levels who have possessed the amount of sensitive information which was given to Dr. Oppenheimer.

Since Dr. Oppenheimer's retirement from the General Advisory Committee he has been employed as a consultant to the Commission. It is true that since 1952 the Commission has used him very little. Commission clearance has, however, been a basis for other agencies using him in connection with delicate problems of national security. It is logical to expect that would continue. For example, the Commission has recently received a letter from Dr. DuBridge, Chairman of the Science Advisory Committee, Office of Defense Mobilization which says:

"Our Committee is planning to undertake during the coming months an intensive study of important matters related to national security on which Dr. Oppenheimer's knowledge and counsel will be of critical importance."

I believe that the outlined facts concerning Dr. Oppenheimer's activities in the scientific profession and employment by the Government demonstrate that the Commission could not decide the matter on any other basis than to grant or deny clearance. Any other action would merely postpone the problem. His activities cannot be compartmented to some particular area of scientific effort. It is only reasonable to expect that he would be used in connection with broad assignments such as he has had in the past. Inevitably the question would arise whether he should be given access to the most sensitive restricted data which is under the Commission's jurisdiction.

Therefore, there must be a determination as to his security status with respect to this data.

As Zuckert says, the A.E.C. had used Oppenheimer's services very little. When Oppenheimer left the General Advisory Committee in 1952 he was appointed consultant to the A.E.C., but his services were used by the Commission only half a dozen times. Nichols reported he had been used only two days—October 16 and 17, 1952—before the renewal of Oppenheimer's contract on June 30, 1953, and since then he had made only a trip to Sandia or Los Alamos in September 1953. Nichols doubted that the A.E.C., "even if the question of his security clearance had not arisen, would have utilized his services to a markedly greater extent during the next few years."

When Oppenheimer left the General Advisory Committee, Gordon Dean, then chairman of the A.E.C., wrote him a letter on October 15, 1952. Let us read it now while we are examining the Commission's decision in 1954.

"Dr. J. Robert Oppenheimer,
  "Institute for Advanced Study,
    "Princeton, N. J.

"Dear Oppy: I cannot let your departure from the General Advisory Committee go by without expressing again my deep appreciation for the time and talent which you have so generously devoted to the work of the committee, and for the immensely valuable contribution you have made to the atomic energy program during the period I have been associated with it and before.

"I know that you are as fully aware as I am of the assistance the General Advisory Committee has given to the Commission during these past 6 formative years, and of the great scientific and technical strides that have been made in that time. I sincerely hope that some day, when the ills of the world are sufficiently diminished, the complete story of this progress can be told, so that the contribution of you and your colleagues may find its rightful place in the chronicle of our times.

"May I say that I shall always be grateful for your past work on behalf of the program, and for your willingness to continue to advise the Commission on a consultative basis.

"With every good wish,
  "Sincerely,

                              "Gordon Dean, Chairman."

"Someday . . ." Dean says, "the contribution of you and your colleagues may find its rightful place in the chronicle of our times." Smyth, in his dissent, refers to the investigation of the past fifteen years of Oppenheimer's life "supplemented by enthusiastic amateur help from powerful personal enemies." The investigation we now have. We must wait for the chronicle.

Oppenheimer's contract was renewed in June of 1953, while Dean was still chairman. Then, as we have seen, early in July, a few days after Strauss succeeded Dean, the Commission "initiated steps to organize the removal of classified documents" from Oppenheimer's custody. Six months later, in December, his clearance was suspended and these proceedings were started.

The A.E.C. did not want Oppenheimer's services. If this were the whole story, the A.E.C. could have simply dropped him, let his contract lapse and engaged someone else in his place. But the scientific profession looked to Oppenheimer as a critic. Students relied on him for leadership and inspiration. Various government agencies turned to him as a top adviser on national-security policies. Wilson, the Secretary of Defense, to be sure, had overridden Dr. Whitman's recommendation and announced, even before the Board made its decision, that he would not have anything to do with Oppenheimer; but here is Dr. DuBridge, the chairman of the Science Advisory Committee of the Department of Defense, asking for Oppenheimer's help in "important matters related to national security" where it would be "of critical importance."

For all these purposes, his access to restricted data had been, of course, essential, and so it would continue to be. Even if the A.E.C. were to let Oppenheimer's contract lapse and the A.E.C. take on another adviser, "inevitably the question would arise whether he should be given access to the most sensitive restricted data which is under the Commission's jurisdiction."

So nothing less than the determination that Oppenheimer is a security risk would prevent others from using the advice and the services which the A.E.C. not only did not itself want but thought other government departments, and the scientific world, had better not have. And if it were done when it is done, then it were well it were done quickly. For otherwise they would never give up asking.

Did the A.E.C. want to make the decision before some other government agency—or some scientific institution or some university wishing to use Oppenheimer's services—asked that Oppenheimer be given access to some of the A.E.C.'s restricted data? Possibly. It is also possible that the A.E.C. felt it must act before Oppenheimer's contract ran out, because after that the A.E.C. would lose jurisdiction under the security regulations to act at all. This would explain why the Commission did not wait two days to let it run out.

And yet I cannot quite get out of my head a picture of the lady of the house who doesn't like her cook, or doesn't like her cooking, but at the same time doesn't quite dare to give her notice. Or perhaps it's rather a grand lady of the house, and it's a chef. But someone opportunely tells her that her chef drinks or at least used to and may still be drinking. She goes to her husband and says, "If this is true, what about your wine cellar?" He expresses concern, and so she tells the chef she cannot have a cook who drinks, and she fires him for cause.

This may be as unjust as it is invidious. The Commission could no more properly funk a decision while it had jurisdiction to make one than Oppenheimer could have accepted Strauss's offer to resign before the charges were brought against him, or any more than Oppenheimer's counsel could properly have loitered through an intermediate board of review while the Commission's jurisdiction and power to make a decision were running out.

At the same time, the A.E.C. may very well have agreed with what Teller said to the Board. You may remember. Gray asked him, "Do you feel that it would endanger the common defense and security to grant clearance to Dr. Oppenheimer?"

After a somewhat guarded statement that he believed Oppenheimer's character to be "such that he would not knowingly and willingly do anything that is designed to endanger the safety of this country," Teller replied in this way: "If it is a question of wisdom and judgment, as demonstrated by actions since 1945, then I would say one would be wiser not to grant clearance. I must say that I am myself a little bit confused on this issue, particularly as it refers to a person of Oppenheimer's prestige and influence. May I limit myself to these comments?"

Gray: "Yes."

Everyone, it seemed to the A.E.C., would be better off with a different adviser, and the A.E.C. took it upon itself to act for the whole Administration. After all, it was the President himself who had "directed that, pending a security review of the material in the file, a blank wall be placed between Dr. Oppenheimer and any secret data and that, without prejudging the outcome, established procedures should be followed." (A.E.C. statement of April 13, 1954.) Zuckert said:

> All of the facts concerning Dr. Oppenheimer's activities, scientific and governmental, and the consequent access to vital information emphasize the degree of his security responsibility.
>
> For the reasons outlined in the first paragraphs of these comments, I conclude that he falls substantially below the standard required by that responsibility. There seems to me no possible alternative to denying Dr. Oppenheimer clearance.

5. THERMONUCLEAR CONTROVERSY DISREGARDED

> There is one final comment which I should add. My decision in this matter was influenced neither by the actions nor by the attitudes of Dr. Oppenheimer concerning the development of thermonuclear weapons. Nor did I consider material any advice given by Dr. Oppenheimer in his capacity as a top level consultant on national security affairs.
>
> In my judgment, it was proper to include Dr. Oppenheimer's activities regarding the thermonuclear program as part of the derogatory allegations that initiated these proceedings. Allegations had been made that Dr. Oppenheimer was improperly motivated.
>
> The Gray Board, although doubting the complete veractiy of Dr. Oppenheimer's explanations, found that these most serious allegations were not substantiated. I have carefully reviewed the evidence and concur in the finding.

We owe to Campbell an admirable example of the cookbook school of administrative and judicial procedure, the school of Follow the Recipe. You can't go wrong if you just follow the recipe. Do you remember how the A.E.C. went about it in 1947? Lilienthal belonged to the other school, the school of Taste before You Serve.

The Commission, Campbell said, had only "an appellate responsibility." He said, "If the security system of the United States Government is to be successfully operated, the recommendations of Personnel Security Boards must be honored in the absence of compelling circumstances. If the General Manager of the Atomic Energy Commission is to function properly, his decisions must be upheld unless there can be shown new evidence, violations of procedure, or other substantial reasons why they should be reversed."

There is much to be said for routine, as every administrator knows. There is even more to be said in favor of a respect for procedure, as every lawyer knows. Neither the administrator nor the lawyer is always, or usually even enough, aware of what a mess they can make of things beyond their grasp. "Ah, but a man's reach should exceed his grasp, Or what's a heaven for?" Browning is still right.

By far the most important and the most interesting of the five opinions—beyond the present case in its reasoning—is Murray's.

Murray concurred in the Commission's decision. "However, I have reached this conclusion by my own reasoning which does not coincide with the majority of the Commission." For he had reached the conclusion that Oppenheimer was "disloyal." He reached it in his own way. I think only Borden and Griggs thought Oppenheimer was "disloyal," each in his own fashion. Murray's way to the same conclusion has no more in common with theirs than my opinion, and perhaps yours, has with his.

> I conclude, therefore, that serious charges were brought against Dr. Oppenheimer; that he was afforded every opportunity to refute them; that a board was appointed, composed of men of the highest honor and integrity, and that in their majority opinion Dr. Oppenheimer did not refute the serious charges which faced him; that the record was reviewed by the General Manager, keenly aware of his serious responsibility in this matter, and that he concurred, and even strengthened the findings of the Personnel Security Board.
>
> If the security system of the United States Government is to be successfully operated, the recommendations of personnel security boards must be honored in the absence of compelling circumstances. If the General Manager of the Atomic Energy Commission is to function properly, his decisions must be upheld unless there can be shown new evidence, violations of procedures, or other substantial reasons why they should be reversed.
>
> Therefore, I voted to reaffirm the majority recommendation of the Personnel Security Board and to uphold the decision of the General Manager. Clearance should be denied to Dr. Oppenheimer.

Before Murray defines loyalty he discards a number of considerations. One is Oppenheimer's opposition to the hydrogen-bomb program. Oppenheimer was in error, he said, and the security interests of the United States may have been adversely affected, but they were errors of judgment. Another is Oppenheimer's moral scruples. Oppenheimer, he said, was "quite right in advancing moral reasons for his attitude to the hydrogen bomb program. A scientist is a man before he is a technician." Still another is Oppenheimer's lack of enthusiasm. Murray said that the Government may command a citizen's services, "but Government cannot command a citizen's enthusiasms for any particular program or policy projected in the national interests." Murray makes it quite clear that Oppenheimer's attitude toward the hydrogen-bomb program does not warrant the denial of security clearance. It would be hard to be clearer or more eloquent.

> There is a preliminary question. It concerns Dr. Oppenheimer's opposition to the hydrogen bomb program and his influence on the development of the program. On this count I do not find evidence that would warrant the denial to Dr. Oppenheimer of a security clearance.
>
> I find that the record clearly proves that Dr. Oppenheimer's judgment was

in error in several respects. It may well be that the security interests of the United States were adversely affected in consequence of his judgment. But it would be unwise, unjust, and dangerous to admit, as a principle, that errors of judgment, especially in complicated situations, can furnish valid grounds for later indictments of a man's loyalty, character, or status as a security risk. It has happened before in the long history of the United States that the national interests were damaged by errors of judgment committed by Americans in positions of responsibility. But these men did not for this reason cease to merit the trust of their country.

Dr. Oppenheimer advanced technical and political reasons for his attitude to the hydrogen-bomb program. In both respects he has been proved wrong; nothing further need be said.

He also advanced moral reasons. Here two comments are necessary. First, in deciding matters of national policy, it is imperative that the views of experts should always be carefully weighed and never barred from discussion or treated lightly. However, Dr. Oppenheimer's opinions in the field of morality possess no special authority. Second, even though Dr. Oppenheimer is not an expert in morality, he was quite right in advancing moral reasons for his attitude to the hydrogen bomb program. The scientist is a man before he is a technician. Like every man, he ought to be alert to the moral issues that arise in the course of his work. This alertness is part of his general human and civic responsibilities, which go beyond his responsibilities as a scientist. When he has moral doubts, he has a right to voice them. Furthermore, it must be firmly maintained, as a principle both of justice and of religious freedom, that opposition to governmental policies, based on sincerely held moral opinions, need not make a man a security risk.

The issue of Dr. Oppenheimer's lack of enthusiasm for the hydrogen bomb program has been raised; so, too, has the issue of his failure to communicate to other scientists his abandonment of his earlier opposition to the program. Here an important distinction is in order. Government may command a citizen's service in the national interest. But Government cannot command a citizen's enthusiasm for any particular program or policy projected in the national interests. The citizen remains free to be enthusiastic or not at the impulse of his own inner convictions. These convictions remain always immune from governmental judgment or control. Lack of enthusiasm is not a justiciable matter.

The point that I shall later make in another connection is pertinent here. The crisis in which we live, and the security regulations which it has rendered necessary in the interests of the common good, have made it difficult to insure that justice is done to the individual. In this situation it is more than ever necessary to protect at every point the distinction between the external forum of action and omission, and the internal forum of thought and belief. A man's service to his country may come under judgment; it lies in the external forum. A man's enthusiasm for service, or his lack of it, do not come under judgment; they are related to the internal forum of belief, and are therefore remote from all the agencies of law.

The citizen's duty remains always that of reasonable service, just as the citizen's right remains always that of free opinion. There is no requirement, inherent in the idea of civic duty, that would oblige a man to show enthusiasm for particular governmental policies, or to use his influence in their favor, against his own convictions; just as there is no permission, inherent in the idea of intellectual freedom, that would allow a man to block established governmental policies, against the considered judgment of their responsible authors.

The conclusion is that the evidence with regard to Dr. Oppenheimer's attitude toward the hydrogen bomb program, when it is rightly interpreted in the light of sound democratic principles, does not warrant the denial to Dr. Oppenheimer of a security clearance.

Then Murray turns to what is to him the primary question:

The primary question concerns Dr. Oppenheimer's loyalty. This idea must be carefully defined, first, in general, and second, in concrete and contemporary terms.

The idea of loyalty has emotional connotations; it is related to the idea of love, a man's love of his country. However, the substance of loyalty does not reside solely in feeling or sentiment. It cannot be defined solely in terms of love.

The English word "loyal" comes to us from the Latin adjective "legalis," which means "according to the law." In its substance the idea of loyalty is related to the idea of law. To be loyal, in Webster's definition, is to be "faithful to the lawful government or to the sovereign to whom one is subject." This faithfulness is a matter of obligation; it is a duty owed. The root of the obligation and duty is the lawfulness of the government, rationally recognized and freely accepted by the citizens.

The American citizen recognizes that his Government, for all its imperfections, is a government under law, of law, by law; therefore he is loyal to it. Furthermore, he recognizes that his Government, because it is lawful, has the right and the responsibility to protect itself against the action of those who would subvert it. The cooperative effort of the citizen with the rightful action of American Government in its discharge of this primary responsibility also belongs to the very substance of American loyalty. This is the crucial principle in the present case.

Murray's etymology makes his thesis clear, but not more convincing than etymology can. No more than the origin of the word itself, which etymologically—*etymos* in Greek means "true"—means the science of true meaning, which does not carry its own conviction. A man is neither a villain nor a hero simply because he looks like his great-grandfather who was one or the other or even both.

Our word *loyal* does indeed derive from the Latin word *legalis,* but it comes to us by way of the French, who endowed it with a richer and a different meaning than our other word—its doublet, that is—the word *legal,* which we took directly from the Latin. It is a pity to reduce the distinction—which itself is another doublet with two meanings—either reduce it or efface it, as Murray does when he says that a man cannot be "loyal" when he does not obey the law. Devotion is not the same thing as obedience. Murray is asking too much of the meaning of the word *loyalty,* and at the same time too little. He is tucking the blanket of its meaning around our feet and pulling it down off our chest. A loyalty which devours every other duty will soon devour itself.

Murray goes on: "This general definition of loyalty assumes a sharper meaning within the special conditions of the present crisis." This, Murray says, is "the fact of the Communist conspiracy," which "has put to American government and to the American people a special problem."

It is the problem of protecting the national security, internal and external, against the insidious attack of its Communist enemy. On the domestic front this problem has been met by the erection of a system of laws and Executive orders designed to protect the lawful Government of the United States against the hidden machinery of subversion.

The American citizen in private life, the man who is not engaged in governmental service, is not bound by the requirements of the security system. However, those American citizens who have the privilege of participating in the operations of Government, especially in sensitive agencies, are necessarily subject to this special system of law. Consequently, their faithfulness to the lawful Government of the United States, that is to say their loyalty, must be judged by the standard of their obedience to security regulations. Dr. Oppenheimer was subject to the security system which applies to those engaged in the atomic energy program. The measure of his obedience to the requirements of this system is the decisive measure of his loyalty to his lawful Government. No lesser test will settle the question of his loyalty.

Murray made certain "distinctions and qualifications." Nevertheless, there remained Murray's "stern test of loyalty," and "Dr. Oppenheimer failed the test."

In order to clarify this issue of the meaning of loyalty, the following considerations are necessary. First, the atomic energy program is absolutely vital to the survival of the Nation. Therefore the security regulations which surround it are intentionally severe. No violations can be countenanced. Moreover, the necessity for exact fidelity to these regulations increases as an individual oper-operates in more and more sensitive and secret areas of the program. Where responsibility is highest, fidelity should be most perfect.

Second, this security system is not perfect in its structure or in its mode of operation. Perfection would be impossible. We are still relatively unskilled in the methods whereby we may effectively block the conspiratorial efforts of the Communist enemy without damage to our own principles. Moreover, the operation of the system is in the hands of fallible men. It is therefore right and necessary that the system should be under constant scrutiny. Those who are affected by the system have a particular right to criticize it. But they have no right to defy or disregard it.

Third, the premise of the security system is not a dogma but a fact, the fact of the Communist conspiracy. The system itself is only a structure of law, not a set of truths. Therefore this system of law is not, and must not be allowed to become, a form of thought control. It restricts the freedom of association of the governmental employee who is subject to it. It restricts his movements and activities. It restricts his freedom of utterance in matters of security import, not in other matters. It restricts his freedom of personal and family life. It makes special demands on his character, moral virtue, and spirit of sacrifice. But no part of the security system imposes any restrictions on his mind. No law or Executive order inhibits the freedom of the mind to search for the truth in all the great issues that today confront the political and moral intelligence of America. In particular, no security regulations set any limits to the free-ranging scientific intelligence in its search for the truths of nature and for the techniques of power over nature. If they were to do so, the result would be disastrous; for the freedom of science is more than ever essential to the freedom of the American people.

Fourth, the preservation of the ordered freedom of American life requires the cooperation of all American citizens with their Government. The indispensable condition of this cooperation is a spirit of mutual trust and confidence. This trust and confidence must in a special sense obtain between governmental officials and scientists, for their partnership in the atomic-energy program and in other programs is absolutely essential to the security interests of the United States. It would be lamentable if conscientious enforcement of security regulations were to become a danger to the atmosphere of trust and confidence which alone can sustain this partnership. In order to avert this danger, there must be on the part of Government a constant concern for justice to the individual, together with a concern for the high interests of the national community. On the part of scientists there should be a generous disposition to endure with patient understanding the distasteful restrictions which the security system imposes on them.

Finally, it is essential that in the operation of the security system every effort should be made to safeguard the principle that no American citizen is to be penalized for anything except action or omission contrary to the well-defined interests of the United States. However stringent the need for a security system, the system cannot be allowed to introduce into American jurisprudence that hateful concept, the "crime of opinion." The very security of America importantly lies in the steady guaranty, even in a time of crisis, of the citizen's right to freedom of opinion and of honest and responsible utterance. The present time of crisis intensifies the civic duty of obedience to the lawful government in the crucial area of security regulations. But it does not justify abridgment of the civic right of dissent. Government may penalize disobedience in action or omission. It may not penalize dissent in thought and utterance.

When all these distinctions and qualifications have been made, the fact remains that the existence of the security regulations which surround the atomic-energy program puts to those who participate in the program a stern test of loyalty.

Dr. Oppenheimer failed the test. The record of his actions reveals a frequent and deliberate disregard of those security regulations which restrict a man's associations. He was engaged in a highly delicate area of security; within this area he occupied a most sensitive position. The requirement that a man in this position should relinquish the right to the complete freedom of association that would be his in other circumstances is altogether a reasonable and necessary requirement. The exact observance of this requirement is in all cases essential to the integrity of the security system. It was particularly essential in the case of Dr. Oppenheimer.

It will not do to plead that Dr. Oppenheimer revealed no secrets to the Communists and fellow travelers with whom he chose to associate. What is incompatible with obedience to the laws of security is the associations themselves, however innocent in fact. Dr. Oppenheimer was not faithful to the restrictions on the associations of those who come under the security regulations.

There is a further consideration, not unrelated to the foregoing. Those who stand within the security system are not free to refuse their cooperation with the workings of the system, much less to confuse or obstruct them, especially by falsifications and fabrications. It is their duty, at times an unpleasant duty, to cooperate with the governmental officials who are charged with the enforcement of security regulations. This cooperation should be active and honest. If this manner of cooperation is not forthcoming, the security system itself, and therefore the interests of the United States which it protects, inevitably suffer. The record proves Dr. Oppenheimer to have been seriously deficient in his cooperation with the workings of the security system. This defect too is a defect of loyalty to the lawful government in its reasonable efforts to preserve itself in its constitutional existence. No matter how high a man stands in the service of his country he still stands under the law. To permit a man in a position of the highest trust to set himself above any of the laws of security would be to invite the destruction of the whole security system.

In conclusion, the principle that has already been stated must be recalled for the sake of emphasis. In proportion as a man is charged with more and more critical responsibilities, the more urgent becomes the need for that full and exact fidelity to the special demands of security laws which in this over-shadowed day goes by the name of loyalty. So too does the need for cooperation with responsible security officers.

Dr. Oppenheimer occupied a position of paramount importance; his relation to the security interests of the United States was the most intimate possible one. It was reasonable to expect that he would manifest the measure of cooperation appropriate to his responsibilities. He did not do so. It was reasonable to expect that he would be particularly scrupulous in his fidelity to security regulations. These regulations are the special test of the loyalty of the American citizen who serves his Government in the sensitive area of the Atomic Energy program. Dr. Oppenheimer did not meet this decisive test. He was disloyal.

I conclude that Dr. Oppenheimer's access to restricted data should be denied.

I do not see how this aspect of the security system, which Gray and Morgan thought "perhaps has had insufficient public attention," could be justified more clearly or more eloquently. Murray is eloquent and he has done his best. It may be my fault, and perhaps yours too, if we still do not really understand. I am not saying that either of us should agree. We may still feel that we need not call a man a robber just because he isn't a cop.

It was my first thought that Murray was smelling brimstone and requiring of loyalty what I think the Church requires of faith. If this be so, of course Murray is right, and Oppenheimer should be excommunicated.

My next thought was also theological. "'Tis rank idolatry, To make the service greater than the God." The identification of the means with the end is always dangerous, particularly when there is only one end and many means. Any absolute is precarious, the more so when we are not dealing with an end but with a means to that end, for one means may have to be reconciled or compromised with others.

Perhaps I am getting only more confused, and yet I know that we do not hire a scientist or a wise man to be a policeman, any more than we ask every G.I. to be an M.P. We want the scientist to think. We want the soldier to fight. We beware of looking too narrowly or myopically at any of their other activities unless they interfere with their work or jeopardize us unnecessarily.

The only fault I have to find with idolatry is that it distracts us from other things. Whether those other things are better than Murray's absolute loyalty I do not know. I do know that loyalty transcends idolatry. Murray would have loyalty stoop to obedience. I would ask it to look higher.

What more is there to be said? But are you not reminded of what the Earl of Warwick—Shaw's Warwick in his *Saint Joan*—said when his chaplain called Bishop Peter Cauchon a traitor? The earl apologized. "My lord, I apologize to you for the word used by Messire John de Stogumber. It does not mean in England what it does in France. In your language traitor means betrayer: one is perfidious, treacherous, unfaithful, disloyal. In our country it means simply one who is not wholly devoted to our English interests." "I am sorry," the bishop said. "I did not understand."

22. SMYTH'S DISSENT

SMYTH dissented. When the decision of the Commission was announced and the reporters came to Oppenheimer for a statement, he referred them to Smyth's dissenting opinion. I won't ask you to read Smyth's summary of those incidents on which the Commission relied. You and I have already gone through the evidence in more detail. Here is the beginning and the end of Smyth's dissent:

I dissent from the action of the Atomic Energy Commission in the matter of Dr. J. Robert Oppenheimer. I agree with the "clear conclusion" of the Gray Board that he is completely loyal and I do not believe he is a security risk. It is my opinion that his clearance for access to restricted data should be restored.

In a case such as this, the Commission is required to look into the future. It must determine whether Dr. Oppenheimer's continued employment by the Government of the United States is in the interests of the people of the United States. This prediction must balance his potential contribution to the positive strength of the country against the possible danger that he may weaken the country by allowing important secrets to reach our enemies.

Since Dr. Oppenheimer is one of the most knowledgable and lucid physicists we have, his services could be of great value to the country in the future. Therefore, the only question being determined by the Atomic Energy Commission is whether there is a possibility that Dr. Oppenheimer will intentionally or unintentionally reveal secret information to persons who should not have it. To me, this is what is meant within our security system by the term security risk. Character and associations are important only insofar as they bear on the possibility that secret information will be improperly revealed.

In my opinion the most important evidence in this regard is the fact that there is no indication in the entire record that Dr. Oppenheimer has ever divulged any secret information. The past 15 years of his life have been investigated and reinvestigated. For much of the last 11 years he has been under actual surveillance, his movements watched, his conversations noted, his mail and telephone calls checked. This professional review of his actions has been supplemented by enthusiastic amateur help from powerful personal enemies.

After reviewing the massive dossier and after hearing some forty witnesses, the Gray Board reported on May 27, 1954, that Dr. Oppenheimer "seems to have had a high degree of discretion reflecting an unusual ability to keep to himself vital secrets." My own careful reading of the complete dossier and of the testimony leads me to agree with the Gray Board on this point. I am confident that Dr. Oppenheimer will continue to keep to himself all the secrets with which he is entrusted.

The most important allegations of the General Manager's letter of December 23 related to Dr. Oppenheimer's conduct in the so-called H-bomb program. I am not surprised to find that the evidence does not support these allegations in any way. The history of Dr. Oppenheimer's contributions to the development of nuclear weapons stands untarnished.

It is clear that Dr. Oppenheimer's past associations and activites are not newly discovered in any substantial sense. They have been known for years to responsible authorities who have never been persuaded that they rendered Dr. Oppenheimer unfit for public service. Many of the country's outstanding men have expressed their faith in his integrity.

In spite of all this, the majority of the Commission now concludes that Dr. Oppenheimer is a security risk. I cannot accept this conclusion or the fear behind it. In my opinion the conclusion cannot be supported by a fair evaluation of the evidence.

Those who do not accept this view cull from the record of Dr. Oppenheimer's active life over the past 15 years incidents which they construe as "proof of fundamental defects in his character" and as alarming associations. I shall summarize the evidence on these incidents in order that their proper significance may be seen.

Smyth summarizes the Chevalier incident, Oppenheimer's continuing associations, the Peters' letter, the Lomanitz deferment, the obstruction of security officers, and the Seaborg letter. He goes on to conclude:

The instances that I have described constitute the whole of the evidence extracted from a lengthy record to support the severe conclusions of the majority that Dr. Oppenheimer has "given proof of fundamental defects in his character" and of "persistent continuing associations." Any implication that these are illustrations only and that further substantial evidence exists in the investigative files to support these charges is unfounded.

With the single exception of the Chevalier incident, the evidence relied upon is thin, whether individual instances are considered separately or in combination. All added together, with the Chevalier incident included, the evidence is singularly unimpressive when viewed in the perspective of the 15 years of active life from which it is drawn. Fed men could survive such a period of investigation and interrogation without having many of their actions misinterpreted or misunderstood.

To be effective a security system must be realistic. In the words of the Atomic Energy Commission security criteria:

"The facts of each case must be carefully weighed and determination made in the light of all the information presented, whether favorable or unfavorable. The judgment of responsible persons as to the integrity of the individuals should be considered. The decision as to security clearance is an overall, commonsense judgment, made after consideration of all the relevant information as to whether or not there is risk that the granting of security clearance would endanger the common defense or security."

Application of this standard of overall commonsense judgment to the whole record destroys any pattern of suspicious conduct or catalog of falsehoods and evasions, and leaves a picture of Dr. Oppenheimer as an able, imaginative human being with normal human weaknesses and failings. In my opinion the conclusion drawn by the majority from the evidence is so extreme as to endanger the security system.

If one starts with the assumption that Dr. Oppenheimer is disloyal, the incidents which I have recounted may arouse suspicion. However, if the entire record is read objectively, Dr. Oppenheimer's loyalty and trustworthiness emerge clearly and the various disturbing incidents are shown in their proper light as understandable and unimportant.

The "Chevalier incident" remains reprehensile; but in fairness and on all of the evidence, this one admitted and regretted mistake made many years ago does not predominate in my overall judgment of Dr. Oppenheimer's character and reliability. Unless one confuses a manner of expression with candor, or errors in recollection with lack of veracity, Dr. Oppenheimer's testimony before the Gray Board has the ring of honesty. I urge thoughtful citizens to examine this testimony for themselves, and not be content with summaries or with extracts quoted out of context.

With respect to the alleged disregard of the security system, I would suggest that the system itself is nothing to worship. It is a necessary means to an end.

Its sole purpose, apart from the prevention of sabotage, is to protect secrets. If a man protects the secrets he has in his hands and his head, he has shown essential regard for the security system.

In addition, cooperation with security officials in their legitimate activities is to be expected of private citizens and Government employees. The security system has, however, neither the responsibility nor the right to dictate every detail of a man's life. I frankly do not understand the charge made by the majority that Dr. Oppenheimer has shown a persistent and willful disregard for the obligations of security, and that therefore he should be declared a security risk. No gymnastics of rationalization allow me to accept this argument. If in any recent instances, Dr. Oppenheimer has misunderstood his obligation to security, the error is occasion for reproof but not for a finding that he should be debarred from serving his country. Such a finding extends the concept of "security risk" beyond its legitimate justification and constitutes a dangerous precedent.

In these times, failure to employ a man of great talents may impair the strength and power of this country. Yet I would accept this loss if I doubted the loyalty of Dr. Oppenheimer or his ability to hold his tongue. I have no such doubts.

I conclude that Dr. Oppenheimer's employment " will not endanger the common defense and security" and will be "clearly consistent with the interests of the national security." I prefer the positive statement that Dr. Oppenheimer's further employment will continue to strengthen the United States.

I therefore have voted to reinstate Dr. Oppenheimer's clearance.

You see, Smyth, like Evans, would not let his best judgment be hobbled and brought to a halt by a doubt. Smyth, too, preferred to follow the Commission's rules and its criteria, which the Commission had made for its own staff and which it had retained through the vicissitudes of the Executive Orders. He too applied an "over-all common-sense judgment." He counted the cost against the risk. He accepted the responsibility which "men of practical affairs" always have to accept. Smyth and Evans followed the rules which the Atomic Energy Commission had told them to follow and these rules bade them be themselves. They refused to be imposed on by a fabricated doubt. They refused to be intimidated by a system.

23. CONCLUSION

"... but man, proud man
Dress'd in a little brief authority,
Most ignorant of what he's most assur'd,
His glassy essence, like an angry ape,
Plays such fantastic tricks before high heaven
As make the angels weep; who, with our spleens,
Would all themselves laugh mortal."

I HAVE SAID that our security system was on trial here. Indeed it is. If there is any excuse, any justification for this decision, it lies in the worship of a system which stultifies our good judgment by subjecting it to the artificial presumption of a doubt. A great and responsible nation, the greatest and therefore the most responsible, is telling itself to fear itself, advising itself to stand on suspicions, to mistake caution for courage and to take prudence to be better than wisdom.

We are telling ourselves that it is dangerous to be ourselves. This is the best I can see that can be said for what Gray and Morgan on the Board did reluctantly, or for what Strauss, Zuckert, Campbell and Murray on the Commission did with a zeal which disregarded their own rules.

Do you remember what Joan's ghost said to Charles the Seventh? In Shaw's epilogue, Charles was telling Joan that her case was being tried over again, as in the chronicles of time Oppenheimer's case will be. Charles was telling Joan that her judges were to be charged with malice and other things besides. Joan would have none of that. Joan said—and her reply was charitable and precise—"Not they. They were as honest a lot of poor fools as ever burned their betters."

Index

A

Acheson, Dean G., 43, 156
Acheson-Lilienthal report, 34, 160, 179
Addis, Thomas, 23, 28, 49, 50, 134
Adelson, David, 23, 24, 28, 29, 51, 53, 114
Adrian, E. D., *quoted*, 157
Advanced Study, Institute for, 8, 34, 43
Alexander, Archibald, 107
Alvarez, Luis W., 142, 159; *quoted*, 124
American-Russian Institute, 22, 48, 49
Architects, Engineers, Chemists, and Technicians, Federation of (FAECT), 32–33, 65, 67, 69, 70, 71
Arts, Sciences and Professions, Independent Citizens Committee of (ICCASP), 24, 35, 53, 55, 114–16
Atomic Energy, Joint Committee of Congress on, 18, 38, 136, 146, 174
Atomic Energy Act (1946), 11, 13, 22, 45, 56, 95, 138, 242; *quoted*, 10
Atomic Energy Commission, United Nations, 34, 207
Atomic Scientists, Bulletin of the, 157

B

Bacher, Robert F., 39, 95, 98, 175, 176, 240, 245; testimony, 212
Barnard, Chester I., 160
Baruch, Bernard, 34, 97, 160, 199
Beckerly, James G., *quoted*, 190
Bethe, Hans A., 30, 39, 128, 130, 131, 132, 163, 164, 176, 177, 229, 250; testimony, 162, 208

Bohm, David, 24, 32, 51, 52, 119–20, 123, 134, 185, 216, 234, 260
Bohr, Niels, 14, 16, 103, 107
Borden, William L., 20–21, 46, 123, 144, 159, 182, 183, 241, 267; letter to FBI, 18–19
Bradbury, Norris E., 13, 33, 39, 164, 176, 177, 245; testimony, 194, 208–209
Bradley, General Omar, 167, 169
Brandeis, Louis D., *quoted*, 241
Bransten, Louise, 50
Bridges, Harry, 27, 50
Brownell, Herbert, 229
Browning, Robert, *quoted*, 266
Buckley, Oliver E., 36, 38, 161, 173, 174; testimony, 211–12
Bundy, McGeorge, 116
Burnham, James, 112
Bush, Vannevar, 6, 8, 30, 96–98, 124, 156, 166, 193, 243, 245; testimony, 137–43, 192, 199–200

C

California Labor School, 22, 48, 49, 114
Calvert, Captain H. K., 84, 91
Campbell, Joseph, 7, 236, 241, 242, 256, 258, 259, 276; *quoted*, 266
Carlson, General, 115
Chevalier, Barbara, 24, 29, 32, 58, 59
Chevalier, Haakon, 21, 23, 24, 29, 32, 33, 50, 58–113, 123, 130, 134, 185, 198, 234, 246–47, 255, 256–58, 260, 274; letter to Wyman, 110
Churchill, Winston, 158, 166
Clifford, Clark, 97, 98, 240
Compton, Arthur, 30, 33
Compton, Karl T., 245; testimony, 207
Conant, James B., 6, 8, 31, 35, 38, 83, 96–98, 124, 161, 163, 164, 173,

About the Author

CHARLES P. CURTIS *began his study of this case with little knowledge of its central character (he had met J. Robert Oppenheimer half a dozen times) but with a scholar's and a practicing lawyer's background in the law and in history. He is a Boston lawyer. For many years he was a member of the Harvard Corporation. Among his published works are two studies of the law,* Lions under the Throne *and* It's Your Law; *a distinguished anthology,* The Practical Cogitator, *which he did with Ferris Greenslet; and* Introduction to Pareto, *with George C. Homans. With his brother, Richard C. Curtis, he also wrote* Hunting in Africa, East and West, *about which Ernest Hemingway, discussing books on Africa, said: "I liked Charlie Curtis's. It was very honest and it made a fine picture."*

Date Due